BERTOLT BRECHT
COLLECTED PLAYS

Volume 1

BERTOLT

Bertolt Brecht: Plays, Poetry, & Prose

Edited by

Ralph Manheim and John Willett

BRECHT

COLLECTED PLAYS

VOLUME 1

Baal

Drums in the Night

In the Jungle of Cities

The Life of Edward the Second
of England

Five One-Act Plays

Pantheon Books, *A Division of Random House, New York*

Library of Congress Catalog Card Number: 71-113718
ISBN: 0-394-40664-8

Manufactured in the United States of America

FIRST AMERICAN EDITION

Contents

Introduction

Brecht in Bavaria 1918–24

1

This volume contains the plays which Brecht wrote in Bavaria before moving to Berlin in the autumn of 1924. In the spring of 1918, when he began work on the first of them, he was just twenty and a new student at Munich University. Six and a half years later he was a recognized, if controversial, writer and the winner of a major literary prize. The best directors and actors of the day were performing his plays; he had also written many poems and short stories and directed one remarkable production. He had just been on the staff of the Munich Kammerspiele, one of the most enterprising small theaters in Germany, where his first and so far most successful play had been performed. Now he was about to go as a "dramaturg," or literary adviser, to Max Reinhardt's Deutsches Theater in Berlin, at that time one of the world's three or four leading theaters.

Born on February 10, 1898, Brecht had been brought up in Augsburg, about forty miles north-west of Munich. His father, a native of the Black Forest, was sales director of the Haindl paper works there; his mother died in May 1920. *Baal*, the first version of which was finished by July 1918, reflects much of the imaginary world of himself and his group of Augsburg friends, as well as the taverns and physical surroundings of the old city. For a few months just before and after the armistice of November 1918 he served as a medical orderly in a local army hospital, but had returned to Munich by February 1919, the early days of the Bavarian Soviet, during which he dashed off the first version of *Drums in the Night*. There he showed both plays to Lion Feuchtwanger, the subsequent author of *Jew Süss,* who was living in Munich and had recently met him for the first time. His own drama professor Arthur Kutscher was always bitterly critical of his work, but Feuchtwanger was encouraging, so that he began to make contact with publishers and, at the end of the summer vacation, to write theater criticism for the Augsburg Socialist paper. The one-act plays are also thought to have been mainly written that year, as well as a wealth of lost or unfinished works.

Baal was accepted by Feuchtwanger's own publisher Georg Müller, who had also published Wedekind's collected plays, but was withdrawn when already in proof for fear of the censorship. *Drums in the Night* was shown by Feuchtwanger to the Kammerspiele "dramaturg" Rudolf Frank, who at some point in the summer of 1920 accepted it for production. Neither publication nor production in fact materialized for another two years, but the encouragement to Brecht was obvious. He left the university in the summer of 1921 and in November set out to try his luck in Berlin, a much more important city from the theatrical point of view.

The expedition was less successful than he had hoped. Neither the Deutsches Theater nor the State Theater under Leopold Jessner would make any promises, and although Brecht was asked to direct Arnolt Bronnen's play *Vatermord* for the experimental Junge Bühne, it ended disastrously with a walkout of the actors. He himself was taken to a hospital suffering from undernourishment, due no doubt in part to the galloping currency inflation. But at least he made many connections or friendships which were to be important for his work: notably Bronnen (with whom he began collaborating on film treatments and various joint theatrical projects); Herbert Ihering, the critic of the *Berliner Börsen-Courier* (a lifelong supporter, whose paper was later to serve as a launching-platform for many of his ideas); and Moritz Seeler, the organizer of the Junge Bühne (who was to produce *Life Story of the Man Baal* in 1926). By the time of his return to Augsburg at Easter he had also completed the first version of *In the Jungle*.

In Bavaria, 1922 was a Brecht year. Soon after his return the Munich Residenztheater accepted *In the Jungle*, thanks to the recommendation of its artistic adviser Jacob Geis and of its new chief director Erich Engel, who had arrived a few months earlier from his native Hamburg. *Baal* was at last published (by Gustav Kiepenheuer of Potsdam), while September 29th saw the pre-

mière of *Drums in the Night.* Clearly this was very different from
later Brecht productions, for Otto Falckenberg, the head of the
Kammerspiele, staged it in expressionist style with angular poses
and sets to match by his own staff designer Otto Reigbert. But
Ihering came from Berlin to review it, and in the *Berliner Börsen-
Courier* of October 5th he wrote that "At twenty-four the writer
Bert Brecht has changed Germany's literary complexion overnight. Bert Brecht has given our time a new tone, a new melody,
a new vision." Here too was "a physical sense of chaos and decay:"

> Hence the unparalleled creative force of his language. It is a
> language you can feel on your tongue, in your gums, your ear,
> your spinal column.

Ihering was known to have been appointed as the judge for that
year's award of the Kleist Prize. This had been founded in 1911 by
a group of Kleist enthusiasts to celebrate the centenary of the
poet's death, and was intended for writers who had yet to establish
themselves. Up to its abolition in 1932 it was probably the most
significant literary award in Germany, having previously been
given to the playwrights Sorge, Unruh, Hasenclever, and Jahnn,
while in 1923–25 it went to Musil, Barlach, and Zuckmayer. On
November 13th the *Berliner Börsen-Courier* announced that it had
gone to Brecht, and not for *Drums in the Night* only but for all
three of his completed plays. "Brecht's linguistic power," said
Ihering's citation,

> is even more richly developed in *Baal* and *In the Jungle.* His
> language is vivid without being deliberately poetic, symboli-
> cal without being over-literary. Brecht is a dramatist because
> his language is felt physically and in the round.

Because *Drums in the Night* was generally regarded as the prize-
winning play it was widely performed all over Germany, notably
in Berlin immediately before Christmas, when Falckenberg again
directed it for the Deutsches Theater with a first-rate cast. Brecht
always claimed that he had only written it to make money, and
certainly it differs in several ways from his other works. Alone of
those in this volume it seems to contain no anticipations of his later
plays.

In Munich for two nights after the première it was followed by a midnight show called *The Red Raisin* (*Die rote Zibebe*, a name at one time given to the tavern in Act 4, and also used of the moon which hangs so conspicuously over the action). This was described as an "improvisation in two scenes by Bert Brecht and Karl Valentin," the latter being a famous Munich music-hall comedian. In the first scene Max Schreck, the actor who played Glubb, was the Freakshow Landlord who opened a series of curtained cabins, each containing a performer who stepped out to do a solo turn. The program shows that these included the sailor-poet Joachim Ringelnatz, the reciter Ludwig Hardt, Brecht himself singing songs, and the dancer Valeska Gert, though for the second performance Brecht seems to have been replaced by his fellow-poet Klabund. The second scene was a sketch called "Christmas Evening" by Valentin, whom a short program note by Brecht compared with Chaplin, among other things for his "virtually complete rejection of mimicry and cheap psychology." Valentin's influence has sometimes been seen in Brecht's farcical one-acters, though Brecht himself acknowledged it rather as affecting his work as a director, particularly his use of grouping.

That October Brecht was appointed to the Kammerspiele's dramaturgical and directing staff, where his main task was the adaptation and production of Marlowe's *Edward II*. The actual writing of this play, which is very largely an original work, must have taken place mainly in the winter of 1922–23, since the Berlin State Theater started showing an interest in it early in the new year. It was done in collaboration with Feuchtwanger, whom Brecht saw frequently throughout 1923 and who is said to have inspired the speech characteristics of Shlink in *In the Jungle*. It was not, however, performed until the next year, and although there were two more Brecht premières in 1923, neither was at the Kammerspiele itself. First *In the Jungle* was staged at the Residenztheater on May 9th by Engel, with settings by Brecht's school friend Caspar Neher: the beginning of a lifelong collaboration among the three men. Jessner of the State Theater came from Berlin, as did Ihering, who again wrote enthusiastically, though not without observing that to anyone insensitive to its language the play must appear a muddle. This the local critics bore out; the three-hour performance was poorly received; it ran for only six evenings, and altogether was a disastrous enough flop to occasion the sacking of the theater's artistic adviser. Nor was *Baal* in Leipzig at the end of the year any more successful. Alwin Kronacher's production at the Old Theater on December 8th was taken off by order of the city council within a week, and the director reprimanded. It brought an interesting press controversy between Ihering and his rival Alfred Kerr as to the relative originality of Brecht and Toller, but Kerr was in the event right when he wrote that "The only hope for a Baalade like this is as a posthumous fragment . . . ." For the text as we have it was not performed again for another forty years.

The rehearsals for *Edward the Second* began that autumn under Brecht's own direction. Brecht also supplied the music; the sets were again by Neher, and as in the two previous Munich Brecht productions the actor Erwin Faber played the lead. The première on March 19, 1924, was somewhat thrown out by the drunkenness of one of the principal actors, but the local critics appreciated Brecht's success in conveying his ballad-like conception of the story (he apparently had the scene titles and dates announced before each episode), while Ihering was impressed by his handling of the ensemble scenes and the careful dissection of the long speeches. Knowing something of Brecht's as yet unformulated theoretical ideas, he realized that the audience with which he most sympathized was that for boxing matches, sporting events and incidents in the street, and attributed to this novel orientation part of the success of the production. Looking back two years later he saw it as something more: a major turning point in the German theater's understanding of the classics. For here had been an attempt at demonumentalization, an appeal for "not so much plaster!!!" (the title of one of Brecht's subsequent essays), in which "He did not analyze the characters; he set them at a distance . . . He called for a report on the events." Viewed from 1926 it seemed like an early example of the "epic" style.

Brecht's Munich period came to an end with the 1923–24 theatrical season, for once established in Berlin he remained based there until he went into exile in 1933. Only the one-acters had not been performed by the time of his move. *Baal, Drums in the Night* and *Edward* were all in print, while the *Hauspostille*, his first book of poems, was enjoying something of an underground reputation, having been announced as early as 1922, five years before its actual publication. That first winter in Berlin he was to have the rare distinction (for a young author) of two productions in the major theaters: *Edward the Second* directed by Jürgen Fehling (this gifted director's only Brecht production) at the State Theater, with Werner Krauss as Mortimer and Faber once more as Edward, and *Jungle* at the Deutsches Theater directed by Engel, who had been lured to Berlin by Max Reinhardt a few months before Brecht. The outstanding young actor Fritz Kortner turned down a part in Reinhardt's *St. Joan* in order to play Shlink: another indication of the interest already stimulated by Brecht's early work.

2

If the Bavarian years made Brecht's name they also established the main lines of argument for and against his work, with Kerr and Ihering, respectively, as counsel for the prosecution and the defense. Already the point at issue was his literary borrowings, and a number of later attacks on him (including that dealt with in the notes to *In the Jungle of Cities*) were foreshadowed in Kerr's *Baal* critique, with its dismissal of the play as secondhand Büchner and Grabbe. "The gifted Brecht," he wrote, "is a frothing plagiarist." To which Ihering countered:

> A writer's productivity can be seen in his relationship with old themes. In *Schweiger* Werfel invented a "hitherto unheard-of story" and was nonetheless imitative in every respect. Brecht was fired by Marlowe's *Edward the Second* and was creative through and through.

At the same time Brecht had been able to build the nucleus of his subsequent team of supporters and collaborators: first and foremost Neher, then Engel, the rather older Feuchtwanger, Kortner, Homolka, Klabund's actress wife Carola Neher, and the playwright Marieluise Fleisser, all of them people who have left their individual mark on the German theater. Here his personal magnetism clearly played a great part: something to which there have been many tributes, starting with Feuchtwanger's fictional picture of him as the engineer Pröckl in his novel *Success*. The first

three plays all bore dedications: to his school friend George Pfanzelt (the "Orge" of the poems), to Bie Banholzer who bore his
illegitimate son Frank (killed in the war), and to Marianne, his first
wife, whom he married in 1922. With *Edward the Second* this
practice came to an end.

These were Brecht's pre-collectivist, indeed in a sense his pre-
political years. He undoubtedly had opinions, many of them
progressive and even revolutionary, but they were far from systematic, and politics and economics were wholly absent from
what we know of his reading. On the other hand it was an extraordinarily tense and eventful time for Germany in general and
Bavaria in particular, and Brecht was much too sensitive a writer
not to reflect this in his work. A good deal has been made of his
supposed pacifism in the First World War—though his schoolboy
writings show that in fact he set out from a conventionally patri-
otic attitude and hardly developed beyond concern at the casual-
ties—and of the impact made on him by his military service,
which in fact was done on his own doorstep and in a hospital for
venereal diseases, and started only a month or two before the end
of the war. Several of the *Hauspostille* poems which are held to
express his postwar sense of release had in fact already been
written by then. Nor is there any evidence that he was more than
a spectator of the revolutionary movements of November 1918,
when the monarchy fell, and the first months of 1919, when Munich and Augsburg were governed by Soviets following Kurt
Eisner's murder and the short-lived Spartacist revolt in Berlin.

Yet the "Legend of the Dead Soldier," which he wrote in 1918
and took into *Drums in the Night* (see pp. 93 and 369) is always
supposed to have earned him a place on the Munich Nazis' black
list, while the play itself, though their paper the *Völkischer Beobachter* thought that it "at any rate showed something of the
idiocy of the November Revolution," struck none of the liberal
critics as an unfair picture. It was certainly a very confused one,
as the muddle over the dating of the action will confirm, and
Brecht himself came to judge it in the severest terms, very nearly
suppressing the play altogether. The revolutionary setting, however, was only a background to the real drama, and it had an
instinctive poetic power which was not to be found in Brecht's
later amendments.

The element of revolt in his writing of this time was largely
directed against his own middle-class background: the satirical
first scene of *Baal,* for instance, and the first two acts of *Drums in
the Night.* Much of his reading, too, was exotic-escapist, as can be
seen from the allusions in this volume to Gauguin and *Treasure
Island* and Rudyard Kipling, and certainly this partly explains
Brecht's interest in Rimbaud, whose elevated prose underlies Garga's "psalmodizing" in *In the Jungle* (cf. Brecht's own semi-prose
"Psalms") and whose relationship with Verlaine was surely the
model for that of Baal and Ekart. "How boring Germany is!" says
a note of June 18, 1920. "It's a good average country, its pale colors
and its surfaces are beautiful, but what inhabitants!" "What's left?"
he concluded. "America!" That year he read two novels about
Chicago, J. V. Jensen's *The Wheel* (which has never appeared in
English) and Upton Sinclair's *The Jungle,* and when he began
work on his own *In the Jungle* it was under their influence, inten-
sified no doubt by his first experience of "the crushing impact of
cities" (about which he wrote an early poem) in the hard winter
of 1921–22.

By the time of its first performance the French occupation of
the Ruhr had given a great stimulus to nationalism throughout
Germany, and not least to the Nazis in Bavaria. The *Völkischer
Beobachter* particularly detested this play, claiming that the audience was full of Jews and that the Chinese characters spoke Yid-
dish. A month later Brecht and Bronnen heard Adolf Hitler
addressing a meeting in a Munich circus, and were inspired (according to Bronnen) to work out what sort of a political show they
could put on in a circus themselves. In November the Beer-Cellar
Putsch interrupted the rehearsals of *Edward the Second* for a day.
Brecht, with his colleague Bernard Reich, went to call on Feuchtwanger, who saw this as the sign that they must leave Bavaria (and
did indeed leave in 1924). But Reich recalls no particular concern
with the Nazis on Brecht's part, and indeed not only was the
putsch quite firmly suppressed—and Hitler jailed—but the stabili-
zation of the currency by the Reich government set the Nazi
movement back for a number of years.

The period covered by this volume saw not only a certain
element of political restoration throughout central and eastern
Europe but also the end of Expressionism in the arts. To the

poet-playwright Iwan Goll, who in 1921 published an essay called
"Expressionism Is Dying," the two phenomena were connected.
"Expressionism was a fine, good, grand thing . . ." he wrote. "But
the result is, alas, and through no fault of the Expressionists, the
German Republic of 1920." Dadaism likewise was breaking up by
1922; at the Bauhaus the semi-mystical Itten was about to be succeeded by the technologically minded Moholy-Nagy; while artists like Grosz, Dix, Beckmann, and Schlichter were evolving the
coolly representational, socially conscious style which in 1924 became known as Neue Sachlichkeit. Brecht was always much too
conscious of his own aims to care to be labeled as part of a movement; nonetheless his works of these years very clearly reflect the
decline of Expressionism and the rise of the new style. He defined
his position admirably in a note of June 27, 1920:

> I can compete with the ultra-modernists in hunting for new
> forms and experimenting with my feelings. But I keep realiz-
> ing that the essence of art is simplicity, grandeur and sen-
> sitivity, and that the essence of its form is coolness.

Baal was written as a kind of counter-play to the Expressionists'
invocations of Humanity with a capital H, yet the wandering poet
remains a romantic-expressionist figure, while the influence of
Georg Büchner is one that is also noticeable in a number of
Expressionist plays. *Drums in the Night* too, with its symbolic use
of the moon, its cinematic third act, and its hero's slightly mad
rhetoric, can reasonably be termed an Expressionist play. *In the
Jungle*, however, was written at the turning point, the watershed
between the two movements. The Rimbaud allusions, the color
references before each scene in the 1922 version, the attic-cum-
undergrowth setting, the use of spotlights referred to in Brecht's
note of 1954: all this is expressionistic, whereas the American
milieu, the preoccupation with the big cities and the very notion
of the "fight" were to become characteristic concerns of the mid-
1920's. A further note of February 10, 1922, even suggests that
Brecht was looking forward to his own 1930's doctrine of "alienation":

> I hope in *Baal* and *Jungle* I've avoided one common artistic
> bloomer, that of trying to carry people away. Instinctively,

I've kept my distance and ensured that the realization of my (poetical and philosophical) effects remains within bounds. The spectator's "splendid isolation" is left intact; it is not *sua res quae agitur;* he is not fobbed off with an invitation to feel sympathetically, to fuse with the hero and seem significant and indestructible as he watches himself in two different versions. A higher type of interest can be got from making comparisons, from whatever is different, amazing, impossible to overlook.

Thus though *In the Jungle* is still wildly romantic it already foreshadows the detached impersonalities of the machine age. And those supporters who, like Ihering and Engel and Geis, thought that Brecht would help lead the theater out of the Expressionist undergrowth can now be seen to have been absolutely right.

3

The final texts of these plays often make Brecht's evolution difficult to follow. He was a restless amender and modifier of his own work, so that any one of them may consist of layer upon layer of elements from different periods. "He is more interested in the job than in the finished work," wrote Feuchtwanger in an article of 1928 called "Portrait of Brecht for the English,"

> in the problem than in its solution, in the journey than in its goal. He rewrites his works an untold number of times, twenty or thirty times, with a new revision for every minor provincial production. He is not in the least interested in seeing a work completed. . . .

Thus between 1922 and its publication in 1927, *In the Jungle* became *In the Jungle of Cities*, the city allusions were strengthened, the boxing foreword was added and various boxing allusions worked into the text, the color references at the start of each scene gave way to mock-precise ("objective") data of time and place, the whole flavor of the play was changed. The same was done still more drastically with *Baal* in 1926, though in this case Brecht later decided to scrap the more "objective," technologically flavored version and go back (more or less) to the 1922–23 text. *Drums in the Night* he seems to have left alone after 1922, perhaps because it was not performed again after the first, largely topical wave of interest had subsided—though the discussion on p. 379 ff. suggests that Piscator was considering it; then for his collected plays in the 1950's he largely rewrote the last two acts.

All this means that each play as we now have it reflects the views and to some extent the spirit of a number of different periods. The performances which have gone into theatrical history were not based on these particular texts. Even Brecht's own notes are difficult to understand without knowing to which version each of them relates.

It is an impossible problem editorially, and our policy has been to print the final text but to provide all the variant material from other versions published in Brecht's lifetime, together with extensive notes on the main unpublished scripts. This is so that the reader should not get false ideas of Brecht's evolution and of his ideas and achievements at any given time. Brecht was a profound believer in change, whom it would be wrong to present statically in a final "authoritative" mold. Indeed opinions might well differ as to whether any such mold is the right one: not only are there fine things in many of the rejected versions, which it would be cruel not to publish, but informed judgment often disagrees with Brecht's last choices. Thus the chief German expert on *Baal* and the author of much the best book on Brecht's early years both prefer the 1919 script of *Baal;* an outstanding West German theater critic wants the 1922 *Drums in the Night;* while Ihering wrote of the (final) published version of *In the Jungle of Cities* in 1927:

> I love the fullness and color of the old *Jungle.* There seemed to be no better evidence of Brecht's richness and gifts than those crackling, exotically pulsating scenes as they shot to and fro. . . . The new *Jungle,* the *Jungle of Cities,* has lost in color and atmosphere. It has gained in clarity and concentration.

Not that there is much chance that Brecht himself would have accepted his own choices as final if he had lived longer, or seen them staged, or looked again at some of the earlier texts which for one reason or another he did not have before him when preparing the collected plays. It is characteristic that he already wanted the 1926 version of *Baal* printed as an appendix. For he was always a man in motion, who progressed best by disagreeing with what had already been said. Often it had been said by himself.

As for the translations, they are as good as translators and editors can make them, but they make no claim to be definitive. Better translations may well appear with time—quite apart from the obvious fact that each time must make its own translations. Generally we are providing different translations of the plays for the British Commonwealth and United States editions; this has been stipulated by Brecht's heirs, though otherwise the plan and much of the material of the two editions are the same. In all the poetry Brecht's rules of punctuation are followed; that is to say there are no commas at the ends of lines, the line break being considered sufficient pause for anything short of a colon. Our aim is that the poetry should so far as possible fit any settings by the main composers with whom Brecht collaborated. A note will normally indicate where this is not the case, though there may be some tunes, particularly of Brecht's own, which we have failed to track down.

With the exception of the 1922 variant material to *Drums in the Night*, of which separate translations have been made for the two editions, all translation in the notes is by the responsible editor, as is the selection of material printed. The aim here has been to include anything of relevance to the understanding or production of the play in question, leaving those notes which comprise more general statements of Brecht's theatrical ideas to be published in the volumes devoted to his theoretical writings. The essay "On Looking Through My First Plays," which he wrote as a foreword to the first two volumes of his collected *Stücke* in 1954 (too late for the first edition), has been split into its component sections, of which that on *A Man's a Man* will follow in the next volume. It can be reconstituted by reading it in the order indicated, starting with (i), the section on *Drums in the Night*.

The German text used throughout, unless otherwise stated, is that of the *Gesammelte Werke* (or Collected Works), edited by Elisabeth Hauptmann and a team comprising Werner Hecht, Rosemarie Hill, Herta Ramthun, and Klaus Völker, and published by Suhrkamp-Verlag, Frankfurt-am-Main, in 1967. This is referred to as GW, plus the appropriate subdivision: *Stücke* (Plays), *Schriften zum Theater* (Writings on the Theater), and so on. When the same terms (*Stücke,* for instance, as above) are used without the prefix GW they refer to the earlier collected edition issued by the same publisher from 1953 on. Particulars of other sources are given in full where reference is made to them. We would like to thank the editors and publisher for the help which they have given with various queries. The Brecht Archive in East Berlin has been generous in supplying material, and we are grateful for the support given us from the outset by Stefan S. Brecht.

THE EDITORS

Baal

Translators: William E. Smith and Ralph Manheim

To my friend George Pfanzelt

CHARACTERS

BAAL, poet
MECH, importer and publisher
EMILIE, his wife
DR. PILLER, critic
JOHANNES SCHMIDT
PSCHIERER, director of the
    water department
A YOUNG MAN
A YOUNG LADY
JOHANNA
EKART
LUISE, a waitress
THE TWO SISTERS
THE LANDLADY
SOPHIE BARGER
THE TRAMP

LUPU
MJURK
THE SOUBRETTE
A PIANO PLAYER
THE PRIEST
BOLLEBOLL
GOUGOU
THE OLD BEGGAR
MAJA, THE BEGGAR WOMAN
THE YOUNG WOMAN
WATZMANN
A WAITRESS
TWO POLICEMEN
TEAMSTERS
PEASANTS
WOODCUTTERS

CHORALE OF THE GREAT BAAL

As Baal grew within his mother's womb so white
Even then the sky was vast and calm and light
Naked, young and hugely marvelous
As Baal loved it when Baal came to us.

And the sky was there in joy and misery
Even when Baal slept, or had no eyes to see:
Nights meant violet sky and drunken Baal
Dawns: Baal good, sky apricottish-pale.

So through hospital, cathedral, bar
Baal trots coolly on, and learns to let it go.
When Baal's tired, boys, Baal will not fall far:
Baal will drag his whole sky down below.

Where the sinners herd in shame together
Baal lies naked soaking up the calm:
Just the sky, but sky to last for ever
Hides his nakedness with its strong arm.

And that lusty woman Earth, who laughs when yielding
To the man who'll stand the pressure of her thighs
Gave him instants of a sweet ecstatic feeling.
Baal survived it; he just raised his eyes.

And when Baal saw corpses all around
Never had he felt less cause for gloom.

Lots of space, said Baal; we aren't enough to count.
Lots of space inside this woman's womb.

Once a woman, Baal says, gives her all
Leave her; that's as far as she can go.
Other men should represent no risk at all;
Even Baal is scared of babies, though.

Vice is not so bad, says Baal. Don't spit
Either on the men who practice it.
Don't say no to any vice as such
Pick out two, for one will be too much.

Slackness, softness: all this you should shun:
Nothing is tougher than pursuing fun.
Powerful limbs are needed, and experience too
Too much gut can spoil it all for you.

Baal will watch the vultures in the star-shot sky
Hovering patiently, waiting for Baal to die.
Sometimes Baal plays dead. The vultures swoop.
Baal, without a word, will dine on vulture soup.

Under mournful stars in our sad vale of trouble
Munching, Baal will graze whole pastures down to stubble.
Once they're cropped, into the forests deep
Baal will trot, singing, to his well-earned sleep.

And when Baal's dragged down to be the dark womb's prize
What's the earth to Baal? For Baal has fed.
Sky enough still lurks behind Baal's eyes
To make just enough sky when he's dead.

As Baal rotted in that tomb as dark as night
Once again the sky was vast and calm and light.
Naked, young and hugely marvelous
As Baal loved it when Baal was with us.

[1] Dining Room

Mech, Emilie Mech, Pschierer, Johannes Schmidt, Dr. Piller, Baal and other guests come through the folding door.

MECH (*to Baal*) Would you care for a sip of wine, Mr. Baal?
(*All sit down—Baal, in the place of honor*)
MECH Do you care for crab? This is the corpse of an eel.
PILLER (*to Mech*) I'm overjoyed that Mr. Baal's immortal poems, which I have had the honor of reading to you, seemed worthy of your approval. (*To Baal*) You must publish your poetry. Mr. Mech will pay liberally. You'll be able to leave your garret.
MECH I buy cinnamon wood. Whole forests of cinnamon wood drift down the rivers of Brazil, just for me. But I'll publish your poetry too.
EMILIE You live in a garret?
BAAL (*eating and drinking*) 64 Klauckestrasse.
MECH To tell you the truth, I'm too fat for poetry. But you have a skull just like a man I knew in the Malay Archipelago, who had himself flogged before starting to work. He couldn't work unless he was foaming at the mouth.
PSCHIERER My dear ladies and gentlemen. I must speak frankly: I was shocked to find a man like him in such straitened circumstances. As you know, I discovered our dear Master in my own office, working as a common clerk. I call it a disgrace to our city, letting a man of his stature work for wages. I congratulate you, Mr. Mech: your salon will be known as the cradle of this genius's—yes, genius's—worldwide fame! Your health, Mr. Baal!
(*Baal makes a disparaging gesture. He eats*)
PILLER I'm going to write an essay about you. Have you any manuscripts? I have influence with the newspapers.

A YOUNG MAN   But how do you manage to be so diabolically naïve, my dear Master? Your naïveté is positively Homeric. In my opinion Homer was one or more highly cultured adapters, who took a sophisticated pleasure in the naïveté of the old folk epics.

A YOUNG LADY   You remind me much more of Walt Whitman. Except that you are more significant. That's my feeling.

ANOTHER MAN   He has rather more of Verhaeren about him, I should say.

PILLER   Verlaine! Verlaine! Even his physiognomy. Let's not forget our Lombroso.

BAAL   A little more eel, if you please.

THE YOUNG LADY   But you have the advantage of being more indecent.

JOHANNES   Mr. Baal sings his poems to the teamsters. In a tavern by the river.

THE YOUNG MAN   My goodness, Master, you lord it over all the names we've mentioned. There's not a poet alive who can hold a candle to you.

THE OTHER MAN   Anyway, he's a bright hope.

BAAL   A little more wine, please.

THE YOUNG MAN   I regard you as the forerunner of the great Messiah of European poetry, whom we all expect most confidently in the immediate future.

THE YOUNG LADY   Honored Master, ladies and gentlemen. Permit me to read you a poem from "Revolution" magazine. I'm sure it will interest you. (*She rises and reads*):

The poet must avoid resplendent harmonies.
He must blow tubas, shrilly flog the drum.
He must arouse the people with chopped phrases.

The new world
Abolishing the world of torment,
Island of happy humanity.
Speeches. Manifestoes.
Singing from platforms.
Let the new holy State
Be preached, inoculated into the blood of the people, blood of their blood.

Coming of Paradise.
—Let us disseminate añ atmosphere of upheaval!
Learn! Make ready! Prepare!

(*Applause*)
THE YOUNG LADY (*hastily*)   If you don't mind. I've found another
poem in the same issue. (*She reads*):

Sun had made him shrivel
And wind had blown him dry.
By every tree rejected
He simply fell away.

Only a single rowan
With berries on every limb,
Red as flaming tongues, would
Receive and shelter him.

So there he hung suspended,
His feet lay on the grass.
The blood-red sunset splashed him
As through his ribs it passed.

It moved across the landscape
And struck all the olive groves.
God in his cloud-white raiment
Was manifest above.

Within the flowering forest
There sang a thousand snakes
While necks of purest silver
With slender murmurs shook.

And they were seized with trembling
All over that leafy domain
Obeying the hands of their Father,
So light in their delicate veins.

CRIES   Brilliant.—Demonic, and yet in good taste.—Just heavenly.
THE YOUNG LADY   In my opinion, that comes very close to Baal's
vision.

MECH   You ought to travel. The Abyssinian mountains. You'd love them.

BAAL   But they won't come to me.

PILLER   No need of that. With your feeling for life! Your poems have had an overpowering effect on me.

BAAL   The teamsters give me money when they like them.

MECH *(drinking)*   I'll publish your poems. I'll let the cinnamon wood drift—or I'll do both at once.

EMILIE   You shouldn't drink so much.

BAAL   I haven't got any shirts. I could use some white shirts.

MECH   You're not interested in the publishing deal?

BAAL   But they'd have to be soft.

PILLER *(ironically)*   And what do you think I might do for you?

EMILIE   You write such wonderful poems, Mr. Baal. You're so tender in your poems.

BAAL *(to Emilie)*   Wouldn't you like to play something on the harmonium?

(Emilie plays)

MECH   I like eating to the harmonium.

EMILIE *(to Baal)*   Don't drink so much, please, Mr. Baal.

BAAL *(looking at Emilie)*   You have cinnamon wood drifting downstream just for you, Mech? Whole forests?

EMILIE   You may drink as much as you like. It was only a request.

PILLER   You're also a very promising drinker.

BAAL *(to Emilie)*   Play higher up! You've got nice arms.

(Emilie stops playing and returns to the table)

PILLER   I take it you don't care much for the music itself?

BAAL   I can't hear the music. You talk too much.

PILLER   You're a strange bird, Baal. Apparently you don't care about being published.

BAAL   Don't you deal in animals too, Mech?

MECH   Do you mind?

BAAL *(stroking Emilie's arm)*   What are my poems to you?

MECH   I wanted to do you a favor. Wouldn't you like to peel some apples, Emilie?

PILLER   He's afraid we'll suck him dry.—Haven't you thought of a way to make use of me?

BAAL   Do you always wear wide sleeves, Emilie?

EMILIE   Now you've really had enough wine.

PSCHIERER   Maybe you ought to go a bit easy on the drinking. Full many a genius . . .

MECH   Wouldn't you like to take a bath? Shall I have a bed made up for you? Haven't you forgotten something?

PILLER   Your shirts are drifting away, Baal. Your poetry has already gone downstream.

BAAL (*drinking*)   Down with monopoly! Go to bed, Mech.

MECH (*rising*)   I delight in every one of the good Lord's animals. But this is one animal you can't do business with. Come, Emilie, come, ladies and gentlemen.

(*All have risen indignantly*)

CRIES   Sir!—Outrageous!—Why, this is . . . !

PSCHIERER   Mr. Mech, I am shocked . . .

PILLER   There's a nasty streak in your poetry, too.

BAAL (*to Johannes*)   What is this gentleman's name?

JOHANNES   Piller.

BAAL   Well, Piller, *you* can send me some old newspapers.

PILLER (*on his way out*)   You don't exist for me! And you don't exist for literature.

(*All go, except Baal*)

SERVANT (*entering*)   Your coat, sir.

[2]   Baal's Garret

Starry night. At the window, Baal and young Johannes. They are looking at the sky.

BAAL   When you lie sprawled in the grass at night, you can tell in your bones that the earth is a ball and that we're flying and that on this star there are animals which eat up its plants. It's one of the smaller stars.

JOHANNES   Do you know anything about astronomy?

BAAL   No.

(*Silence*)

JOHANNES   I have a sweetheart, she's the most innocent girl in the world, but once I saw her in a dream, being loved by a juniper tree. I mean: her white body was lying outstretched on the juniper tree, clasped in the gnarled branches. Since then I haven't been able to sleep.

BAAL   Have you ever seen her white body?

JOHANNES   No. She's innocent. Even her knees—there are so many degrees of innocence, aren't there? And yet, sometimes at night when I hold her in my arms for a moment, she trembles like a leaf, but only at night. But I can't do it. She's only seventeen.

BAAL   Did she enjoy making love in your dream?

JOHANNES   Yes.

BAAL   Has she white linen next to her body? A snow-white shift between her knees? Once you've slept with her, maybe she'll turn into a heap of flesh without a face.

JOHANNES   You're only saying what I've always felt. I thought I must be a coward. Now I see: you agree that sexual intercourse is dirty.

BAAL   That's the cry of the swine who are no good at it. When you embrace those virgin thighs in the fear and joy of created man, you'll be a god. Just as the juniper has many roots, all intertwined, so the two of you will have many limbs in one bed, and beating hearts and blood flowing from limb to limb.

JOHANNES   But the law punishes it! And so do our parents!

BAAL   Your parents (*He reaches for the guitar*) are has-beens. How dare they open their mouths, showing their rotten teeth, to talk against love, that any man can die of? Because, if you people can't endure love, there's nothing left but vomit and disgust. (*He tunes the guitar*)

JOHANNES   You mean pregnancy?

BAAL   (*with a few hard chords*)   Once the pale mild summer has ebbed and they have soaked up love like sponges, they turn back into animals, cross and childish, ungainly, with fat bellies and flowing breasts, and with damp, clinging arms like slimy squid, and their bodies degenerate and become heavy unto death. And with enormous screams, as though bringing forth a cosmos, they give birth to a tiny fruit. They spit out with pain what they sucked in with joy. (*He plays scales*) You've got to have teeth; then love is like biting into an orange until the juice spurts between your teeth.

JOHANNES   You have teeth like an animal's: grayish-yellow, massive, sinister.

BAAL   And love is like letting your bare arm float on the surface of a pond with water weeds between your fingers: like the pain of a drunken tree that sets it creaking and singing as the wild wind rides it; like drowning in swigs of wine on a hot day, and her body presses into every fold of your skin, like very cool wine; her limbs are as gentle as plants in the wind; and the force of the impact, to which you must yield, is like flying into a storm; and her body rolls over you like cool pebbles. But love is also like a coconut that's good as long as it's fresh; but you have to spit it out once its juice is squeezed dry, and all that remains is the meat, which is bitter. (*Throws away the guitar*) But now I'm sick of this aria.

JOHANNES   Then you think I should do it, if it's so wonderful?

BAAL   I think *you* should keep away from it, Johannes!

[3]   Tavern

Morning. Baal. Teamsters. Ekart upstage with Luise, the waitress. Through the window white clouds can be seen.

BAAL (*telling the teamsters a story*)   He threw me out of his white rooms, because I vomited up his wine. But his wife came running after me, and that night there was a celebration. Now I'm stuck with her and I'm fed up.

TEAMSTERS   She ought to have her backside smacked.—They're all as hot as mares, only stupider. Let her eat plums!—I always beat mine black and blue before I give her what she wants.

JOHANNES (*entering, with Johanna*)   This is Johanna.

BAAL (*to the teamsters, who go to the rear*)   I'll come over and sing for you later on. Hello, Johanna.

JOHANNA   Johannes has read me some of your songs!

BAAL   Mm. How old are you?

JOHANNES   She was seventeen in June.

JOHANNA   I'm jealous of you. He's always raving about you.

BAAL   You're in love with your Johannes! Spring has come. I'm expecting Emilie.—Better to love than to enjoy.

JOHANNES   I can see how you win men's hearts, but how can *you* get anywhere with women?

(*Emilie enters quickly*)

BAAL   There she comes. Hello, Emilie. Johannes has brought his fiancée. Sit down!

EMILIE   How can you ask me to come to such a dive? What riffraff!—It's just like you.

BAAL   Luise! A schnapps for the lady!

EMILIE   Are you trying to make me look ridiculous?

BAAL   No. Why shouldn't you have a drink? It's only human.

EMILIE   But you're not human.

BAAL   How do you know? (*He holds out his glass to Luise*) Not too stingy, young lady. (*Puts his arm around her*) You're mighty soft today, like a plum.

EMILIE   How boorish you are!

BAAL   Shout it louder, sweetheart!

JOHANNES   Anyway, it's interesting here. The simple folk. The way they drink and enjoy their fun! And the clouds in the window!

EMILIE   I suppose he's dragged you here too? To see the white clouds?

JOHANNA   Wouldn't it be better if we went to the meadows by the river, Johannes?

BAAL   Nothing doing! You stay right here! (*Drinks*) The sky is violet, especially if you're drunk. And beds are white. Before. That's where love is, between earth and sky. (*Drinks*) Why are you such cowards? The sky is wide open, you puny shadows! Full of bodies! Pale with love!

EMILIE   You've drunk too much again, and it makes you talk nonsense. And he uses that awful, wonderful nonsense to drag girls to his trough!

BAAL   Sometimes the sky (*Drinking*) is yellow, too. And full of vultures. (*Looks under the table*) Who's kicking me in the shin? Is it you, Luise? Oh, I see: it's Emilie! Well, it doesn't matter. Drink up!

EMILIE (*half rising*)   I don't know what's wrong with you today. Maybe I shouldn't have come here.

BAAL   Has that just dawned on you? Well, now there's no reason for you to leave. Relax.

JOHANNA   You shouldn't act like that, Mr. Baal.

BAAL   You have a good heart, Johanna. You'd never be unfaithful to your husband, would you?

FIRST TEAMSTER (*neighing wildly*)   Bitch of trumps! Takes!

SECOND TEAMSTER   Keep it up, said the whore, we're over the top! (*Laughter*) Let her eat plums!

THIRD TEAMSTER   You unfaithful bastard! said the wife, when she caught the hired man in bed with the maid. (*Laughter*)

JOHANNES (*to Baal*)   If only for Johanna's sake—she's a child!

JOHANNA (*to Emilie*)   Would you like to leave with me? We can both go.

EMILIE (*sobbing, bent over the table*)   Now I'm ashamed.

JOHANNA (*puts an arm around her*)   I understand you perfectly. It doesn't matter.

EMILIE   Don't look at me like that! You're still so young. You don't know anything yet.

BAAL (*standing up, ominously*)   A comedy: Two Sisters in Hades! (*He goes to the teamsters, takes his guitar from the wall and tunes it*)

JOHANNA   He's been drinking, dear. Tomorrow he'll be sorry.

EMILIE   If you only knew. He's always like this. And I love him.

BAAL (*sings*)

Orge said to me:

The spot on earth he most had come to crave
Was not the grass plot by his parents' grave

Or any whore's bed or confession stool
Or snowy bosom, soft and warm and full.

Orge said to me: His best retreat
On earth had always been the toilet seat.

For there a man can sit, content to know
That stars are overhead, and dung below.

A lovely place it is where even on
His wedding night a man can be alone.

A humble place where you will humbly know
You're only human, so you may as well let go.

A place of wisdom, where you clear the way
For the drink and victuals of the coming day.

A place where by exerting gentle pressure
A man can benefit while reaping pleasure.

You find out what you are in these dank pits
A man who feeds his face and meanwhile—sits.

TEAMSTERS (*applauding*) Hurray!—A fine song!—A cherry
brandy for Mr. Baal, if you'll accept it!—And he made it up all
by himself!—Hats off!

LUISE (*in the center of the room*) You're something, Mr. Baal!

FIRST TEAMSTER If you went into something useful—you'd be a
big success. You could be running a trucking business.

SECOND TEAMSTER What a brain!

BAAL The brain's nothing! You need a backside to go with it—
and the rest. A toast, Luise! (*Goes back to his table*) A toast,
Emmi! Come on, drink something, even if you can't do anything else! Drink, I say!

(*Emilie, with tears in her eyes, sips at her glass of schnapps*)

BAAL That's more like it. That'll put some fire into you!

EKART (*has risen and, crossing behind the bar, comes slowly over to
Baal. He is rawboned and powerful*) Baal! Stop this! Come with
me, brother! To the roads, with their hard dust—in the evening
the air will be violet. To the bars filled with drunken men—
while the bitches you've knocked up drop into the black rivers.
To the cathedrals, with their small white women; you will say:
May I breathe here? To the cow barns, to sleep among the cattle
—dark and full of the mooing of cows. And to the forests, where
the brazen gong rings above you and you forget the light of
the sky—and God has forgotten you. Do you remember what
the sky looks like? You've turned into a tenor! (*Spreads out his
arms*) Come with me, brother! Dancing and music and drinking! Drenched to the skin with rain! Drenched to the skin with
sun! Darkness and light! Women and dogs! Have you sunk so
low?

BAAL   Luise! Luise! An anchor! Don't leave me with him! (*Luise goes to him*) Come help me, my friends.

JOHANNES   Don't be led astray!

BAAL   That's a good boy!

JOHANNES   Think of your mother and your art! Be strong! (*To Ekart*) You ought to be ashamed! You're the devil himself!

EKART   Come, brother Baal! We'll fly into the blue as blissfully as two white doves! Rivers in the morning light! Graveyards in the wind and the smell of the endless fields before they've been cut down!

JOHANNA   Be strong, Mr. Baal!

EMILIE (*clings to him*)   You can't! Do you hear? You're too good for that!

BAAL   It's too soon, Ekart! I'm still all right like this. They won't let me, brother!

EKART   Then go to the devil! You've got the head of a baby and a heart of pure fat! (*He goes*)

TEAMSTERS   Out with the ten of clubs!—Damn it! Reckon up!—I'm through!

JOHANNA   This time you won, Mr. Baal!

BAAL   A narrow squeak! Are you free tonight, Luise?

EMILIE   You shouldn't talk like that, Baal! You don't know what you're doing to me.

LUISE   Oh, leave the lady alone, Mr. Baal. She's not herself, a child can see that.

BAAL   Calm down, Luise! Horgauer!

A TEAMSTER   What can I do for you?

BAAL   Here's a woman who's being mistreated and wants some love. Give her a kiss, Horgauer!

JOHANNES   Baal!

(*Johanna embraces Emilie*)

TEAMSTERS (*laughing, pounding the table*)   Go ahead, Andreas!—Go to it! She's high class.—Blow your nose first, Andy!—You're okay, Mr. Baal!

BAAL   Are you cold, Emilie? Do you love me? He's shy, Emmi! Give him a kiss! If you disgrace me in front of all these people, it's all over. One. Two.

(*The teamster bends down*)

(*Emilie raises her tear-stained face toward him. He kisses her noisily. Much laughter*)

JOHANNES   That was evil, Baal! Drinking makes him evil, and then he feels good. He's too strong.

TEAMSTERS   Good for him! Why is she running around in bars? —There's a man for you!—She's an adulteress!—She had it coming to her. (*They begin to leave*) Let her eat plums!

JOHANNA   Ugh! Shame on you!

BAAL (*goes to her*)   Why are your knees trembling, Johanna?

JOHANNES   What are you up to?

BAAL (*a hand on his shoulder*)   Why do you have to write poems, too? When life is so good: when you can rush down a raging stream on your back, naked under the orange sky, seeing nothing but the way the sky turns violet, and then black as a hole . . . when you can trample down your enemy . . . or make music out of mourning . . . or, eat an apple as you sob with love-sickness . . . or bend a woman's body back onto the bed . . . (*Johannes silently leads Johanna out*)

BAAL (*leaning on the table*)   Did you all feel it? Did it get under your skin? That was a circus! The animal has to be coaxed out! Get the animal out into the sunlight! Luise, the check! Get love out into the daylight! Naked in the sunlight, under the sky!

TEAMSTERS (*shaking his hand*)   So long, Mr. Baal!—Most humble servant, Mr. Baal.—Listen, Mr. Baal: I've always figured: something's wrong with Mr. Baal, upstairs. Those songs of his, and in general. But there's one sure thing: your heart's in the right place.—You got to know how to handle women!—Well, today we had a show: a white ass.—A good morning to you, Mr. Circus! (*They go*)

BAAL   Good morning, my friends! (*Emilie has thrown herself down on the bench, sobbing. Baal passes the back of his hand across her forehead*): Emmi! Now you can relax. It's all over now. (*Lifts her face, pulls her hair away from her wet face*) Forget it! (*Throws himself heavily on top of her and kisses her*)

[4]   Baal's Garret

1

Dawn. Baal and Johanna sitting on the edge of the bed.

JOHANNA   Oh, what have I done! I'm wicked.
BAAL   Better wash yourself.
JOHANNA   I still don't know how it happened.
BAAL   It's all Johannes's fault. Dragging you up here, then running out like a fool when it dawns on him why your knees are trembling.
JOHANNA (*standing up, in a lower voice*)   When he comes back . . .
BAAL   And now for a little literature. (*Lying back*) Dawn on Mount Ararat.
JOHANNA   Should I get up?
BAAL   After the flood. Stay where you are!
JOHANNA   Wouldn't you like to open the window?
BAAL   I like the smell.—What do you say to a second edition? What's lost is lost.
JOHANNA   How can you be so coarse?
BAAL (*lazily, on the bed*)   White, washed clean by the flood, Baal lets his thoughts fly away like doves, over the black waters.
JOHANNA   Where's my blouse? I can't . . .
BAAL (*holds it out to her*)   Here!—Can't what, sweetheart?
JOHANNA   Go home like this. (*Drops it, but then begins dressing*)
BAAL (*whistles*)   A wild colt! I can feel every single bone in my body. Give me a kiss!
JOHANNA (*at the table in the center of the room*)   Say something! (*Baal is silent*) Do you still love me? Say it! (*Baal whistles*) Can't you say it?
BAAL (*looks at the ceiling*)   I've got it up to here.
JOHANNA   Then what about last night? And just now?
BAAL   Johannes is liable to make trouble. Emilie is running around like a stove-in clipper. I could starve here. None of you would lift a finger for a man. You only care about one thing.

JOHANNA (*bewildered, clearing the table*)   And you—didn't you ever feel differently about me?

BAAL   Have you washed? No common sense! You got something out of it, didn't you? Go on home! You can tell Johannes I took you home yesterday. And tell him I spit gall on him. It was raining. (*Wraps himself up in the blanket*)

JOHANNA   Johannes? (*Goes heavily to the door and out*)

BAAL (*turns over brusquely*)   Johanna! (*Gets out of bed, goes to the door*) Johanna! (*Goes to the window*) There she goes! There she goes!

2

Noon. Baal is lying on the bed.

BAAL (*singing in an undertone*)

The sky turns violet, dark and gloomy
Above the drinking man at night:
Besides, the bed is white and roomy . . .

(*Enter the two sisters, with their arms around each other*)

OLDER SISTER   You said to come and see you again.

BAAL (*goes on singing*)

Your half-dressed body wants a fight.

OLDER SISTER   We've come, Mr. Baal.

BAAL   Now they come fluttering up to the dovecote in pairs. Take your clothes off!

OLDER SISTER   Last week Mother heard the stairs creak. (*She opens her sister's blouse*)

YOUNGER SISTER   It was getting light on the stairs when we slipped back to our room.

BAAL   One of these days I'll have you both on my neck.

YOUNGER SISTER   I'd drown myself, Mr. Baal!

OLDER SISTER   We're both here . . .

YOUNGER SISTER   I'm ashamed, Sister.

OLDER SISTER   It's not the first time . . .

YOUNGER SISTER   But it's never been so light, Sister. It's broad daylight outside.

OLDER SISTER   It's not the second time, either . . .

YOUNGER SISTER   You've got to undress, too.

OLDER SISTER   I am.

BAAL   When you're through, you can come over. Then everything will be darkness.

YOUNGER SISTER   You've got to go first today, Sister.

OLDER SISTER   I went first last time . . .

YOUNGER SISTER   No, I did.

BAAL   I'll take you both on at once.

OLDER SISTER   (*standing with her arm around the younger sister*) We're ready, but it's so light in here.

BAAL   Is it warm outside?

OLDER SISTER   It's only April.

YOUNGER SISTER   But today there's a warm sun.

BAAL   Did you like it last time?

(*Silence*)

OLDER SISTER   A girl drowned herself: Johanna Reiher.

YOUNGER SISTER   In the Laach. I'd never go in there. There's such a current.

BAAL   Drowned? Does anybody know why?

OLDER SISTER   People are talking. Things get around.

YOUNGER SISTER   She went out in the evening, and stayed out all night.

BAAL   Didn't she go home this morning?

YOUNGER SISTER   No, she jumped in the river. They haven't found her yet.

BAAL   Still floating . . .

YOUNGER SISTER   What's wrong, Sister?

OLDER SISTER   Nothing. Maybe I've got a chill.

BAAL   I feel so lazy today. You can go home.

OLDER SISTER   You can't do that, Mr. Baal. You can't treat her like that!

(*Knocking*)

YOUNGER SISTER   Someone's knocking. It's Mother.

OLDER SISTER   For God's sake don't open the door!

YOUNGER SISTER   Sister, I'm scared.

OLDER SISTER   Here, take your blouse!

(*Louder knocking*)

BAAL   If it's your mother, you'll see what you've let yourselves in for.

OLDER SISTER (*quickly dressing*)   Don't open yet! Bolt the door, please, for God's sake!

THE LANDLADY (*fat, enters*)   Ooh, would you look at that! Just as I thought! So now he's taking them two at a time! Haven't you any shame? The two of you in his swamp at once! From morning till night, from night till morning, his bed never gets cold! But now I've got something to say: My attic isn't a whorehouse! (*Baal rolls over to face the wall*)

THE LANDLADY   Sleepy, is it? Seems to me you get plenty of meat. Doesn't it fill you up? I can practically see through you, you look like a ghost. All skin and bones!

BAAL (*moving his arms*)   They come fluttering into my wood like swans!

THE LANDLADY (*clapping her hands*)   Some swans! The way you talk! You could be a poet! If your knees don't rot away first!

BAAL   I wallow in white bodies.

THE LANDLADY   White bodies! You *are* a poet! That's all you're good for! And these sweet young things! You're sisters, I suppose? Poor little orphans, ready to burst into tears. Maybe I ought to give you a thrashing? On those white bodies? (*Baal laughs*)

THE LANDLADY   You think it's a laughing matter? Ruining poor girls by the dozen, dragging them into your cave! Ugh! You beast! I'm giving you notice. All right, now, get going, home to Mother, we can go together. (*The younger sister cries harder*)

OLDER SISTER   It isn't her fault, ma'am.

THE LANDLADY (*taking both by the hand*)   There go the waterworks. You little fools! Well, you aren't the only ones! He's had a whole flock of swans! He's brought bliss to dozens and thrown their skins on the garbage heap! Well, now it's time for you to take the air! No salt water needed! (*Taking them both by their shoulders*) I know what kind of man he is all right! I know the type. Stop blubbering, it shows in your eyes! Just go home to

Mother like good girls, hand in hand, and don't do it again. (*Pushes them to the door*) And as for you: I'm giving you notice! You can set up your swannery somewhere else! (*Pushes the two sisters out, and goes*)

BAAL (*standing up, stretching*)   A bitch with a good heart!—I feel damnably lazy today anyway. (*He throws some paper onto the table and sits down before it*) I'll make a new Adam. (*Draws large capital letters on the paper*) I'll see what I can do with the inner man. I'm all hollowed out, but I'm as hungry as a wild beast. I have nothing but skin over my bones. Bitch! (*Leans back, stretches his arms and legs, emphatically*) Now I'm going to make the summer. Red. Scarlet. Voracious. (*He hums the tune again*)

3

Evening. Baal is sitting at the table.

BAAL (*clasping the bottle of schnapps. With many pauses*)   Four days now, I've been smearing the red summer all over: wild, pale, and voracious, and fighting the schnapps bottle. There have been defeats, but the bodies have started retreating back to the walls, into the black Egyptian darkness. I'll nail them to the wooden walls; only I mustn't drink any schnapps. (*He begins to babble*) This white schnapps is my rod and my staff. It's been reflecting my paper since the snow started dripping from the gutter, and I haven't touched it. But now my hands are shaking. As if they still had bodies in them. (*He listens*) My heart is pounding like a horse's hoof. (*He daydreams*) Oh, Johanna, one more night with you in your aquarium, and I'd have rotted away among the fishes! But now the smell of soft May nights is in me. I am a lover without a sweetheart. I am defeated. (*Drinks, stands up*) I've got to move. But first I'll get a woman. It's sad to move alone. (*Looks out the window*) It doesn't matter who! As long as she has a face like a woman! (*Goes out, humming*)

(*Below, a harmonium plays* Tristan)

(*Johannes, pale and wasted, comes in. He rummages among the
papers on the table. He lifts the bottle. Timidly, he goes back to the
door and waits*)
(*Noise on the stairs. Whistling*)
BAAL (*dragging in Sophie Barger, whistles*)   Be nice, sweetheart!
This is my room. (*Sits her down. Sees Johannes*) What are you
doing here?
JOHANNES   I only wanted . . .
BAAL   Oh? You only wanted? To stand there? A tombstone for
my lost Johanna? The corpse of Johannes, come from another
world, is that it? I'll throw you out! Get out of here! (*Circles
around him*) This is an outrage! I'll beat you to a pulp! Why not?
It's spring! Get out!
(*Johannes looks at him and goes*)
(*Baal whistles*)
SOPHIE   What did that young man do to you? Let me go!
BAAL (*opening the door wide*)   One floor down, then turn right!
SOPHIE   They ran after us when you caught me in front of that
door. They'll find me.
BAAL   Nobody will find you here.
SOPHIE   I don't even know you. What are you going to do to me?
BAAL   If that's all you have to say, you can leave.
SOPHIE   You pounced on me right in the street. I thought you
were an orangutan.
BAAL   But it's spring. There had to be something white in this
damned cave! A cloud! (*Opens the door, listens*) Those idiots got
lost.
SOPHIE   They'll throw me out if I get home too late.
BAAL   Especially if . . .
SOPHIE   If what?
BAAL   If you look like somebody I've been making love to.
SOPHIE   I don't know why I'm still here.
BAAL   I can tell you.
SOPHIE   Please don't think I'm bad.
BAAL   Why not? You're a woman like any other. The faces vary.
But they all have weak knees.
SOPHIE (*half inclined to go, looks around at the door. To Baal who is
watching her, straddling a chair*)   Good-bye!
BAAL (*indifferently*)   Aren't you getting enough air?

SOPHIE I don't know. I feel so weak. (*Leans against the wall*)
BAAL I know. It's April. It's getting dark, and you can smell me.
It's the same with the animals. (*Stands*) And now, white cloud,
you belong to the wind! (*Goes to her quickly, slams the door shut,
takes Sophie Barger in his arms*)
SOPHIE (*breathlessly*) Let me go!
BAAL My name is Baal.
SOPHIE Let me go!
BAAL You've got to comfort me. The winter took my strength
away. And you look like a woman.
SOPHIE (*looking up at him*) Your name is Baal . . . ?
BAAL You don't want to go home any more?
SOPHIE (*looking up at him*) You're so ugly, so ugly that it's fright-
ening . . . But . . .
BAAL Hm?
SOPHIE But it doesn't matter.
BAAL (*kissing her*) Have you got strong knees. Hm?
SOPHIE You know my name? It's Sophie Barger.
BAAL You'll have to forget it. (*Kisses her*)
SOPHIE No . . . no . . . Nobody has ever . . .
BAAL Are you a virgin? Come! (*He leads her back to the bed. They
sit down*) Cascades of bodies have lain in this wooden attic—but
now I want a face. At night we'll go outside. We'll lie down
among the plants. You are a woman. I have become unclean.
You must love me, for a while!
SOPHIE So that's the kind of man you are? . . . I love you.
BAAL (*laying his head on her breast*) Now the sky is above us, and
we are alone.
SOPHIE But you must lie still.
BAAL As a child!
SOPHIE (*straightening up*) But—at home—my mother! I've got to
go home.
BAAL Is she old?
SOPHIE She's seventy.
BAAL Then she's accustomed to wickedness.
SOPHIE Even when the earth swallows me up? When I'm
dragged into a cave at night and never come back again?
BAAL Never? (*Silence*) Have you any brothers or sisters?
SOPHIE Yes. They need me.

BAAL   The air in this room is like milk. (*Gets up, goes to the window*) The willows by the river, dripping wet, frowzy with the rain. (*Holds her*) You must have pale thighs.

[5]   Whitewashed Houses with Brown Tree Trunks

Somber bells. Baal. The tramp, a pale, drunken individual.

BAAL (*takes long steps in a semicircle around the tramp, who is sitting on a stone, holding his pale face upward*) Who nailed these defunct trees to the walls?

THE TRAMP   The pale ivory air around the defunct trees. Corpus Christi.

BAAL   Not to mention ringing bells when plants die!

THE TRAMP   The bells give me moral uplift.

BAAL   But don't the trees depress you?

THE TRAMP   Bah! Tree cadavers! (*Drinks from a bottle of schnapps*)

BAAL   Women's bodies are no better!

THE TRAMP   What have women's bodies got to do with processions?

BAAL   They're both obscene! You aren't in love!

THE TRAMP   The white body of Jesus—that's what I love! (*Hands the bottle up to him*)

BAAL (*more calmly*)   I put songs down on paper. But now they'll be hung in the toilet.

THE TRAMP (*transfigured*)   To serve!! My Lord Jesus. I see the white body of Jesus. I see the white body of Jesus. Jesus loved evil.

BAAL (*drinking*)   Like me.

THE TRAMP   Do you know the story about him and the dead dog? Everybody said: It's carrion, it stinks! Call the police! It's unbearable! But he said: He has beautiful white teeth.

BAAL   Maybe I'll turn Catholic.

THE TRAMP   He didn't. (*Takes the bottle away from him*)

BAAL (*rushing around excitedly again*)   But the women's bodies he nails to the walls—I'd never do that.

THE TRAMP   Nailed to the walls! They didn't drown in the river! They were slaughtered for him, for the white body of Jesus.

BAAL (*taking the bottle from him, turning away*)   You're too full of religion, or too full of schnapps. (*Goes off with the bottle*)

THE TRAMP (*wildly calling after him*)   So you won't stand up for your ideals, mister! You won't join the procession? You love plants and you won't do anything for them?

BAAL   I'll go down to the river and wash. I never bother with corpses. (*Goes*)

THE TRAMP   But I've got schnapps in me and I can't stand it. I can't stand these damned dead plants. Maybe, if I had a lot of schnapps in me, I could stand it.

[6]   May Night, Under the Trees

Baal, Sophie.

BAAL (*lazily*)   It's stopped raining now. The grass must still be wet . . . The water couldn't get through our leaves . . . The young leaves are dripping wet, but here, in among the roots, it's dry. (*Angrily*) Why can't a man sleep with plants?

SOPHIE   Listen!

BAAL   The howling of the wind in the wet black leaves! Do you hear the rain dripping through the leaves?

SOPHIE   I feel a drop on my neck . . . Oh, darling, don't!

BAAL   Love tears a man's clothes from his body like a whirlpool, and buries him naked in among the leaf corpses, after he's seen the sky.

SOPHIE   I wish I could crawl away inside you, because I'm naked, Baal.

BAAL   I'm drunk, and you're wobbling. The sky is black, and we're on a swing, with bodies full of love, and the sky is black. I love you.

SOPHIE   Oh, Baal! My mother is crying over my corpse now; she thinks I've drowned myself. How many weeks is it now? It was still April. It must be three weeks now.

BAAL   It's been three weeks now, said his sweetheart among the roots of the trees, after thirty years had passed. And she was half rotted away by then.

SOPHIE   It feels good to lie here like a captive, with the sky over-head, and I'll never be alone any more.

BAAL   And now I'll lift up your shift again.

[7]   Night Spot: "Night Cloud"

A small filthy café; whitewashed dressing room. To the left, rear, a dark brown curtain. To the right, a door made of whitewashed boards, leading to the toilet. Right rear, a door. When it opens, the blue night is visible. Backstage in the café, a soubrette is singing.

Baal, stripped to the waist, is walking around drinking and humming.

LUPU (*a fat young man with an egg-shaped head and with black, glossy hair, plastered on either side of his sweaty, pale face, is seen in the door, at right*)   They've knocked the street lamp down again.

BAAL   Only pigs come to this place. Where's my ration of schnapps?

LUPU   You've drunk it all.

BAAL   Watch your step.

LUPU   Mr. Mjurk was saying something about a sponge.

BAAL   So I don't get any schnapps?

LUPU   Mr. Mjurk says there won't be any more schnapps for you before the show. I feel sorry for you.

MJURK (*coming through the curtain*)   Make yourself scarce, Lupu!

BAAL   I've got to have my ration, Mjurk, or no poetry for you.

MJURK   You shouldn't drink so much. One of these nights you won't be able to sing at all.

BAAL   What do you think I sing for?

MJURK   Aside from Savettka, the soubrette, you're the best act the "Night Cloud" has got. I discovered you personally. Who ever saw such a sensitive soul in such a lump of fat? It's the lump of fat that sends them, not the songs. Your drinking is ruining me.

BAAL   I'm sick of this fight every night about schnapps when it's in the contract. I'm clearing out.

MJURK   I have influence with the police. What you need, man, is a good night's sleep; you stagger around as if you'd been ham-strung. Give your girl the air! (*Applause in the café*) But now it's time for you to go on.

BAAL   I've got it up to here.

THE SOUBRETTE (*coming through the curtain with the pale, apathetic piano player*)   Time to knock off.

MJURK (*forcing Baal to take a dress coat*)   You can't appear on our stage half naked.

BAAL   Idiot! (*Throws away the coat and goes through the curtain, dragging his guitar after him*)

THE SOUBRETTE (*sitting down and drinking*)   He only works for the girl he lives with. He's a genius. Lupu imitates him disgust-ingly. Same tone, same girl.

THE PIANO PLAYER (*leaning against the door to the toilet*)   His songs are heavenly, but he's been fighting with Lupu for the last eleven nights about his schnapps ration.

THE SOUBRETTE (*drinking*)   It's a hard life.

BAAL (*behind the curtain*)   I'm a child, I'm undefiled, always happy, always wild. (*Applause. Baal goes on, to the guitar*):

Through the room the cold wind comes
The little girl eats dark blue plums
Holds her soft white body still
Ready and waiting, come what will.

(*Applause in the café, with cries of "Boo!" Baal goes on singing, and the commotion continues to grow as the song becomes more indecent. At the end, an enormous tumult in the café*)

THE PIANO PLAYER (*listlessly*)   What the hell. He's going too far! Call an ambulance! Now Mjurk is talking—but they'll tear him apart. He gave them the naked truth.

(*Baal comes through the curtain, dragging the guitar after him*)

MJURK (*behind him*)   You swine, I'll get you for this. You're going to sing your number! As your contract stipulates! Or I'll call the police! (*Goes back into the café*)

THE PIANO PLAYER   You'll ruin us, Baal.

(*Baal clutches his throat, goes to the toilet door on the right*)

THE PIANO PLAYER (*standing in his way*)   Where do you think you're going?

(*Baal shoves him aside. Goes out through the door, with the guitar*)

THE SOUBRETTE   Taking your guitar to the can with you? You're divine!

GUESTS (*sticking their heads through the curtain, rear*)   Where is that son of a bitch?—Sing some more!—No intermission!—That damned son of a bitch! (*They go back into the café*)

MJURK (*coming through the curtain*)   I spoke to them like a Salvation Army major. We have no problem with the police. But those people are banging the tables for him. Where is that bastard? He's got to get out there.

THE PIANO PLAYER   Our star has gone to the can.

SHOUT BACKSTAGE   Baal!

MJURK (*pounding the door*)   Hey! Say something! Damn it, I forbid you to lock yourself in! And on my time! What do you think I'm paying you for? I have it in black and white! You crook! (*Pounds ecstatically*)

LUPU (*in the doorway at right. The blue night is visible*)   The toilet window is open. The bird has flown. No schnapps, no poetry.

MJURK   Empty? Flown? Out through the can? Cutthroat! I'll call the police. (*Rushes out*)

CRIES (*rhythmic, from backstage*)   Baal! Baal! Baal!

[8]   Green Fields, Blue Plum Trees

Baal, Ekart.

BAAL (*walking slowly through the fields*)   The sky is green and pregnant: July air, wind, no shirt in my pants! (*Going back toward Ekart*) They brush against my bare thighs. My head is blown up with wind, the scent of the fields hangs in the hair of my armpits. The air is trembling as if drunk.

EKART (*behind him*) Why are you running away from the plum trees, like an elephant?

BAAL Put your paw on my skull! With every pulse beat, it swells, and then shrinks again, like a blister. Can't you feel it?

EKART No.

BAAL You don't understand my soul.

EKART Why don't we go lie in the water?

BAAL My soul, brother, is the groaning of the wheat fields when they toss in the wind, and the gleam in the eyes of two insects that want to devour each other.

EKART A July-crazed boy, with immortal guts—that's what you are. A dumpling that will some day leave grease spots on the sky!

BAAL That's a lot of words. But it doesn't matter.

EKART My body is as light as a tiny plum in the wind.

BAAL The pale summer sky does that, brother. Shall we soak up the mild warm water of some blue pool? If we don't, the white country roads will pull us up to heaven like ladders of angels.

[9] Village Tavern

Evening. Peasants surrounding Baal. Ekart in a corner.

BAAL I'm glad to have you all together. My brother's coming out here tomorrow evening. The bulls had better be here by then.

A PEASANT (*open-mouthed*) How can we know if a bull is the kind your brother wants?

BAAL Only my brother can know that. I want none but the best bulls. Otherwise, there's no point. Landlord, a schnapps!

SECOND PEASANT Will you buy him right away?

BAAL The one that has the strongest loins.

THIRD PEASANT They'll be bringing in bulls from eleven villages for the price you're offering.

FIRST PEASANT   Take a look at *my* bull!

BAAL   Landlord, another schnapps!

THE PEASANTS   My bull is the best! Tomorrow evening, you say?
(*They begin to leave*) Are you spending the night here?

BAAL   Yes. In a bed!

(*The peasants go*)

EKART   Just what are you trying to do? Have you gone crazy?

BAAL   Wasn't it marvelous the way they blinked and gaped, and
finally caught on, and started figuring?

EKART   At least it got us a few glasses of schnapps. But now we'd
better make tracks!

BAAL   Make tracks, now? Are you out of your mind?

EKART   Then you really are crazy? Think of those bulls!

BAAL   Why do you think I handed them that line?

EKART   For a couple of drinks, I suppose.

BAAL   Don't be silly! I'm going to give you a treat, Ekart. (*He
opens the window, behind him. It is growing dark. He sits down
again*)

EKART   You're drunk, on six glasses of schnapps. You ought to be
ashamed!

BAAL   It will be wonderful. I love these simple people. I'm going
to give you a divine spectacle, brother! Prost!

EKART   It amuses you to play dumb. Those poor fellows will split
my skull—and yours.

BAAL   It's part of their education. I'm thinking of them now, on
this warm evening, with a kind of tenderness. They're coming
to cheat me in their simple way—and that appeals to me.

EKART   (*rising*)   Then it's the bulls or me. I'm going before the
landlord smells a rat.

BAAL   (*ominously*)   It's such a warm evening. Just wait an hour.
Then I'll go with you. You know I love you. I can smell the
manure in the fields. Do you think the landlord might have one
more schnapps for the men who arranged this business with the
bulls?

EKART   I hear footsteps.

THE PRIEST   (*enters. To Baal*)   Good evening. Are you the man
with the bulls?

BAAL   I am.

THE PRIEST   Tell me, why did you perpetrate this swindle?

BAAL   We have nothing else in the world. How strong the hay smells here! Is it always like this in the evening?

THE PRIEST   Your world seems very threadbare!

BAAL   My heaven is full of trees and bodies.

THE PRIEST   Don't talk about that! The world isn't your circus.

BAAL   What is the world then?

THE PRIEST   You'd better be going! I'm a very good-natured man. I won't hold it against you. I've already straightened the whole thing out.

BAAL   The man of God has no sense of humor, Ekart!

THE PRIEST   Don't you realize how childish your plan was? (*To Ekart*) What does he want?

BAAL (*leaning back*)   In the evening twilight—it has to be evening, of course, and the sky has to be clouded over of course—when the air is warm and there's a little breeze, then the bulls will come. Trotting from all directions. It will be an impressive sight. And then the poor men will stand around, and won't know what to do with their bulls. They've miscalculated. There's nothing in it for them but the impressive sight. I love people who have miscalculated. And where can a man see so many animals all at once?

THE PRIEST   And just for that you were going to round up seven villages?

BAAL   What are seven villages compared to such a sight!

THE PRIEST   Now I see. You're a poor devil. And I presume that you're very fond of bulls?

BAAL   Come, Ekart! He's spoiled it all. Christians don't love animals any more.

THE PRIEST (*laughing, then seriously*)   Well, you can't have your fun. Please leave, and don't attract any more attention! It seems to me that I'm doing you a great service!

BAAL   Come, Ekart! You won't get your treat, brother! (*Goes out slowly with Ekart*)

THE PRIEST   Good evening! Landlord, I'll pay for these gentlemen!

LANDLORD (*behind the bar*)   Eleven glasses of schnapps, Your Reverence.

[10]   Trees at Evening

Six or seven woodcutters sit leaning against trees. Among them,
Baal. In the grass, a corpse.

FIRST WOODCUTTER   It was an oak. He didn't die right away. He
suffered a while.

SECOND WOODCUTTER   Early this morning he said the weather
seemed to be getting better. He liked it this way: green, with
a little rain. And the wood not too dry.

THIRD WOODCUTTER   Teddy was a good fellow. Used to have a
little shop somewhere. Those were his good days. He was as fat
as a priest then. But his business went broke because he had an
affair with some woman, and he came up here and lost his
paunch with the years.

ANOTHER WOODCUTTER   Didn't he ever talk about his affair with
the woman?

THIRD WOODCUTTER   No. I don't even know if he wanted to go
back down there. He had saved quite a lot, but then he was a
temperate sort. We only tell lies up here. It's much better that
way.

A WOODCUTTER   A week ago he said he'd be going up north in the
winter. Seems he had a hut up there somewhere. Hey, Elephant, didn't he tell you where? (*To Baal*) You were talking
about it, weren't you?

BAAL   Leave me alone. I don't know anything.

SAME WOODCUTTER   I guess you'd like to take it over yourself, eh?

SECOND WOODCUTTER   You can't trust him. Remember how he
hung our boots in the water overnight to keep us from going
to the woods, just because he was feeling lazy, as usual.

ANOTHER WOODCUTTER   He doesn't lift a finger for his money.

BAAL   Don't fight today! Can't you think about poor Teddy a
little?

A WOODCUTTER   Where were you when he got through dying?
(*Baal rises and crosses the grass to Teddy. He sits down by him*)

SAME WOODCUTTER   Baal isn't walking straight, boys!

ANOTHER WOODCUTTER   Leave him alone! The Elephant's had a shock.

THIRD WOODCUTTER   Really, you might be a little quieter today, with him still lying there.

THE OTHER WOODCUTTER   What are you doing with Teddy, Elephant?

BAAL (*over him*)   He has his rest, and we have our unrest. Both are good. The sky is black. The trees are trembling. Clouds are swelling somewhere. That's the setting. We can eat. When we've slept, we wake up. He doesn't. We do. That's doubly good.

THE OTHER WOODCUTTER   What's that about the sky?

BAAL   The sky is black.

THE OTHER WOODCUTTER   You aren't strong in the head. It's always the wrong ones that get it.

BAAL   Yes, friend, that is a funny thing, you're right.

A WOODCUTTER   It can't ever happen to Baal. He never goes near where the work is.

BAAL   But Teddy was hard-working. Teddy was generous. Teddy was congenial. And nothing is left but: Teddy *was*.

SECOND WOODCUTTER   I wonder where he is now?

BAAL (*pointing to the dead man*)   There he is.

THIRD WOODCUTTER   I always think that lost souls are the wind, especially on spring evenings, but sometimes I think it in the autumn, too.

BAAL   And in the summer, in the sunlight, over the fields of grain.

THIRD WOODCUTTER   No, that doesn't fit. It has to be dark.

BAAL   It has to be dark, Teddy.

(*Silence*)

A WOODCUTTER   What's to become of him now, boys?

THIRD WOODCUTTER   He has nobody that wants him.

THE OTHER WOODCUTTER   He was all alone in the world.

A WOODCUTTER   And his things?

THIRD WOODCUTTER   There isn't much. He took his money away somewhere, to the bank. There it'll lie, even if nobody ever comes for it. Do you know of anything, Baal?

BAAL   He hasn't started to stink yet.

A WOODCUTTER   Boys, I've got a really good idea.

THE OTHER WOODCUTTER   Let's hear it!

THE MAN WITH THE IDEA   The Elephant isn't the only one with ideas, boys. How would it be if we had a drink to Teddy's health?

BAAL   That's indecent, Bergmeier.

THE OTHERS   Indecent, hell!—What do you want us to drink? Water?—Shame on you, boy!

THE MAN WITH THE IDEA   Schnapps!

BAAL   I'll vote for that proposal. Schnapps is decent. What schnapps?

THE MAN WITH THE IDEA   Teddy's.

THE OTHERS   Teddy's?—That's an idea.—His ration! Teddy was thrifty.—That's a good idea for an idiot, boy!

THE MAN WITH THE IDEA   Good idea, eh? Something for you blockheads! Teddy's schnapps, to celebrate Teddy's funeral! Fitting and proper! Has anybody made a speech for Teddy yet! Wouldn't that be the right thing?

BAAL   I did.

SEVERAL WOODCUTTERS   When?

BAAL   Just now. Before you started talking big. It began with: Teddy has his rest . . . You never notice anything until it's all over.

THE OTHERS   Bonehead!—Let's get the schnapps!

BAAL   It's disgraceful.

THE OTHERS   Bah!—And why, great Elephant?

BAAL   It's Teddy's property. We've no right to break into that keg. Teddy has a wife and five poor orphans.

A WOODCUTTER   Four. There's only four.

ANOTHER WOODCUTTER   All of a sudden it comes out.

BAAL   Would you do that to Teddy's five poor orphans—drink up their poor father's schnapps? Is that Christian?

SAME WOODCUTTER   Four. Four orphans.

BAAL   To Teddy's four orphans—drink the schnapps right out of their mouths?

A WOODCUTTER   Teddy had no family at all.

BAAL   But orphans, my friends, orphans.

ANOTHER WOODCUTTER   The crazy Elephant is pulling our legs. Do you think Teddy's orphans would drink Teddy's schnapps? I admit it's Teddy's property . . .

BAAL (*interrupting*)   It was . . .

THE OTHER WOODCUTTER   What do you mean by that?

A WOODCUTTER   He's just shooting off his mouth. He's weak in the head.

THE OTHER WOODCUTTER   I say, it was Teddy's property, and so we'll pay for it. With money, good money, boys. Then the orphans can come ahead.

ALL   That's a good suggestion. The Elephant is overruled.—He must be crazy if he doesn't want any schnapps.—Let's leave him here and go drink Teddy's schnapps!

BAAL (*calling after them*)   Come back here at least, you damned scavengers! (*To Teddy*) Poor Teddy! And the trees are pretty strong today, and the air is good and soft, and I feel a swelling inside me—poor Teddy, don't you feel a tickling? You're done for altogether, let me tell you, soon you'll begin to stink, and the wind goes on, everything goes on, and I know where your shack is, and the living will take away your belongings, you've abandoned them, and all you wanted was peace. Your body wasn't so bad, Teddy, it still isn't, just a little damaged on one side, and the legs—you'd have been washed up with the women, you can't go between a woman with legs like that. (*He lifts the dead man's leg*) But all in all, you could have gone on living in this body if you'd really wanted to—but your soul was used to nothing but the best, the dwelling place was defective, and rats desert a sinking ship; you were simply the victim of your habits, Teddy.

THE OTHERS (*coming back*)   Hey, Elephant, now you're in for it! Where's the keg of brandy that was under Teddy's old bed?— Where were you while we were busy with poor Teddy? How about it, mister? Teddy wasn't quite dead yet, mister.—Where were you, you son of a bitch, you defiler of the dead, you protector of Teddy's poor orphans, eh?

BAAL   That proves nothing, my friends!

THE OTHERS   Then where's the schnapps? Are you going to claim that it drank itself?—This is a damn serious business, boy.— Come on, you, stand up, get up! Take four steps, and then try to deny that you're shaken, that you're a wreck, inside and outside, you swine!—Up with him, tickle him, boys, the defiler of Teddy's poor honor! (*They stand Baal on his feet*)

BAAL   You bastards! Don't trample poor Teddy at least! (*He sits down and takes the corpse's arm in his own*) If you manhandle me, Teddy'll fall on his face. Call that piety? I'm doing this in self-defense. There are seven of you, se-ven, and you haven't been drinking, I'm only one man and I have been drinking. Is that decent, is it honorable, seven to one? Calm down! Look at Teddy, he's calmed down.

SEVERAL WOODCUTTERS (*sadly and indignantly*)   Nothing is holy to that boy.—God have mercy on his drunken soul!—He's the most hardened sinner that ever ran around between God's fingers.

BAAL   Sit down, I can't stand preaching. Some people will always be smarter and some softer in the head. The softheads are the best workers. You know me—I work with my brain. (*He smokes*) You never had the proper respect, my friends! If you bury that good schnapps inside you, what inspiration will it bring you? But I discover truths, I tell you! I've been saying some very significant things to Teddy. (*He takes papers out of his breast pocket and examines them*) But you had to go running after your wretched schnapps. Sit down: look up at the sky, between the trees, it's getting dark. Is that nothing? Then there's no religion in you!

[11]   A Hut

Rain is heard. Baal. Ekart.

BAAL   Here our white bodies hibernate in the black mud.
EKART   You haven't gone for the meat yet!
BAAL   I suppose you're busy with your Mass?
EKART   Do you have to think about my Mass? Think of your woman! Where have you driven her again in this rain?
BAAL   She keeps running after me in despair and hanging on my neck.
EKART   You're sinking lower and lower.

BAAL   I'm too heavy.

EKART   Don't you ever expect to kick in?

BAAL   I'll fight to the last ditch. I'll go on living without my skin; I'll retreat all the way to my toes. I'll drop like a bull into the grass, where it's softest. I'll gulp death down, and I won't know a thing.

EKART   Ever since we've been lying here, you've been getting fatter.

BAAL   (*feels in his left armpit, under his shirt, with his right hand*) But my shirt is getting looser—the dirtier it gets, the looser. Somebody else could fit in here with me. But not with a fat body. And why are you just lazing around, resting your bones?

EKART   I've got a kind of sky inside my skull, very green and terribly high, and under it thoughts move, like light clouds in the wind. In no particular direction. I've got all that inside me.

BAAL   That's just delirium. You're an alcoholic. Now you see— it doesn't pay.

EKART   When the delirium comes, I can tell by my face.

BAAL   You've got a face with room for plenty of wind. It's concave. (*Looks at him*) You have no face. You're nothing. You're transparent.

EKART   I'm getting more and more mathematical.

BAAL   You never tell anybody your story. Why don't you ever talk about yourself?

EKART   I probably haven't got one. Who's running around outside?

BAAL   You have good ears. You've got something inside you that you cover up. You're evil, just like me, a devil. But some day you're going to see rats. Then you'll be good again.

(*Sophie is in the doorway*)

EKART   Is that you, Sophie?

BAAL   What do you want this time?

SOPHIE   May I come in now, Baal?

[12]   A Plain. Sky

Evening. Baal. Ekart. Sophie.

SOPHIE   My knees are giving out. Why are you running so desperately?

BAAL   Because you hang on my neck like a millstone.

EKART   How can you treat her like that, when you got her pregnant?

SOPHIE   I wanted it myself, Ekart.

BAAL   She wanted it herself. And now she's hanging on my neck.

EKART   That's bestial. Sit down here, Sophie.

SOPHIE (*sitting down heavily*)   Let him go on!

EKART (*to Baal*)   If you drop her, I'll stay with her.

BAAL   She won't stay with you. But you'll be deserting me. On account of her—it's just like you.

EKART   Twice you took my place in bed. My sweethearts left you cold—you filched them away from me although I loved them.

BAAL   Because you loved them. I violated corpses twice, because I wanted to keep you clean. I need that. I didn't get any pleasure out of it, God knows!

EKART (*to Sophie*)   And you still love this obvious beast?

SOPHIE   I can't help it, Ekart. I still love his corpse. I still love his fists. I can't help it, Ekart.

BAAL   I never want to know what you two did while I was in jail.

SOPHIE   We stood in front of the white prison together, and looked up at your cell window.

BAAL   But you were together.

SOPHIE   Beat me for it.

EKART (*shouting*)   Didn't you force her on me?

BAAL   I didn't give a damn about you in those days.

EKART   I haven't got your elephant's hide!

BAAL   That's why I love you.

EKART   At least keep your damn mouth shut about that, while she's here.

BAAL   Let her run along! She's turning into a bitch. (*Runs his hands over his throat*) She washes her dirty linen in your tears.

Can't you see the way she goes naked between us? I have the patience of a lamb, but I can't climb out of my own skin.

EKART (*sits down beside Sophie*)   Go home to your mother!

SOPHIE   I can't.

BAAL   She can't, Ekart.

SOPHIE   Beat me if you like, Baal. I'll stop asking you to slow down. I didn't mean it. Let me go with you, as long as I can —then I'll lie down in the bushes and you won't have to look. Don't send me away, Baal.

BAAL   Throw your swollen body in the river! You disgust me, and it's your own doing.

SOPHIE   Are you going to leave me lying here? You're not going to leave me lying here. You don't know that yet, Baal. You're like a child to be thinking such things.

BAAL   I'm sick and tired of you.

SOPHIE   But not at night, not at night, Baal. I'm afraid to be alone. I'm afraid of the dark. I'm afraid.

BAAL   In your condition? Nobody'll touch you.

SOPHIE   But tonight. Won't you stay with me tonight?

BAAL   Go to the raftsmen. It's Midsummer Night. They'll be drunk.

SOPHIE   Only a few minutes.

BAAL   Come, Ekart!

SOPHIE   But where will I go?

BAAL   To heaven, sweetheart!

SOPHIE   With my child?

BAAL   Bury it!

SOPHIE   I only pray that you'll never have to remember these things you're saying under the beautiful sky that you love so much. On my knees I pray for it.

EKART   I'll stay with you. And later on I'll take you to your mother—if you'll only say that you've stopped loving this beast.

BAAL   She loves me.

SOPHIE   I love this beast.

EKART   Are you still here, you beast? Haven't you got knees! Are you drunk on schnapps or on poetry? Degenerate beast! Degenerate beast!

BAAL   Fool!

(*Ekart rushes at him wildly; they wrestle*)

SOPHIE   Mother of God! They're wild beasts!

EKART (*wrestling*)   Did you hear what she said? In the woods—
and now it's getting dark? Degenerate beast! Degenerate beast!
BAAL (*pressing Ekart close*)   Now I've got you close. I've got you.
Can you smell me? It's better than women! (*Lets go*) Look,
Ekart, you can see stars over the woods.
EKART (*stares at Baal, who is looking at the sky*) I can't hit this beast.
BAAL (*putting an arm around him*)   It's getting dark. We need a
place to sleep in. In the woods there are hollows where there's
no wind. Come, I'll tell you about the beasts.
(*He draws him away*)
SOPHIE (*alone in the dark, screams*)   Baal!

[13]   Brown Wooden Bar

*Night. Wind. At tables, Gougou, Bolleboll. The old beggar and Maja,
with a child in a crate.*

BOLLEBOLL (*playing cards with Gougou*)   I'm out of money. Let's
play for our souls!
THE BEGGAR   Brother Wind wants to come in. But we don't know
our cold Brother Wind. Heh, heh, heh.
(*The child cries*)
MAJA (*the beggar woman*)   Listen! There's something creeping
around the house! If only it's not some big animal!
BOLLEBOLL   Why? You got hot pants again?
(*Pounding on the door*)
MAJA   Listen! I won't open!
THE BEGGAR   Yes, you will.
MAJA   No, no! Dear Mother of God, no!
THE BEGGAR   Bouque la Madonne! Open!
MAJA (*cringing, to the door*)   Who's there?
(*The child cries*)
(*Maja opens the door*)
BAAL (*entering with Ekart, wet with rain*)   Is this the Hospital Bar?
MAJA   Yes, but there's no bed free. (*More boldly*) And I'm sick.
BAAL   We've brought champagne with us.
(*Ekart has gone to the stove*)

BOLLEBOLL   Come right in! Anybody who knows what champagne is is all right with us.

THE BEGGAR   Only the best people are here today, my boy!

BAAL (*moving to the table, pulling two bottles out of his pockets*) Hm?

THE BEGGAR   It's an apparition.

BOLLEBOLL   I know where you got that champagne. But I won't tell anybody.

BAAL   Come on, Ekart! Any glasses?

MAJA   Cups, my dear sir! Cups! (*She brings some*)

GOUGOU   I need a cup of my own.

BAAL (*suspiciously*)   Are you allowed to drink champagne?

GOUGOU   Please!

(*Baal pours*)

BAAL   What's wrong with you?

GOUGOU   A cold in the lungs. It's nothing. A slight inflammation. Nothing serious.

BAAL (*to Bolleboll*)   And you?

BOLLEBOLL   Stomach ulcers. Not worth mentioning.

BAAL (*to the beggar*)   I trust you have some affliction, too?

THE BEGGAR   I'm insane.

BAAL   Prost!—We understand each other. I'm healthy.

THE BEGGAR   I once knew a man who thought he was healthy. That's what he thought. He was born in a forest, and one time he went back because there was something he had to think over. The forest seemed very strange to him, he'd lost his kinship with it. He walked for many days, all the way on into the wilderness, he wanted to see exactly how dependent he was, and how much strength he still had in him to keep on going. But there wasn't much left. (*Drinks*)

BAAL (*restlessly*)   What a wind! And we have to go on tonight, Ekart.

THE BEGGAR   Yes, the wind. One day, at dusk, when he didn't feel so alone any more, he was walking through the great silence between the trees, and he stopped under one of them, a big tall one. (*Drinks*)

BOLLEBOLL   The ape in him did that.

THE BEGGAR   Yes, maybe it was the ape. He leaned against it, very close, he felt the life inside it, or thought he did and said: You are taller than I, you stand fast, and you know the earth deep down underneath, and it holds you up. I can run and move about better, but I don't stand fast, and I can't reach into the depths, and nothing holds me up. And to me the great stillness over the silent treetops in the endless heavens is unknown. (*Drinks*)

GOUGOU   And what did the tree say?

THE BEGGAR   Yes. The wind blew. A tremor ran through the tree, the man felt it. He threw himself to the ground, hugged the wild, hard roots, and wept bitterly. But he did the same with many trees.

EKART   Did he ever get well?

THE BEGGAR   No, but his death was easier.

MAJA   I don't understand.

THE BEGGAR   We never understand. But we feel certain things. Stories we understand are just badly told.

BOLLEBOLL   Do you believe in God?

BAAL (*with an effort*)   I've always believed in myself. But it's possible to become an atheist.

BOLLEBOLL (*with a ringing laugh*)   It's time to make merry! God! Champagne! Love! Wind and rain! (*Makes a grab at Maja*)

MAJA   Leave me alone! Your mouth stinks!

BOLLEBOLL   And I suppose you haven't got syphilis? (*Takes her on his lap*)

THE BEGGAR   Careful! (*To Bolleboll*) I'm getting gradually drunk. And you can't go out in the rain today if I'm completely drunk.

GOUGOU (*to Ekart*)   He was better looking, that's how he got her.

EKART   And your intellectual superiority? Your psychic ascendancy?

GOUGOU   She didn't care about such things. She was pure and innocent.

EKART   And what did you do?

GOUGOU   I felt ashamed.

BOLLEBOLL   Listen! The wind! It's begging God for peace.

MAJA (*singing*)

Lullaby, baby, outside blows the storm
While we in here are so drunk and warm.

BAAL   Whose child is that?

MAJA   My daughter, kind sir.

THE BEGGAR   A Virgo Dolorosa!

BAAL (*drinking*)   That was the past, Ekart. Yes, that was beautiful too.

EKART   What?

BOLLEBOLL   He's forgotten.

BAAL   Past. What a strange word!

GOUGOU (*to Ekart*)   Best of all is nothingness.

BOLLEBOLL   Shh! Now comes Gougou's aria! The singing bag of worms!

GOUGOU   It's like the trembling air on summer evenings. Sunlight. But it doesn't tremble. Nothing. Nothing at all. You just stop. The wind blows, you're never cold. The rain falls, you never get wet. Funny things happen, you don't laugh. You rot, there's no more waiting. General strike.

THE BEGGAR   That's the paradise of hell!

GOUGOU   Yes, that's paradise. No more unfulfilled desires. All gone. You get over all your habits. Even the habit of desire. That's the way to be free.

MAJA   And what happens at the end?

GOUGOU (*grinning*)   Nothing. Nothing at all. The end never comes. Nothing lasts forever.

BOLLEBOLL   Amen.

BAAL (*has risen, to Ekart*)   Ekart, stand up! We've fallen in with murderers. (*Holding on to Ekart by the shoulders*) The worms are swelling. Crawling decomposition. The worms are glorifying themselves.

EKART   This is the second time you've been like this. Is it only from drinking?

BAAL   My guts will be on exhibit here . . . This is no mud bath.

EKART   Sit down! Drink till you're full! Warm yourself!

MAJA (*singing, rather drunk*)

Summer and winter, snowstorms and rain—
If we are stinko, we don't feel pain.

BOLLEBOLL (*has seized Maja, scuffling*)   That aria always tickles me, little Gougou . . . Kitchy, kitchy, little Maja.
(*The child cries*)

BAAL (*drinking*)   Who are you? (*Irritably, to Gougou*) Bag-of-Worms, that's your name. Have the doctors given you up? Prost! (*Sits down*)

THE BEGGAR   Watch out, Bolleboll! Champagne doesn't agree with me.

MAJA (*leaning on Bolleboll, sings*)

Shut your eyes, dear, to see is to weep
Shut them to sorrow and sleep, baby, sleep.

BAAL (*brutally*)

Float down the river, with rats in your hair,
Everything's lovely. The sky is still there.

(*He stands up, cup in hand*) The sky is black. What are you afraid of? (*Drums on the table*) You've got to stay with the merry-go-round. It's wonderful. (*Sways*) I want to be an elephant in the circus, that passes water when everything isn't just right . . . (*Begins dancing, sings*) Dance with the wind, poor dead body, sleep with the cloud, you run-down god! (*Swaying, he comes back to the table*)

EKART (*drunk, rising*)   I won't go any further with you. I have a soul too. You've corrupted my soul. You corrupt everything. Now I'm going to start on my Mass.

BAAL   I love you. Prost!

EKART   But I won't go with you! (*Sits down*)

THE BEGGAR (*to Bolleboll*)   Hands off, you swine!

MAJA   What business is it of yours?

THE BEGGAR   Be still, you miserable thing!

MAJA   You lunatic! You're raving!

BOLLEBOLL (*venomously*)   Lies! He isn't even sick. That's right! It's a fraud!

THE BEGGAR   And you've got cancer!

BOLLEBOLL (*strangely calm*)   I've got cancer?

THE BEGGAR (*intimidated*)   I haven't said a thing. Leave the poor creature alone!

(*Maja laughs*)

BAAL   Why is it crying? (*Strolls over to the crate*)

THE BEGGAR (*angrily*)   What do you want with it?

BAAL (*bending over the crate*)   Why are you crying? Haven't you
  seen all this before? Or do you cry every single time?
THE BEGGAR   Leave it alone, man! (*Throws his cup at Baal*)
MAJA (*jumping up*)   You swine!
BOLLEBOLL   He only wants to look under its clothes.
BAAL (*slowly standing*)   Oh you pigs! You've lost all humanity!
  Come, Ekart, we'll wash ourselves in the river! (*Goes with
  Ekart*)

[14]   Green Leafy Thicket. The River
Behind It

Baal. Ekart.

BAAL (*sitting among the leaves*)   The water is warm. We can lie on
  the sand like crabs. And then there are the bushes, and the
  white clouds in the sky. Ekart?
EKART (*hidden*)   What do you want?
BAAL   I love you.
EKART   I'm too comfortable.
BAAL   Did you see those clouds a while ago?
EKART   Yes. They're shameless. (*Silence*) A woman passed by just
  now.
BAAL   I don't care for women any more . . .

[15]   Country Road. Willows

Wind. Night. Ekart is asleep, on the grass.

BAAL (*coming across the fields, as if drunk, his clothes open, like a
  sleepwalker*)   Ekart! Ekart! I've got it! Wake up!
EKART   What have you got? Are you talking in your sleep again?
BAAL (*sitting down beside him*)   This:

Once she had drowned, and started her slow descent
Downstream to where the river broadens

The opal sky shone most magnificent
As if it had to be her body's guardian.

Wrack and seaweed cling to her as she swims
Slowly their burden adds to her weight
Cool the fishes play about her limbs
Creatures and growths encumber her in her final state.

Then in the evening the sky grew dark as smoke
And at night the stars kept the light still soaring
But soon it cleared, as dawn again broke
To maintain her sequence of evening and morning.

As her pale body decayed in the water there
It happened (very slowly) that God gradually forgot it
First her face, then her hands, then right at the end her hair.
Then she rotted in rivers where much else is rotted.

(*Wind*)

EKART   Is the ghost walking so soon? It's not as bad as you are.
But sleep has gone to hell, and the wind is playing the organ
again in the willows. Nothing is left but the white bosom of
philosophy, darkness and dampness, until the end of our days;
and even old women have nothing left but second sight.

BAAL   In this wind you don't need schnapps to make you drunk.
I see the world in a gentle light; it's the good Lord's excrement.

EKART   The good Lord, who revealed himself completely, once
and for all, in the combination of the urethra and the sex organ.

BAAL (*lying down*)   All this is so beautiful.

(*Wind*)

EKART   The willows are like stumps of rotten teeth in the sky's
black mouth.—I'll be starting work on my Mass soon.

BAAL   Is the Quartet finished?

EKART   Where would I find the time?

(*Wind*)

BAAL   There's a pale, red-haired woman; you go around with her.

EKART   She has a soft, white body; she brings it down to the
willows at noon. They have branches that hang down like hair,
and there we fuck like squirrels.

BAAL   Is she more beautiful then I am?

(*Darkness. The wind continues to play the organ*)

[16]   Young Hazelnut Bushes

Long red withes hanging down. Baal sits among them. Noon.

BAAL   I'll satisfy her—that's all.—The white dove . . . (*Looking around*) There's a good view of the clouds through willow branches . . . Then, if he comes, he'll only see her skin. These love affairs of his make me sick. Be still, my precious soul! (*A young woman comes out of the thicket: red hair, full figure, pale*)

BAAL (*not looking around*)   Are *you* the one?

THE YOUNG WOMAN   Where is your friend?

BAAL   He's writing a Mass in E-flat minor.

THE YOUNG WOMAN   Tell him I was here!

BAAL   He's becoming too obvious. He's soiling himself. He's regressing to zoology. Sit down! (*He looks around*)

THE YOUNG WOMAN   I'd rather stand.

BAAL (*pulling himself up by the willow branches*)   He's been eating too many eggs lately.

THE YOUNG WOMAN   I love him.

BAAL   What do I care about you! (*Holds her*)

THE YOUNG WOMAN   Don't touch me! You're too dirty.

BAAL (*slowly touching her throat*)   Is this your neck? Do you know how they silence doves, or wild ducks, in the woods?

THE YOUNG WOMAN   Mother of God! (*Pulls back*) Leave me alone!

BAAL   With those weak knees of yours? You're going to fall. You want me to lay you down among the willows. A man's a man; in that respect we're almost all the same. (*Takes her in his arms*)

THE YOUNG WOMAN (*trembling*)   Please let me go! Please!

BAAL   A shameless quail! Let's go! A desperate man is saving his life! (*Holds her by both arms, drags her into the bushes*)

[17]   Maple Tree in the Wind

Baal and Ekart, sitting among the roots.

BAAL   We need a drink, Ekart; have you any money left?
EKART   No. Look at that maple tree in the wind!
BAAL   It's trembling.
EKART   Where's that girl you were taking around to all the taverns?
BAAL   Turn into a fish and look for her.
EKART   You're overeating, Baal. You'll burst.
BAAL   That's an explosion I'd be glad to hear.
EKART   Don't you look down into the water sometimes, when it's black and deep, and there are no fish? Never fall in. You'd better be on your guard. You're so very heavy, Baal.
BAAL   I'll be on my guard against somebody else. I've made up a song. Want to hear it?
EKART   Read it—then I'll know you.
BAAL   It's called: Death in the Woods.

And a man died in the primeval woods
Where the storm blew in torrents around him.
Died like an animal scrabbling for roots
Stared up through the trees, where the wind skimmed the
    woods
As the howl of the thunderstorm drowned him.

And his comrades stood there in a row
And they tried to make his passage smoother
Saying: We'll get you home all right, brother.
But he threw them off him with a blow
Spat and cried: And where is home, d'you know?
That was home, and he hadn't any other.

Is your toothless mouth choked up with pus?
How's the rest of you: can you still tell?
Must you die so slowly and with so much fuss?

We've just had your horse carved up as meat for us.
Hurry up! They're waiting down in hell.

And the forest roared above his head
Clinging to a tree in desperation
And they heard his screams and what he said.
And they felt an overwhelming dread
Clenched their fists with frightful agitation:
So like them, and yet so nearly dead!

You're mad, useless, putrid! To your lair!
You're a sore, a chancre, you're excreta!
Selfish beast, you're breathing up our air
So they said. And he, the cancer there:
Let me live! Your sun was never sweeter!
Lovely radiance all of us can share!

This is what no friend can understand
How they're shocked to silence and they shiver.
Earth holds out to him her naked hand
In the breeze from sea to sea lies land:
Here I lie in solitude for ever.

Our poor life, by some inherent weight
Held him so that even half-decayed
He pressed his dead body ever deeper:
At the dawn of day he fell dead in the grassy shade.
Numb with shock they buried him, and cold with hate
Hiding him with undergrowth and creeper.

And they rode in silence from that place
Turning round to see the tree again
Under which his body once had lain
Who felt dying was too cruel a pain:
The tree stood in the sun ablaze
As each made the mark of the Cross on his face
And then rode swiftly out to the plain.

EKART   Hm. It certainly looks bad.
BAAL   Whenever I can't sleep at night, I look up at the stars. It's
just as good.
EKART   Really?

BAAL (*suspiciously*) But I don't do it very often. It makes me weak.

EKART (*after a while*) You've been writing a lot of poetry lately. I suppose you haven't had a woman for quite a while?

BAAL Why?

EKART That's what I thought. Say you haven't.

(*Baal stands up, stretches, looks at the crown of the maple tree, laughs*)

[18]   Tavern

Evening. Ekart. The waitress. Watzmann. Johannes, ragged, in a shabby coat with a turned-up collar, hopelessly run down. The waitress looks like Sophie.

EKART It's been eight years now.

(*They drink. The wind blows*)

JOHANNES They say life begins at twenty-five. That's when they grow wider and get children.

(*Silence*)

WATZMANN His mother died yesterday. He's running around trying to borrow money for the funeral. He'll bring it back here. Then we'll be able to pay for the schnapps. The landlord is a decent fellow; he gives credit for a corpse that once was a mother. (*Drinks*)

JOHANNES Baal! He hasn't got the wind in his sails any more.

WATZMANN (*to Ekart*) I daresay he gives you a lot to put up with.

EKART I can't spit in his face. He's sinking.

WATZMANN (*to Johannes*) Does it make you unhappy? Does it upset you?

JOHANNES It's a pity, if you ask me. (*Drinks*)

(*Silence*)

WATZMANN He's getting more and more disgusting.

EKART Don't say that. I don't want to know. I love him. I don't mind anything he does. Because I love him. He's a child.

WATZMANN He only does what he has to. He's so lazy.

EKART (*stepping into the doorway*) It's a mild night. A warm wind.

Like milk. I love it all. People shouldn't drink. Or not so much. (*Goes back to the table*) The night is mild. At the moment—and for three more weeks of autumn—I'd be all right on the road. (*Sits*)

WATZMANN You're leaving tonight? I suppose you want to get rid of him? You're sick of him?

JOHANNES You'd better watch your step!

(*Baal enters slowly*)

WATZMANN   Is it you, Baal?

EKART (*hard*) What do you want now?

BAAL (*comes in, sits down*) What a stinking hole this place has turned into!

(*The waitress brings him schnapps*)

WATZMANN Nothing has changed. Only you seem to have become more refined in your tastes.

BAAL Is it still you, Luise?

(*Silence*)

JOHANNES Yes, I like it here.—I need to drink, to drink a lot. It gives me strength. Even so, the road to hell is over knives. I admit it. But not exactly. As if your knees were caving in: no resistance! So you hardly feel the knife. With springy knee joints. You know, I never used to have such comical ideas when I was leading a comfortable middle-class life. But now I get ideas. Now I'm a genius. Hm.

EKART (*in an outburst*) I want to be back in the woods again, in the early morning! The light is lemon-colored between the tree trunks! I want to go back up to the forests.

JOHANNES That's something I don't understand. Baal, you've got to pay for another schnapps. This is really a nice place.

BAAL A schnapps for—

JOHANNES No names! We know each other. You know, I sometimes dream such awful things at night. But only now and then. Yes, it's really nice. (*The wind blows. They drink*)

WATZMANN (*singing in an undertone*)

There are plenty of trees you can turn to
All very conveniently made—
For hanging yourself from their branches
Or stretching yourself in their shade.

BAAL   Where was it ever like that? It was like that once.

JOHANNES   She's still drifting. Nobody ever found her. Only
sometimes I get the feeling that she's drifting down my throat
in all this schnapps, a small corpse, half rotted away. She was
already seventeen after all. Now she has rats and water weeds
in her green hair; rather becoming . . . a little bloated, and
whitish, full of stinking river muck, all black. She was always
so clean. That's why she drowned herself and began to stink.

WATZMANN   What is flesh? It decays, like spirit. Gentlemen, I am
completely drunk. Two times two is four. So I'm not drunk.
But I have intimations of a higher world. Bow down, be hum
—humble! Set aside the old Adam. (*Drinks, shakily and vio-*
lently) I haven't quite gone under yet, as long as I have my
intimations and I can still figure out that two times two . . . Isn't
two a funny word? Two! (*Sits down*)

BAAL (*reaching for his guitar and smashing the light with it*)   Now
I'll sing. (*Sings*)

Sick from sun, and shredded raw by the weather
A looted wreath crowning his tangled head
He called back the dreams of a childhood he had lost altogether
Forgot the roof, not the sky that was overhead.

(*Speaking*) My voice isn't exactly as clear as a bell.

EKART   Go on singing, Baal!

BAAL (*goes on singing*)

O you whose life it has been always to suffer
You murderers they expelled from heaven and hell
Why did you not remain in the womb with your mother
Where it was quiet, and you slept, and all was well?

(*Speaking*) The guitar isn't tuned right, either.

WATZMANN   That's a good song. Just the kind for me! Romantic!

BAAL (*goes on singing*)

Still he explores and scans the absinthe-green ocean
Though his mother gave him up for lost

Grinning and cursing, or weeping at times with contrition
Always in search of that land where life is best.

WATZMANN   Now I can't find my glass. The table is wobbling
idiotically. Put on the light. You can't even find your mouth in
here!

EKART   Nonsense! Can you see anything, Baal?

BAAL   No. I don't want to. It's fine in the dark. With champagne
inside, and nostalgia without memory. Are you my friend,
Ekart?

EKART (*with an effort*)   Yes, but sing!

BAAL (*singing*)

Loafing through hells and flogged through paradises
Calm and grinning, with expressionless stare
Sometimes he dreams of a small field he recognizes
With blue sky overhead and nothing there.

JOHANNES   Now I'll stay with you always. Don't worry—I won't
be a burden to you. I hardly eat anything now.

WATZMANN (*with an effort, has struck a light*)   Let there be light.
Heh, heh, heh.

BAAL   It's blinding. (*Stands*)

EKART (*with the waitress on his lap, stands up with an effort and tries
to loosen her armhold around his neck*)   What's the matter with
you? It doesn't mean a thing. It's ridiculous.
(*Baal crouches, ready to spring*)

EKART   You can't be jealous of her?
(*Baal gropes his way forward. A mug falls*)

EKART   Why shouldn't I have women?
(*Baal looks at him*)

EKART   Am I your sweetheart?
(*Baal throws himself at Ekart, chokes him. The light goes out.
Watzmann laughs drunkenly. The waitress screams. Other guests
come in from the next room, with a lamp*)

WATZMANN   He's got a knife.

THE WAITRESS   He's killing him. Mother of God!

TWO MEN (*throwing themselves on top of the struggling men*)   What

the hell, man! Let go!—The bastard's stabbed him! Lord God
in heaven!
BAAL (*rising. Suddenly the dawn breaks in and the lamp goes out*)
Ekart!

[19]   Longitude 10° East of Greenwich

Forest. Baal is on his way with his guitar, his hands in his pockets.

BAAL   The pale wind in the black trees! They're like Lupu's wet
hair. Around eleven o'clock, the moon will come out. Then it
will be bright enough. This is a little forest. I'll trot down to the
big one. I don't mind the rough going now that I'm alone again,
in my own skin. I've got to head north. Toward the veined side
of the leaves. Put that little business behind me. On! (*Sings*):

Baal will watch the vultures in the star-shot sky
Hovering patiently, waiting for Baal to die.

(*He moves on*)

Sometimes Baal plays dead. The vultures swoop.
Baal, without a word, will dine on vulture soup.

(*Gust of wind*)

[20]   Country Road

Evening. Wind and rain. Two policemen are fighting the wind.

FIRST POLICEMAN   The black rain, and this All Souls' wind! That
damned tramp!
SECOND POLICEMAN   He seems to me to be heading further and
further north, toward the forests. Nobody'll ever find him up
there.

FIRST POLICEMAN   Who is he anyway?

SECOND POLICEMAN   In the first place: a murderer. Started out as a cabaret performer and poet. Then merry-go-round owner, woodcutter, millionairess's lover, jailbird and pimp. After the murder, they caught him, but he has the strength of an elephant. It was on account of a waitress, a registered whore. He stabbed his best friend on account of her.

FIRST POLICEMAN   A man like that has no soul. He's a wild beast.

SECOND POLICEMAN   And yet he's like a child. He carries wood for old women, and it nearly gets him caught. He never had anything. The waitress was the last straw. That's probably why he killed his friend, another shady character to tell the truth.

FIRST POLICEMAN   If there was only some place to get schnapps, or a woman! Let's go! It's spooky around here. And there's something moving! (*Both go*)

BAAL (*coming out of the bushes with his pack and guitar. Whistling through his teeth*)   Dead, eh? Poor little beast! Getting in my way! Now it's beginning to be interesting. (*Goes on, after the policemen. Wind*)

[21]   Wooden Hut in the Forest

Night. Wind. Baal, on a dirty bed. Men are playing cards and drinking.

A MAN (*next to Baal*)   What do you want? You're on your last legs. A child can see that—and who's interested in you? Have you got anybody? See? See? Grit your teeth! Have you any teeth left? Sometimes people kick in who could still have had a lot more fun—millionaires! But you haven't even got any papers. Don't worry, the world will roll on, round as a ball; tomorrow morning the wind will whistle. Try to look at things more objectively. Tell yourself that a rat is dying. See? Just don't make a fuss! You have no teeth left.

THE MEN   Is it still raining? We'll have to stay up all night with the corpse.—Shut up! Trump!—Any breath left, fatso? Sing something? "Within his mother's womb so white . . ."—Leave him alone. He'll be cold before this black rain is over. Go on playing!—He drank like a sponge, but there's something about that pale lump of fat that makes a man think. Nobody sang him that tune in his cradle.—Ten of clubs! Shut up, gentlemen! That's no way to play. If you want a decent game, you'll have to be more serious.

(*Silence, except for cursing*)

BAAL   What time is it?

THE SAME MAN   Eleven. Are you leaving?

BAAL   Soon. Are the roads bad?

THE SAME MAN   Rain.

THE MEN (*getting up*)   The rain has stopped now. It's time.— Everything will be dripping wet.—Now he's got another excuse for not working. (*They pick up their axes*)

A MAN (*stopping in front of Baal, spitting*)   Good night and goodbye. You going to croak?

ANOTHER MAN   Going to kick in? Incognito?

THIRD MAN   Try to schedule your stinking tomorrow. We'll be cutting until noon and then we'll want to eat.

BAAL   Couldn't you stay here a little while?

ALL (*laughing loudly*)   Want us to mother you? Want to sing your swan song?—Want to confess, you schnapps barrel?—Can't you puke on your own?

BAAL   If you'd stay half an hour.

ALL (*laughing loudly*)   You know what you can do? Croak by yourself!—Let's go, boys! The wind has died down.—What's wrong with you?

THE FIRST MAN   I'll come later.

BAAL   It can't be much longer, gentlemen. (*Laughter*) You wouldn't want to die all alone, gentlemen! (*Laughter*)

ANOTHER MAN   You old woman! Here's a souvenir! (*Spits in his face*)

(*All go to the door*)

BAAL   Twenty minutes!

(*The men go out through the open door*)

THE FIRST MAN (*in the doorway*)   Stars.

BAAL   Wipe off the spit!

FIRST MAN (*goes to him*)   Where?

BAAL   On my forehead.

FIRST MAN   All right. Why are you laughing?

BAAL   It tastes good.

FIRST MAN (*angrily*)   You're through. Addio! (*Goes to the door with his ax*)

BAAL   Thank you.

FIRST MAN   Can I do anything else for you . . . but I've got to go to work. Damn it all! Corpses!

BAAL   You! Come closer! (*First man bends down*) It's been beautiful . . .

FIRST MAN   What? You lunatic! Eunuch, I mean.

BAAL   Everything.

FIRST MAN   Each man to his taste! (*Laughs loudly, goes. The door is still open. The blue night can be seen*)

BAAL (*nervously*)   Hey, you!

FIRST MAN (*in the window*)   Huh?

BAAL   Are you going?

FIRST MAN   To work!

BAAL   Where?

FIRST MAN   What's it to you?

BAAL   What time is it?

FIRST MAN   Quarter past eleven. (*Goes*)

BAAL   He's gone. (*Silence*) One, two, three, four, five, six. That's no help. (*Silence*) Mama! Make Ekart go away. The sky is so damned close now, close enough to touch. Everything is dripping wet again. Sleep. One. Two. Three. Four. It's stifling in here. It must be light outside. I want to go out. (*Raises himself*) I will go out. Dear Baal. (*Sharply*) I'm not a rat. Outside it must be light. Dear Baal. At least I can get to the door. I've still got knees, it's better in the doorway. Hell! Dear Baal! (*He crawls to the threshold on all fours*) Stars . . . Hm. (*He crawls out*)

[22]   Morning in the Forest

Woodcutters.

FIRST   Give me the schnapps! You can listen to the birds!

SECOND   It's going to be a hot day.

THIRD   A lot of trees are still standing that have got to come down by nightfall.

FOURTH   I guess he's cold by now?

THIRD   Yes. Yes. He's cold.

SECOND   Yes. Yes.

THIRD   We could have had those eggs now if he hadn't eaten them on us. That's really something—stealing eggs on his deathbed! I was sorry for him at first, but then it got to be too much. Thank God he didn't get wind of the schnapps those last three days. No consideration. Eggs—in a corpse!

FIRST   The way he lay down in the dirt! He wasn't ever going to get up again, and he knew it. He lay down as if it was a made-up bed. Carefully! Did anybody know him? What was his name? What did he do?

FOURTH   We'll have to bury him anyway. Give me the schnapps!

THIRD   When he'd begun to rattle deep down in his throat, I asked him: "What are you thinking about?" I always like to know what a dying man is thinking about. And he said: "I'm still listening to the rain." It gave me gooseflesh. "I'm still listening to the rain." That's what he said.

Drums in the Night

A Comedy

Translators: William E. Smith and Ralph Manheim

CHARACTERS

ANDREAS KRAGLER

ANNA BALICKE

KARL BALICKE, her father

AMALIA BALICKE, her mother

FREDERICK MURK, her fiancé

BABUSCH, a journalist

TWO MEN

PICCADILLY-BAR MANKE,
   a waiter

RAISINS MANKE, his brother,
   a waiter

GLUBB, the gin mill owner

THE DRUNK

BULLTROTTER, a newspaper
   vendor

A WORKER

LAAR, a peasant

AUGUSTA AND MARIE, prostitutes

A MAID

A WOMAN NEWSPAPER VENDOR

The two Manke brothers are played by the same actor.

In this play a small circle in the margin [o] has been used to indicate the position for insertion of variant material. See Notes and Variants, p. 386 ff. for further explanation.

ACT ONE

(AFRICA)

At the Balickes'

Dark room with muslin curtains. Evening.

BALICKE (*shaving at the window*) Four years since he was reported missing. He'll never come back now. The times are so
damned uncertain. Any man is worth his weight in gold. Two
years ago I'd have given my blessing. You took me in with your
damned sentimentality. But now I'd walk over dead bodies.

MRS. BALICKE (*facing a photograph, on the wall, of Kragler as an
artilleryman*) He was such a good man. Such a childlike man.

BALICKE He's rotted away by now.

MRS. BALICKE What if he comes back?

BALICKE Nobody comes back from heaven.

MRS. BALICKE By all the heavenly hosts, Anna would drown
herself.

BALICKE If she says that, she's a goose, and I've never seen a
goose drown itself.

MRS. BALICKE Besides, she's been throwing up all the time.

BALLICKE She shouldn't eat so much blackberries and pickled
herring. That Murk is a fine boy. We can thank God on our
knees for him.

MRS. BALICKE He does make money. But compared to the other!
It brings the tears to my eyes.

BALICKE Compared to a corpse? I tell you it's now or never.
What's she waiting for? The Pope? Does she want a nigger? I'm
sick of this romantic stuff.

MRS. BALICKE But suppose this corpse that you say is rotting does

come back from heaven or hell—"My name is Kragler"—who's
going to tell him he's a corpse and his girl is in bed with another
man?

BALICKE   I'll tell him. And you tell that little fool that I'm sick and
tired of this and it's time to play the Wedding March, and Murk
is the man. If I tell her, she'll drown us in tears. And now will
you kindly give us some light?

MRS. BALICKE   I'll get the adhesive. You always cut yourself in the
dark.

BALICKE   Cuts are free of charge. Light costs money.
(*Calling*) Anna!

ANNA (*in the doorway*)   What's the matter, Father?

BALICKE   Kindly listen to your mother, and no bawling on your
big day.

MRS. BALICKE   Come here, Anna! Father thinks you're looking
pale, as if you didn't sleep at night.

ANNA   I sleep fine.

MRS. BALICKE   See here. This can't go on forever. He'll never
come back now. (*Lights the candles*)

BALICKE   Now she's making those big crocodile eyes again!

MRS. BALICKE   It's been hard on you. He was a good man, but he's
dead now.

BALICKE   Buried and rotting away!

MRS. BALICKE   Karl! And now there's Murk. He's got a head on
his shoulders, he'll go far.

BALICKE   See what I mean?

MRS. BALICKE   So say yes, for goodness' sake.

BALICKE   And no dramatics.

MRS. BALICKE   Just take him, for goodness' sake!

BALICKE (*furious, busy with the adhesive tape*)   Yes, damn it, do
you think a man can be kicked around like a football? Yes or
no! It's stupid to keep ogling up at heaven.

ANNA   Y-yes, Papa.

BALICKE (*irritated*)   All right, go ahead and bawl, open the flood-
gates, I'll get my lifebelt.

MRS. BALICKE   But don't you love Murk just a little bit?

BALICKE   It's immoral if you ask me.

MRS. BALICKE   Karl! Tell me, Anna, aren't you and Frederick
getting along?

ANNA   Of course we are. But don't you realize . . . ? And I'm so sick to my stomach.

BALICKE   I don't know a thing. I'm telling you, the man has rotted away, his bones have fallen apart! Four years! And no sign of life! And the whole battery blown sky-high! To smithereens! Missing! It doesn't take a genius to say where he is now. It's just that you're so damn scared of ghosts! Get yourself a man and you won't have to worry about ghosts. (*Going toward Anna, broadly*) Are you a brave girl or aren't you? All right, so come to Papa.

(*The doorbell rings*)

ANNA   (*frightened*)   It's him.

BALICKE   Keep him outside. Talk to him.

MRS. BALICKE   (*in the doorway with a laundry basket*)   Haven't you got anything to put in the wash?

ANNA   Yes. No. No, I don't think so . . .

MRS. BALICKE   But this is the eighth.

ANNA   The eighth? Already?

MRS. BALICKE   Of course it's the eighth!

ANNA   And what if it were the eighteenth?

BALICKE   What's all this chatter in the doorway? Come inside.

MRS. BALICKE   All right, just see that you put something in the wash! (*Goes out*)

BALICKE   (*sits down, takes Anna on his lap*)   See here, a woman without a man is blasphemy. You miss this fellow who's been gathered to the High Command. But do you really remember him? Nonsense, my dear. Death has turned him into a figure for the waxworks, he's had a three-year beauty treatment. Even if he weren't as dead as a doornail, he'd be very different from what you think. Anyway, he's rotted away and lost his looks! No more nose! And you miss him! Take another man, I tell you! That's nature, see. You'll wake up feeling like a rabbit in a cabbage patch! You're sound of body and limb, nothing wrong with your appetite! There's no blasphemy in that.

ANNA   But I can't forget him! Never! You're trying to talk me into it, but I can't!

BALICKE   Take Murk. He'll help you get over him.

ANNA   I do love him, and some day I won't love anybody else. But the time hasn't come yet.

BALICKE   Never mind, he'll bring you around, but he needs certain privileges. Marriage will do the trick. I can't tell you exactly what I mean, you're too young. (*Tickles her*) There! Is it
a deal?

ANNA (*laughs salaciously*)   I don't even know if Frederick wants
to.

BALICKE   Come in, woman.

MRS. BALICKE   Won't you come into the parlor? Do come in, Mr.
Murk.

BALICKE   Evening, Murk! Say, you look like a washed-up corpse!

MURK   Good evening, Anna!

BALICKE   What's the matter? Business trouble? You're green
around the gills. Is it the shooting in the streets tonight? (*Silence*) All right, Anna, you cheer him up. (*Goes out ostentatiously
with his wife*)

ANNA   What *is* the matter, Frederick? You really do look pale.

MURK (*sniffing*)   I suppose he needs the wine to celebrate our
engagement. (*Silence*) Has somebody been here? (*Coming closer
to Anna*) Has someone been here? Why are you suddenly as
white as a sheet? Who's been here?

ANNA   Nobody. Nobody's been here. What's got into you?

MURK   Then why are they in such a hurry? You can't put anything over on me. All right, if that's what he wants. But I'm not
getting engaged in this joint.

ANNA   Who said anything about getting engaged?

MURK   The old lady. The Lord's eye maketh the cattle fat.
(*Pacing around restlessly*) Oh well, why not?

ANNA   You act as if this meant something to my parents. God
knows it doesn't mean a thing to my parents. Nothing at all.

MURK   Tell me, when did you take your first communion?

ANNA   I only meant you were taking things a little too much for
granted.

MURK   Oh! Because of the other fellow?

ANNA   I didn't say anything about the other fellow.

MURK   But there he hangs. There he is, he haunts the place.

ANNA   That was entirely different. That was something you'll
never understand; it was spiritual.

MURK   And what's between us is physical?

ANNA   What's between us is nothing at all.

MURK   It is now! It's something now.

ANNA   How would you know?

MURK   You'll soon be singing a different tune.

ANNA   That's what you think.

MURK   But I'm proposing.

ANNA   And this is your declaration of love?

MURK   No, that comes later.

ANNA   There is a box factory after all.

MURK   You really are a bitch. And last night again, they didn't catch on?

ANNA   Oh, Frederick. They sleep like logs. (*Presses close to him*)

MURK   We don't.

ANNA   You rascal!

MURK   (*takes hold of her, but kisses her nonchalantly*)   Bitch!

ANNA   Shh! A train in the night! Do you hear it? Sometimes I'm afraid he'll come back. It gives me the cold shivers.

MURK   The mummy? I'll take care of him. But let me tell you this. You've got to get rid of him. I'm not putting up with a stiff between us in bed.

ANNA   Don't get excited! Come on, Frederick, forgive me.

MURK   St. Andreas? A ghost. He won't be any more alive after we're married than after he was buried. Want to bet? (*Laughs*) I'll bet you a baby.

ANNA   (*hiding her face against his chest*)   Oh, Frederick, you mustn't say such things.

MURK   (*gaily*)   You'll see. (*In the direction of the door*) Come in, Mother. Hello, Father.

MRS. BALICKE   (*right behind the door*)   Oh, children! (*Starting to sob*) And out of a clear blue sky!

BALICKE   A rough delivery, eh? (*General embrace, with emotion*)

MURK   Triplets! When do we have the wedding? Time is money!

BALICKE   In three weeks as far as I'm concerned. The bed is ready. Mother, let's have some supper.

MRS. BALICKE   Right away, right away, Papa, just let me catch my breath. (*Runs out*) And out of a clear blue sky!

MURK   Let me invite you out. We'll have a bottle at the Piccadilly Bar. I'm for getting engaged right away. What do you think, Anna?

ANNA   If we must.

BALICKE   But here! Why the Piccadilly Bar? Have you got a screw loose?

MURK   (*uneasily*)   Not here. Nothing doing!

BALICKE   Why not?

ANNA   He's so funny. Never mind, we'll go to the Piccadilly Bar.

BALICKE   Tonight? We'd be taking our life in our hands.

MRS. BALICKE   (*enters with the maid, bearing platters*)   Ah, my dears! Life is full of surprises! Be seated, gentlemen!
    (*They start gobbling*)

BALICKE   (*raising his glass*)   To the young couple! (*Clinking glasses*) The times are uncertain. The war is over. The pork is too fat, Amalia. Demobilization is sweeping disorder, greed and inhuman brutality over the oases of peaceful labor.

MURK   Where we make ammunition boxes, prost! Prost, Anna!

BALICKE   Shady, disreputable characters are springing up all around us. The government is too lax about combating the vultures of revolution. (*Unfolds a newspaper*) The incited masses have no ideals. But the worst of the lot, between ourselves, are the soldiers back from the front, brutalized, degenerate adventurers who've lost the habit of working. Nothing is sacred to them. Yes, these are hard times. A real man is worth his weight in gold, Anna. Hold on to him. Fight your way upward, but always together, upward, but always together, prost! (*He winds up the phonograph*)

MURK (*wiping away the sweat*)   That's talking! A real man always gets ahead. You need elbows, you need hobnailed boots and a square jaw, and don't look down. That's what it takes, Anna. I came up from the bottom myself. Errand boy, machine shops, here a trick, there a trick, I picked up things as I went along. That's how this Germany of ours got where it is. We didn't always wear gloves, but God knows we always worked hard. And now we're on top. Prost, Anna! (*The phonograph plays: "I Worship the Power of Love"*)

BALICKE   Right you are! What's the matter now, Anna?

ANNA (*has risen, half turned away*)   I don't know. It's all happening so fast. Maybe that's bad. What do you think, Mother?

MRS. BALICKE   What's the matter, child? What a silly goose! Enjoy yourself. What can be bad about it?

BALICKE   Sit down. Or wind the phonograph as long as you're up. (*Anna sits down. Pause*)

MURK   Prost! (*Clinks glasses with Anna*) What's wrong with you?

BALICKE   Well, Fritz, about the business, ammunition boxes are going to be washed up pretty soon. Another few weeks of civil war is the most we can expect, and then what? I've got a great idea. I mean it. Baby carriages. The factory is in good shape all around. (*He takes Murk by the arm and draws him toward the rear. Pulls back the curtains*) Annex Two and Annex Three. Good solid construction, and modern. Anna, wind the phonograph. It moves me every time. (*The phonograph plays: "Deutschland, Deutschland über Alles"*)

MURK   There's a man in the factory yard. Say, what's going on?

ANNA   It's scary. I think he's looking up here.

BALICKE   Probably the watchman. What are you laughing about, Fritz? Something stuck in your throat? The women are all pale.

MURK   I've got a funny feeling: the Spartacists . . .

BALICKE   Nonsense. No Spartacists around here. (*Nevertheless turns away in embarrassment*) Well, that's the factory. (*Goes to the table. Anna draws the curtains*) The war brought me prosperity. There it was, lying in the street, why not take it? I'd have been crazy not to. If I hadn't someone else would have. The end of the pig is the beginning of the sausage. If you look the facts in the face, the war was a lucky break for us. We've piled up some nice cozy capital. We can start making baby carriages with an easy mind. There's no hurry. Am I right?

MURK   Dead right, Papa! Prost!

BALICKE   And you can make babies with an easy mind. Ha-ha-ha!

MAID   Mr. Balicke, Mr. Babusch is here.

BABUSCH (*trots in*)   Friends, the Reds are having a witches' sabbath, but you're nicely fortified in here. Spartacus is mobilizing. The negotiations have been broken off. In twenty-four hours the artillery will be firing on Berlin.

BALICKE (*with his napkin tied around his neck*)   Damnation! Aren't those devils satisfied?

MRS. BALICKE   Artillery? Oh, my goodness gracious! What a night! I'm going down in the cellar, Balicke.

○   BABUSCH It's quiet downtown. But I hear they're planning to take over the newspapers.

BALICKE What! And here we are celebrating an engagement. Today of all days! We're out of our minds.

MURK They should all be lined up against the wall.

BALICKE Anybody that's dissatisfied, shoot him.

BABUSCH Are *you* getting engaged, Balicke?

MURK Babusch, meet my bride-to-be!

MRS. BALICKE Out of a clear blue sky! But when do you think they'll start shooting?

BABUSCH (*shakes hands with Anna and Murk*) The Spartacists have stored up mountains of arms. Shady rabble! So Anna's getting engaged! Go right ahead, they won't come here. The sanctity of the hearth! The family! The German family! "My home is my castle."

MRS. BALICKE Did it have to be today of all days? Your big day, Anna!

BABUSCH But my dear friends, it's damned interesting.

BALICKE Not to me. Not in the least. (*Passes his napkin over his lips*)

MURK Say, why don't you come to the Piccadilly Bar with us? To celebrate our engagement.

BABUSCH And the Spartacists?

BALICKE Let 'em wait, Babusch. Let 'em shoot somebody else in the belly, Babusch. Come along to the Piccadilly Bar. Go get dressed, girls.

MRS. BALICKE The Piccadilly Bar? Tonight? (*Sits down in a chair*)

BALICKE It used to be called the Piccadilly Bar. Now it's called the Café Fatherland. Frederick has invited us. What's wrong with tonight? What are cabs for? Get a move on, woman. Put on your glad rags.

MRS. BALICKE I'm not setting foot outside these four walls. What's got into you, Fritz?

ANNA When Frederick makes up his mind to something . . . (*All look at Murk*)

MURK Not here! Certainly not. I . . . I want music and light. It's really a nice place. It's so dark here. I've dressed especially for the occasion. How about it, Mother?

MRS. BALICKE   It's beyond me. (*Goes out*)

ANNA   Wait for me, Frederick. I won't be a minute.

BABUSCH   There's so much going on. The whole nickelodeon is exploding. Babes in arms, organize! And say, for ten marks you can get a pound of apricots, flesh-colored, juicy, so tender they melt in your mouth. Idlers, don't respond to provocation! Gangs of shady characters on all sides, two fingers in their mouths, whistling into the brightly lit cafés! The emblem on their banner is the golden brick! And high society is dancing in the night spots! Well, here's to the wedding!

MURK   Don't change, ladies. Equality is the word these days. You'll only attract attention with too much glitter.

BALICKE   Right! In these grave times. Our oldest clothes are good enough for the mob. Come on down, Anna.

MURK   We'll go on ahead. Don't change.

ANNA   Brute! (*Goes out*)

BALICKE   Forward march! . . . To paradise with a brass band! But first let me change my shirt.

MURK   You'll come later with Mother. And we'll take Babusch with us as a chaperon. (*Sings*) "Babusch, Babusch, Babusch, goes trotting around the hall."

BABUSCH   Don't you ever get sick of that young lunatic's stupid jingle? (*Goes out with him, arm in arm*)

MURK   (*outside, still singing*)   "Stop sucking your fingers, boys, we're going to have a ball." Anna!

BALICKE   (*alone, lights a cigar*)   Thank God it's all settled. Like pulling teeth! That girl has to be driven into bed! Pining away for a corpse! My clean shirt is soaked in sweat. Now I don't care what happens. Baby carriages forever! (*Goes out*) Woman, get me a shirt!

ANNA   (*outside*)   Frederick! Frederick! (*Hurrying in*) Frederick!

MURK   (*in the doorway*)   Anna! (*Dryly, uneasily, his arms dangling like an orangutan's*) Are you coming?

ANNA   What's the matter? You look so strange.

MURK   Are you coming? I know what I'm saying. Don't be difficult. Speak up!

ANNA   Yes, of course, I'm coming. Surprise!

MURK   Fine, fine. I'm not so sure. For twenty years I lived in garrets, chilled to the bone. Now I wear buttoned shoes, just

take a look at them. I sweated in the dark, by gaslight, the sweat
ran down into my eyes. Now I have a tailor. But I still feel
shaky, there's a wind blowing down below, there's an icy
breeze down below, a man's feet get cold down below. (*Approaches Anna, but does not take hold of her; he stands teetering
before her*) The lump of flesh is growing. Now the wine flows.
I've made it! Bathed in sweat, eyes closed, fists clenched so hard
that my nails cut into my flesh. That's all over now. Security!
Warmth! No more overalls! A white bed, soft and wide! (*Passing
the window, he looks out quickly*) Come here now! I open my
fists. I relax in the sunshine, and I've got you.

ANNA (*rushing to him*) Darling!

MURK Cuddle bunny!

ANNA Now you've got me.

MURK Isn't she down yet?

BABUSCH (*from outside*) How about it? I'm the bridesmaid, children.

MURK (*winds the phonograph. It starts worshipping the power of love
again*) I'm not a bad sort as long as I get my own way.
(*They go out, pressed close together*)

MRS. BALICKE (*scurries in, in black. Stands at the mirror arranging
her bonnet*) The moon is so big and red . . . And the young
people, goodness! Oh my! . . . Tonight we really have something to be thankful for.
(*At this moment a man in a muddy dark-blue artillery uniform
steps into the doorway. He is smoking a stubby pipe*)

THE MAN My name is Kragler.

MRS. BALICKE (*weak at the knees, supporting herself on the dressing
table*) My God!

KRAGLER What are you looking so unearthly about ? Been wasting money on wreaths? Too bad! Beg leave to report that I set
up in business as a ghost in Algiers. But right now the corpse
is starving. I could eat worms! What's the matter, Mother Balicke? Idiotic song! (*Turns off the phonograph*)
(*Mrs. Balicke, still speechless, just stares at him*)

KRAGLER Don't pass out on me. Here's a chair. A glass of water
is available. (*Goes humming to the cupboard*) I still know my way
around here pretty well. (*Pours wine into a glass*) Wine! Nier-

steiner! Pretty chipper for a ghost, eh? (*Busies himself over Mrs. Balicke*)

BALICKE   Come on, old woman! Marchons! How lovely you are, little chickadee! (*Enters, stands transfixed*) What's this?

KRAGLER   Good evening, Mr. Balicke. Your wife isn't feeling well. (*He tries to pour wine into her mouth, but she averts her head in horror. Balicke looks on for a time uneasily*)

KRAGLER   Take it, take it! Why not? Make you feel better. I didn't think you'd remember me so well. Just got back from Africa. Via Spain. Phony passport and all that rot. But now: where's Anna?

BALICKE   Leave my wife alone, for God's sake. You're drowning her.

KRAGLER   Whatever you say.

MRS. BALICKE (*runs to Balicke, who is standing rigid*)   Karl!

BALICKE (*severely*)   Mr. Kragler, if you're the person you claim to be, may I ask what you want here?

KRAGLER (*taken aback*)   But I've been a prisoner of war in Africa.

BALICKE   Damn it! (*Goes to a wall cupboard, takes a drink of schnapps*)   That's rich. It's just like you. Disgusting! What do you want anyway? What do you want? My daughter promised her hand less than half an hour ago.

KRAGLER (*sways, uncertainly*)   What do you mean?

BALICKE   You were gone four years. She waited four years. We waited four years. That's all over now, and you haven't a chance. (*Kragler sits down. Balicke is shaken, but is making an effort to keep up his dignity*) Mr. Kragler, I have certain obligations for this evening.

KRAGLER (*looks up*)   Obligations . . . ? (*Absently*) Mm . . . (*Slumps back into his chair*)

MRS. BALICKE   Don't take it so hard, Mr. Kragler. The world is full of girls. You know how it is. You must learn to suffer in silence.

KRAGLER   Anna . . .

BALICKE (*harshly*)   Woman! (*She goes over to him hesitantly. He, with sudden firmness*) Let's not have any more sentimentality. Marchons! (*Out with his wife. The maid appears in the doorway*)

KRAGLER   Hm . . . (*Shakes his head*)

MAID   The masters have gone out. (*Silence*) The masters have gone to the Piccadilly Bar to celebrate the engagement. (*Silence. Wind*)

KRAGLER (*looking up at her*)   Hm. (*He stands up clumsily, looks at the room, goes about stooped, saying nothing, looks out the window, turns around, and goes slowly out, whistling, without his cap*)

MAID   Here! Your cap! You forgot your cap!

ACT TWO
(PEPPER)

The Piccadilly Bar

In the rear a large window. Music. In the window a red moon. When the door opens, wind.

BABUSCH   Come on into the menagerie, friends. The moon is big enough. Hurrah for Spartacus! Flimflam! Red wine!

MURK (*enters with Anna on his arm, they take their coats off*)   A night out of a book. The shouting in the newspaper district, the fiancés in the cab.

ANNA   I've got such a sick feeling today, I can't get rid of it. I'm shaking all over.

BABUSCH   Prost, Frederick!

MURK   I feel at home here. You get sick of it after a while, but it's so elegant. Go take care of the older generation, Babusch.

BABUSCH   Sure. (*Takes a drink*) And you take care of the next one. (*Goes out*)

ANNA   Kiss me!

MURK   Don't be silly. Half Berlin is watching.

ANNA   Who cares? When I want something, nothing else matters. Aren't you like that?

MURK   No. Neither are you for that matter.

ANNA   You're vulgar.

MURK   Right.

ANNA   Coward!

(*Murk rings, Manke, the waiter, enters*)

MURK   Attention! (*He bends over the table, upsetting some glasses, and gives Anna a violent kiss*)

ANNA   Darling!

MURK   Dismissed! (*The waiter goes out*) Am I a coward? (*Looks under the table*) Now you don't have to play footsie with me any more.

ANNA   What do you mean by that?

MURK   And he shall be thy lord and master.

BALICKE (*entering with Babusch and Mrs. Balicke*)   There they are! Waiter!

ANNA   Where have you been?

MRS. BALICKE   The moon is so red. I'm all upset because it's so red. And they're shouting again in the newspaper district.

BABUSCH   Wolves!

MRS. BALICKE   Just be sure you two get together.

BALICKE   In bed, Frederick, see?

ANNA   Aren't you feeling well, Mother?

MRS. BALICKE   When are you planning to be married?

MURK   In three weeks, Mama.

MRS. BALICKE   Shouldn't we have invited more people to the celebration? This way nobody knows about it. People ought to know.

BALICKE   Nonsense. Pure nonsense. You mean because the wolf is howling? Let him howl. Until his tongue hangs red between his knees. I'll shoot him dead.

BABUSCH   Murk, help me uncork this bottle. (*In an undertone*) He's here, he came with the moon. The wolf with the moon. From Africa.

MURK   Andry Kragler?

BABUSCH   The wolf. Damn nuisance, isn't it?

MURK   He's dead and buried. Draw the curtains.

MRS. BALICKE   Your father has been dropping into every other bar. He's as drunk as a lord. There's a man for you! What a man! He'd drink himself to death for his children.

ANNA   But why should he?

MRS. BALICKE   Don't ask, child. Just don't ask! Everything is topsy-turvy. It's the end of the world. I need a drink of kirsch this minute, child.

BALICKE   It's only the red moon, Mother. Draw the curtain. (*The waiter does so*)

BABUSCH   You had a hunch this was going to happen?

MURK   Forewarned is forearmed. Has he been to see them?

BABUSCH   Yes, a little while ago.

MURK   Then he'll be coming here.

BALICKE   What are you plotting behind those wine bottles? Come join us. This is a party. (*All sit down around the table*) Let's have some action! I haven't time to be tired.

ANNA   Oh, that horse! It was so funny! In the middle of the street he just stopped. "Frederick, get out, the horse won't move." And there stood the horse in the middle of the street. Quivering. With eyeballs like gooseberries, all white; Frederick poked him in the eye with his cane, and he reared. It was like a circus.

BALICKE   Time is money. It's damn hot in here. I'm sweating again. This will be the second shirt today.

MRS. BALICKE   All this laundry will put you in the poorhouse.

BABUSCH (*eating prunes that he takes from his pocket*)   A pound of apricots costs ten marks now. Oh well. I'll write an article about the high cost of living. And then I'll be able to buy apricots. If the world comes to an end, I'll write an article about it. But what are other people supposed to do? If the Tiergarten section blows up, I'll be all set. But what about you?

MURK   Shirts, apricots, the Tiergarten section. When's the wedding?

BALICKE   In three weeks. Wedding in three weeks. Ahem! Those words have been heard in heaven. Are we agreed? All agreed about the wedding? Well then, my lovebirds, go to it!
(*They clink glasses. The door has opened, Kragler is standing in the doorway. The candles flutter in the wind and grow dim*)

BALICKE   Why is your glass shaking, Anna? Do you take after your mother?
(*Anna, who is sitting across from the door, has seen Kragler. She slumps down and stares at him*)

MRS. BALICKE   Holy Mary, what's wrong with you, child?

MURK   Where's that wind coming from?

KRAGLER (*in a hoarse voice*)   Anna.
(*Anna cries out feebly. All look around and jump up. Tumult. Simultaneously*)

BALICKE   Damnation! (*Pours wine down his throat*) Mother, it's the ghost.

MRS. BALICKE   Heavenly saints! Kra . . .

MURK   Throw him out! Throw him out!

(*Kragler has stood for some time swaying in the doorway. He looks sinister. During the brief tumult he moves clumsily, but rather quickly toward Anna, who alone is still seated, her glass trembling before her face. He takes the glass away from her, leans against the table and stares at her*)

BALICKE   He must be drunk.

MURK   Waiter! This man has no business here. Throw him out! (*Runs along the wall and in so doing pulls back the curtain. Moon.*)

BABUSCH   Careful! He's still got raw flesh under his shirt. It stings him. Don't touch him. (*Strikes the table with his cane*) Let's not have any trouble. Just leave quietly. One by one.

ANNA (*has meanwhile run away from the table and thrown her arms around her mother*)   Mother! Help!

(*Kragler staggers around the table toward Anna*)

MRS. BALICKE (*almost simultaneously with the following*)   Spare my child's life. They'll send you to prison. Good God, he's going to kill her.

BALICKE (*puffs himself up at a safe distance from Kragler*)   Are you drunk? Pauper! Anarchist! Soldier! Pirate! Moon ghost! Where'd you leave your sheet?

BABUSCH   If you have a stroke, he'll marry her. Shut up, you people! He's the injured party. Get out the whole lot of you! He's entitled to make a speech. That's his right! (*To Mrs. Balicke*) Have you no feelings? He's been away four years. It's a question of feelings.

MRS. BALICKE   She can hardly stand up. She's as white as a sheet.

BABUSCH (*to Murk*)   Look at his face! She's already seen it. It used to be like peaches and cream. Now it's a rotten fig. There's nothing to worry about.

(*They go out*)

MURK (*on his way out*)   If you're thinking of jealousy, don't make me laugh. Ha!

BALICKE (*is still standing between door and table, somewhat tipsy, his legs bent, a glass in hand*)   The nigger tramp! He's got a face like a, like a bankrupt elephant! He's down and out! It's an outrage! (*Goes out, only the waiter is left standing in front of the door right, with a tray in his hands. Gounod's "Ave Maria." The light dims*)

KRAGLER (*after a while*)   It's as if everything in my head had been wiped away, there's nothing but sweat left in it, I don't understand anything any more.

ANNA (*picks up a candle, rises unsteadily, shines it in his face*)   So the fish haven't eaten you?

KRAGLER   I don't know what you mean.

ANNA   You weren't blown up?

KRAGLER   I don't understand.

ANNA   They didn't shoot you through the face?

KRAGLER   Why are you looking at me like that? Is that what I look like? (*Silence, he looks toward the window*) I've come to you like an old dog. (*Silence*) I've got skin like a shark. Black. (*Silence*) And I used to be pink and white. (*Silence*) And I'm always bleeding, it just runs out of me . . .

ANNA   Andry!

KRAGLER   Yes.

ANNA (*goes to him hesitantly*)   Oh, Andry, why did you stay away so long? Did they keep you away with guns and sabers? And now I can't get through to you any more.

KRAGLER   Have I really been away?

ANNA   In the beginning you were with me a long time, your voice was still fresh. When I went down the hall, I brushed against you, and out in the meadow you called me from behind the maple tree. Even though they wrote that you'd been shot through the face and buried two days later. But then one day it was different. When I went down the hall, it was empty, and the maple tree didn't speak. When I stood up from bending over the wash trough, I still saw your face, but when I spread the washing out on the grass, I didn't see it, and all that time I didn't know what you looked like. But I should have waited.

KRAGLER   You should have had a picture.

ANNA   I was afraid. Even with my fear I should have waited, but I'm no good. Let go my hand, everything about me is bad.

KRAGLER (*looking at the window*)   I don't know what you're talking about. But maybe it's the red moon. I've got to think out what it means. My hands are swollen, there are webs between my fingers, I'm not refined, and I break glasses when I drink. I can't talk to you properly any more, I've got some nigger language in my throat.

ANNA   Yes.

KRAGLER   Give me your hand. Do you think I'm a ghost? Come here to me, give me your hand. Won't you come?

ANNA   You want my hand?

KRAGLER   Let me have it. Now I'm not a ghost any more. Now do you see my face? Is it like crocodile skin? I can hardly see. I've been in salt water. It's only the red moon.

ANNA   Yes.

KRAGLER   Take my hand too. Why don't you press it? Give me your face. Do you mind?

ANNA   No! No!

KRAGLER (*puts his arms around her*)   Anna! A vagrant nigger, that's what I am! With muck in my throat! Four years! Will you have me? Anna! (*Swings her around and sees the waiter. Grins and stares at him*)

WAITER (*thrown off balance, drops his tray. Stammering*)   The main thing is has she . . . has she still got . . . her lily . . . her lily . . .

KRAGLER (*holding Anna in his arms, guffaws*)   What did he say? Lily? (*The waiter runs out*) Don't go away. He's been reading novels. Something popped out of him. Lily! Something has happened to him! Lily! Did you hear that? He must have been deeply moved.

ANNA   Andry!

KRAGLER (*he has let go of her. Bowed down, he looks at her*)   Say it again. That was your voice. (*He runs to the right*) Waiter! Come here.

BABUSCH (*in the doorway*)   What a fleshy laugh you have! A flesh-colored laugh! How are you feeling?

MRS. BALICKE (*behind him*)   Anna, my child! We've been so worried about you! (*The "Lady from Peru" has been playing for some time in the next room*)

BALICKE (*slightly sobered, runs in. To Kragler*)   Sit down! (*He draws the curtain, a metallic sound is heard*) Over in Babusch's newspaper district they've got a red moon with them and rifles to back them up. They're a force to be reckoned with. (*He relights all the candles*) Sit down.

MRS. BALICKE   Your face, child! My legs are shaking again. Waiter! Waiter!

BALICKE   Where's Murk?

BABUSCH   Frederick Murk is dancing the boston.

BALICKE (*in a subdued tone*)   Just make him sit down. Once he's sitting down, half the fight will be out of him. The sitting position is no good for dramatics. (*Aloud*) Sit down, the whole lot of you! Calm down! Pull yourself together, Amalia. (*To Kragler*) You sit down too, for God's sake.

MRS. BALICKE (*taking a bottle of kirsch from the waiter's tray*)   I've got to have some kirsch or I'll die. (*She brings it to the table*) (*Mrs. Balicke, Balicke and Anna have sat down. Babusch has scurried about, making them sit down. Now he pushes Kragler, who has been standing there helplessly, down into a chair*)

BABUSCH   Sit down, you're weak in the knees. Do you want some kirsch? Why do you laugh that way? (*Kragler stands up again. Babusch pushes him down. He remains seated*)

BALICKE   What do you want, Andreas Kragler?

MRS. BALICKE   Mr. Kragler, our Kaiser has said: "Learn to suffer in silence."

ANNA   Don't get up.

BALICKE   Shut up! Let him speak. What do you want?

BABUSCH (*stands up*)   Would you like a drop of kirsch? Speak up.

ANNA   Think before you say anything, Andry.

MRS. BALICKE   You'll be the death of me. Hold your tongue. You don't understand anything.

KRAGLER (*tries to stand up, is pushed back by Babusch. Very earnestly*)   Now that you ask me, it's not so simple. And I don't want any kirsch. There's too much at stake.

BALICKE   Don't beat about the bush. Say what you have to say. And then I'll throw you out.

ANNA   No! No!

BABUSCH   You'd better drink something. You're parched. That will make it easier, believe me.

(*At this moment Frederick Murk dances in at the left with a prostitute by the name of Marie*)

MRS. BALICKE   Murk!

BABUSCH   Even genius has its limits. Sit down.

BALICKE   Good for you, Fritz. Show this man what it is to be a man. Fritz doesn't tremble. Fritz enjoys himself. (*Applauds*)

MURK (*gloomily—he has been drinking. He leaves Marie and comes to the table*)   Hasn't this stupid argument been settled yet?

BALICKE (*drags him to a chair*)   Shut your trap!

BABUSCH   Go on, Kragler. Don't let him bother you.

KRAGLER   His ears are mangled.

ANNA   He used to lay chickie.

MURK   He's got an egg in his head.

KRAGLER   Make him go away.

MURK   And they hit him on the head.

KRAGLER   I've got to be very careful what I say.

MURK   So now he has mayonnaise on the brain.

KRAGLER   Yes, they hit me on the head. I was gone for four years. I couldn't write. I didn't have an egg in my brain. (*Silence*) That was four years ago, I've got to be very careful. You didn't know me any more, you're still in doubt, you don't feel it yet. But I'm talking too much.

MRS. BALICKE   His brain is all dried up. (*Shakes her head*)

BALICKE   So you had a bad time, fighting for Kaiser and country? I feel sorry for you. Is there anything you want?

MRS. BALICKE   The Kaiser said: "Be strong in suffering." Have a drink! (*Pushes the kirsch in his direction*)

BALICKE (*drinking, with emphasis*)   You stood up under shellfire? Like an iron man? Splendid! Our men did big things. Died like heroes, laughing. Have a drink! What do you want? (*Offers him a box of cigars*)

ANNA   Andry, didn't they give you another uniform? You're still wearing the old blue one. Nobody wears them any more.

MRS. BALICKE   There are so many women. Waiter, another kirsch! (*Passes Kragler the kirsch*)

BALICKE   We were no slackers on the home front either. So what's the complaint? You haven't a cent to your name? You're high and dry? The Fatherland has nothing for you but a barrel organ? Impossible. Such things don't happen any more. What do you want?

MRS. BALICKE   Don't worry. You won't be pushing a barrel organ.

ANNA   "Stormy the night and the sea runs high." (*She shudders*)

KRAGLER (*has stood up*)   Since I feel that I have no rights here I ask you from the bottom of my heart to go with me, to walk at my side.

BALICKE   What kind of talk is that? What's he saying? Bottom of
my heart! Walk at my side! Where did he get such expressions?
(*The others laugh*)

KRAGLER   Because no man has a right . . . Because I can't live
without you . . . From the bottom of my heart. (*Loud laughter*)

MURK (*putting his feet on the table. Cold, malignant, drunk*)   Sunk
to the bottom. Fished out. With mud in his mouth. Take a look
at my shoes. I once had shoes like yours. Go buy a pair like mine
and come again. Do you know what you are?

MARIE (*suddenly*)   Were you in the army?

WAITER   Were you in the army?

MURK   Shut your traps! (*To Kragler*) The steam roller passed over
you? It's passed over a lot of people. We didn't set it rolling.
You've no face left, eh? You want us to make you a present of
one? You want the three of us to outfit you? Was it for us that
you crawled under it? You still don't know what you are?

BABUSCH   Calm down!

WAITER (*steps forward*)   Were you in the army?

MURK   No. I'm one of the people who are expected to pay for
your heroism. The steam roller has broken down.

BABUSCH   Cut the dramatics. It's disgusting. You made your pile,
didn't you? And stop talking about your shoes.

BALICKE   But look, that's the whole point. It's not dramatics, it's
realpolitik. That's what we need more of in Germany. It's
perfectly simple. Have you the wherewithal to support a wife?
Or have you got webs between your fingers?

MRS. BALICKE   You hear that, Anna? He hasn't got a cent to his
name.

MURK   I'll marry his mother if he has. (*Jumps up*) He's just a
common fortune-hunter, that's all.

WAITER (*to Kragler*)   Say something! Speak up!

KRAGLER (*has stood up, trembling. To Anna*)   I don't know what to
say. When we were down to skin and bones and we had to keep
drinking schnapps so we could pave the roads, we often had
nothing left but the evening sky, that's very important, because
that was the time of day when I'd lain in the bushes with you
in April. I told the others about it. But they were collapsing like
flies.

ANNA   You mean horses?

KRAGLER   Because it was so hot and we were drinking the whole time. But why do I keep telling you about the evening sky, I didn't mean to, I don't know . . .

ANNA   Did you always think of me?

MRS. BALICKE   Listen to him talk like a child. It makes you feel ashamed for him.

MURK   Would you sell me your boots? For the Army Museum. I'll pay forty marks.

BABUSCH   Go on, Kragler. You're on the right track.

KRAGLER   We had no shirts left either. That was the worst, believe me. Do you understand how that can be the worst?

ANNA   Andry, they're all listening to you.

MURK   In that case I offer sixty marks. Sell!

KRAGLER   So, now you're ashamed for me, because they're all watching like in a circus, and the elephant passes water because he's scared. And they don't know what it's all about.

MURK   Eighty marks!

KRAGLER   I'm not a pirate. What's the red moon to me? It's just that I can't get my eyes open. I'm a chunk of flesh in a clean shirt. I'm not a ghost!

MURK (*jumps up*)   All right, a hundred marks!

MARIE   You ought to be ashamed to the bottom of your soul!

MURK   Now the swine refuses to sell me his old boots for a hundred marks!

KRAGLER   Anna, something is talking. What can that voice be?

MURK   You've got sunstroke! Can you leave on your own steam?

KRAGLER   Anna, it thinks it shouldn't be stepped on.

MURK   Is this your real face now?

KRAGLER   Anna, God made this thing!

MURK   Is that you? What do you actually want? You're a corpse! You stink! (*Holds his nose*) Haven't you any sense of cleanliness? Do you want to be set up in a shrine because you've swallowed the African sun? I've worked! I've slaved till there was blood in my shoes! Look at my hands. You get all the sympathy because you've been beaten, I didn't beat you! You're a hero and I'm a worker! And this is my fiancée!

BABUSCH   Say it sitting down, Murk. You're just as much of a worker sitting down. Kragler, history would be different if people spent more time on their asses.

KRAGLER   When I look at him I can't see anything. He's like a shithouse wall. With smut scribbled on it. The wall can't help it. Anna, do you love him, do you love this thing? (*Anna laughs and drinks*)

BABUSCH   You're leading with your chin, Kragler.

KRAGLER   No, I'm squeezing his filthy pimples. Do you love him? With his face as green as an unripe nut? Are you going to throw me over for him? He has an English suit, and his chest is stuffed with paper, and he has blood in his shoes. I've only got my old clothes, with moths in them. Say you can't marry me because of my clothes. Say it! I'd rather have it that way.

BABUSCH   Sit down, damn it! There's going to be trouble.

MARIE (*clapping her hands*)   That's him. And the way he danced with me I was ashamed. Poking his knees into my belly.

MURK   You shut up! So that's the kind you are. Haven't you got a knife in your boot top to cut my throat with because you got blisters on the brain in Africa? Pull it, I'm fed up. Cut my throat!

MRS. BALICKE   Anna! How can you stand it?

BALICKE   Waiter, bring me four glasses of kirsch. To hell with it all.

MURK   You'd better not pull that knife. Calm down, don't try the hero act around here. You'll end up in jail.

MARIE   Were you in the army?

MURK (*furious, throws a glass at her*)   Why weren't you?

KRAGLER   Now I'm here.

MURK   Who called you?

KRAGLER   I've come.

MURK   Swine!

ANNA   You pipe down.
   (*Kragler crouches*)

MURK   Bandit!

KRAGLER (*tonelessly*)   Thief!

MURK   Ghost!

KRAGLER   Watch your step!

MURK   Careful with your knife! Does it itch? Ghost! Ghost! Ghost!

MARIE   You swine! You swine!

KRAGLER   Anna, Anna! What's happening to me? Staggering over a sea of corpses: it doesn't drown me. Rolling southward in dark cattle cars: nothing can happen to me. Burning in the fiery furnace: I myself am hotter still. A man goes mad in the sun: not I. Two fall into the water hole: I go on sleeping. I shoot niggers. I eat grass. I'm a ghost.

(*At this moment the waiter rushes to the window and throws it open. The music suddenly breaks off, excited cries are heard: "They're coming!" "Keep calm!" The waiter blows out the candles. The "Internationale" is heard from outside*)

A MAN (*enters left*)   Ladies and gentlemen, we must ask you to keep calm. You are requested not to leave the premises. Rioting has broken out. There's fighting in the newspaper district. The situation is uncertain.

BALICKE (*sitting down heavily*)   Spartacus! Your friends, Mr. Andreas Kragler! Your criminal accomplices! Your comrades, shouting in the newspaper district and stinking of murder and arson. Beasts! (*Silence*) Beasts! Beasts! Beasts! Anybody want to know why you're beasts? Because you eat flesh! You've got to be exterminated.

WAITER   By you who have gorged yourself fat.

MURK   Where's your knife? Pull it.

MARIE (*bearing down on him with the waiter*)   Will you shut up!

WAITER   That thing isn't human. It's a beast!

MURK   Draw the curtain! Ghosts!

WAITER   Are we to be lined up against the wall that we built with our own hands? The wall behind which you swill kirsch?

KRAGLER   Here's my wrist and here's the artery. Cut it! There'll be plenty of blood when I kick off.

MURK   Ghost! Ghost! What are you anyway? You expect me to crawl into a hole because you've got an African hide, because you bellow in the newspaper district? Can I help it if you were in Africa? Can I help it if I wasn't in Africa?

WAITER   He's got to get his woman back! It's inhuman!

MRS. BALICKE (*furious, facing Anna*)   They're all of them sick. They've all got something. Syphilis! Syphilis! They've all got syphilis!

BABUSCH (*strikes the table with his cane*)   That's the last straw!

MRS. BALICKE   Will you leave my child alone! Will you leave her alone! You hyena! You swine!

ANNA   Andry, I can't stand it! You're killing me!

MARIE   You're the swine!

WAITER   It's not human. There must be some justice.

MRS. BALICKE   Hold your tongue! You flunky! You scoundrel! I'm ordering kirsch, do you hear? You're going to be fired!

WAITER   It's a question of humanity! It concerns us all! He's got to get his woman.

KRAGLER   Out of my way! I'm fed up. What do you mean, human? What does this drunken cow want? I've been alone and I want my woman. What does this boozing archangel want? You want to sell her belly like a pound of coffee? If you take her away from me with iron hooks, you'll only tear her to pieces.

WAITER   You'll tear her to pieces.

MARIE   That's right. Like a pound of coffee.

BALICKE   And not a red cent to his name.

BABUSCH   You're bashing his teeth in and he's spitting them in your face.

MURK   (*to Anna*)   Why do you sit there looking like puked-up milk? Letting him lick you with his eyes! With a face like you'd been pissing in nettles!

BALICKE   Is that a way to talk about your fiancée?

MURK   Fiancée? Is she? Is she my fiancée? Isn't she running out on me? He's come back, has he? You love him? Is the green nut on his way down? Itching for African legs? Is that how the wind blows?

BABUSCH   You wouldn't have said that sitting down.

ANNA   (*moving closer to Kragler, looks disgustedly at Murk. In an undertone*)   You're drunk.

MURK   (*pulls her to him*)   Show your face! Bare your teeth! Whore!

KRAGLER   (*picks Murk up, the glasses on the table rattle, Marie claps her hands at length*)   You're shaky on your pins. Go outside and throw up. You've had too much to drink. You're going to capsize. (*Pushes him to the floor*)

MARIE   Give it to him! Oh, give it to him!

KRAGLER   Let him stay there. Come here to me, Anna. I want you now. He wanted to buy my boots, but now I'll take my coat off.

The icy rain went through my skin, it's red now, it bursts in the sun. My pockets are empty, I haven't a red cent. I want you. I'm not good to look at. Up to now I've been scared shitless, but now I'm going to drink. (*Drinks*) And then we'll go. Come!

MURK (*in total collapse, his shoulder drooping, says almost calmly to Kragler*) Don't drink. You don't know the whole story. Let's be reasonable. I was drunk. But you don't know the whole story. Anna, (*Totally sober*) tell him. What are you going to do? In your condition?

KRAGLER (*doesn't hear him*) Don't be afraid, Anna. (*Pouring kirsch*) You'll be all right, don't be afraid. We'll be married. I've always managed.

WAITER   That's the way to talk.

MRS. BALICKE   You scoundrel!

KRAGLER   If you've got a conscience, the birds shit on your roof. If you've got patience, the vultures get you in the end. The whole thing is a hoax.

ANNA (*suddenly starts running, falls over the table*)   Andry! Help me! Help me, Andry!

MARIE   What's the matter? What's wrong?

KRAGLER (*looks after her in astonishment*)   What is it?

ANNA   I don't know, Andry. I'm so miserable, Andry. I can't tell you why, you mustn't ask. (*Looks up*) I can't belong to you, God knows, I can't. (*Kragler drops his glass*) Andry, please, I beg you, go. (*Silence. In the next room the man who appeared before is heard asking: "What's going on?" The waiter answers, speaking toward the outside from the doorway left*)

WAITER   The crocodile-skinned lover from Africa has been waiting four years, and his fiancée still has her lily in her hand. But her other lover, a man with buttoned shoes, won't let her go, and the fiancée, who still has her lily in her hand, doesn't know which way to turn.

VOICE   Is that all?

WAITER   The revolution in the newspaper district has something to do with it, and besides the fiancée has a secret, something that the lover from Africa, who has been waiting four years, doesn't know. The outcome is still undecided.

VOICE   There's been no decision?

WAITER   No. No decision.

BALICKE   Waiter! Who are these riffraff? Do you expect us to drink with bedbugs? (*To Kragler*) Did you hear that? Are you satisfied now? Hold your tongue! The sun was hot, wasn't it? That's to be expected in Africa. It's in the geography books. You were a hero? That will be in the history books. But the account books are blank. So the hero will go back to Africa. Period. Waiter! Take this thing away!

(*The waiter takes Kragler in tow. Slowly and clumsily Kragler follows. To the left of him trots the prostitute Marie*)

BALICKE   Silly farce! (*Feeling that it's too quiet, shouts after Kragler*) Was it flesh you wanted? This isn't a meat market. Pack up your red moon and go sing to your chimpanzees. Who gives a damn for your fig trees? You're only something out of a novel anyway. Where's your birth certificate? (*Kragler has gone out*)

MRS. BALICKE   Just have a good cry. But what have you got there, are you going to drink yourself under the table on kirsch?

BALICKE   And the face on you! Like paper!

MRS. BALICKE   Heavens, just look at the child! What's got into you, this has got to stop!

(*Anna sits motionless behind the table, almost hidden by the curtains. She has a glass in front of her and looks malignant*)

MURK (*goes up to her, sniffs at her glass*)   Pepper! Ugh! (*She takes it away from him with a look of contempt*) Is that it?! What in hell is the pepper for? Why not a hot sitz bath too? Or do you want it done by hand? Disgusting! (*Spits and throws the glass on the floor. Anna smiles*)

(*Machine guns are heard*)

BABUSCH (*at the window*)   This is it. The masses are rising. Spartacus is attacking. Murder marches on.

(*All stand rigid, listening to the noise outside*)

ACT THREE

(RIDE OF THE VALKYRIES)

o ## Street Leading to the Newspaper District

Red brick barracks wall extending from upper left to lower right. Behind it in the dim starlight the city. Night. Wind.

MARIE Where are you going?

KRAGLER (*without a cap, his collar turned up, his hands in his pockets, has come in whistling*) What's that red fig?

MARIE Why do you have to walk so fast?

KRAGLER Can't you keep up?

MARIE Do you think somebody's following you?

KRAGLER Want to make a little money? Where's your room?

MARIE That wouldn't be any good.

KRAGLER No. (*About to go on*)

MARIE I've got trouble with my lungs.

KRAGLER Do you have to run after me like a dog?

o MARIE But your . . .

KRAGLER Shh! That's all over. Washed up. Crossed out.

MARIE And what are you going to do until morning?

o KRAGLER There are knives.

MARIE Christ . . .

KRAGLER Take it easy. I don't want you screaming like that.

o There's liquor too. What do you want me to do? I can try laughing if it amuses you. Say, did they lay you on the stairs before your first communion? Cross that out. Do you smoke?

o (*He laughs*) Let's get going.

o MARIE They're shooting in the newspaper district.

KRAGLER Maybe they can use us. (*Both go out. Wind*)

(*Two men appear, going in the same direction*)

FIRST   This would be a good place.

SECOND   Maybe we won't get a chance down there . . .
(*They pass water*)

o FIRST   Cannon.

o SECOND   Hell! On Friedrichstrasse!

FIRST   Where you cut liquor with wood alchohol.

SECOND   Just that moon could send a man out of his mind.

FIRST   If he's been selling contaminated tobacco.

SECOND   Yes, I've sold contaminated tobacco. But you stuffed
people into rat holes.

FIRST   A lot of good that does you!

SECOND   I won't hang by myself!

o FIRST   Do you know what the Bolsheviks have been doing? "Put
out your hand! No calluses?" Bang bang! (*The second man examines his hand*) Bang bang! You're starting to stink already!

SECOND   Good God!

FIRST   Won't it be sweet if they see you with that bowler!

SECOND   But you're wearing a bowler yourself.

FIRST   But mine's got a dent in it, friend.

SECOND   I can make one in mine.

FIRST   Your stiff collar is worse than a greased rope.

SECOND   I can soften it up with sweat. But you've got buttoned
shoes!

FIRST   And your paunch!

SECOND   Your voice!

FIRST   The look in your eyes! Your walk! Your manner!

SECOND   Yes, that will get me strung up, but you've got a face
with a high-school education.

FIRST   My dear sir, I've got a mangled ear with a bullet hole in
it.

SECOND   Damn! (*Both go out. Wind.*)

(*From left to right, the Ride of the Valkyries: Anna, as though in
flight. Beside her in tails but hatless, Manke, the waiter from the
Piccadilly Bar, who acts drunk. Behind them Babusch, dragging
Murk, who is drunk, pale and bloated*)

MANKE   Don't stop to think. He's gone. Blown away. Maybe the
o   newspaper district has already swallowed him up. They're
shooting all over the place, anything can happen down there

tonight, he might even be shot. (*To Anna emphatically as though drunk*) When the shooting starts, a man can run away or not run away. Either way, in an hour nobody'll be able to find him, he'll disintegrate like paper in water. The moon has gone to his head. He runs after every drum. Get a move on! Save the man who was, no, is, your lover.

BABUSCH (*flings himself in Anna's path*) Halt, all you riding Valkyries! Where do you think you're going? It's cold, the wind's blowing, and he's probably holed up in some gin mill. (*Imitates the waiter*) The man who has waited four years, but now nobody can find him.

MURK   Nobody. No one. (*He sits down on a stone*)

BABUSCH   And look at him now!

MANKE   Who cares about him? Give him a coat! But don't waste any time! The man who waited four years is running faster than those clouds are moving! He'll be gone sooner than this wind!

MURK (*apathetically*)   There was artificial coloring in that punch! And now this has to happen when everything was ready. The apartment rented, the linen all bought. Come here beside me, Babusch.

MANKE   Why are you standing there like Lot's wife? This isn't Gomorrah. Does this lump of drunken misery impress you? Do you think you can still turn back? Is it the linen? Is that going to stop the clouds?

BABUSCH   What's all this to you, may I ask? What are the clouds to you? You're only a waiter.

MANKE   What business is it of mine? The stars are thrown off course when injustice leaves a man cold! (*Clutches his throat*) I'm being hunted down too! We have no right to be petty when a man is scared shitless.

BABUSCH   What? Shitless? Where does the Good Book say that? Take it from me, you'll hear a bull roaring in the newspaper district before the night is out. That will be the rabble who think the time has come to settle old scores.

MURK (*stands up, whimpering*)   Why are you dragging me around in this wind? I'm sick as a dog. Why are you running away? What's going on? I need you. It's not the linen.

ANNA   I can't.

MURK   My legs won't carry me any more.

MANKE   Sit down! You're not the only one! It all hangs together. The father is down with a stroke, the drunken kangaroo is crying her eyes out. But the daughter's going down to the slums. To her lover who has waited four years.

ANNA   I can't.

MURK   Your linen's all ready. The rooms are all furnished.

MANKE   The linen is folded, but the bride isn't coming.

ANNA   My linen is bought, I've put it in the closet, piece by piece. But now I don't need it. The apartment is rented, the curtains are up, and the walls are papered. But the man has come who has no shoes and only one coat, and the moths are in it.

MANKE   And the newspaper district is swallowing him up! The gin mill is waiting for him! And night! And misery! And the dregs of humanity! Save him!

BABUSCH   The whole thing is a play: The Angel of the Waterfront Dives.

MANKE   That's it, the angel!

MURK   And you're going down there? To Friedrichstadt? And nothing will hold you back?

ANNA   Nothing I know of.

MURK   Nothing? You don't want to think of the "other thing"?

ANNA   No, not any more.

MURK   You don't want it any more?

ANNA   It's a chain.

MURK   And it doesn't hold you?

ANNA   It's broken now!

MURK   Your child means nothing to you?

ANNA   Nothing.

MURK   Because the man who has no coat has come?

ANNA   I didn't know him.

MURK   He's not the same any more. You didn't know him!

ANNA   He stood in the ring like an animal. And you all beat him like an animal.

MURK   And he cried like an old woman.

ANNA   And he cried like a woman.

MURK   And went off and left you flat.

ANNA   And went off and left me flat.

MURK   He's done for!

ANNA   And he's done for!

MURK   He's gone away . . .

ANNA   But when he went away and he was done for . . .

MURK   Nothing happened. Nothing at all.

ANNA   There was an eddy behind him, it pulled gently, and then it was very strong, stronger than everything else. And now I'm going away, and now I'm coming, and we're done for, both of us. Because where has he gone? God knows where he is. The world is so big and where is he? (*She looks calmly at Manke and says lightly*) Go back to your bar, thank you, and take him with you. But you, Babusch, come with me. (*She runs out to the right*)

○   MURK (*whining*)   Where has she gone?

○   BABUSCH   The Ride of the Valkyries is shot to hell, son.

MANKE   The lover is missing, but the beloved is hurrying after him on wings of love. The hero has fallen, but everything is ready for the ascent to heaven.

BABUSCH   But the lover will kick the beloved into the gutter, he'd rather go down to hell. You and your romantic claptrap!

○   MANKE   She's vanishing, hurrying to the newspaper district. She is still visible, like a white sail, like an idea, like a last stanza, like a drunken swan flying over the water . . .

BABUSCH   What are we going to do with this wet blotter?

MURK   I'm staying right here. It's cold. When it gets colder, they'll come back. You don't know a thing, because you don't know about the other thing. Let them go. He won't take two of them. He left one behind, now two are running after him. (*Laughs*)

○   BABUSCH   And now, by God, she has vanished like a last stanza! (*Trudges after her*)

○   MANKE (*calls after him*)   Glubb's gin mill on Chausseestrasse! The prostitute with him hangs out at Glubb's gin mill! (*Spreads both arms wide*) The revolution is swallowing them up. Will they find each other?

ACT FOUR

o (A DAWN WILL COME)

A Small Gin Mill

Glubb, the proprietor, in white, is singing "The Ballad of the Dead Soldier," (see p. 369) accompanying himself on the guitar. Laar and a sinister-looking drunk are staring at Glubb's fingers. A short, thick-set man by the name of Bulltrotter is reading the paper. Manke the waiter, brother of Manke at the Piccadilly Bar, is drinking with Augusta, a prostitute. All are smoking.

BULLTROTTER   I don't want any dead soldiers, I want booze, I want to read the paper, and, hell, without booze I can't make head or tail of it.

GLUBB (*in a cold, glassy voice*)   You don't like it here?

BULLTROTTER   Sure, but there's a revolution going on.

GLUBB   What's the good of that? In my gin mill the scum make themselves at home, and Lazarus sings.

o THE DRUNK   I'm the scum, you're Lazarus.

A WORKER (*comes in and goes to the bar*)   Hi, Karl.

GLUBB   In a hurry?

WORKER   Eleven o'clock at Hausvogteiplatz.

GLUBB   A lot of rumors going around.

WORKER   The guards division has been at Anhalt station since six o'clock. All quiet at the *Forward.* We could use your Paul today, Karl.

(*Silence*)

MANKE   We don't usually talk about Paul around here.

WORKER (*paying*)   Today is unusual. (*Goes out*)

MANKE (*to Glubb*)   What about November? Wasn't that

unusual? You need a gun in your hands and a tight feeling in your fingers.

GLUBB (*coldly*) The gentleman wants something.

BULLTROTTER Freedom! (*He removes his jacket and collar*)

GLUBB Drinking in shirt sleeves is prohibited.

BULLTROTTER That's reactionary.

MANKE They're rehearsing the "Internationale" in four parts with tremolo. Freedom! Now I suppose any man with white cuffs will have to scrub out the toilet.

GLUBB You're going to ruin the marble, it's made of wood.

AUGUSTA Why shouldn't the men with white cuffs scrub out the toilet?

BULLTROTTER Up against the wall with you, kid!

AUGUSTA Then the men with white cuffs can just tie up their assholes.

MANKE Augusta, you're vulgar.

AUGUSTA Shame on you, you pigs, they ought to rip out your guts and hang you from the lamp post, you with the cuffs. "Couldn't you lower your prices, miss, we've lost the war." Forget about love if you haven't any cash, and don't make war if you don't know how! Put your feet on the floor when ladies are present! Do I have to smell your sweaty feet, you creep?

GLUBB His cuffs aren't white.

THE DRUNK What's that rumbling?

MANKE Cannon.

THE DRUNK (*pale, grins at the others*) What's that clanking? (*Glubb goes to the window and opens it. They hear cannon hurrying through the streets. All to the window*)

BULLTROTTER That's the June-Bug Regiment.

AUGUSTA Christ Almighty, where are they going?

GLUBB To the newspaper offices! They're the readers! (*He closes the window*)

AUGUSTA Christ Almighty, who's that standing in the doorway? (*Kragler is in doorway, swaying as though drunk, rocking on the balls of his feet*)

MANKE Are you going to lay an egg in that doorway?

AUGUSTA Who are you?

KRAGLER (*with a malignant grin*) Nobody.

AUGUSTA   The sweat's running down his neck! You been running as fast as all that?

THE DRUNK   You got the trots?

KRAGLER   No, I haven't got the trots.

MANKE (*crossing over to him*)   Then what have you been up to, boy? I know a guilty face when I see one.

MARIE (*appears behind him*)   He hasn't been up to anything. I invited him here, Augusta, he has no place to go. He's been in Africa. Sit down.

(*Kragler remains standing in the doorway*)

MANKE   Prisoner?

MARIE   Yes. And missing.

AUGUSTA   Missing too?

o   MARIE   And a prisoner. And meanwhile they swiped his girl.

AUGUSTA   In that case, come to Mamma. Sit down, soldier. (*To Glubb*) Karl, five double kirsches! (*Glubb fills five glasses and Manke puts them on a table*)

GLUBB   Last week they swiped my bicycle.

(*Kragler moves toward the table*)

AUGUSTA   Tell us something about Africa.

o   (*Kragler doesn't answer, but takes a drink*)

BULLTROTTER   Go on, spill your guts. The owner's a Red.

GLUBB   What am I?

BULLTROTTER   A Red.

MANKE   Watch your step, mister, there's nothing Red around here if you please.

BULLTROTTER   Anything you say.

AUGUSTA   And what did you do down there?

KRAGLER (*to Marie*)   Shot niggers in the gut. Paved roads . . . Trouble with your lungs, eh?

AUGUSTA   How long were you there?

KRAGLER (*still to Marie*)   Twenty-seven.

MARIE   Months.

AUGUSTA   And before that?

KRAGLER   Before that? Lying in a mudhole.

BULLTROTTER   What did you do there?

KRAGLER   Stink.

GLUBB   You fellows certainly knew how to take it easy.

BULLTROTTER   What's the ass like in Africa? (*Kragler says nothing*)

AUGUSTA   Don't be vulgar.

BULLTROTTER   And when you came home, she wasn't there, is that it? Did you expect her to wait for you every day from morning to night, outside the barracks with the dogs?

KRAGLER (*to Marie*)   Should I slap him on the mouth?

GLUBB   No, not for the moment. But you can start the nickelodeon. That's what you can do.

KRAGLER (*stands up swaying and salutes*)   Yes, sir!
(*He goes over and starts the nickelodeon*)

BULLTROTTER   A lot of sentimentality.

AUGUSTA   It's just that he feels like a corpse; he's dead but he doesn't know it.

GLUBB   Yes, yes. He's suffered a slight injustice. Nothing time won't heal.

BULLTROTTER   What is this? Aren't you a Red, Glubb? Wasn't there some talk about a nephew of yours?

GLUBB   Yes, there's been some talk. But not around here.

BULLTROTTER   No, not here. At the Siemens works.

GLUBB   For a time.

BULLTROTTER   At the Siemens works for a time. He was a machinist. He operated a lathe for a while. He operated a lathe there until November, is that it?

THE DRUNK (*who has only been laughing up to now, sings*)

All my brothers now are dead,
I came through, I don't know how.
In November I was Red,
But it's January now.

GLUBB   Mr. Manke, this gentleman isn't trying to molest anybody. Make sure he doesn't.

KRAGLER (*takes hold of Augusta and hops around with her*)

A dog went to the kitchen
To find a bone to chew.
The cook picked up his chopper
And chopped the dog in two.

THE DRUNK (*shaking with laughter*)   A lathe for a while.

GLUBB   Please, don't break my glasses, soldier!

MARIE   He's drunk now. He feels better.

KRAGLER   Does he feel better? Console yourself, Brother Brandykeg. Tell yourself that such things don't happen.

AUGUSTA   Have a drink yourself.

THE DRUNK   Wasn't there some talk about a nephew?

KRAGLER   What's a pig in the eyes of God, Sister Prostitute? Nothing.

THE DRUNK   Not around here.

KRAGLER   Why not? Can you abolish the army or God? Can you abolish the torment of pain, Mr. Red, and the torments that men have taught the devil? You can't abolish them, but you can serve liquor. So drink and shut the door, and don't let the wind in, the wind is shivering too. Shut the door and bolt it!

BULLTROTTER   The owner here says you've suffered a slight injustice, and time will heal it, he says.

KRAGLER   Heal it? Did you say injustice, Brother Red? Injustice: there's another funny word. They make up a lot of those little words and blow them into the air, then they can lie back and time starts healing. And big brother punches little brother in the jaw, and the rich man makes off with the rich milk, and time heals it all!

THE DRUNK   Even the nephew—the one we don't talk about.

KRAGLER

The other dogs came running
And dug that dog a grave.
They chiseled this inscription
Upon the stone above:
"A dog went to the kitchen . . ."

And so make yourselves comfortable on this little star. It's cold here and kind of dark, Mr. Red, and the world is too old for better days, and heaven's already been rented out, my friends.

MARIE   Then what should we do? He says he wants to go down to the newspaper district, that's where things are happening. But what *is* happening in the newspaper district?

KRAGLER   A cab is driving to the Piccadilly Bar.

AUGUSTA   Is she in it?

KRAGLER   She's in it. My pulse is perfectly normal. You can feel it. (*Holds out his hand, drinks with the other*)

MARIE   His name's Andry.

KRAGLER   Andry. Yes, they used to call me Andry. (*He is still absently feeling his pulse*)

LAAR   They were mostly pine trees. Little ones.

GLUBB   The stone is opening its mouth.

BULLTROTTER   And you sold them, you idiot?

LAAR   Me?

BULLTROTTER   Ah, business! Interesting, Glubb, but not around here.

GLUBB   You feel offended? Just control yourselves. Or if you can't, I'll control you! Hold still when they skin you, soldier, or your skin will come apart, and it's the only one you've got. (*Still busy washing the glasses*) Sure, you feel offended, they slaughtered you with cannon and sabers, and swindled you and spat on you a little. So what?

BULLTROTTER   (*referring to the glasses*)   Aren't they clean yet?

THE DRUNK   Wash me, Lord, and make me white. Wash me, make me as white as the snow. (*Sings*)

All my brothers now are dead, yes, dead.
I've come through alive, I don't know how.
In November I was Red, yes Red.
But it's January now.

GLUBB   That'll do.

AUGUSTA   You cowards!

WOMAN SELLING NEWSPAPERS (*entering*)   Spartacus in newspaper district! Red Rosa addresses open-air meeting in Tierpark! How long will mob disorder be tolerated? Where's the army? Ten pfennigs, soldier! Where's the army? Ten pfennigs. (*No one wants a paper and she leaves*)

AUGUSTA   And no Paul!

KRAGLER   Are they shooting again?

GLUBB   (*closes the liquor closet and wipes his hands*)   I'm closing up.

MANKE   Let's go, Augusta. He doesn't mean you, but let's go! (*To Bulltrotter*)   What about you, sir? Two marks sixty.

BULLTROTTER   I was at Jutland. That was no bed of roses either.
(*All prepare to leave*)
THE DRUNK (*with his arms around Marie*)

Sinful Sadie was good as gold
She sheltered him through tears and cold.

KRAGLER   On to the newspaper district!

A dog went to the kitchen
To find a bone to chew.
The cook picked up the chopper
And chopped the dog in two.

(*Laar staggers to the nickelodeon, pulls out the drum, and, playing drumrolls, goes out after the others*)

ACT FIVE

(THE BED)

Wooden Bridge

Screams. Large red moon.

BABUSCH You'd better go home.

ANNA I can't any more. What's the use, I waited four years with his picture. Then I took another man. I was afraid at night.

BABUSCH I'm out of cigars. Aren't you ever going home?

ANNA Listen!

BABUSCH They're ripping up newspapers and throwing them into puddles, they're screaming at machine guns and shooting in each other's ears. They think they're making a new world. There comes another bunch of them.

ANNA It's him!

(*A great turbulence invades the streets as the group approaches. The sound of shooting from all directions*)

ANNA I'm going to tell him now!

BABUSCH I'll stop your mouth!

ANNA I'm not an animal. I'm going to scream.

BABUSCH And I'm out of cigars.

(*Glubb, Laar, the drunk, the two prostitutes, Manke, the waiter from the gin mill, and Andreas Kragler emerge from between the houses*)

KRAGLER I'm hoarse. I've got Africa up to here. I'm going to hang myself.

GLUBB Couldn't you hang yourself tomorrow and come to the newspapers now?

KRAGLER (*staring at Anna*) Yes.

AUGUSTA Seen a ghost?

MANKE   Good God, man, your hair's standing on end.

GLUBB   Is it her?

KRAGLER   What's wrong? Why are you stopping? I'll have you stood up against the wall. Forward march! And keep marching!

ANNA *(steps in his way)*   Andry!

THE DRUNK   Lift your leg. Love is calling.

ANNA   Andry, stop. It's me, there's something I want to say. *(Silence)* I've got to tell you something. Stop just a minute. I'm not drunk. *(Silence)* But you haven't got a cap and it's cold. I've got to whisper something in your ear.

KRAGLER   Are you drunk?

AUGUSTA   Here comes the bride, and the bride is drunk.

ANNA   Yes, what do you think of that? *(Takes a few steps)* I'm going to have a baby. *(Augusta laughs shrilly. Kragler staggers, glances toward the bridge, teeters about as though learning how to walk)*

AUGUSTA   Are you a fish? The way you gasp for air?

MANKE   Maybe you think you're asleep?

KRAGLER *(at attention, his hands to the seams of his trousers)*   Yes, sir!

MANKE   She's going to have a baby. Having babies is her job. Let's go!

KRAGLER *(stiffly)*   Yes, sir! Where to?

MANKE   He's gone crazy.

GLUBB   Weren't you in Africa at one time?

KRAGLER   Morocco, Casablanca, Hut 10.

ANNA   Andry!

KRAGLER *(listening)*   Listen! My fiancée, the whore! She's come, she's here. With her belly full!

GLUBB   Isn't she a little anemic?

KRAGLER   Sh! It wasn't me! Not me!

ANNA   Andry, we're not alone!

KRAGLER   Is your belly bloated with air, or have you turned whore? I was away, I couldn't keep an eye on you. I was lying in the mud. Where were you lying while I was lying in the mud?

MARIE   You shouldn't talk like that. What do you know about it?

KRAGLER   And I wanted to see you! Or I'd be lying where I belong, with wind in my skull and dust in my mouth, and I wouldn't know a thing. But I had to see this first. I wouldn't settle for less. I ate husks. They were bitter. I crawled out of the mudhole on all fours. Wasn't that bright of me! I'm a pig. (*Opens his eyes wide*) You all enjoying the show? You got free tickets? (*He picks up lumps of dirt and throws them in all directions*)

AUGUSTA   Hold him down!

ANNA   Throw it, Andry! Throw it! Throw some at me!

MARIE   Take her away. He'll kill her.

KRAGLER   Go to hell! You're getting all you need. Open your mouths. That's all there is.

AUGUSTA   Get his head down! His head! In the mud! (*The men hold him down*) And now make tracks, lady.

GLUBB (*to Anna*)   Right, go on home. The morning air is bad for the ovaries.

BABUSCH (*plods across the battlefield. Chewing his mangled cigar butt, to Kragler*)   Now you know where the shoe pinches. You're God Almighty. You've done your thundering. The woman, on the other hand, is pregnant, she can't stay here on that stone, the nights are cool. Maybe you could say something . . .

GLUBB   Yes, maybe you could say something.

(*The men let Kragler up.*)

(*Silence. A gust of wind. Two men pass hurriedly*)

FIRST   They've taken the Ullstein Building.

SECOND   And the artillery is pulling up in front of Mosse's.

FIRST   There aren't nearly enough of us.

SECOND   A lot more are coming.

FIRST   Much too late. (*They are gone*)

AUGUSTA   Did you hear that? Let's get going!

MANKE   That bourgeois with his whore! Shove the answer down his throat!

AUGUSTA (*tries to pull Kragler along*)   Come along to the newspapers, boy! That'll put the hair back on your chest.

GLUBB   Leave her there on her stone. The subway will be running at seven.

AUGUSTA   There won't be any subway today.

DRUNK   Forward! On to Glory!

(*Anna has stood up again*)

MARIE (*looks at her*)   White as a sheet.

GLUBB   A trifle pale. A trifle thin.

BABUSCH   She's shot to hell.

o   GLUBB   It only looks that way. In this unflattering light. (*Looks at the sky*)

AUGUSTA   Here they come from Wedding.

GLUBB (*rubbing his hands*)   You came with the cannon. Maybe you belong with them. (*Kragler is silent*) You're not talking.
o   That's wise. (*Walking around him*) Your coat's kind of faded, you look kind of pale and wrung out. But that doesn't matter. Only your shoes—yes, maybe your shoes make a bad impression. They squeak. But you can grease them. (*He sniffs the*
o   *air*) Yes, of course, a few constellations have drifted out of sight
o   since eleven o'clock, and a few Saviours have been eaten by sparrows. But I'm glad to see you're still here. The only thing that worries me is your digestion. But the light doesn't shine through you yet. At least we can see you.

KRAGLER   Come here, Anna.

MANKE   "Come here, Anna."

o   ANNA   Where's the subway, somebody?

AUGUSTA   There won't be any subway today. No subway, no elevated, no nothing all day. This is going to be a day of rest, sweetie, all the trains will be standing still, and we'll be roaming around like human beings until nightfall.

o   KRAGLER   Come here to me, Anna.

GLUBB   Won't you come a little further with us, Brother Soldier? (*Kragler is silent*) Some of us would have liked another drink of gin, but you were against it. Some of us would have liked to lie in a bed one more time, but you had no bed, so we gave up the idea of going home. (*Kragler is silent*)

ANNA   Aren't you going, Andry? Your friends are waiting.

MANKE   For God's sake, man, take that hand out of your pocket.

KRAGLER   Throw stones at me, here I stand. I'll give you the shirt off my back, but I won't hold out my neck to the knife.

THE DRUNK   Heavenly blazing assholes!

AUGUSTA   But but but the newspapers?

KRAGLER   It's no use. You can't drag me to the newspaper district in my shirt sleeves. I'm through with being a lamb. I don't want to die. (*Takes his pipe from his pants pocket*)

GLUBB   Isn't that rather contemptible?

KRAGLER   They'll shoot a bull's-eye in your chest. Anna! Why are
you looking at me like that, damn it! Do I have to justify myself
to you too? (*To Glubb*) They shot your nephew, but I've got my
woman back. Anna, come!

GLUBB   We'd better go on without him, if you ask me.

AUGUSTA   Then it was all a lot of lies? Africa and all that?

KRAGLER   No, it was true. Anna!

MANKE   He was yelling like a stockbroker, and now he wants to
go to bed.

KRAGLER   I've got my woman now.

MANKE   Have you?!

KRAGLER   Come here, Anna! She's damaged, she's lost her innocence. Did you behave yourself? Or have you got a kid inside
you?

ANNA   A kid. Yes, I've got a kid.

KRAGLER   That's it.

ANNA   He's in here. The pepper didn't help and my hips will
never be the same.

KRAGLER   See? That's the way she is.

MANKE   And what about us? Soaked to the heart in booze, stuffed
to the gills with doubletalk. And these knives in our fists! Who
put them there?

KRAGLER   I did. (*To Anna*) Yes, that's how you are.

ANNA   That's how I am.

AUGUSTA   I suppose you didn't yell: "On to the newspapers!"

KRAGLER   I did. I did. (*To Anna*) Come along.

MANKE   You sure did. You'll never live that down, boy. "On to
the newspapers!" That's what you yelled.

o   KRAGLER   And now I'm going home. (*To Anna*) Get going!

AUGUSTA   You stinker!

ANNA   Forget about me! I fooled my father and mother and went
to bed with a bachelor.

o   AUGUSTA   You're another stinker.

KRAGLER   What did you do?

ANNA   I bought the curtains with him. And I slept in the bed with
him.

KRAGLER   Shut up!

MANKE   Boy, if you back down, I'll hang myself.
(*Distant shouting from the rear*)

o   AUGUSTA   Now they're closing in on Mosse's.

ANNA   And I forgot you completely in spite of the picture. Every inch of you.

KRAGLER   Shut up!

ANNA   Forgot! Forgot!

o KRAGLER   And I don't give a damn. Must I go after you with my knife?

ANNA   Yes, go after me. Yes, with your knife!

o MANKE   Throw her in the water! The slut!
(They fling themselves on Anna)

AUGUSTA   Yes, take the bitch away from him.

MANKE   Hold her by the neck!

AUGUSTA   Drown the profiteer's whore!

ANNA   Andry!

KRAGLER   Hands off!
(Only panting is heard. In the distance muffled irregular cannon fire)

MANKE   What's that?

AUGUSTA   Artillery.

MANKE   Cannon.

o AUGUSTA   God help anybody who's there! They'll explode like fish!

KRAGLER   Anna!
(Augusta, stooped over, runs to the rear)

o BULLTROTTER   *(appears on the bridge rear)*   Christ, where have you been?

GLUBB   He's going to the can.

MANKE *(on his way out)*   Bastard!

KRAGLER   And now, my boy, I'm going home.

o GLUBB *(already on the bridge)*   Sure. You've still got your balls if nothing else.

KRAGLER *(to Anna)*   They're shooting again. Hold on to me, Anna.

ANNA   I'll make myself very little.

GLUBB   You'll see, you'll hang yourself in the can tomorrow morning.
(Augusta has disappeared with the others)

KRAGLER   You're going to your death, man.

o GLUBB   Yes, my boy, a lot of things will be happening in the morning. But perhaps certain people will save their skins. *(He disappears)*

KRAGLER   They practically drowned in their tears for me, and I
only washed my shirt in their tears. Do they want my flesh to
rot in the gutter so their ideas can win out? Are they drunk?

ANNA   Andry! It doesn't matter.

KRAGLER (*not looking in her face, staggers around, clutches his
throat*)   I've got it up to here. (*He laughs angrily*) It's all a lot
of make-believe. A few boards and a paper moon. The only
thing that's real is the butcher's block in the background. (*He
runs around again, his arms hanging down to the ground, and fishes
up the drum from the nickelodeon*) They forgot their drum. (*He
pounds on it*) "The Half-baked Spartacist, or the Power of
Love." "The Blood Bath in the Newspaper District, or Every
Man Is Best Off in his Own Skin." (*Looks up, blinking*) "With
your Shield or Without It." (*Drumming*) The bagpipes play, the
poor people die in the newspaper district, the houses fall on
them, the day dawns. They lie in the street like drowned cats,
I'm a stinker, and the stinker goes home. (*He takes a breath*) I'll
put on a clean shirt, I've still got my skin, I'll take off my
uniform, I'll grease my boots. (*Laughs malignantly*) The shouting will all be over tomorrow morning, but I'll lie in bed tomorrow morning and multiply, so as not to perish from the earth.
(*Drumming*) Stop that romantic gaping, you usurers! (*Drumming*) You cutthroats! (*Laughing loudly, almost choking*) You
bloodthirsty cowards! (*His laughter sticks in his throat. He can't
go on. He staggers around and throws the drum at the moon which
turns out to be a Japanese lantern. Drum and moon fall in the river,
which has no water in it*) Drunken foolishness! Now's the time
for bed, for the big, white, broad bed. Come!

ANNA   Oh, Andry!

KRAGLER (*leads her toward the rear*)   Aren't you cold?

ANNA   But you haven't got your coat on. (*She helps him on with
it*)

KRAGLER   It's cold. (*He puts his scarf around her neck*)   Come
now!

(*They walk side by side, without contact, Anna a little behind him.
High in the air, very distant, white, wild screams. They come from
the newspaper district*)

KRAGLER (*stops, listens, puts his arm around Anna*)   Four years!
(*As the screams continue, they walk off*)

In the Jungle of Cities

*The Fight Between Two Men in the
Gigantic City of Chicago*

Translator: Gerhard Nellhaus

You are in Chicago in 1912. You will witness an inexplicable wrestling match between two men and observe the downfall of a family that has moved from the prairies to the jungle of the big city. Don't worry your heads about the motives for the fight, keep your minds on the stakes. Judge impartially the technique of the contenders, and be prepared to concentrate on the finish.

CHARACTERS

SHLINK THE LUMBER DEALER, a Malay

GEORGE GARGA

JOHN GARGA, his father

MAE GARGA, his mother

MARY GARGA, his sister

JANE LARRY, his girl friend

SKINNY, a Chinese, Shlink's clerk

COLLIE COUCH, known as BABOON, a pimp

J. FINNAY, known as WORM, hotel owner

PAT MANKY, a first mate

A SALVATION ARMY PREACHER

TWO SALVATION ARMY GIRLS

THE PUG-NOSED MAN

THE BARTENDER

C. MAYNES, owner of a lending library

WAITER

RAILROAD WORKERS

1

The Lending Library of C. Maynes in Chicago

THE MORNING OF AUGUST 8, 1912

Garga behind the counter. The doorbell rings. Enter Shlink and Skinny.

SKINNY   If we read the sign right, this is a lending library.   We'd like to borrow a book.

GARGA   What kind of a book?

SKINNY   A fat one.

GARGA   For yourself?

SKINNY (*who looks at Shlink before each answer*)   No, not for me; for this gentleman.

GARGA   Your name?

SKINNY   Shlink, lumber dealer, 6 Mulberry Street.

GARGA (*taking down the name*)   Five cents a week per book. Take your pick.

SKINNY   No, you choose one.

GARGA   This is a detective story, it's no good. Here's something better—a travel book.

SKINNY   Just like that you say the book is no good?

SHLINK (*stepping up to him*)   Is that your personal opinion? I'll buy your opinion. Is ten dollars enough?

GARGA   Take it as a gift.

SHLINK   You mean you've changed your opinion and now it's a good book?

GARGA   No.

SKINNY   Ten dollars will buy you some fresh linen.

GARGA   My job here is wrapping books, that's all.

SKINNY   It drives the customers away.

GARGA   What do you want of me? I don't know you. I've never seen you before.

SHLINK   I never heard of this book and it doesn't mean a thing to me. I'm offering you forty dollars for your opinion of it.

GARGA   I'll sell you the opinions of Mr. J. V. Jensen and Mr. Arthur Rimbaud but I won't sell you my own opinion.

SHLINK   Your opinion is just as worthless as theirs, but right now I want to buy it.

GARGA   I indulge in opinions.

SKINNY   Are your family millionaires?

GARGA   My family live on rotten fish.

SHLINK   (*obviously pleased*)   A fighter! I'd have expected you to come across with the words that would give me pleasure and get your family something better than fish.

SKINNY   Forty bucks! That's a lot of linen for you and your family.

GARGA   I'm not a prostitute.

SHLINK   (*with humor*)   I hardly think my fifty dollars would interfere with your inner life.

GARGA   Raising your offer is one more insult and you know it.

SHLINK   (*naïvely*)   A man's got to know which is better, a pound of fish or an opinion. Or two pounds of fish or the opinion.

SKINNY   Dear sir, your stubbornness will get you into trouble.

GARGA   I'm going to have you thrown out.

SKINNY   Having opinions shows you don't know anything about life.

SHLINK   Miss Larry says you wanted to go to Tahiti!

GARGA   How do you know Jane Larry?

SHLINK   She's starving. She's not getting paid for the shirts she sews. You haven't been to see her in three weeks.

(*Garga drops a pile of books*)

SKINNY   Watch your step! You're only an employee.

GARGA   You're molesting me. But there's nothing I can do about it.

SHLINK   You're poor.

GARGA   I live on fish and rice. You know that as well as I do.

SHLINK   Sell!

SKINNY   Are you an oil king?

SHLINK   The people in your neighborhood feel sorry for you.

GARGA   I can't shoot down the whole neighborhood.

SHLINK   Your family that came from the prairies . . .

GARGA   Sleep three in a bed by a broken drain pipe. I smoke at night, it's the only way I can get to sleep. The windows are closed because Chicago is cold. Are you enjoying this?

SHLINK   Of course your sweetheart . . .

GARGA   Sews shirts for two dollars a piece. Net profit: twelve cents. I recommend her shirts. We spend Sundays together. A bottle of whiskey costs us eighty cents, exactly eighty cents. Does this amuse you?

SHLINK   You're not coughing up your secret thoughts.

GARGA   No.

SHLINK   Nobody can live on twelve cents profit.

GARGA   Each man to his taste. Some people like Tahiti, if you don't mind.

SHLINK   You're well informed. That's the simple life. On Cape Hay there are storms. But farther south you've got the Tobacco Isles, and green rustling fields. You live like a lizard.

GARGA (*looking out the window, dryly*)   Ninety-four degrees in the shade. Noise from the Milwaukee Bridge. Traffic. A morning like every other morning.

SHLINK   But this morning is different; I'm starting my fight with you. I'm going to start by rocking the ground you stand on. (*The bell rings, Maynes enters*) Your man has gone on strike.

MAYNES   Why aren't you taking care of these gentlemen, George?

SKINNY (*bitingly*)   His relations with us are strained.

MAYNES   What do you mean by that?

SKINNY   We don't care for his greasy shirt.

MAYNES   How dare you come to work like that, George? Is this a hash house? It won't happen again, gentlemen.

SKINNY   He's saying something. He's cursing up his sleeve! Speak up, man, use the voice God gave you!

GARGA   I must ask you for some new shirts, Mr. Maynes. You can't be a gigolo on five dollars a week.

SHLINK   Go to Tahiti. Nobody washes there.

GARGA   Thanks. Your concern is touching. I'll send my sister to pray for you in church.

SHLINK   Please do. She has nothing else to do anyhow. Manky's the right man for her. He runs himself ragged for her. Your parents are starving and she doesn't bat an eyelash.

GARGA   Are you running a detective agency? Your interest in us is flattering, I hope.

SHLINK   You're just shutting your eyes. Your family is headed for disaster. You're the only one who's making any money and you indulge in opinions! When you could be on your way to Tahiti. (*Shows him a sea chart that he has with him*)

GARGA   I've never seen you before in all my life.

SHLINK   There are two passenger lines.

GARGA   You just bought this map, didn't you? It's brand-new.

SKINNY   Think it over, the Pacific!

GARGA   (*to Maynes*)   Please ask these gentlemen to leave. They didn't come to buy anything. They're driving the customers away. They've been spying on me. I don't even know them. (*J. Finnay, called Worm, enters. Shlink and Skinny step back, pretending not to know him*)

WORM   Is this C. Maynes's lending library?

MAYNES   In person.

WORM   Shady establishment, if you ask me.

MAYNES   Are you looking for books, magazines, stamps?

WORM   So these are books? Filthy business. What's the point in it? Aren't there enough lies? "The sky was blue, the clouds flew east." Why not south? What people won't swallow!

MAYNES   Let me wrap this book for you, sir.

SKINNY   Why not let him catch his breath? And I ask you, does this gentleman look like a bookworm?

GARGA   It's a plot.

WORM   You don't say! Listen to this. She says, "When you kiss me I always see your beautiful teeth." How can you see when you're kissing? But that's the way she is. Recorded for posterity. The lewd bitch! (*He grinds his heels on the books*)

MAYNES   Look here, sir, you've ruined those books, you'll have to pay for them.

WORM   Books! What good are they? Did libraries stop the San Francisco earthquake?

MAYNES   George, get the sheriff.

WORM   I've got a liquor store. That's an honorable business.

GARGA   He isn't even drunk.

WORM   The sight of such loafers makes me tremble like a leaf.

GARGA   It's a put-up job. They're out to get me.

(*Couch, called Baboon, enters with Jane Larry. Worm steps back pretending not to know them*)

BABOON   Come on in, my little white chick. This is Maynes's rental library.

GARGA   You better close the shop, Mr. Maynes. Strange vermin are crawling into your papers, moths are eating your magazines.

WORM   I always say: Look life straight in the eyes.

BABOON   Get your face out of my way! I can't stand paper, especially newspaper.

GARGA   Get the gun!

SHLINK   (*steps forward*)   I ask you again, will you sell?

GARGA   (*noticing Jane*)   No!

JANE   George, is this your shop? Why are you staring at me? I was just going for a little walk with this gentleman.

GARGA   Keep walking.

BABOON   Say, let's not get rough. Don't you trust her? If I get excited, this book will end up in a thousand pieces. You still don't trust her?

MAYNES   I'll fire you if you won't trust her. My books are being ruined.

GARGA   Go home, Jane, please. You're drunk.

JANE   What's wrong with you, George? These gentlemen are being nice to me. (*She drinks out of Baboon's bottle*) They've bought me drinks. It's hot today—ninety-four. You know, George, it rips through you like lightning.

GARGA   Go on home now. I'll come tonight.

JANE   You haven't shown up for three weeks. I'm not going home any more. I'm fed up sitting around with those shirts.

BABOON   (*pulling Jane onto his lap*)   That's all over now.

JANE   Oh, you're tickling me. Stop that! George doesn't like it.

BABOON   In brief, she's got a body that's worth a few bucks. Can you afford it, sir? It's a question of love and it's a question of drinks.

WORM   Maybe you'd like to keep her a virgin? What do you want her to do? Scrub floors? Wash clothes?

SKINNY   You expect a nice little pigeon like her to be an angel?

GARGA (*to Shlink*)   Are you trying to turn this place into the Wild West? Knives? Guns? Cocktails?

WORM   Hold on! You can't leave your job here. Maybe somebody will fall by the wayside. Sell!

GARGA   Strange. Everybody knows what's going on except me. —Jane!

BABOON   Tell him!

JANE   Don't look at me that way, George! This may be my only chance. Can you buy me drinks? Oh, it's not for the drinks! It's like this, George: every morning I look in the mirror. It's been two years now. You always go off and work for four weeks. When you were sick of it and needed liquor, you thought of me. I can't take it any more. The nights, George! That doesn't make me bad, not me. Don't look at me that way, it's not fair!

BABOON   That's smart. Have another drink and you'll be even smarter.

GARGA   Whiskey's rotting your brain. Can you hear what I'm saying? Let's go away! Together! To Frisco! Anywhere you want. I don't know if a man can love forever, but I can tell you this much: I'll stick by you.

JANE   You can't, Georgie.

GARGA   I can do anything. I can even make money if that's it. I've got a special feeling for you. There are no words for it! But we'll get together again. I'll come tonight. This very evening!

JANE   I hear every word; you don't need to shout and you don't need to tell these gentlemen here you didn't love me. You're only saying the bitterest things you know, and naturally I've got to listen. You know it as well as I do.

WORM   Cut the comedy! Just tell him you were in bed with this gentleman from nine to ten-thirty.

JANE   That might not be so good. But now at least you know, George, it's not the whiskey or the heat!

SHLINK   Sell! I'll double the price again. This is so unpleasant.

GARGA   That doesn't count. What's nine to eleven against two years?

SHLINK   I assure you, two hundred dollars means nothing to me. I hardly dare make such an offer.

GARGA   Would you be kind enough to send your friends away.

SHLINK   As you wish. Consider the ways of this planet and sell.

MAYNES   You're a fool and a dishrag and a lazy coolie; just think of . . .

SKINNY   Your innocent careworn parents!

WORM   Your sister!

BABOON   Your sweetheart! This lovely young girl.

GARGA   No, no, no!

SHLINK   Tahiti!

GARGA   I refuse.

MAYNES   You're fired!

SHLINK   Your economic existence! The ground you stand on! It's shaking!

GARGA   This is freedom! Here is my coat! (*Takes it off*) Share it among you! (*Takes a book from the shelf and reads*) "Idolatry! Lies! Lechery! I'm a beast, a black. But I can be saved. You're phony niggers, maniacs, savages, misers! Merchant, you are a nigger and, General, you are a nigger, Emperor, you old leper, you're a nigger, you drink untaxed liquor from Satan's still. This people inspired by fever and cancer!" (*Drinks*) "I'm unversed in metaphysics, understand no laws. I have no moral sense, I'm a brute; you are mistaken!"

(*Shlink, Skinny, Worm and Baboon have gathered around Garga and applaud as at a theatrical performance*)

SHLINK (*smoking*)   Why get so excited? Nobody's doing anything to you.

JANE (*her arms around his neck*)   Is it that bad, George?

GARGA   Here are my shoes! Are you smoking your little black cigar, sir? It might make you dribble. Here, my handkerchief. Yes, yes, I'll auction off this woman! I'm throwing these papers in your face. I want the tobacco fields of Virginia and a ticket to the Islands. I want, I want my freedom. (*He runs out in his pants and shirt*)

SHLINK (*calls after him*)   My name's Shlink, Shlink the lumber dealer! Six Mulberry Street!

SKINNY   He'll toe the line. What's all this paper cost?

WORM   You're really going to pay?

MAYNES   The books are worth ten dollars.

SKINNY   Here's twenty.

BABOON (*to Jane, who is crying*)   Aha, now comes the awakening! Go weep in the gutter.

WORM   You've got to look life straight in the eyes.

SHLINK   How much is this stuff?

MAYNES   The clothes? Jacket? Tie? Shoes? They're not really for sale. Ten dollars.

SKINNY   We finally drove him out of his skin. Let's take it with us.

(Shlink goes out slowly toward the back, Skinny follows him with the bundle of clothes)

2

Chicago. The office of C. Shlink, lumber dealer

AUGUST 22, SHORTLY BEFORE 7 P.M.

Shlink at his little table.

SKINNY *(voice from left rear)*   Kentucky—seven carloads.

WORM *(in the rear)*   Right.

SKINNY   Stripped logs—two carloads.

WORM   There's a man asking to see Mr. Shlink.

SHLINK   Send him in.

WORM   Here's Mr. Shlink!

(Garga enters)

SHLINK *(pleased)*   So here you are! Here are your clothes. Put them on.

GARGA   You've been waiting for me? You've brought my clothes here? Filthy rags. *(Kicks the bundle of clothes away)*

(Shlink strikes a small gong)

MARY *(enters)*   George!

GARGA   You here, Mary?

MARY   Where've you been, George? They were worried about you. And the way you look!

GARGA   Just what are you doing here?

MARY   I take care of the linen. We can live on that. Why are you

looking at me like that? You look as if you'd been having a hard
time. I'm doing fine here. They told me they'd fired you.

GARGA   Mary, pack your things and go home. (*Pacing around*) I
don't know what they want of me. They've harpooned me and
pulled me in. I can feel the ropes. I may have to depend on you,
sir. But leave my sister out of it!

SHLINK   As you wish. (*To Mary*) But first get him a clean shirt,
and a suit. If you don't mind.

MARY   I can't understand my brother. He wants me to leave you.

SHLINK   And when you've finished, please go home. I don't know
anything about linen.

(*Mary leaves*)

SHLINK   Have you been drinking?

GARGA   Kindly tell me if that doesn't fit in with your plans.

SHLINK   I only have saki. But I'll get you anything you like. You
prefer cocktails?

GARGA   I do everything in one fell swoop. I'm in the habit of
doing nothing for weeks but drink, make love, and smoke, all
at the same time.

SHLINK   And leaf through the *Britannica* . . .

GARGA   You know everything.

SHLINK   When I heard about your habits, I thought to myself:
There's a good fighter.

GARGA   What's the holdup with those clothes?

SHLINK   Excuse me . . . (*He stands up and strikes the little gong*)

MARY (*enters*)   Here's your linen, George, and your suit.

GARGA   Wait and we'll leave together. (*He changes clothes behind
a screen*)

MARY   I have to say good-bye, Mr. Shlink. I couldn't quite finish
the linen. Thanks for letting me stay at your house.

GARGA (*from behind the screen*)   This suit has no pockets.

(*Shlink whistles*)

GARGA (*coming out*)   Who are you whistling for? In the last few
weeks you've got left, I want you to stop whistling for people.

SHLINK   I accept your orders.

GARGA   You opened up this western. I'll accept the challenge.
You skinned me alive for the fun of it. You won't make amends
by giving me a new skin. I'm going to wipe you out. (*Pulls a
gun*) An eye for an eye, a tooth for a tooth.

SHLINK   Then the fight's on?

GARGA   Yes! Without obligation, of course.

SHLINK   And no question why?

GARGA   No question why. I don't want to know why you need a fight. If you've got a reason, I'm sure it's rotten. For me it's enough that you think you're the better man.

SHLINK   Well, let's think it over. Owning a house and a lumber business, for instance, puts me in a position to sick the dogs on you. Money is everything. Right? But my house is yours now, and so is the lumber business. From now on, Mr. Garga, my fate's in your hands. I don't know you! From now on I'm going to be your slave. Every look that comes into your eyes will trouble me. Every one of your wishes, known or unknown, will find me willing. Your cares will be my cares, my strength will be yours. My feelings will be dedicated to you alone, and you will be an evil master.

GARGA   I accept your challenge. I hope you'll have nothing to laugh about.

(*Baboon, Skinny and Worm enter silently. Garga notices with a grin that their suits are the same as his*)

SHLINK   This house and this lumber business, carried on the Chicago Register of Deeds as the property of Shlink, are being transferred this day to Mr. George Garga of Chicago.

GARGA (*to Shlink*)   That's me. All right. How many stripped logs have you in stock?

SHLINK   Maybe four hundred. I don't know exactly.

SKINNY   They belong to Broost and Company of Virginia.

GARGA   Who sold them?

WORM   I, known as Worm, owner of the Chinese Hotel in the coal district.

GARGA   Sell them again.

WORM   Sell them twice! That's fraud.

GARGA   Right.

WORM   And who'll be responsible for this order?

GARGA   Sell those logs in Frisco under the name of Shlink. Turn the money over to Mr. Shlink, who'll hold it for me until I ask him for it. Any objections, Mr. Shlink?

(*Shlink shakes his head*)

WORM   That's barefaced fraud. We'll have the law on us in no time.

GARGA How soon?

SHLINK Six months at the most. (*He brings Garga the ledger*)

BABOON This is a bog.

GARGA Storks thrive on bogs.

BABOON It's better to work with a switchblade than with phony papers. Can you forget that Chicago is cold?

GARGA You meant your actual lumber business, didn't you, Shlink? The house, the logs, the whole inventory?

SHLINK Of course. Here's the ledger.

GARGA Pour ink over the ledger. You!

SKINNY Me?

(*Shlink hands him a bottle of ink*)

SKINNY (*over the ledger*) All these entries! All our transactions!

GARGA Go ahead, pour!

(*Skinny pours carefully*)

BABOON That's that.

WORM What an ending after twenty years! Some joke! I don't get it. This used to be a lumber business.

GARGA And now turn off the saws and that will be the end of this lumber business.

BABOON Anything you say, boss! (*Goes out*)

(*The sound of the saws outside stops. Shlink's cronies put on their coats and stand against the wall. Garga laughs loudly*)

MARY What are you doing, George?

GARGA Shut up! Fire that man, Mr. Shlink!

SHLINK You may leave.

SKINNY Leave? After working in this place for twenty years come April?

SHLINK You're fired.

MARY I don't think you're doing right, George.

GARGA I want you to go home, Mary.

MARY And I want you to come with me. You'll only come to grief around here. Let him go, Mr. Shlink.

SHLINK Give me your orders, Garga.

GARGA Certainly. As long as there's nothing left for you to do around here, my orders are to set up a little poker game with your former staff.

(*Shlink and his cronies sit down to play poker*)

MARY You're coming home with me, George. This whole thing is a joke, can't you see that?

GARGA   We grew up on the prairies, Mary. Here we're being sold out.

MARY   We? What do they want of us?

GARGA   You're of no consequence in all this. They're only trying to rope you in. Two weeks ago, a man spat a small cherry pit into my eye. I come to see him. With a gun in my pocket. And he only bows and scrapes and offers me his lumber business. I don't understand a thing, but I accept. I'm alone on the prairie, and, Mary, I can't help you.

WORM (*addressing Garga and Mary from behind*)   He plays like a paper god. I swear he cheats.

GARGA (*to Shlink*)   I don't understand a thing, sir, I'm like a nigger in all this. I came with a white flag, but now I'm attacking. Give me the papers that are your fortune and hand over your personal assets. I'll put them in my pocket.

SHLINK   Paltry things, I beg you not to despise them.

(*Shlink and Garga go out*)

SKINNY   Things were bad around here and the rain came in on us, but being fired is always an injustice.

WORM   Don't talk like a fool. (*Mocking him*) He thinks we've been talking about the mildew in the floor.

SKINNY   I love you, lady. You have a way of holding out your hand . . .

WORM   Christ! He's lost his bed, and he wants a woman to share it.

SKINNY   Come with me. I'll work for you. Come with me.

BABOON (*also comes forward*)   Pitiful! There are all sorts of women, black and golden-yellow and white like apples! Black women. Straight as a die from hip to foot! Full thighs, by God, not chicken legs like this! Oh Papua! Forty dollars for Papua!

SHLINK (*appears in the doorway and turns to call off stage*)   Yes, that's all.

WORM (*to Baboon*)   You're a barbarian. Ungrateful! The lady's innocent. Does she smoke a pipe? She's inexperienced, but who's to say she has no fire? Forty dollars, and all for the lady.

SKINNY   As much as you want for her!

BABOON   Without make-up, naturally, uncooked, the naked flesh. Ah, the tropics! Seventy dollars for toi cha!

MARY   Protect me, Mr. Shlink.

SHLINK I'm ready to protect you.

MARY Do you think I should go with him?

SHLINK Here nobody loves you. He loves you.

GARGA (*has entered*) Do you like being for sale? There's a lot of lumber here, and now they've put a few pounds of flesh up for auction! And isn't jujitsu known as the gay and easy art?

SHLINK (*walks up to Garga, troubled*) But aren't you making things too easy for yourself?

MARY (*to Garga*) You should have helped me. Come with me, George, this minute. Something terrible has happened. Even if I go away now, this thing may not be over. You must be blind not to see that you're losing.

(*In the background, the sound of two guitars and a drum. Salvation Army girls sing: "Christ receiveth sinful men."*)

GARGA I can see you're ready to lose yourself. It's the bog that's sucking you in. Here's something for you, Mary. The Salvation Army! Marching in here for you. (*He gets up from the table and goes to the rear*) Hey! Salvation Army! This way!

WORM (*to Mary*) A river has drained off here, and at night the place is haunted by the ghosts of drowned rats. Go home to your parents!

GARGA (*coming back*) Clean this joint up. Get rid of that whiskey! (*Shlink starts to do so, but Mary does it for him*) Come in, you people.

(*Shlink, bowing low, opens the wooden gate. A young Salvation Army preacher enters, followed by two girls with guitars and an old sinner with a drum*)

PREACHER Did you want me?

WORM Hallelujah! The Salvation Army!

GARGA I don't think much of what you people are doing. You could use a house though. Here, take this one.

PREACHER The Lord will bless you.

GARGA Maybe. (*To Shlink*) Did you inherit this house and these papers?

SHLINK No.

GARGA You worked forty years for them?

SHLINK Worked my fingers to the bone. I never slept more than four hours.

GARGA Were you poor when you came over?

SHLINK   I was seven. I've worked ever since.

GARGA   You don't own anything else?

SHLINK   Not a thing.

GARGA (*to the preacher*)   I'll give you this man's property on one condition. For the sake of the orphans and drunks whose shelter this will be, you must let me spit in your insufferable face.

PREACHER   I'm a man of God.

GARGA   Then take the consequences.

PREACHER   I have no right.

GARGA   Snow falls on the orphans, the drunks die like flies, and you take care of your face.

PREACHER   I'm ready. I've kept my face clean; I'm twenty-one. You must have your reasons. I beg you to understand me: please ask the lady to turn around.

MARY   I'll despise you if you accept.

PREACHER   I expect that. There are better faces than mine. But none too good for this.

GARGA   Spit in his face, Shlink, if you please.

MARY   This isn't right, George. I don't like it.

GARGA   A tooth for a tooth, if you please.

(*Shlink steps coolly up to the preacher and spits in his face. Worm bleats like a goat. The reformed sinner plays a drum roll.*)

PREACHER (*shaking his fists, in tears*)   Excuse me.

GARGA (*throws the papers at him*)   Here is the deed of gift. For the Salvation Army. And this is for you. (*Gives him his gun*) Now get out, you swine!

PREACHER   I thank you in the name of my mission. (*He leaves, bowing awkwardly. The hymn-singing fades with striking speed*)

GARGA   You spoiled my fun. Your brutality has no equal. I'll keep some of the money. But I'm not staying here, because this is the point of the whole thing, Mr. Shlink from Yokohama: I'm going to Tahiti.

MARY   You're yellow, George. When the preacher left, you winced. I saw you. How desperate you are!

GARGA   I came here peeled to the bones. Trembling from the spiritual debauches of the last two weeks. I spat in his face many times. Each time he swallowed it. I despise him. It's all over.

MARY   Disgusting!

GARGA   You left me in the lurch. A tooth for a tooth.

MARY And now you're going to carry on the fight with me? You never knew where to stop. God will punish you. I want nothing from you, only my peace.

GARGA And to find bread for your parents in a whore's bed. And to offer your horse's smell for sale and say: It's not me! That you may prosper in bed and dwell long upon the earth. (*He goes out with the others*)

MARY I don't really understand you, Mr. Shlink. But you can go in all four directions, while others have only one. A man has many possibilities, hasn't he? I can see that a man has many possibilities.

(*Shlink shrugs his shoulders, turns around and leaves. Mary follows him*)

3

Living room of the Garga Family

AUGUST 22, AFTER 7 P.M.

A filthy attic. In the rear a curtain hangs in front of a small balcony. John Garga and his wife Mae. Manky is singing a song.

JOHN Something has happened here that's hard to talk about.

MANKY They say your son George is mixed up in the kind of deal that never ends. They say he's mixed up with a yellow man. The yellow man has done something to him.

MAE We can't interfere.

JOHN If he's been fired, we can eat hay.

MAE Ever since he was a little boy, he's had to have things his way.

MANKY They say you shouldn't have hired out your daughter, Mary, to this yellow man.

MAE Yes, Mary's been gone two weeks now, too.

MANKY   People must be beginning to see that it all hangs together.

MAE   When our daughter left, she told us she'd been offered a job
in a lumber business. Ten dollars a week and only linen to
attend to.

MANKY   Linen for a yellow man!

JOHN   In cities like this nobody can see the next house. When
people read a newspaper, you never know what it means.

MANKY   Or when you buy a ticket.

JOHN   Riding in these electric trolleys probably gives people . . .

MANKY   Stomach cancer.

JOHN   Nobody knows. Here in the States wheat grows summer
and winter.

MANKY   But suddenly, without warning, there's no dinner for
you. You walk in the street with your children, observing the
fourth commandment to the letter, and suddenly you've only
got your son's or daughter's hand in your hand, and your son
and daughter themselves have sunk into a sudden gravel pit.

JOHN   Hello, who's there?

(*Garga stands in the doorway*)

GARGA   Still chewing the fat?

JOHN   Have you finally got the money for the two weeks?

GARGA   Yes.

JOHN   Have you still got your job or not? A new jacket! Looks
like you've been well paid for something? Huh? There's your
mother, George. (*To Mae*) Why are you standing there like
Lot's wife? Your son's here. Our son has come to take us out
to dinner at the Metropolitan Bar. Your darling son looks pale,
doesn't he? Slightly drunk maybe. Come on, Manky, let's go.
We'll smoke our pipes on the stairs!

(*Both go out*)

MAE   Tell me, George, are you mixed up with somebody?

GARGA   Has somebody been here?

MAE   No.

GARGA   I've got to go away.

MAE   Where?

GARGA   Any place. You always get scared right away.

MAE   Don't go away.

GARGA   I've got to. One man insults another. That's disagreeable for the man who gets insulted. But under certain circumstances the first man is willing to give up a whole lumber business for the pleasure of insulting the other. That's even more disagreeable for the second man. Maybe when he's been insulted like that, he'd better leave town. But since that might be too pleasant for him, even that may no longer be possible. In any case, he's got to be free.

MAE Aren't you free?

GARGA No. (*Pause*) We're none of us free. It starts in the morning with our coffee, and we're beaten if we play the fool. A mother salts her children's food with her tears and washes their shirts with her sweat. And their future is secure until the Ice Age, and the root sits in their heart. And when you grow up and want to do something, body and soul, they pay you, brainwash you, label you and sell you at a high price, and you're not even free to fail.

MAE But tell me what's getting you down.

GARGA You can't help me.

MAE I can help you. Don't run away from your father. How are we going to live?

GARGA (*giving her money*) I've been fired. But here's enough money for six months.

MAE We're worried about not hearing from your sister. We hope she's still got her job.

GARGA I don't know. I advised her to leave the yellow man.

MAE I know you won't let me talk to you the way other mothers do.

GARGA Oh, all those other people, the many good people, all the many other good people who stand at their lathes and earn their bread and make all the good tables for all the many good bread-eaters; all the many good table-makers and bread-eaters with their many good families, so many, whole armies of them, and nobody spits in their soup, and nobody sends them into the next world with a good kick in the pants, and no flood comes over them to the tune of "Stormy the night and the sea runs high."

MAE Oh, George!

GARGA No! Don't Oh, George me! I don't like it and I don't want to hear it any more.

MAE   You don't want to hear it any more? But what about me? How am I to live? With these filthy walls and the stove that won't last through the winter.

GARGA   It's plain as day, Mother. Nothing can last long now, neither the stove nor the walls.

MAE   How can you say that? Are you blind?

GARGA   And neither will the bread in the cupboard or the dress on your back, and neither will your daughter for that matter.

MAE   Sure, go ahead and shout, so everybody can hear. How everything is useless and anything that takes an effort is too much and wears you down. But how am I to live? And I've still got so much time ahead of me.

GARGA   If it's as bad as all that, speak up. What makes it so bad?

MAE   You know.

GARGA   Yes, I know.

MAE   But the way you say that! What do you think I said? I won't have you looking at me like that. I gave you birth and fed you milk, I gave you bread and beat you, so don't look at me like that. A husband is what he wants to be, I won't say a word to him. He has worked for us.

GARGA   I want you to come with me.

MAE   What's that?

GARGA   Come south with me. I'll work, I can cut down trees. We'll build a log cabin and you'll cook for me. I need you terribly.

MAE   Who are you saying that to? The wind? When you come back, you can come by and see where we spent our last days. (*Pause*) When are you leaving?

GARGA   Now.

MAE   Don't say anything to them. I'll get your things together and put your bundle under the stairs.

GARGA   Thank you.

MAE   Don't mention it.

   (*Both go out*)

   (*Worm enters cautiously and sniffs around the room*)

MANKY   Hey, who's there? (*Comes in with John*)

WORM   Me, a gentleman. Mr. Garga, I presume? Mr. John Garga?

MANKY   What do you want?

WORM Me? Nothing. Could I speak to your son—I mean, if he's had his bath?

JOHN What's it all about?

WORM (*sadly shaking his head*) What inhospitality! If it's not too much of an effort, could you tell me where your excellent son is taking his nap?

JOHN He's gone away. Go to the devil. This isn't an information bureau.

(*Mae enters*)

WORM Too bad! Too bad! We miss your son terribly, sir. And it's about your daughter, too, in case you're interested.

MAE Where is she?

WORM In a Chinese hotel, milady, in a Chinese hotel.

JOHN What?

MAE Holy Mary!

MANKY What's the meaning of this? What's she doing there?

WORM Nothing, just eating. Mr. Shlink wants me to tell you and your son that he should come and get her. She's too expensive, it's running into money, the lady's got a healthy appetite. She doesn't lift a finger. But she pursues us with immoral propositions. She's demoralizing the hotel. She'll have the police after us.

MAE John!

WORM (*shouting*) We're sick of her.

MAE Christ!

MANKY Where is she? I'll get her right away.

WORM Sure, you'll get her. Are you a bird dog? How do you know where the hotel is? You young fool! It's not so simple. You should have kept an eye on the lady. It's all your son's fault. Tell him to call for the bitch and kindly look after her. Or tomorrow night we'll get the police on the move.

MAE Good God. Just tell us where she is. I don't know where my son is. He's gone away. Don't be hardhearted. Oh, Mary! John, plead with him. What's happened to Mary? What's happening to me? Oh, George! John, what a city this is! What people! (*Goes out*)

(*Shlink appears in the doorway*)

WORM (*mutters in a fright*) Yes, I . . . this place has two entrances . . . (*Sneaks out*)

SHLINK (*simply*)   My name is Shlink. I used to be a lumber dealer, now I catch flies. I'm all alone in the world. Can you rent me a place to sleep? I'll pay board. On the door plate downstairs I recognized the name of a man I know.

MANKY   Your name is Shlink? You're the man who's been holding these people's daughter.

SHLINK   Who's that?

JOHN   Mary Garga, sir. My daughter, Mary Garga.

SHLINK   I don't know her. I don't know your daughter.

JOHN   The gentleman who was just here . . .

MANKY   Sent by you, I presume.

JOHN   Who slipped away the moment you came in.

SHLINK   I don't know the gentleman.

JOHN   But you and my son . . .

SHLINK   You're making fun of a poor man. Of course there's no danger in insulting me. I've gambled away my fortune; often you don't know how these things happen.

MANKY   What I say is, when I steer my ship into port, I know my channel.

JOHN   You can't trust anybody.

SHLINK   Lonely through sheer bungling at an age when the ground must close if snow is not to fall into the crevices, I see you deserted by your breadwinner. I'm not without compassion; and if you'll keep me, my work would have a purpose.

JOHN   Reasons won't fill anybody's stomach. We're not beggars. We can't eat fish heads. But our hearts aren't made of stone, we feel for your loneliness. Your elbows are looking for a family table. We're poor people.

SHLINK   I like everything, I can digest gravel.

JOHN   It's a small room. We're already packed in like sardines.

SHLINK   I can sleep on the floor, and a space half my length is good enough for me. I'm as happy as a child as long as my back's protected from the wind. I'll pay half the rent.

JOHN   All right, I understand. You don't want to wait out in the wind. You may share our roof.

MAE (*comes in*)   I've got to hurry downtown before dark.

JOHN   You're always gone when I need you. I'm taking this man in. He's lonely. There's room now that your son has run away. Shake hands with him.

MAE   Our home was on the prairies.

SHLINK   I know.

JOHN   What are you doing in the corner?

MAE   I'm making up my bed under the stairs.

JOHN   Where's your bundle?

SHLINK   I have nothing. I'll sleep on the stairs, ma'am. I won't intrude. My hand will never touch you. I know the skin on it is yellow.

MAE   (*coldly*)   I'll give you mine.

SHLINK   I don't deserve it. I meant what I said. I know you didn't mean your skin. Forgive me.

MAE   I open the window over the stairs at night. (*Goes out*)

JOHN   She's a good soul under that skin.

SHLINK   God bless her. I'm a simple man, don't expect words from my mouth. I've only teeth in it.

4

The Chinese Hotel

THE MORNING OF AUGUST 24

Skinny, Baboon and Jane.

SKINNY   (*in the doorway*)   Aren't you even thinking of starting a new business?

BABOON   (*lying in a hammock, shakes his head*)   All the boss does is walk along the waterfront, checking the passengers on the ships bound for Tahiti. Some fellow has run off with his soul and his entire fortune, maybe to Tahiti. It's him he's looking for. He's brought what was left of his belongings here for safekeeping, down to the last cigar butt. (*Referring to Jane*) And he's been feeding this here free of charge for the last three weeks. He's even taken the fellow's sister in. What he means to do with her is a mystery to me. He often sits up all night, talking to her.

SKINNY   You've let him put you out in the street, and now you feed him and his hangers-on too?

BABOON   He makes a few dollars hauling coal, but he gives them to the fellow's family; he's taken up lodging with them, but he can't live there, they don't like having him around. That fellow really took him for a ride. He got himself a cheap trip to Tahiti and hung a tree trunk over the boss's head that's likely to come crashing down any minute; because in five months at the most they're going to drag him into court for selling the same lumber twice.

SKINNY   And you bother to feed a wreck like that?

BABOON   He had to have his little joke. A man like him can always get credit. If that fellow stays lost, the boss will be back at the top of the lumber business in three months.

JANE (*half-dressed, making up*)   I've always thought I'd end up like this: in a Chinese flophouse.

BABOON   You've no idea what's in store for you.

(*Two voices are heard from behind a screen*)

MARY   Why don't you ever touch me? Why are you always wearing that smoky sack? I've got a suit for you, like other men wear. I can't sleep; I love you.

JANE   Pst! Listen! You can hear them again.

SHLINK   I am unworthy. I don't know anything about virgins. And I've been conscious of the smell of my race for years.

MARY   Yes, it's a bad smell. Yes, it's bad.

SHLINK   Why cut yourself in pieces like that? Look: my body is numb, it even affects my skin. Man's skin in its natural state is too thin for this world, that's why people do their best to make it thicker. The method would be satisfactory if the growth could be stopped. A piece of leather, for instance, stays the way it is. But a man's skin grows, it gets thicker and thicker.

MARY   Is it because you can't find an opponent?

SHLINK   In the first stage a table has edges; later on, and that's the nasty part of it, the same table is like rubber, but in the thick-skinned stage, there's neither table nor rubber.

MARY   How long have you had this disease?

SHLINK   Since I was a boy on the rowboats on the Yangtze Kiang. The Yangtze tortured the junks and the junks tortured us. There was a man who trampled our faces every time he stepped into the boat. At night we were too lazy to move our faces away. Somehow the man was never too lazy. We in turn had a cat to torture. She was drowned while learning to swim, though she'd eaten the rats that were all over us. All those people had the disease.

MARY   When were you on the Yangtze Kiang?

SHLINK   We lay in the reeds in the early morning and felt the disease growing.

WORM (*enters*)   The wind has swallowed the fellow. There's neither hide nor hair of him in all Chicago.

SHLINK   You'd better get some sleep. (*Steps out*) Still no news? (*Shlink goes out; through the open door the sound of Chicago waking is heard, the shouts of the milkmen, the rumbling of meat wagons*)

MARY   Chicago is waking up. The shouting of milkmen, the rumbling of meat wagons, the newspapers and the fresh morning air. It would be good to go away, it's good to wash in water, there's something good about the prairie and the asphalt. Right now, for instance, there's surely a cool wind in the prairies where we used to live.

BABOON   Do you still know your shorter catechism, Jane?

JANE (*droning*)   Things are getting worse, things are getting worse, things are getting worse. (*They begin to straighten the room, pull up the blinds and stand the sleeping mats up*)

MARY   For my part, I'm a little out of breath. I want to sleep with a man and I don't know how. Some women are like dogs, yellow and black ones. But I can't do it. I'm all torn apart. These walls are like paper. You can't breathe. You've got to set it all on fire. Where are the matches, a black box, to make the water come in. Oh, if I swim away, I'll be in two parts, swimming in two different directions.

JANE   Where has he gone?

BABOON   He's looking into the faces of all the people who are leaving town because Chicago's too cruel.

JANE   There's an east wind. The Tahiti-bound ships are weighing anchor.

5

Same Hotel

A MONTH LATER, THE 19TH OR 20TH OF SEPTEMBER

A filthy bedroom. A hallway. A glass-enclosed bar. Worm, George Garga, Manky and Baboon.

WORM (*from the hallway toward the bar*)   He never sailed after all. The harpoon is in deeper than we thought. We thought the earth had swallowed him up. But now he's in Shlink's room, licking his wounds.

GARGA (*in the bedroom*)   That dog Shlink. "In my dreams I call him my infernal bridegroom. We are parted from bed and board, he has no room any more. His little bride smokes stogies, and tucks money away in her stocking." That's me! (*Laughs*)

MANKY (*in the bar behind the glass partition*)   Life is strange. I knew a man who was really tops, but he loved a woman. Her family was starving. He had two thousand dollars, but he let them starve before his eyes. Because with those two thousand dollars he loved the woman, without them he couldn't get her. That was infamous, but he can't be held responsible.

GARGA   "Behold, I am a sinner. I loved deserts, burnt orchards, run-down shops, and hot drinks. You are mistaken. I am a little man." I'm through with Mr. Shlink from Yokohama.

BABOON   Take that lumber dealer. He never had any heart. But one day a passion made him wreck his whole lumber business. And now he's hauling coal down there. He had the whole neighborhood by the throat.

WORM   We took him in the way you might take in an exhausted pedigreed dog. But now by some stroke of luck his lost bone has turned up again, and if he won't let it go, our patience will be at an end.

GARGA   "One day I'll be his widow. That day, I know, has already been marked on the calendar. And I in clean underwear shall walk behind his corpse, swinging my legs lustily in the warm sun."

MARY (*enters with a lunch basket*)   George.

GARGA   Who's that? (*Recognizing her*) Good God! You look like a soiled rag!

MARY   I know.

WORM (*in the direction of the bar*)   He's dead drunk. And now his sister has come to see him. He's told her that she's soiled. Where's the old man?

BABOON   He's coming today. I've brought Jane. For bait, I suppose. There won't be any punches pulled in this fight.

JANE (*shakes her head*)   I don't understand you. Give me a drink. Gin.

MARY   I'm glad to see you had a better opinion of me. Or you wouldn't be surprised to see me here now. Besides, I remind you of the days when you were the pride of women, dancing the shimmy and ragtime with a crease in your pants on Saturday night, when your only vices were tobacco, whiskey, and the love of women, the legitimate vices of men. I wish you'd think of that, George. (*Pause*) How do you live?

GARGA (*lightly*)   It gets cold here at night. Do you need anything? Are you hungry?

MARY (*lightly, shaking her head and looking at him*)   Oh, George, we've had vultures over our heads for some time now.

GARGA (*lightly*)   When were you home last? (*Mary is silent*) I heard you were spending your time around here.

MARY   Did you? I wonder who's looking after them at home?

GARGA (*coldly*)   You needn't worry. I've heard that somebody's taking care of them. And I know what you've been doing. And I know something about a certain Chinese hotel too.

MARY   Does it make you feel good to be so cold-hearted, George? (*Garga looks at her*)

MARY   Don't look at me like that. I know you expect a confession.

GARGA   Go ahead!

MARY   I love him. Why don't you say something?

GARGA   Go ahead and love him. That will weaken him.

MARY   For God's sake, stop looking at the ceiling. I can't win him.

GARGA   That's disgraceful.

MARY   I know.—Oh, George, I'm torn in two. Because I can't win him. I tremble under my dress when I see him and I say the wrong thing.

GARGA   I can't tell you the right thing. A rejected woman! I had one once who wasn't worth a bottle of rum, but she knew how to attract men. She got paid for it too. And she knew her power.

MARY   You say such biting things. They swim in my head like gin. But are they good? You ought to know if they're good. But I understand you now.

(*Shlink enters the hallway*)

WORM   I can tell you from experience: humanity has fallen fist over calluses for a lot of paper dreams. And nothing is so much like paper as real life. (*Mary Garga turns around and bumps into Shlink*)

SHLINK   You here, Miss Garga?

MARY   It's considered wrong for a woman to tell a man she loves him. But I'd like to tell you that my love for you doesn't prove a thing. I don't want anything from you. It's not easy for me to tell you that. Maybe you knew it all along.

GARGA (*comes out of the bedroom*)   Stay here, Mary. We've got the prairies written on our faces, and here we've been tossed into the city. Don't hold back. Do what you want to do.

MARY   Yes, George.

GARGA   He works like a horse, and I lie lazily in a pool of absinthe.

SHLINK   The men who conquer the world like to lie on their backs.

GARGA   And those who own it work.

SHLINK   Are you worried?

GARGA (*to Shlink*)   Every time I look at you, you're sizing me up. Have you backed the wrong horse? Your face has grown old.

SHLINK   Thank you for not forgetting me. I was beginning to think you had gone south. Forgive me. I have taken the liberty of supporting your unfortunate family with the work of my hands.

GARGA   Is that true, Mary? I didn't know that. You've wormed your way in? Does supporting my family make you enjoy your vileness? You hand me a laugh. (*Goes left into the bedroom, lies down and laughs*)

SHLINK (*follows him*)   Go ahead and laugh, I like to hear you

laugh. Your laughter is my sunshine, it was misery here. It's
been dismal without you. It's been three weeks, Garga.

GARGA I've been satisfied, all in all.

SHLINK Of course. You've been rolling in clover.

GARGA Only my back is getting thin as a rail from lying on it.

SHLINK How pitiful life is! You're rolling in clover and the clover's not sweet enough.

GARGA I expect more out of life than to wear my shoes out
kicking you.

SHLINK Kindly take no notice of my insignificant person or my
intentions. But I'm still here. If you have to quit, you won't
leave the ring in innocence.

GARGA I'm quitting though. I'm going on strike. I throw in the
towel. Do I have to keep on chewing at you? You're a small hard
betel nut, I ought to spit it out, I know it's harder than my teeth
and that it's only a shell.

SHLINK (*pleased*) I'm doing my best to give you all the light you
need. I show myself in every possible light, Mr. Garga. (*Goes
under the lamp*)

GARGA You want to auction off your pock-marked soul? Are you
hardened to all suffering? Utterly callous?

SHLINK Crack the nut.

GARGA You're withdrawing into my corner. You're staging a
metaphysical fight, but leaving a slaughterhouse behind you.

SHLINK You mean this business with your sister? I haven't butchered anything your hands protected.

GARGA I have only two hands. Whatever is human to me you
devour like a chunk of meat. You open my eyes to possible
sources of help by choking them off. You use my family to help
yourself. You live on my reserves. I'm getting thinner and
thinner. I'm getting metaphysical. And on top of everything,
you vomit all this in my face.

MARY Please, George, can't I go now? (*She retreats toward the
rear*)

GARGA (*pulling her forward*) No, certainly not! We've just started
talking about you. I've just noticed you.

SHLINK It's my misfortune to tread on delicate ground. I'll retreat. You're never aware of your affections until their objects
are in the morgue, and I feel the need of acquainting you with

your affections. But please proceed, I understand you perfectly.

GARGA   But I am making sacrifices. Have I refused?

MARY   Let me go. I'm afraid.

GARGA   This way, sir! (*Runs into the hallway*) Let's start a family!

MARY   George!

GARGA   Stay here! (*In the direction of the bedroom*) I demand a little human involvement on your part, sir.

SHLINK   I wouldn't say no for a minute.

GARGA   You love this man? And he's indifferent? (*Mary weeps*)

SHLINK   I hope you're not overestimating your power. (*Runs back to the bedroom*)

GARGA   Don't worry. This will be a step forward. Let's see now, this is Thursday night. This is the Chinese hotel. And this is my sister, Mary Garga. (*Runs out*) Come here, Mary. My sister. This is Mr. Shlink from Yokohama. He has something to tell you.

MARY   George!

GARGA   (*goes out to get drinks*)   "I fled into the suburbs, where women with crooked orange mouths cower white in glowing thorn bushes."

MARY   It's dark in the window and I want to go home now.

SHLINK   I'll go with you if you like.

GARGA   "Their hair was black-lacquered shells, ever so thin, their eyes were dulled by the winds of debauch in the drunken night and by sacrifices in the open fields."

MARY   (*softly*)   Please don't ask me that.

GARGA   "Their thin dresses, like iridescent snake skins drenched with never-ending rain, slapped against their forever excited limbs."

SHLINK   I meant it when I asked you. I have no secrets from anyone.

GARGA   "They cover their legs to the very toenails, which are incrusted with molten copper; the madonna in the clouds turns pale at the sight of her sisters." (*Comes back, hands Shlink a glass*) Won't you drink? I find it necessary.

SHLINK   Why do you drink? Drinkers lie.

GARGA   It's fun talking with you. When I drink, half my thoughts float downward. I guide them to the ground and then they seem lighter. Drink!

SHLINK   I'd rather not. But if you insist.

GARGA   I'm inviting you to drink with me and you refuse.

SHLINK   I don't refuse, but my brain is all I've got.

GARGA   (*after a moment*)   Forgive me, let's go halves: you'll cut down on your brain. When you've drunk, you'll make love.

SHLINK   (*drinks as in a ritual*)   When I have drunk, I'll make love.

GARGA   (*calls from the bedroom*)   Won't you have a drink, Mary? No? Why don't you sit down?

BABOON   Shut up. I could hear them talking before. Now they're not saying anything.

GARGA   (*to Mary*)   This is the Black Pit. Forty years are passing. I don't say no. The ground is giving way, the water of the sewers rises to the surface, but the tide of their lusts is too weak. For four hundred years I have dreamed of mornings on the ocean, I had the salt wind in my eyes. How smooth it was! (*He drinks*)

SHLINK   (*submissively*)   I ask you for your hand, Miss Garga. Shall I throw myself humbly at your feet? Please come with me. I love you.

MARY   (*runs into the bar*)   Help! They're selling me!

MANKY   Here I am, beautiful!

MARY   I knew you'd be wherever I am.

GARGA   "As at the opera, a breeze opens gaps in the partitions."

SHLINK   (*bellowing*)   Will you kindly come out of the bar, Mary Garga! (*Mary comes out of the bar*) I beg you, don't throw yourself away, Miss Garga.

MARY   All I want is a little room with nothing in it. I've stopped wanting very much, Pat, I promise you that I never will again.

GARGA   Fight for your chance, Shlink.

SHLINK   Think of the years that won't pass, Mary Garga, and think how sleepy you are.

MANKY   Come with me, I've got four hundred pounds, that means a roof in the winter and no more ghosts except in the morgues.

SHLINK   I implore you, Mary Garga, come with me if you please. I shall treat you like my wife and wait on you and hang myself without any fuss if ever I hurt you.

GARGA   He's not lying. I promise you that. That's what you'll get if you go with him. Down to the last cent. (*Goes into the bar*)

MARY   Tell me, Pat, even if I don't love you, do you love me?

MANKY   I think so, beautiful. And it's not written anywhere between heaven and earth that you don't love me.

GARGA   Is that you, Jane? Polishing off the cocktails? You don't
look exactly yourself. Have you sold everything?

JANE   Get rid of him, Baboon. I can't stand his face. He's molesting me. Even if I'm not living in milk and honey these days,
I don't have to put up with ridicule.

BABOON   I'll crack the nose of any man who says you're an old
shoe.

GARGA   Did they feed you too? Your face looks like lemon ice
that's been left standing. Damn it all, you used to wear glad rags
like an opera singer, and now you look as if they'd sprinkled you
with black powder. But I'll say this much: you didn't come of
your own accord when only the flies made spots on you, my
drunken chick.

MARY   Let's go then. I'd have gladly obliged you, Shlink, but I
can't. It's not pride.

SHLINK   Stay if you like. I won't repeat my offer if it displeases
you. But don't let the pit swallow you up. There are many
places to get away from a man.

GARGA   Not for a woman. Forget it, Shlink. Don't you see what
she's driving at? If you'd preferred a roof in the winter, Jane,
you'd still be sewing shirts.

SHLINK   Drink before you make love, Mary Garga.

MARY   Come, Pat. This isn't a good place. Is this your woman,
George? Is she? I'm glad I had a chance to see her. (*Out with
Manky*)

SHLINK (*calls after her*)   I won't forsake you. Come back when
you've found out.

BABOON   An old shoe, gentlemen, well worn. (*He laughs*)

GARGA (*shining a candle in Shlink's face*)   Your face is in good
shape. But where does your good will get me?

SHLINK   The sacrifices on both sides have been considerable.
How many ships do you need to get to Tahiti? Do you want
me to hoist my shirt for a sail, or your sister's? I hold you
responsible for your sister's fate. You showed her that men
would always treat her as an object. I haven't spoiled anything
for you, I hope. I almost got her as a virgin, but you wanted me

to have leftovers. And don't forget your family that you're abandoning. Now you've seen what you are sacrificing.

GARGA   I want to slaughter them all now. I know that.—I think I'll get the jump on you. And now I understand why you've fattened them on what you earn hauling coal. I won't let you do me out of my fun. And now I'm taking delivery of this little animal that you've been keeping for me.

JANE   I refuse to be insulted. I stand on my own feet, I support myself.

GARGA   And now I request you to hand over the money you made selling that lumber twice. I hope you've been keeping it for me. The time has come.

(*Shlink takes out the money and gives it to Garga*)

GARGA   I'm dead drunk. But drunk or sober, I've got a good idea, Shlink, a very good idea. (*Goes out with Jane*)

BABOON   That was your last money, sir. And where did it come from? They'll be asking you about it. Broost and Company have demanded delivery of the lumber they paid for.

SHLINK   (*not listening to him*)   A chair. (*They have occupied the chairs and do not stand up*) My rice and water.

WORM   There's no more rice for you, sir. Your account is overdrawn.

6

Lake Michigan

THE END OF SEPTEMBER

Woods: Shlink and Mary.

MARY   The trees look draped in human dung, the sky is close enough to touch, but what is it to me? I'm cold. I'm like a half-frozen quail. I can't help myself.

SHLINK   If it will do you any good, I love you.

MARY   I've thrown myself away. Why has my love turned to bitter fruit? Others have their summer when they love, but I'm withering away and tormenting myself. My body is soiled.

SHLINK   Tell me how low you feel. It will relieve you.

MARY   I lay in bed with a man who was like an animal. My whole body was numb, but I gave myself to him, many times, and I couldn't get warm. He smoked stogies in between, a seaman. I loved you every hour I spent between those papered walls, I was so obsessed that he thought it was love and wanted to stop me. I slept into the black darkness. I don't owe you anything, but my conscience cries out to me that I've soiled my body, which is yours even if you scorned it.

SHLINK   I'm sorry you're cold. I thought the air was warm and dark. I don't know what the men of this country say to the women they love. If it will do you any good: I love you.

MARY   I'm such a coward, my courage has gone with my innocence.

SHLINK   You'll wash yourself clean.

MARY   Maybe I ought to go down to the water, but I can't. I'm not ready yet. Oh, this despair! This heart that won't be appeased! I'm never anything more than half, I can't even love, it's only vanity. I hear what you say, I have ears and I'm not deaf, but what does it mean? Maybe I'm asleep, they'll come and wake me, and maybe it's just that I'd do the most shameful things to get a roof over my head, that I lie to myself and close my eyes.

SHLINK   Come, it's getting cold.

MARY   But the leaves are warm and shelter us from the sky that's too close. (*They go out*)

MANKY (*enters*)   Her tracks point this way. You need a good sense of humor in a September like this. The crayfish are mating, the rutting cry of the deer is heard in the thicket, and the badger season is open. But my flippers are cold and I've wrapped my black stumps in newspaper. Where can she be living? That's the worst of it. If she's lying around like a fishbone in that greasy saloon, she'll never have a clean petticoat again. Only stains. Oh, Pat Mankyboddle, I'm going to court-martial you. Too weak to defend myself, I'd better attack. I'll devour the good-for-nothing with skin and bones, I'll speed up my digestion with prayers, the vultures will be shot at sunrise and hung up in the Mankyboddle Museum. Brrr! Words! Toothless phrases! (*He takes a revolver from his pocket*) This is the coldest answer! Stalk through the jungle looking for a woman, will you, you old swine! Down on all fours! Damn, this underbrush is suicide. Watch yourself, Paddy. Where can a woman go when it's all up with her? Let her go, Paddy boy, have a smoke, take a bite to eat, put that thing away. Forward, march! (*Goes out*)

MARY (*coming back with Shlink*) It's loathsome before God and man. I won't go with you.

SHLINK Moldy sentiments. Air out your soul.

MARY I can't. You're making a sacrifice of me.

SHLINK You've always got to have your head in some man's armpits, no matter whose.

MARY I'm nothing to you.

SHLINK You can't live alone.

MARY You took me so quickly, as if you were afraid I'd get away. Like a sacrifice.

SHLINK You ran into the bushes like a rabid bitch and now you're running out again like a rabid bitch.

MARY Am I what you say? I'm always what you say. I love you. Never forget that, I love you. I love you like a rabid bitch. That's what you said. But now pay me. Yes, I'm in the mood to get paid. Give me your money, I'll live on it. I'm a whore.

SHLINK Something wet is running down your face. What kind of a whore is that?

MARY Don't make fun of me, just give me the money. Don't look at me. It's not tears that make my face wet, it's the fog. (*Shlink gives her money*) I won't thank you, Mr. Shlink from Yokohama. It's a straight business deal, no need for thanks.

SHLINK You'd better be going. You won't make money here. (*Goes out*)

7

The Garga Family's Living Room

SEPTEMBER 29, 1912

The room is full of new furniture. John Garga, Mae, George, Jane, Manky, all dressed in new clothes for the wedding dinner.

JOHN   Ever since that man we don't like to speak of, who has a different skin but who goes down to the coal yards to work night and day for a family he knows; ever since the man in the coal yards with the different skin has been watching over us, things have been getting better for us every day, in every way. Today, without knowing of the wedding, he's made it possible for our son George to have a wedding worthy of the director of a big business. New ties, black suits, the breath of whiskey on our lips—amid new furniture.

MAE   Isn't it strange that the man in the coal yards should make so much hauling coal?

GARGA   I make the money.

MAE   From one day to the next you decided to get married. Wasn't it a little sudden, Jane?

JANE   The snow melts, and where is it then? And you can pick the wrong man, it often happens.

MAE   Right man, wrong man, that's not the question. The question is whether you stick to him.

JOHN   Nonsense! Eat your steak and give the bride your hand.

GARGA (*takes Jane by the wrist*)   It's a good hand. I'm all right here. Let the wallpaper peel, I've got new clothes, I eat steak, I can taste the plaster, I've got half an inch of mortar all over me, I see a piano. Hang a wreath on the picture of our dear sister, Mary Garga, born twenty years ago on the prairies. Put immor-

telles under glass. It's good to sit here, good to lie here, the black
wind doesn't come in here.

JANE (*stands up*)   What's the matter, George? Have you a fever?

GARGA   I feel fine in my fever, Jane.

JANE   I keep wondering what your plans are for me, George.

GARGA   Why are you so pale, Mother? Isn't your prodigal son
back again under your roof? Why are you all standing against
the wall like plaster statues?

MAE   Perhaps because of the fight you keep talking about.

GARGA   It's only flies in my brain. I can shoo them away. (*Shlink
enters*) Oh, Mother, get a steak and a glass of whiskey for our
welcome guest. I was married this morning. My dear wife, tell
him!

JANE   Me and my husband, out of bed this morning, we went to
the sheriff and said: Can we be married here? He said: I know
you, Jane,—will you always stay with your husband? But I saw
that he was a good man with a beard, he had nothing against
me, so I said: Life isn't exactly the way you think.

SHLINK   Congratulations, Garga. You're a vindictive man.

GARGA   There's a hideous fear in your smile! For good reason.
Don't eat too fast. You have plenty of time. Where's Mary? I
hope she's being taken care of. Your satisfaction must be complete. Unfortunately there's no chair for you at the moment,
Shlink. We're one chair short. Otherwise our furnishings are
new and complete. Look at the piano. A delightful place. I
mean to spend my evenings here with my family. I've started
a new life. Tomorrow I'm going back to C. Maynes's lending
library.

MAE   Oh, George, aren't you talking too much?

GARGA   Do you hear that? My family doesn't want me to have
anything more to do with you. Our acquaintance is at an end,
Mr. Shlink. It has been most profitable. The furniture speaks for
itself. My family's wardrobe speaks loud and clear. There's
plenty of cash. I thank you. (*Silence*)

SHLINK   May I ask just one favor of you? A personal matter. I
have a letter here from the firm of Broost and Company. It bears
the seal of the Attorney General of the State of Virginia. I
haven't opened it yet. You would oblige me by doing so. Any

news, even the worst, would be more acceptable to me from your lips. (*Garga reads the letter*) Of course this is my own private affair, but a hint from you would make things much easier for me.

MAE   Why don't you say something, George? What are you planning to do, George? You look as if you were planning something. There's nothing that frightens me more. You men hide behind your unknown thoughts as if they were smoke. And we wait like cattle before slaughter. You say: Wait a while, you go away, you come back, and you're unrecognizable. And we don't know what you've done to yourselves. Tell me your plan, and if you don't know what it is, admit it, so I'll know what to do. I've got to plan my life too. Four years in this city of steel and dirt! Oh, George!

GARGA   You see, the bad years were the best, and now they're over. Don't say anything to me. You, my parents, and you, Jane, my wife, I've decided to go to jail.

JOHN   What are you saying? Is that where your money comes from? It was written on your face when you were five years old that you'd end up in jail. I never asked what went on between the two of you, I knew it was rotten. You've both lost the ground from under your feet. Buying pianos and going to jail, dragging in whole armloads of steak and robbing a family of its livelihood is all the same to you. Where's Mary, your sister? (*He tears off his jacket and throws it on the floor*) There's my jacket, I never wanted to put it on. But I'm used to the kind of humiliations this city still has in store for me.

JANE   How long will it be, George?

SHLINK   (*to John*) Some lumber was sold twice. Naturally that means jail, because the sheriff isn't interested in the circumstances. I, your friend, could explain certain things to the sheriff as neatly and simply as Standard Oil explains its tax returns. I am prepared to listen to your son, Mrs. Garga.

JANE   Don't let them talk you into anything, George, do what you see fit, regardless. I, your wife, will keep the house running while you're gone.

JOHN   (*laughing loudly*) She's going to keep the house running! A girl who was picked off the streets only yesterday. We're to be fed by the wages of sin!

SHLINK (*to Garga*) You've given me to understand that your family means a great deal to you. You'd like to spend your evenings among this furniture. You'll have a thought or two for me, your friend, who is busy making things easier for you all. I am prepared to save you for your family's sake.

MAE You can't go to jail, George.

GARGA I know you don't understand, Mother. It's so hard to harm a man, to destroy him is utterly impossible. The world is too poor. We wear ourselves out cluttering it with things to fight about.

JANE (*to Garga*) There you go philosophizing with the roof rotting over our heads.

GARGA (*to Shlink*) Search the whole world, you'll find ten evil men and not one evil action. Only trifles can destroy a man. No, I'm through. I'll draw a line under the account, and then I'll go.

SHLINK Your family would like to know if they mean anything to you. If you won't hold them up, they'll fall. One little word, Garga!

GARGA I give them all their freedom.

SHLINK They'll rot, and you'll be to blame. There aren't many of them left. They might take a notion, just like you, to make a clean sweep, to cut up the dirty tablecloth and shake the cigar butts out of their clothes. The whole lot of them might decide to imitate you, to be free and indecent, with slobber on their shirts.

MAE Be still, George, everything he says is true.

GARGA Now at last, if I half-close my eyes, I see certain things in a cold light. Not your face, Mr. Shlink, maybe you haven't got one.

SHLINK Forty years have been written off as so much dirt, and now there will be a great freedom.

GARGA That's how it is. The snow tried to fall, but it was too cold. My family will eat leftovers again, and again they'll be hungry. But I, I will strike down my enemy.

JOHN All I see is weakness, nothing else. Since the day I first laid eyes on you. Go ahead and leave us. Why shouldn't they take the furniture away?

GARGA I've read that feeble waters erode whole mountains. And

I still want to see your face, Shlink, your damned invisible, frosted-glass face.

SHLINK   I have no desire to talk with you any further. Three years. For a young man that's no more than a swing of the door. But for me! I've drawn no profit from you if that's any comfort to you. But you're not leaving a trace of sadness in me, now that I'm going back into the noisy city to carry on my business as I did before we met. (*Goes out*)

GARGA   All that remains for me to do now is phone the police. (*Goes out*)

JANE   I'm going to the Chinese bar. I can do without the police. (*Goes out*)

MAE   Sometimes I think Mary will never come back either.

JOHN   She has only herself to blame. Can we be expected to help them when they live in vice?

MAE   Is there any better time to help them?

JOHN   Don't talk so much.

MAE   (*sits down next to him*)   I wanted to ask you: what are you going to do now?

JOHN   Me? Nothing. This part of our life is over.

MAE   You understand, don't you, what George is going to do to himself?

JOHN   Yes. More or less. It won't help us any.

MAE   And what are you going to live on?

JOHN   On the money that's still left. And we'll sell the piano.

MAE   No, they'll take it away, it was come by dishonestly.

JOHN   Maybe we'll go back to Ohio. We'll do something.

MAE   (*stands up*)   There's something else I wanted to tell you, John, but I can't. I've never believed that a man could suddenly be damned. It's decided in heaven. This is a day like any other, and nothing has changed, but from this day on you're damned.

JOHN   What are you going to do?

MAE   I'm going to do a certain thing, John, something I want very much to do. Don't imagine I have any special reason. But first I'll put some coal on the fire, you'll find your supper in the kitchen. (*Goes out*)

JOHN   Take care that the ghost of a shark doesn't eat you on the stairs.

WAITER (*enters*)   Mrs. Garga has ordered you a grog. Do you wish
to drink it in the dark, or should I put the light on?

JOHN   What do you think? Give us some light.

(*The waiter goes out*)

MARY (*enters*)   Don't make any speeches. I've brought money.

JOHN   You dare to set foot here? A fine family. And look at you!

MARY   I look all right. But where did you get all this new furniture? Have you taken in some money? I've taken in some
money too.

JOHN   Where did you get the money?

MARY   Do you want to know?

JOHN   Hand it over. You people have brought me to this with
hunger.

MARY   So you're taking my money? In spite of your new furniture? Where's Mother?

JOHN   Deserters are stood up against the wall.

MARY   Did you send her out on the streets?

JOHN   Be cynical, wallow in the gutter, drink grog. But I'm your
father, you can't let me starve.

MARY   Where has she gone?

JOHN   You can go, too. I'm used to being left.

MARY   When did she leave here?

JOHN   At the end of my life I'm condemned to being poor and
licking my children's spittle, but I won't have any truck with
vice. I have no hesitation about throwing you out.

MARY   Give me back my money. It wasn't meant for you.

JOHN   Not a chance. You can sew me up in a shroud, I'll still beg
for a pound of tobacco.

MARY   So long. (*Goes out*)

JOHN   They've no more to say to a man than can be said in five
minutes. Then they run out of lies. (*Pause*) Actually everything
there is to say could be covered in two minutes of silence.

GARGA (*comes back*)   Where's Mother? Gone? Did she think I
wasn't coming back up again? (*He runs out and comes back*) She
won't be back, she's taken her other dress. (*He sits down at the
table and writes a letter*) "To *The Examiner*. I wish to call your
attention to C. Shlink, the Malay lumber dealer. This man
molested my wife, Jane Garga, and raped my sister, Mary

Garga, who was in his employ. George Garga."—I won't say anything about my mother.

JOHN   That wipes out our family.

GARGA   I've written this letter. I'll put it in my pocket and forget the whole business. And in three years—that's how long they'll hold me—a week before I'm discharged, I'll send my letter to the newspaper. This man will be exterminated from this city, and when I come back, he'll have vanished from my sight. But for him the day of my release will be marked by the howl of the lynch mobs.

8

C. Shlink's Private Office

OCTOBER 20, 1915, 1 P.M.

Shlink and a young clerk.

SHLINK (*dictating*)   Write to Miss Mary Garga, who has applied for a position as secretary, that I will never again have anything to do with either her or her family. To Standard Real Estate. Dear Sirs: As of today not a single share of our stock is in the hands of any outside firm and our business situation is secure. Consequently, there is nothing to prevent us from accepting your offer of a five-year contract.

AN EMPLOYEE (*brings a man in*)   This is Mr. Shlink.

THE MAN   I've got three minutes to give you some information. You've got two minutes to understand your situation. Half an hour ago *The Examiner* received a letter from one of the state penitentiaries, signed by one Garga, showing you've committed a number of crimes. In five minutes the reporters will be here. You owe me a thousand dollars.

(*Shlink gives him the money. The man goes out*)

SHLINK (*carefully packing his suitcase*)   Carry on the business as
long as you can. Mail these letters. I'll be back. (*Goes out
quickly*)

9

Bar across the Street from the Prison

OCTOBER 28, 1915

*Worm, Baboon, the pug-nosed man, the Salvation Army preacher,
Jane, Mary Garga. Noise from outside.*

BABOON   Do you hear the howling of the lynch mob? These are
dangerous days for Chinatown. A week ago the crimes of a
Malayan lumber dealer came to light. Three years ago he sent
a man to prison, for three years the man kept quiet, but a week
before his release he wrote a letter to *The Examiner*, telling the
whole story.

THE PUG-NOSED MAN   The human heart!

BABOON   The Malay himself, naturally, has skipped town. But
he's done for.

WORM   You can't say that about anybody. Consider the conditions on this planet. A man never gets finished off all at once,
but at least a hundred times. A man has too many possibilities.
For instance, let me tell you the story of G. Wishu, the bulldog
man. But I'll need the nickelodeon. (*The nickelodeon is played*)
This is the story of the dog, George Wishu. George Wishu was
born on the Emerald Isle. When he was eighteen months old,
a fat man took him to the great city of London. His own
country let him go like a stranger. In London he soon fell into
the hands of a cruel woman, who subjected him to gruesome
tortures. After much suffering he ran away to the country,
where he was hunted down between green hedges. Men shot
at him with big dangerous guns, and strange dogs chased him.

He lost a leg and from then on he limped. After several of his undertakings had failed, weary of life and half starved, he found refuge with an old man who shared his bread with him. Here, after a life full of disappointments and adventures, he died at the age of seven and a half with great serenity and composure. He lies buried in Wales.—Now tell me, sir, how are you going to fit all that under one roof?

THE PUG-NOSED MAN   Who is this man that's wanted?

WORM   It's the Malay they're looking for. He went bankrupt once before, but in three years he managed by all sorts of dodges to recover his lumber business, and that made him a lot of enemies in his neighborhood. But no court could have touched him if a man in jail hadn't brought his sex crimes to light. (*To Jane*) When is your husband getting out?

JANE   Yes, that's it: I knew it a while ago. Gentlemen, don't go thinking I don't know. It's on the twenty-eighth, yesterday or today.

BABOON   Cut the comedy, Jane.

THE PUG-NOSED MAN   And who's that woman in the indecent dress?

BABOON   That's the victim, the sister of the man in jail.

JANE   Yes, that's my sister-in-law. She pretends not to know me, but when I was married she never came home a single night.

BABOON   The Malay ruined her.

THE PUG-NOSED MAN   What's she dropping into the sink behind the bar?

WORM   I can't see. She's saying something, too. Keep still, Jane.

MARY (*lets a banknote flutter into the sink*)   When I held the bills in my hand that day, I saw God's eye watching me. I said: I've done everything for him. God turned away, there was a sound like tobacco fields rustling in the wind. I kept them though. One bill! Another! Pieces of myself! I'm giving my purity away. Now the money's gone! I don't feel any better . . .

GARGA (*enters with C. Maynes and three other men*)   I've asked you to come with me so you could see with your own eyes that I've been done an injustice. I've brought you with me, Mr. Maynes, to witness the kind of place I find my wife in after three years of absence. (*He leads the men to the table where Jane is sitting*) Hello, Jane. How are you?

JANE   George! Is this the twenty-eighth? I didn't know. I'd have been home. Did you notice how cold it is there? Did you guess I'd be sitting here just to get warm?

GARGA   This is Mr. Maynes. You know him. I'm going back to work in his store. And these are neighbors who take an interest in my situation.

JANE   How do you do, gentlemen. Oh George, it's awful for me that I missed your day. What will you gentlemen think of me? Ken Si, wait on the gentlemen.

BARTENDER (*to the pug-nosed man*)   That's the fellow from the pen who informed on him.

GARGA   Hello, Mary. Have you been waiting for me?—My sister's here too, as you can see.

MARY   Hello, George. Are you all right?

GARGA   Let's go home, Jane.

JANE   Oh, George, you're just saying that. But if I go with you, you'll scold me when we get home. I'd better tell you right away that the housework hasn't been done.

GARGA   I know that.

JANE   That's mean of you.

GARGA   I'm not chiding you, Jane. We're going to make a fresh start. My fight is finished. I've driven my opponent from the city, and that's the end of it.

JANE   No, George. Things will keep getting worse and worse. People say things are going to get better, but they keep getting worse, they can do that. I hope you like it here, gentlemen. Of course we could go somewhere else . . .

GARGA   What's the matter, Jane? Aren't you glad I've come for you?

JANE   You know perfectly well, George. And if you don't, I can't tell you.

GARGA   What do you mean?

JANE   Don't you see, George, I'm different from what you think, even if I'm almost done for. Why did you bring these gentlemen? I've always known I'd end like this. When they told me in Sunday school what happens to the weak, I said to myself: That's what will happen to me. You don't have to prove it to anybody.

GARGA   Then you won't come home?

JANE   Don't ask me, George.

GARGA   But I am asking you, my dear.

JANE   Then I'll have to put it a different way. I've been living with
this man. (*Points to Baboon*) I admit it, gentlemen. And what's
the use? Nothing's going to get any better.

BABOON   She's out of her mind.

MAYNES   Dreadful!

GARGA   Listen to me, Jane. This is your last chance in this city.
I'm ready to wipe the slate clean. These gentlemen are my
witnesses. Come home with me.

JANE   It's nice of you, George. It certainly is my last chance. But
I won't take it. Things aren't right between us, you know that.
I'm going now, George. (*To Baboon*) Come.

BABOON   That's that. (*Both go out*)

ONE OF THE MEN   That fellow has nothing to laugh about.

GARGA   I'll leave the apartment open, Jane. You can ring at night.

WORM (*steps up to the table*)   You've probably noticed: there's a
family here in our midst, or what's left of it. Moth-eaten as it
is, this family would gladly give its last cent to find out where
the mother, the mainstay of the household, is keeping herself.
The fact is, I saw her one morning at about seven o'clock, a
woman of forty, scrubbing a fruit cellar. She's started a new
business. She'd aged but she was looking all right.

GARGA   But you, sir, didn't you work in the lumber business of
the man they're combing every inch of Chicago for?

WORM   Me? No, I've never laid eyes on the man. (*Goes out, on his
way inserting a coin in the nickelodeon. It starts playing Gounod's
"Ave Maria"*)

THE PREACHER (*at a corner table reads the liquor list aloud in a hard
voice, savoring each word*)   Cherry Flip, Cherry Brandy, Gin
Fizz, Whiskey Sour, Golden Slipper, Manhattan, Curaçao extra
dry, Orange, Maraschino Cusenier, and the specialty of the
house, Eggnog. This drink is made of raw egg, sugar, cognac,
Jamaica rum, and milk.

THE PUG-NOSED MAN   Are you familiar with those drinks, sir?

PREACHER   No!

(*Laughter*)

GARGA (*to the men with him*)   It has been necessary to show you
my broken family, but you can see how humiliating it is for me.

You will also have realized that that yellow weed must never again be allowed to take root in our city. My sister Mary, as you know, was in Shlink's employ for some time. In speaking to her now, of course, I shall have to proceed as carefully as possible, because even in her deepest misery my sister has preserved a certain trace of delicacy. (*He sits down beside Mary*) Won't you let me see your face?

MARY   It's not a face anymore. It's not me.

GARGA   No. But I remember once in church—when you were nine years old—you said: Let him come to me beginning tomorrow. We thought you meant God.

MARY   Did I say that?

GARGA   I still love you, soiled and wasted as you are. But even if I knew that you knew you could do as you pleased with yourself if I told you I still loved you, I'd tell you all the same.

MARY   And you can look at me when you say that? At this face?

GARGA   That face. People remain what they are even if their faces fall apart.

MARY (*stands up*)   But I won't have it. I don't want you to love me that way. I like myself the way I was. Don't say I was never any different.

GARGA (*in a loud voice*)   Do you earn money? Do you live entirely on what you get from men?

MARY   And you've brought people to hear about it? Can I have some whiskey? With plenty of ice. All right, I'll tell them. All right; I threw myself away, but as soon as I'd done it I asked for money, to make it plain what I am and that I can live on it. It's only a business arrangement now. I've got a nice body, I never let a man smoke when he's with me, but I'm not a virgin any more, love is my job. I've got money here. But I'm going to earn more, I want to spend money, it's a craving I have; when I've made money, I don't want to save, here, I throw it down the sink. That's the way I am.

MAYNES   Horrible!

ANOTHER MAN   You wouldn't dare to laugh.

PREACHER   Man is too durable. That's his main fault. He can do too much to himself. He's too hard to destroy. (*Goes out*)

MAYNES (*standing up with the other three men*)   We've seen, Garga, that you've suffered an injustice.

THE PUG-NOSED MAN (*approaches Mary*) Whores! (*He guffaws*) Vice is a lady's perfume.

MARY You call us whores. With this powder on our faces you can't see the eyes that were blue. The men who do business with crooks make love to us. We sell our sleep, we live on abuse. (*A shot is heard*)

BARTENDER The gentleman has shot himself in the neck.

(*The men bring in the preacher and lay him down on the table among the glasses*)

FIRST MAN Don't touch him. Hands off.

SECOND MAN He's trying to say something.

FIRST MAN (*bending over him, in a loud voice*) Do you want any-thing? Have you any relatives? Where should we take you?

PREACHER (*mumbles*) "La montagne est passée: nous irons mieux."

GARGA (*standing over him, laughing*) He's missed, and in more ways than one. He thought those were his last words, but they're somebody else's, and anyway they're not his last words, because his aim was bad and it's only a small flesh wound.

FIRST MAN So it is. Tough luck. He did it in the dark, he should have done it in the light.

MARY His head is hanging down. Put something under it. How thin he is. I recognize him now. He spat in his face one time.

(*All except Mary and Garga go out with the wounded man*)

GARGA His skin is too thick. It bends anything you can stick into it. There aren't blades enough.

MARY He's still on your mind?

GARGA Yes, to you I can admit it.

MARY Love and hate! How low they bring us!

GARGA So they do.—Do you still love him?

MARY Yes . . . yes.

GARGA And no hope of better winds?

MARY Yes, now and then.

GARGA I wanted to help you. (*Pause*) This fight has been such a debauch that today I need all Chicago to help me stop it. Of course it's possible that he himself wasn't planning to go on. He himself intimated that at his age three years can mean as much as thirty. In view of all these circumstances I've destroyed him with a very crude weapon. I didn't even have to be there in person. In addition, I've made it absolutely impossible for him to see me. This last blow will not be discussed between us, he won't be able to find me. You could call it a technical knockout, and on every street corner the taxi drivers are watching to make sure that he won't show up in the ring again. Chicago has thrown in the towel for him. I don't know where he is, but he knows what's what.

BARTENDER   The lumber yards on Mulberry Street are on fire.

MARY   If you've shaken him off, it's a good thing. But now I'm going.

GARGA   I'll stay here in the middle of the lynch mob. But I'll be home tonight. We'll live together. (*Mary goes out*) Now I'll drink hot black coffee again in the morning, wash my face in cold water, and put on clean clothes, first of all a shirt. I'll comb a good many things out of my brain in the morning; there will be fresh noise and many things happening all around me in the city, now that I'm rid of that passion. It was all set to drag me down to hell, but I've still got things to do. (*Opens the door wide and listens laughing to the howling of the lynch mob that has grown louder*)

SHLINK   (*enters, wearing an American suit*)   Are you alone? It was hard to get here. I knew you were getting out today, I've looked for you at your place. They're close at my heels. Quick, Garga, come with me.

GARGA   Are you out of your mind? I informed on you to get rid of you.

SHLINK   I'm not a brave man. I died three times on the way here.

GARGA   Yes, I hear they're hanging yellow men like linen on Milwaukee Bridge.

SHLINK   All the more reason for hurrying. You know you've got to come. We're not through yet.

GARGA   (*very slowly, aware of Shlink's haste*)   Unfortunately your request comes at a bad time. I have company. My sister, Mary Garga, ruined in September three years ago, taken by surprise. My wife, Jane Garga, debauched at the same time. Last of all, a Salvation Army preacher, name unknown, spat on and destroyed, though it doesn't matter much. But most of all, my mother, Mae Garga, born in 1872 in the South, who disappeared three years ago this October and has vanished even from memory, now faceless. Her face fell off her like a yellow leaf. (*Listens*) That howling!

SHLINK (*also absorbed in listening*)   Yes, but it's not the right kind of howling yet, the white kind. Then they'll be here. Then we'll still have a minute. Listen! Now! Now it's the right kind—white! Come!

(*Garga quickly leaves with Shlink*)

10

A deserted tent, formerly used by railroad workers, in the gravel pits of Lake Michigan

NOVEMBER 19, 1915, BEFORE 2 A.M.

Shlink, Garga.

SHLINK   The perpetual roar of Chicago has stopped. Seven times three days the skies have paled and the air turned gray-blue like grog. Now the silence has come, that conceals nothing.

GARGA (*smoking*)   Fighting comes as easy to you as digestion. I've been thinking about my childhood. The blue flat fields. The polecat in the gulches and the light-frothing rapids.

SHLINK   Right. All that was in your face. But now it's as hard as amber, which is transparent; here and there dead insects can be seen in it.

GARGA   You've always been alone?

SHLINK   Forty years.

GARGA   And now, toward the end, you've succumbed to the black plague of this planet, the lust for human contact.

SHLINK (*smiling*)   Through enmity?

GARGA   Through enmity.

SHLINK   Then you understand that we're comrades, comrades in a metaphysical conflict. Our acquaintance has been brief, for a

time it overshadowed everything else, the time has passed
quickly. The stations of life are not those of memory. The end
is not the goal, the last episode is no more important than any
other. Twice in my life I've owned a lumber business. For the
last two weeks it has been registered in your name.

GARGA   Have you premonitions of death?

SHLINK   Here is the ledger of your lumber business; it begins
where ink was once poured over the figures.

GARGA   You've been carrying it next to your skin? Open it yourself, it's sure to be filthy. (*He reads*) A clean account. Nothing
but withdrawals. On the seventeenth: the lumber deal, $25,000
to Garga. Just above: $10 for clothing. Below: $22 for Mary
Garga, "our" sister. At the very end: the whole business burned
to the ground again.—I can't sleep any more. I'll be glad when
you're covered with quicklime.

SHLINK   Don't deny the past, George! What's an account?
Remember the question we raised. Brace yourself: I love you.

GARGA (*looks at him*)   That's disgusting! You're terrifyingly loathsome. An old man like you!

SHLINK   Maybe I'll never get an answer. But if you get one, think
of me when my mouth is full of dry rot. What are you listening
for?

GARGA (*lazily*)   You show traces of feeling. You're old.

SHLINK   Is it so good to bare your teeth?

GARGA   If they're good teeth.

SHLINK   Man's infinite isolation makes enmity an unattain-
able goal. But even with the animals understanding is not
possible.

GARGA   Speech isn't enough to create understanding.

SHLINK   I've observed the animals. Love, the warmth of bodies in
contact, is the only mercy shown us in the darkness. But the
only union is that of the organs, and it can't bridge over the
cleavage made by speech. Yet they unite in order to produce
beings to stand by them in their hopeless isolation. And the
generations look coldly into each other's eyes. If you cram a
ship full to bursting with human bodies, they'll all freeze with
loneliness. Are you listening, Garga? Yes, so great is man's
isolation that not even a fight is possible. The forest! That's
where mankind comes from. Hairy, with apes' jaws, good ani-

mals who knew how to live. Everything was so easy. They simply tore each other apart. I see them clearly, with quivering flanks, staring into the whites of each other's eyes, sinking their teeth into each other's throats and rolling down. And the one who bled to death among the roots was the vanquished, and the one who had trampled down the most undergrowth was the victor. Are you listening for something, Garga?

GARGA   Shlink, I've been listening to you now for three weeks. I've been waiting the whole time for a rage to take hold of me, under any pretext, however slight. But now, looking at you, I realize that your drivel irritates me and your voice sickens me. Isn't this Thursday night? How far is it to New York? Why am I sitting here wasting my time? Haven't we been lying around here for three weeks now? We thought the planet would change its course on our account. But what happened? Three times it rained, and one night the wind blew. (*Stands up*) Shlink, I think the time has come for you to take off your shoes. Take your shoes off, Shlink, and let me have them. Because I doubt if you've got much money left. Shlink, here in the woods of Lake Michigan, I'm putting an end to our fight now going into its fourth year, because its substance is used up: it's ending right now. I can't finish it off with a knife, I see no need for high-sounding words. My shoes are full of holes and your speeches don't keep my toes warm. It's the old story, Shlink: the younger man wins.

SHLINK   Today we've heard the shovels of the railroad workers from time to time. I saw you pricking up your ears. You're standing up, Garga? You're going there, Garga? You're going to betray me?

GARGA (*lying down lazily*)   Yes, Shlink, that's exactly what I'm going to do.

SHLINK   And there will never be an outcome to this fight, George Garga? Never an understanding?

GARGA   No.

SHLINK   But you'll come out of it with nothing to show but your bare life.

GARGA   Bare life is better than any other kind of life.

SHLINK   Tahiti?

GARGA   New York. (*Laughing ironically*) "I will go and I will return with iron limbs and dark skin, with fury in my eyes. My face will make people think I come of a strong race. I will have gold, I will be lazy and brutal. Women love to nurse wild, sick men, returned from the hot countries. I will swim, trample grass, hunt, and most of all smoke. And down drinks as hot as boiling metal. I will mingle with life and be saved."—What nonsense! Words on a planet that's not in the center. Long after lime has covered you through the natural elimination of the obsolete, I shall be choosing the things that amuse me.

SHLINK   What kind of an attitude is that? Kindly take your pipe out of your filthy mouth. If you're trying to tell me you've gone impotent, take a different tone at least.

GARGA   Whatever you say.

SHLINK   That gesture shows me you're unworthy to be my opponent.

GARGA   I was only deploring the fact that you bored me.

SHLINK   What's that? You deploring? You! A hired pug! A drunken salesman! Whom I bought for ten dollars, an idealist who couldn't tell his two legs apart, a nobody!

GARGA (*laughing*)   A young man! Be frank.

SHLINK   A white man, hired to drag me down, to stuff my mouth with disgust or dry rot, to give me the taste of death on my tongue. Six hundred feet away in the woods I'll find all the men I need to lynch me.

GARGA   Yes, maybe I'm a leper, but what of it? You're a suicide. What more have you to offer me? You hired me, but you never paid up.

SHLINK   You got what a man like you needs. I bought you furniture.

GARGA   Yes, I got a piano out of you, a piano that had to be sold. I ate meat *once*. I bought one suit, and for your idiotic talk I gave up my sleep.

SHLINK   Your sleep, your mother, your sister and your wife. Three years off your stupid life. But how annoying! It's all ending in banality. You never understood what it was all about. You wanted me dead. But I wanted a fight. Not of the flesh, but of the spirit.

GARGA   And the spirit, you see, is nothing. The important thing is not to be stronger, but to come off alive. I can't defeat you,

I can only stamp you into the ground. I'll carry my raw flesh into the icy rains, Chicago is cold. I'm going there now. Possibly I'm doing the wrong thing. But I have plenty of time. (*Goes out*)

(*Shlink falls down*)

SHLINK (*standing up*)   Now that the last sword thrusts have been exchanged as well as the last words that occurred to us, I thank you for the interest you have shown in my person. A good deal has fallen away from us, we have hardly more than our naked bodies left. In four minutes the moon will rise, then your lynch mob will be here. (*He notices that Garga has gone and follows him*) Don't go, George Garga! Don't quit because you're young. The forests have been cut down, the vultures are glutted, and the golden answer will be buried deep in the ground. (*Turns. A milky light is seen in the brush*) November 19th. Three miles south of Chicago. West wind. Four minutes before the rising of the moon, drowned while fishing.

MARY (*enters*)   Please don't drive me away. I'm an unhappy woman.

(*The light grows stronger in the brush*)

SHLINK   It's all piling up. Fish swimming into your mouth . . . What's that crazy light? I'm very busy.

MARY (*removing her hat*)   I'm not pretty any more. Don't look at me. The rats have gnawed at me. I'm bringing you what's left.

SHLINK   That strange milky light! Ah, that's it! Phosphorescent rot, that's it!

MARY   Does my face look bloated to you?

SHLINK   Do you realize you'll be lynched if the mob catches you here?

MARY   It's all the same to me.

SHLINK   I beg you, leave me alone in my last moments.

MARY   Come. Hide in the underbrush. There's a hiding place in the quarry.

SHLINK   Damn it! Are you out of your mind? Don't you see that I have to cast one last look over this jungle? That's what the moon is rising for. (*Steps into the entrance of the tent*)

MARY   All I see is that you've lost the ground from under your feet. Have pity on yourself.

SHLINK   Can't you do me this one last kindness?

MARY I only want to look at you. I've found out that this is where I belong.

SHLINK Maybe so! Then stay. (*A signal is heard in the distance*) Two o'clock. Time to be thinking about my safety.

MARY Where's George?

SHLINK George? He's run away. What a miscalculation! My safety. (*He tears off his scarf*) The barrels are beginning to stink. Good fat fish, I caught them myself. Well dried, packed up in crates. Salted. First set out in ponds, bought at a high price, fattened! Fish eager for death, suicidal fish, that swallow hooks like holy wafers. Phoo! Quick now! (*He goes to the table, sits down. Drinks from a flask*) I, Wang Yeng, known as Shlink, born in Yokohama in northern Peiho under the sign of the Tortoise. I operated a lumber business, ate rice, and dealt with all sorts of people. I, Wang Yeng, known as Shlink, aged fifty-four, ended three miles south of Chicago, without heirs.

MARY What's the matter?

SHLINK (*seated*) You here? My legs are getting cold. Throw a cloth over my face. Have pity. (*He collapses*)
(*Panting in the underbrush. Footsteps and hoarse curses from behind*)

MARY What are you listening for? Answer me. Are you asleep? Are you still cold? I'm here, close to you. What did you want with the cloth?
(*At this moment knives cut openings in the tent. The lynchers step silently through the openings*)

MARY (*going toward them*) Go away. He just died. He doesn't want anyone to look at him.

11

The private office of the late C. Shlink

A WEEK LATER

The lumber yard has burned down. Signs here and there saying: "Business for Sale." Garga, John Garga, Mary Garga.

JOHN   It was stupid of you to let this place burn down. Now all you've got is charred beams. Who's going to buy them?

GARGA (*laughing*)   They're cheap. But what are you two planning to do?

JOHN   I thought we'd stay together.

GARGA (*laughing*)   I'm leaving. Are you going to work?

MARY   I'm going to work. But not scrub stairs like my mother.

JOHN   I'm a soldier. We slept in watering troughs. The rats on our faces never weighed less than seven pounds. When they took away my rifle and it was over, I said: From now on we'll all sleep with our caps on.

GARGA   You mean: we'll all sleep.

MARY   We'd better go now, Father. Night's coming on, and I still have no room.

JOHN   Yes, let's go. (*Looks around*) Let's go. A soldier at your side. Forward march! Against the jungle of the city.

GARGA   I've got it behind me. Hello!

MANKY (*comes in beaming, with his hands in his pockets*)   It's me. I read your ad in the paper. If your lumber business doesn't cost too much, I'll buy it.

GARGA   What's your offer?

MANKY   Why are you selling?

GARGA   I'm going to New York.

MANKY   And I'm moving in here.

GARGA   How much can you pay?

MANKY   I'll need some cash for the business.

GARGA   Six thousand, if you'll take the woman too.

MANKY   All right.

MARY   I've got my father with me.

MANKY   And your mother?

MARY   She's not here any more.

MANKY (*after a pause*)   All right.

MARY   Draw up the contract.

   (*The men sign*)

MANKY   Let's all have a bite. Want to come along, George?

GARGA   No.

MANKY   Will you still be here when we get back?

GARGA   No.

JOHN   Good-bye, George. Take a look at New York. You can come back to Chicago if the going gets too rough.

   (*The three go out*)

GARGA (*putting the money away*)   It's a good thing to be alone. The chaos is used up. That was the best time.

The Life of
Edward the Second
of England

(After Marlowe)

A History

I wrote this play with Lion Feuchtwanger.

BERTOLT BRECHT

Translators: William E. Smith and Ralph Manheim

Here will be publicly performed the history of the troubled reign of Edward the Second, King of England, and his lamentable death / Along with the good fortune and end of Gaveston, his favorite / Moreover, the tangled fate of Queen Anne / Likewise, the rise and fall of the great Earl Roger Mortimer / All of which came to pass in England, especially in London, more than six hundred years ago

CHARACTERS

KING EDWARD THE SECOND
QUEEN ANNE, his wife
KENT, his brother
YOUNG EDWARD, his son, later
    KING EDWARD THE THIRD
GAVESTON
ARCHBISHOP OF WINCHESTER
BISHOP OF COVENTRY, later
    ARCHBISHOP OF WINCHESTER
MORTIMER
LANCASTER
RICE AP HOWELL

BERKELEY
SPENCER
BALDOCK
THE ELDER GURNEY
THE YOUNGER GURNEY
LIGHTBORN
JAMES
PEERS
SOLDIERS
A BALLAD-SELLER
TWO RAGGED MEN
A MONK

December 14, 1307. Return of the favorite, Daniel Gaveston, on the occasion of Edward II's coronation.

LONDON

GAVESTON (*reading a letter from King Edward*)
"My father, old Edward, is dead. Come quickly, Gaveston, and share the kingdom with your dearest friend, King Edward the Second."

And here I am. These loving lines of yours
Blew aft my brig from Ireland.
The sight of London to an exile is
Like heaven to a new-come soul.
My father often said to me: "Only eighteen
And already fat from drinking ale!"
And my mother said: "When you are buried
Those who mourn you will be scarcer
Than a hen's teeth." And now a king
Is down on his knees for their son's friendship.
Hey, reptiles!
Who are these first crawlers in my path?
(*Enter two ragged men*)

FIRST MAN
Men who would gladly serve your lordship.

GAVESTON
What can you do?

FIRST MAN
I can ride.

GAVESTON
  I have no horse.
  What are you?
SECOND MAN
  A soldier. I served in the Irish war.
GAVESTON
  I have no war. And so, gentlemen, Godspeed.
SECOND MAN
  Godspeed?
FIRST MAN (*to the second*)
  England has nothing
  To offer old soldiers.
GAVESTON
  But England offers them St. James's Hospital.
FIRST MAN
  Where they die like dogs.
GAVESTON
  That's a soldier's fate.
SECOND MAN
  Think so?
  Then die like a dog in this England
  Of yours, and I hope you die by a soldier's hand!
  (*Both go out*)
GAVESTON (*alone*)
  That fellow talks like my father.
  Oh, well!
  His words impress me about as much
  As a goose that tried to play the porcupine
  Thrusting out with its feathers, imagining
  It could stab me to the heart. Stab away!
  But many a man will soon be repaid in full.
  For all my ale-drinking and whist-playing
  I've not forgotten that paper on which they wrote
  That I am Edward's whore and therefore banished.
  But here comes my fresh-dipped king
  With a herd of Peers. I'll stand aside.
  (*He hides*)
  (*Enter Edward, Kent, Mortimer, the Archbishop of Winchester,
  Lancaster*)

ARCHBISHOP
My lord! In haste, while on my way to read
The Mass over the immortal remains
Of your father, Edward King of England
I bring you this message:
On his deathbed, Edward required your Peers—
LANCASTER
Already he's turned whiter than his sheets—
ARCHBISHOP
To swear an oath. That man must never come
To England.
GAVESTON (*concealed*)
Mort dieu!
ARCHBISHOP
If you love us, my lord, hate Daniel Gaveston!
(*Gaveston whistles between his teeth*)
LANCASTER
If that man crosses the water, many swords
Will be bared in England.
EDWARD
I will have Gaveston.
GAVESTON
Well spoken, Ned.
LANCASTER
We're only saying that no one likes to be forsworn.
ARCHBISHOP
My lord, why do you so provoke your Peers
Whose nature bids them love you and respect you?
EDWARD
I will have Gaveston.
LANCASTER
It looks as if swords may be drawn in England
My lords.
KENT
If swords are drawn in England, Lancaster
There will be heads, I think, to set on poles
Because the tongues within them are too long.
ARCHBISHOP
Our heads!

EDWARD
Yes, yours. And so I hope you'll change your minds.
LANCASTER
We have hands, it seems to me, to guard our heads.
(*The Peers go out*)
KENT
Abandon Gaveston, brother, but check those Peers.
EDWARD
Brother, I'll stand or fall with Gaveston.
GAVESTON (*comes forward*)
I can hold back no longer, dearest lord.
EDWARD
What, Danny! Dearest!
Come, embrace me, Danny, as I do you.
Since you were banished, all my days were parched.
GAVESTON
And since I left, no soul in hell has suffered
More than poor Gaveston.
EDWARD
I know it. Now, rebellious Lancaster
Arch-heretic Winchester, plot and be damned.
Gaveston, We appoint you Lord High Chamberlain
Lord Chancellor, Earl of Cornwall, Lord of Man.
KENT (*darkly*)
Brother, you're going too far.
EDWARD
Brother, be still.
GAVESTON
My lord, don't crush me. What will the people say?
Might they not say: "This is too much
For a common butcher's son."
EDWARD
Are you afraid? You shall have bodyguards.
Do you need money? Go to my treasure vault.
Do you wish to be feared? Here, my ring and seal.
Command in Our name whatever gives you pleasure.
GAVESTON
Your love has put me on a plane with Caesar.
(*Enter the Bishop of Coventry*)

EDWARD

Where are you going, Lord Bishop of Coventry?

BISHOP

To your father's Requiem Mass, my lord.

EDWARD (*pointing at Gaveston*)

My dead father has a guest from the Irish Sea.

BISHOP

What? Here again? That scoundrel Gaveston?

GAVESTON

Yes, my good man. And London's filled
With wailing and the chattering of teeth.

BISHOP

I did no more than I was bound to do.
But if you're here unlawfully, Gaveston
I'll take your case to Parliament again
And back you'll go aboard that Irish ship.

GAVESTON (*seizing hold of him*)

Just come with me. There's water in the gutter.
For setting hand to that petition, priest
I'll dip you in the gutter, you, a bishop
As you once dipped me in the Irish Sea.

EDWARD

A good thing too. Whatever you do is good.
Yes, duck him, Gaveston, wash his face for him
And shave your enemy in slops.

KENT

Brother, brother, don't lay violent hands on him!
He'll lodge a protest with the Pope in Rome.

EDWARD

Spare his life, but take his gold and livings!
You will be bishop, him we'll banish.

BISHOP

King Edward, God will surely punish you
For this offense.

EDWARD

But meanwhile, Gaveston, go quickly
And take possession of his house and goods.

GAVESTON

Why would a priest need such a mansion anyway?

Mismanagement under King Edward's rule in the years 1307 to 1312. A war in Scotland is lost by the King's negligence.

LONDON

Spencer, Baldock, the two ragged men, soldiers.

BALDOCK
The Archbishop of Winchester said in his sermon: "The grain this year is wormy." That must mean something.

SECOND MAN
But not to us. Winchester eats all the grain.

FIRST MAN
And now it seems some Yorkshireman has seized the provisions for the Scottish troops.

BALDOCK
But to make up for it, Ned and his friends start drinking beer at eight in the morning.

SPENCER
Ned fainted yesterday.

FIRST SOLDIER
How so?

SPENCER
The Earl of Cornwall told him he'd decided to grow a beard.

BALDOCK
The other day Ned puked on Tanner Street.

SECOND SOLDIER
How so?

BALDOCK
A woman crossed his path.

SECOND MAN

Have you heard the latest about the Earl of Cornwall? He's taken to wearing a bustle.

(*Laughter. Enter a ballad-seller*)

BALLAD-SELLER

Ned's strumpet has hair on his chest.
Pray for us, pray for us, pray for us.
That's why the war in Scotland had to be laid to rest.
Pray for us, pray for us, pray for us.
The Earl of Cornwall has too much gold in his stocking.
Pray for us, pray for us, pray for us.
That's why O'Nelly has a stump and Paddy's arms are lacking.
Pray for us, pray for us, pray for us!
Ned's delousing his Gavvie, that keeps him occupied.
Pray for us, pray for us, pray for us.
That's why Johnny fell in the rushes of Bannockbride.
Pray for us, pray for us, pray for us.

SPENCER

That song is worth its ha'penny, my good man.

(*Enter Edward and Gaveston*)

EDWARD

Dear Gaveston, you have no friend but me.
Forget them! We will go to Tynemouth Pond.
We'll fish, eat fish, and ride, and stroll upon
The battlements together, knee to knee.

SPENCER (*seizing hold of the ballad-seller*)

That's high treason, my good man. You may tear my aunt's nephew to pieces, but my mother's son will never tolerate an insult to his dear Earl of Cornwall.

GAVESTON

What do you want, my friend?

SPENCER

I enjoy a well-turned couplet as much as the next man, my lord, but high treason sticks in my craw.

GAVESTON

Which one was it?

SPENCER

This worm-eaten pegleg, my lord.

(*The ballad-seller leaves quickly*)

GAVESTON (*to the King*)
   Calumniare audacter, semper aliquid haeret.
SPENCER
   Or in plain English, hanging's too good for him.
GAVESTON (*to Spencer*)
   Follow me.
   (*He goes out with the King. Spencer motions Baldock and they go along. The others laugh*)
   (*Enter the Archbishop and Lancaster*)
ARCHBISHOP
   London is mocking us. The tax farmers are wondering how long the Parliament and Peers will stand for it. In every street there's talk of civil war.
LANCASTER
   One harlot doesn't make a war.

LONDON

MORTIMER (*at home with his books, alone*)
   Plutarch relates that Gaius Julius Caesar
   Could read and write and dictate all at once
   And beat the Gauls as well. Men of his stamp
   Would seem to draw their fame from a peculiar
   Absence of insight into the futility
   Of human affairs, compounded with
   An amazing lack of seriousness: in short
   From their superficiality.
   (*Enter the Archbishop and Peers*)
ARCHBISHOP
   While in seclusion, Mortimer, you wallow
   In classical literature and meditate
   On bygone times.
   London is seething like a roused-up ant hill
   And needs you.
MORTIMER
   London needs grain.

ARCHBISHOP

    If God the Father should let a hundred swine
    Die in St. James's Hospital for lack
    Of grain, you may be certain, Mortimer
    We wouldn't take you from your books for that.
    But when one special swine grows fat in Westminster
    Suckled upon the nation's milk, by the man
    Who should be the nation's guardian, the King
    Then I believe it's time to let the classics
    Be classics.

MORTIMER

    The classics tell us that Alexander the Great
    Loved his Hephaestion, that wise Socrates
    Loved Alcibiades, that Achilles sickened
    For Patroclus. Why then should I
    For a mere sport of nature show myself
    To the sweaty rabble in the marketplace?

ARCHBISHOP

    Ned has long arms, catapults. Once he's shortened
    You by a head, I doubt if you'll enjoy
    Your hard-won leisure. You will have come in
    Out of the rain only to drown in the flood.
    You are a man of cold passion, at the age
    When cool reflection prompts auspicious acts.
    Your books and tumultuous life have given you
    Keen knowledge of all human weaknesses.
    Great, moreover, in name, in wealth, in troops
    You are the man to raise your voice
    In Westminster.

MORTIMER

    If you mean to cook your soup on the fire of Etna
    You've come to the wrong man. You start
    By plucking a rooster, either to eat it or
    Because it wakes you with its crowing. But soon
    The habit gets the best of you, and in the end
    You want to skin a tiger. Have you thought of that?

ARCHBISHOP

    Even if we have to level Westminster Castle
    We've got to pluck that commoner from our flesh.

MORTIMER
  My lords, I see one remedy for our distress:
  To frame an order for his banishment
  And force the King to sign it.
ARCHBISHOP (*hurriedly*)
  And you will press our cause in Parliament.
  In England's name we thank you, Mortimer
  For sacrificing your learned studies
  To England's welfare.
  (*The Archbishop and Peers go out*)
MORTIMER (*alone*)
  Because a few have groveled before a dog
  The men of England are preparing
  To hurl their island into the abyss.

LONDON

Mortimer, Archbishop, Lancaster, two Peers.

LANCASTER
  The King of England is showing the Earl of Cornwall his
  catapults.
ARCHBISHOP
  He's showing them to us.
LANCASTER
  Are you afraid, Archbishop?
MORTIMER
  Ah, Lancaster, this shows how base we are.
  Had the ancients witnessed such a spectacle
  He'd have been torn from the King's bosom long ago.
  Toothless and slightly swollen with poison
  The butcher's son would be swinging from a dog's gallows.
LANCASTER (*after a catapult projectile has struck home*)
  Well aimed, Edward. A shot like that is food
  For thought. Those catapults
  Are Edward's long arms. Archbishop

He can reach into your Scottish castles
With his catapults.
(*Enter Queen Anne*)
MORTIMER
Where is Your Majesty going in such haste?
ANNE
Into the forest, noble Mortimer
To live in grief and bitterness.
My lord the King no longer looks at me
He has eyes only for this Gaveston.
He hangs about his neck, and when I come
He frowns as if to say: "Leave me, you see
That I have Gaveston."
MORTIMER
My lady, you've been made a widow by
A butcher's son.
ARCHBISHOP
Mortimer is comforting my lady.
LANCASTER
She loves the wicked Edward.
A cruel fate! God help her.
ANNE
My Mortimer, can there be greater bitterness
Than that the sister of the King of France should be a widow
Yet not a widow, for her husband lives.
Worse than a widow. She'd be better off
Under the earth. She walks in the shadow
Of disgrace, a woman, yet not a woman.
For her bed is barren.
MORTIMER
Madam, too many tears are bad for the skin.
Orphaned nights age you. Blubbery feelings
Slacken the body. My lady, seek satisfaction.
As a general rule, tough flesh
Needs to be sprinkled.
ANNE (*aside*)
O wretched Edward, see how low you've brought me
That instead of slapping this beast in the face
I stand here helpless, afraid to say a word

While he assaults me with his lechery.
(*Aloud*)
You take advantage of my suffering, Mortimer.

MORTIMER

Lady Anne, go back to the court.
Our Peers know what to do. Before the moon
Changes, the butcher's son will be on shipboard bound
For Ireland.

ARCHBISHOP

My lady, Gaveston is
A thorn in our flesh too. We'll pull him out.

ANNE

But do not take up arms against your King.
Edward's beyond our understanding. Oh, my love
Bewilders me. How can I go off to the woods
If they are going to fall upon King Edward?
On far-off paths I'd hear men threatening him
And hurry back to help him in his need.

LANCASTER

Gaveston will never leave England without bloodshed.

ANNE

Then let him stay. Rather than know my lord
In danger, I will bear my life
And let him have his Gaveston.

LANCASTER

Patience, my lady.

MORTIMER

My lords, let us escort the Queen
Back to Westminster.

ANNE

And for my sake
Do not take up arms against the King.
(*All go out*)
(*Enter Gaveston*)

GAVESTON

The mighty Earl of Lancaster, the Archbishop
Of Winchester, the Queen, and certain vultures
From the city are laying plots against
Various people.

LONDON

GAVESTON (*alone in his house, writing his testament*)
For no good reason, on a common Thursday
And through no special love of slaughter, men
Are often obliterated, painfully.
Therefore I write, in ignorance
Of what I had too little or too much of
That Edward, who now is King of England
Should have kept after me.
For my own mother never found in me
Anything out of the ordinary, no caul, no goiter.
Therefore, because I know not
Which way to turn, but blockhead that I am
Know this:
That nothing can help you live when everyone
Wants you dead, that I shall never leave
This London other than feet foremost—
Therefore I write my testament:
I, Daniel Gaveston, a butcher's son
Now in my twenty-seventh year, laid low
By smiling circumstance, extinguished
By lavish fortune, do hereby bequeath
My clothes and boots to those who are with me
At the end.
To the giddy women of St. James's Street
The Bishopric of Coventry, to the good
Ale-drinking folk of England my narrow grave.
To good King Edward, my friend
God's forgiveness.
For I am most unhappy that I did not
Simply turn to dust.

May 9, 1 3 1 1. King Edward refuses to sign the order banishing Gaveston, his favorite, and a thirteen-years war breaks out.

WESTMINSTER

Mortimer, Lancaster, the Archbishop, and Peers sign the document one by one.

MORTIMER
This parchment sets the seal on his banishment.
(*Enter the Queen, Gaveston, who sits down beside the King's chair, Kent, then Edward*)

EDWARD
Are you so angry to see Gaveston sitting here?
It is Our wish, and that's the way We want it.

LANCASTER
Your Grace does well to seat him next to you
For nowhere else is the new peer so safe.

ARCHBISHOP
Quam male conveniunt!

LANCASTER
The British lion fawning upon vermin.

FIRST PEER
See how the fellow lounges in his chair!

SECOND PEER
People of London, come and feast your eyes:
Behold King Edward with his pair of wives.
(*The Parliament is opened in the presence of the people*)

KENT
Roger Mortimer has the floor.

MORTIMER
  When Paris ate the bread of Menelaus
  And salt in Menelaus's house, he slept—
  Or so the ancient chronicles relate—
  With Menelaus's wife, and on the ship
  That took him back to Troy, she shared his bed.
  Troy laughed. To laughing Troy and Greece as well
  It seemed good sense to give that willing flesh
  That bore the name of Helen, back to her Greek
  Husband, because she was a whore.
  Only Lord Paris, understandably
  Objected. Said she was unwell. Meanwhile
  Greek ships turned up, and multiplied like fleas.
  One morning Greeks came barging into
  Paris's house, intent on seizing the
  Greek strumpet. Paris shouts
  Out of the window: This place is my house
  My castle; and the Trojans, thinking
  Him not entirely wrong, grin and applaud.
  The Greeks lower their sails, lie down and fish
  Till one day in an ale-house in the port
  Someone punches someone in the nose
  And then explains that it was done for Helen.
  And in the next few days, before
  Anyone realized what was happening
  Too many hands reached for too many throats.
  From shattered ships men speared the drowning
  Like tuna fish. And as the moon waxed
  More and more men were missing from their tents.
  Many were found headless in the houses. The crabs
  Grew fat that year in the Skamander River
  But no one ate them. Men who in the morning
  Looked out for signs of storm, thinking of nothing
  But whether the fish would bite that afternoon
  Had fallen by midnight through confusion and purpose
  Every last one.
  Seen at ten o'clock
  With human faces
  By eleven o'clock

Forgetting the language of their country
Trojan sees Troy and Greek sees Greece no more.
Instead they feel human lips
Turned into tiger jaws. At noon
Beast sinks its fangs into the flanks
Of moaning beast.
But if on the beleaguered walls one man
Had kept his wits and
Called them by name and species, many
Would even then have frozen in their tracks.
Better if they had gone down fighting
Aboard a vessel suddenly grown old
Sinking beneath their feet at nightfall
Nameless.
They were to kill each other more horribly:
That war dragged on ten years—
The Trojan War it's called—
And was ended by a horse.
And so if reason, by and large, were not inhuman
And human ears not plugged—
Regardless whether Helen was a whore
Or grandmother to a flourishing line—
Troy, which was four times bigger than our London
Would still be standing, Hector would not
Have died in the blood of his genitals, dogs
Would not have spat upon the aged hair
Of tearful Priam, an entire race
Would not have perished in its prime.
Quod erat demonstrandum. True
We would not have had the Iliad.
(*He sits down. A pause. Edward weeps*)
ANNE
What's the matter? Do you want water, husband?
KENT
The King has taken sick. The session's closed.
(*The Parliament is closed*)
EDWARD
Why do you look at me? Don't look at me. God grant
Your lips are not deceitful, Mortimer.
Don't worry about me. Think nothing of it

If I look dejected. It's only
A pallor of the temples, a momentary
Stoppage of the blood in the brain.
Nothing more.
Lay hands on that traitor, Mortimer.

ARCHBISHOP
We'll answer with our heads for what he says.

LANCASTER
Sire, send Gaveston from our sight.

MORTIMER
Read
What we have written for you on this parchment.

ANNE (*to Edward*)
Listen to reason, my lord.
This is Thursday, this is London.

MORTIMER
Sign your name
To the banishment of Daniel Gaveston
Son of a butcher in the city of London
Banished long years ago by the English
Parliament, returned illegally, and now
Banished again by the English Parliament.
Sign, Sire!

LANCASTER
Sign, my lord!

ARCHBISHOP
Sign, my lord!

GAVESTON
Things have moved faster than you expected, Sire.

KENT
Brother, let Gaveston go!

MORTIMER
This is Thursday, this is London. Sign!
(*Lancaster, Archbishop, and Peers set a table before the King*)
Sign!

EDWARD
Never, never, never!
Before I let my Gaveston be taken
I'll leave the island.
(*He tears the document*)

ARCHBISHOP

There's England torn in two.

LANCASTER

Plenty of blood will flow in England now
King Edward.

MORTIMER (*sings*)

The maids of England in widow's weeds
Their lovers are rotting in Bannockbride's reeds
Cry aheave and aho!
The King's drums roll to override
The lament of the widows of Bannockbride
With a rom rombelow.

EDWARD

Won't you sing some more? Do you look upon
A king as your ox to slaughter?
Is this a life for royalty?
Come, Gaveston, I'm still here
I have a foot to plant on vipers' heads.
(*Goes out with Gaveston*)

MORTIMER

This means war.

LANCASTER

Neither the angels of heaven nor the devils of the sea
Will save the butcher's son from England's infantry.

The Battle of Killingworth (August 15 and 16, 1320). Battlefield near Killingworth.

ABOUT SEVEN O'CLOCK IN THE EVENING

Mortimer, Lancaster, Archbishop, troops.

LANCASTER
Here! The tattered banner of St. George
That has waved from Ireland to the Dead Sea!
Alarm!
(*Enter Kent*)

KENT
My lords, for love of England I enlist
Under your banner and renounce the King
My brother. His infamous attachment
To Gaveston is the ruin of our country.

ARCHBISHOP
Your hand, Kent!

LANCASTER
March!
(*Drums*)
Let no one lay a hand upon King Edward!

ARCHBISHOP
And a hundred shillings for the head of Gaveston.
(*They march off*)

ABOUT SEVEN O'CLOCK IN THE EVENING

Marching troops. Edward, Gaveston.

FIRST SOLDIER
  Come, Sire. The battle's on.
EDWARD
  Continue, Gaveston.
GAVESTON
  A good many people in London are saying
  This war will never end.
EDWARD
  Gaveston, We are deeply moved to see
  You standing here unarmed at such a time
  Trusting in Us, bare of leather or metal
  Wearing only your usual Irish dress.
SECOND SOLDIER
  Order the march, my lord. The battle's on.
EDWARD
  As in the sky that wedge of storks, though flying
  Seems to stand still, so stands your image firm
  Within Our heart, unscathed by time.
GAVESTON
  My lord, before he sleeps, a fisherman reckons
  Counting his nets and fish, and adding up
  The shillings earned that day. And I myself
  Even by daylight can't help pondering
  Such simple sums: many are more than one
  And one lives many days but not forever.
  Then set no heavy stake upon your heart
  For fear of the losing of your heart.
THIRD SOLDIER
  Sire, to battle!
EDWARD
  Your lovely hair!

EIGHT O'CLOCK AT NIGHT

GAVESTON (*fleeing*)
  Ever since those drums started, and this swamp engulfing
  Horses and catapults, my mother's son
  Seems to have lost his wits. Stop panting. Can
  They all be drowned and done for and nothing left
  But noise, still hovering between
  Heaven and earth. I won't run any more
  For it's only a matter of minutes. I won't stir
  A finger, but simply lie down on the ground
  To keep from living till the end of time.
  And when tomorrow morning King Edward rides
  By to torment me, calling, "Daniel!
  Where are you?" I won't be there. And now
  Gavvy, untie your shoelaces and stay
  Right where you are.
  (*Enter Lancaster, Mortimer, Archbishop, Peers, James, troops*)
LANCASTER
  Take him, soldiers!
  (*The Peers laugh*)
  Welcome, Lord Chamberlain.
FIRST PEER
  Welcome, beloved Earl of Cornwall.
ARCHBISHOP
  Welcome, Lord Bishop!
LANCASTER
  Running to cool your poisoned blood, Your Grace?
ARCHBISHOP
  Most worthy Peers! His trial need not be long.
  The verdict: whereas Daniel Gaveston
  Son of a butcher in the city of London
  Has been King Edward's whore and has seduced him
  To lechery and many other crimes
  And whereas though twice banished he did not
  Desist, he shall be hanged from a branch. Hang him.

JAMES

    He's stopped moving. He's as stiff as a
    Frozen codfish, my lords. That's a good branch.
    Two hempen ropes. He's heavy.

MORTIMER (*aside*)

    This man alive would be worth the half of Scotland
    I myself would have traded the whole army
    For this watery codfish. But
    Branch, rope, and neck are here, and blood is cheap.
    At a time when catapults with men appended
    Are pounding irresistibly and herds
    Of mounted horses, shying from the roll of drums
    Are clashing; when night and walls of dust
    Seal up the exit from the battle: at
    A time when catapults are pounding, drums
    Drumming, manned herds of horses
    Devouring each other, a red and reeling moon
    Draws reason from men's minds, and out of man
    There crawls a naked beast.
    The situation calls for a hanging.

JAMES

    Pass the plank.

GAVESTON

    The rope's not right.

JAMES

    Never fear, we'll soap it.

SOLDIERS (*singing in the background*)

    Ned's strumpet has hair on his chest.
    Pray for us, pray for us, pray for us.

A SOLDIER (*to Gaveston*)

    How does it feel, sir?

GAVESTON

    First bring the drum.

SOLDIER

    Will you scream, sir?

GAVESTON

    I beg you, take the drum away. I will
    Not scream.

JAMES

    Good, sir. Now shut your mouth.

    Put the noose on him. His neck is short.

GAVESTON

    One thing I ask you: get it over with.

    But first I'd like to hear the sentence read.

JAMES (*reads the sentence, then*)

    Now, proceed.

GAVESTON

    Edward! My friend Edward! Help me

    If you are still alive.

    Edward!

    (*A soldier enters*)

SOLDIER

    Stop! A message from the King.

GAVESTON

    He's still alive.

ARCHBISHOP (*reads*)

    "Having learned that you have taken Gaveston

    I beg of you, before he dies

    To let me see him—for I know

    That he will die. I send my word

    And seal: He will come back.

    And if you grant me this request

    I shall be grateful for your courtesy.

    Edward."

GAVESTON

    Edward!

ARCHBISHOP

    What now?

LANCASTER

    This paper, my lords, is as good as a battle won.

GAVESTON

    Edward. The name revives me.

LANCASTER

    It needn't. We could send the King

    Your heart, for instance.

GAVESTON

    Our good King Edward pledges his word and seal.

He only wants to see me, then he'll send
Me back.

LANCASTER

When?

(*Laughter*)

For his Danny, once he sees him, he will break
The seal of the kingdom before the eyes of God.

ARCHBISHOP

Before the King of England breaks an oath
The island will break and sink into the ocean.

LANCASTER

Good. Send him Gaveston. But hang him later.

MORTIMER

Don't hang Gaveston, but don't send him either.

ARCHBISHOP

It may be fitting to cut down the King
But never to turn down the King's request.

LANCASTER

That's it. Kill him, skin him, but be sure
Not to deny him the slightest courtesy.
And now to battle with Edward Gloucester
Wife of the butcher's son.

ARCHBISHOP

Cut the man loose.
And you, Lord Mortimer, see to his conveyance.

GAVESTON

Another night watch and a last round trip.
And death goes with me like my moon.

JAMES

What a to-do for a common butcher's son!

(*All go out except Mortimer, James, Gaveston*)

MORTIMER

This butcher's son is the alpha of this war
And its omega too
A rope in a swamp, a shield to ward off arrows.
And I've got him. James!
Lead this man in a circle. And if someone asks
You where you're going, say: to potter's field. But
Handle him like a bag of eggs. And bring him

Tomorrow morning at eleven to
Killingworth Wood. I'll be there.

JAMES

  And if something happens to you, my lord?

MORTIMER

Use your own judgment.

JAMES

  Come, sir.
(Goes out with Gaveston)

MORTIMER

Those orders seem to emanate a faint
Odor of carrion. But since the moon
Began to draw forth blood like water vapor
And death crept into the faces of these Peers, I
Who know what's what and disregard the moon
Am nothing but a lump of cowardice.
One man's enough to kill
Another, who's able to kill thousands.
Therefore, as circumspectly as one burned
I'll wrap myself in someone else's skin
To wit: the skin of Gaveston, the butcher's son.

ABOUT TEN O'CLOCK AT NIGHT

ANNE *(alone)*

Oh, most unhappy Queen!
If only when I left fair France and was
Embarked, the sea had turned to stone.
If only the arms that twined about my neck
Had stifled me upon my wedding night!
For here I am pursuing King Edward
Who, widowing me, went off to fight this battle
Of Killingworth for that devil Gaveston.
My skin crawls when I look at him. But Edward
Steeps his heart in him like a sponge.
And so I am forever miserable.
O God, why have you brought me, Anne

Of France, so low, and so exalted
That devil Gaveston?
(*Enter Gaveston, James, soldier*)
JAMES (*steps forward*)
Ho, there!
ANNE
Are you King Edward's men?
JAMES
Certainly not.
ANNE
Who is that man in Irish dress?
JAMES
It's Gaveston, the King of England's whore.
ANNE
Where are you taking him?
JAMES
To potter's field.
GAVESTON (*in the rear*)
If only I had water for my feet.
SOLDIER
Here's some water.
ANNE
I beg you, don't refuse him.
GAVESTON
Let me speak to her. It's the Queen.
Take me with you, my lady.
JAMES
No, stop. Just wash your feet. I have my orders.
ANNE
Why won't you let him speak with me?
JAMES
Just stand aside, Your Highness, and let him wash.
(*Pushes her away*)
GAVESTON
Stay, dear lady, stay!
Poor Gaveston! Where are you going now?

ONE O'CLOCK IN THE MORNING

Lancaster, Peers, and troops on the march to Boroughbridge.

A SOLDIER
  To Boroughbridge.
  (*Word is passed down the line*)
SOLDIERS (*singing*)
  The maids of England in widow's weeds
    (In the night)
  Their lovers are rotting in Bannockbride's reeds
    (In the night)
  Cry aheave and aho.
  The King's drums roll to override
    (In the night)
  The lament of the widows of Bannockbride
    (In the night)
  With a rom, rombelow.
LANCASTER
  All's well. We'll take Boroughbridge before the night's out.

TWO O'CLOCK IN THE MORNING

Edward, Spencer, Baldock, young Edward, the sleeping army.

EDWARD
  I long to hear an answer from the Peers
  Touching my friend, my dearest Gaveston.
  Ah, Spencer, all the gold in England
  Can't ransom him now. The mark of death
  Is on him. I know Mortimer's vile nature
  I know the Archbishop is ruthless
  And Lancaster unbending. Never again

Will I lay eyes on Daniel Gaveston.
And in the end they'll crush me too.

SPENCER

If I were Edward, Sovereign of England
Son of great Edward Longshanks, I would not
Bear that lewd rabble, suffer those knavish Peers
To threaten me in my own kingdom.
Cut off their heads and set them up on poles!
That method never fails.

EDWARD

Yes, my good Spencer, We have been much too gentle
Too kind to them. But that's all over now.
If they don't send me Gaveston, their heads
Will roll.

BALDOCK

An excellent plan, my lord; it becomes you well.

YOUNG EDWARD

Father, why are they making so much noise?

EDWARD

They're mangling England, child.
I would have sent you over to them, Edward
To make them yield up Gaveston. Would
You have been frightened of the maddened Peers?

YOUNG EDWARD

Yes, Father.

EDWARD

That's a good answer.
The field is full of hungry birds tonight.
(*Enter the Queen*)

ANNE

Are you King Edward's soldiers?
Is this the limestone quarry of Killingworth?
Where is King Edward, soldiers?

SPENCER

Who's there?

A SOLDIER

A woman looking for King Edward.

ANNE

I've come from London, two full days on horseback.

I've searched for you through thicket, swamp, and battle.

EDWARD

You are not welcome.

SPENCER

The battle's been in labor for two days.
A painful birth: the armies look alike
And both cry out St. George and England. Crying
St. George, brother mangles brother. Army
Is meshed with army like two salamanders
Knotted in battle. English villages burn
For England. At nightfall in the swamp, amid
Catapults and drowning men, in the
Same spot where Gaveston was taken, Lord
Arundel is reported to have fallen.
A strong rain fell. The night was loud with skirmishes.
The King was chilled, but now he's feeling better.
Our position isn't bad, unless the Peers
Have taken Boroughbridge. This day will be
Decisive. As for Gaveston, the Peers
Have promised to send him here.

ANNE (*aside*)

And instead are dragging him to death.
Perhaps it's for the best. But I am not
The one to tell him that most likely
His friend's already dead.
(*Aloud*)
Edward, this day it's you they're hunting.

EDWARD

Yes.
And my friend Daniel Gaveston's been taken.
And who comes here through swamp and thicket? You!

ANNE

If you desire to spit on me, my lord
Here is my face.

EDWARD

Your face is like a tombstone. I can read the writing:
"Here lies poor Gaveston." But haven't you
Some little word of comfort? "Take heart, my lord
For Gaveston squinted in one eye."

And here's my answer: "All skin repels me:
Yours, for instance."
I, Edward of England, mindful that only a few
Hours stand between
Me and my end, have this to say: I do
Not care for you. In the sight of death:
I love Gaveston.

ANNE

Though I shall not forget this hard offense—
For the little I have in this poor head of mine
Sits fast and is very slow to fade—
Still it's a good thing that he's gone.

EDWARD

You must get him back for me. They say
Mortimer holds the power. Go to him.
He's vain. His kind is child's play for a queen.
Wheedle him. Bring your wiles, your special wiles
To bear. The world's about to end.
What is a vow? I give you absolution.

ANNE

Jesus! I cannot.

EDWARD

Then I banish you from my sight.

ANNE

At such a time, convulsed with war which
So they say, will never end, you mean to send me
Back through those rough and murderous armies?

EDWARD

Yes, and I'll give you an errand, too—to raise
An army in Scotland for your young son Edward.
For fortune isn't smiling on his father.

ANNE

Cruel Edward!

EDWARD

He also tells you this: such is your fate.
He may be cruel, but he knows
You from your heart down to your intimate parts.
And you'll be bound to him until the day
You perish like a wild beast in a snare.

ANNE
> Are you so sure it will always be so?

EDWARD
> You are a thing, bequeathed by testament
> My property, conveyed on me unasked.
> Never without my consent will you be free.

ANNE
> You send me away and bind me, both in one?

EDWARD
> Yes.

ANNE
> Heaven is my witness. I love only you.
> To hold you I once thought my arms could reach
> Across all England.
> But now I fear they may grow tired.
> You bind me even as you send me away?

EDWARD
> Is there no news of Gaveston?

ANNE
> You bid me go and will not let me go.
> I pray that all desert you yet not let you go.
> I pray that flayed of skin you'll roam, imploring
> The end that doesn't come.
> I pray that when you need a human hand
> That hand may be skinless with leprosy
> And when you try to run from them and die
> They'll hold you and not let you go.

EDWARD
> Is there no news of Gaveston?

ANNE
> Edward, if you're still waiting for your darling
> Gaveston, cut short your hope. In the swamp
> I saw a man in Irish dress, and heard
> Them saying he was bound for potter's field.

SPENCER
> Oh bloody perjury!

EDWARD (*on his knees*)
> By the mother of you all, the earth
> By heaven, by the purposes of the stars

By this hard and dried-out hand
By all the iron in this island
By the last vows of an emptied breast
By all the honors in England, by my teeth:
I will take all your misbegotten bodies
And change them till your mothers wouldn't know you
To white and headless stumps.

ANNE

I see it now. He's fallen heart and bones
Into the snares of that devil Gaveston.
(*Goes out with young Edward. A soldier enters*)

SOLDIER

The Peers send answer:
We have Boroughbridge, the battle's over.
Should you desire help and comfort
Without bloodshed, England bids you:
Forget Gaveston who is gone from the battle—

EDWARD

Gone from the world—

SOLDIER

And forswear his memory. You will have peace.

EDWARD

Good. Tell your Peers this:
Since you have Boroughbridge, and therefore I
Am powerless to fight; and since my friend
Gaveston is no longer of this world
I accept your offer; let there be peace
Between us. Come at noon to the limestone quarry
Of Killingworth, where I will meet your wish
And forswear his memory. But come unarmed
For weapons would offend Our royal eye.
(*The soldier goes out*)
(*To his soldiers*)
Wake up, you sluggards. Lie down in the quarry
Like corpses. Edward Softhand
Is expecting guests. And when they come
Go for their throats!

FIVE O'CLOCK IN THE MORNING

Gaveston, James, the other soldier.

GAVESTON
  Where the devil are we going?
  This is the quarry again.
  We keep going in a circle.
  Why those cold stares?
  Fifty silver shillings!
  Five hundred!
  I don't want to die.
  (*Throws himself on the ground*)
JAMES
  When you've finished whimpering, we'll go on.
  (*Enter two soldiers*)
SHOUTS
  St. George and England.
FIRST SOLDIER
  What's that over there?
SECOND SOLDIER
  Fire.
FIRST SOLDIER
  That's Boroughbridge. And what's that sound?
SECOND SOLDIER
  Bells.
FIRST SOLDIER
  Those are the bells of Bristol, ringing because the King of
  England and his Peers are making peace.
SECOND SOLDIER
  That's sudden. How so?
FIRST SOLDIER
  They say, to stop the country from being mangled.
JAMES
  If that's the case, you're likely to come off with minor bruises,
  sir. What time is it?
SOLDIER
  About five.

ELEVEN O'CLOCK IN THE MORNING

Edward, Spencer, Baldock.

SPENCER
The Peers of England are coming from the hills—
Unarmed.
EDWARD
Are the guards posted?
SPENCER
Yes.
EDWARD
Have you got ropes?
SPENCER
Yes.
EDWARD
Are the troops in place, ready to fall
On the headless army?
SPENCER
Yes.
(*Enter Archbishop, Lancaster, Peers*)
BALDOCK
My lord, your Peers.
EDWARD
Tie them with ropes.
THE PEERS (*bellowing*)
Treason! A trap! Your oath!
EDWARD
Perjury thrives in this kind of weather.
ARCHBISHOP
You swore an oath.
EDWARD
Drums!
(*The cries of the Peers are drowned out by drums. The Peers are led away bound*)

SPENCER

Mortimer didn't come.

EDWARD

Then get him.
Have you crossbows and slings and catapults?
Bring out the maps!
Sweep the plain with iron! Comb it through.
And tell each one before you strangle him
That the King of England has turned tiger
In Killingworth wood.
Forward!
(*A great battle*)

TWELVE NOON

Gaveston, James, the other soldier.

JAMES

Shovel, boy. The battle's mounting. Your friend is winning.

GAVESTON

What do you need a hole for?

JAMES

It's time to save our skins. But first we have to carry out our
orders. Shovel, my lord. If you'd like to pass water first, you can
do it here, sir.

GAVESTON

The battle's moving toward Bristol. When the wind blows, you
can hear the Welshmen's horses. Have you ever read about the
Trojan War? A lot of blood is going to be spilled for my mother's son too. Ned must be asking what's become of his friend.

JAMES

I doubt it, sir. Everybody in Killingworth must be telling him
not to expect you any more. Shovel, my lord. The rumor is
going around, sir, that your honorable Irish corpse has been
seen in Killingworth's potter's field. If rumor's to be trusted,
your head is off, sir.

GAVESTON
  Whom is this hole for?
  (*James says nothing*)
  Am I never to see the King again, James?
JAMES
  The King of Heaven, perhaps. But hardly the King of England.
SOLDIER
  Many men have fallen by soldiers' hands today.
JAMES
  What time is it?
SOLDIER
  About noon.

SEVEN O'CLOCK IN THE EVENING

Edward, Spencer, Baldock, the captive Peers, among them Mortimer.
Spencer is counting the prisoners, taking down their names.

EDWARD
  The hour has come, the time
  To avenge the murder of Daniel Gaveston
  My dearest friend to whom, as you all know
  I was devoted heart and soul.
KENT
  Brother, it was done for you and England.
EDWARD (*sets him free*)
  There, sir. You've said your piece. Now go away.
  (*Kent goes out*)
  Peers, it is not always fortune
  That wins the day. Sometimes the good cause triumphs.
  You seem to hang your heads. But never mind
  We'll find a way to lift them up again.
  Scoundrels! Rebels! Accursed wretches!
  Have you butchered him?
  When We sent heralds to find him, bearing
  Our seal and word, requesting you in writing

To let him come and speak with Us
Did you consent? Well? Did you? Have you butchered him?
Beheaded him? You've such a big head, Winchester,
I want to see it overtop the rest,
Just as your fury overtopped their fury.

ARCHBISHOP
When I look into that perjured face of yours
I give up hope of reaching you with words.
Your kind of man would scarcely take the word
Of one professing innocence of crime
Even if it be the truth. You have destroyed
All evidence and so confused the issue
Between us, you and Gaveston, that all
Eternity will never sort it out.
Your version, Edward, will not long have credit.

EDWARD
And what do you think, Lancaster?

LANCASTER
The worst of all is death, but rather death
Than to live with you in such a world.

MORTIMER (*aside*)
But with me
Though I'm their butcher more than Edward
They'll gladly start decaying hand in hand.

EDWARD
Take them away! Behead them!

LANCASTER
Good-bye to time!
When the thin crescent rose two nights ago
God was with us. And now that the moon
Is rising a little fuller, it's all over.
Good-bye, my Mortimer.

ARCHBISHOP
My Mortimer, good-bye.

MORTIMER
For those who love their country as we love it
It is not hard to die.
England will mourn us. England will not forget.
(*Archbishop, Lancaster, and Peers except Mortimer are led away*)

EDWARD

Is a certain Mortimer who was wisely absent
When I invited them to Killingworth
Quarry, now present?

SPENCER

Quite so, my lord. He is here.

EDWARD

Dispatch the others. Our Majesty has plans
For this man who dislikes forgetfulness.
Unbind him. We desire to keep the memory
Of Killingworth Day alive in England.
You Mortimers are bleary-eyed with reckoning.
You are at home in books. Like worms. But books
Say nothing about Edward, who neither reads
Nor reckons, who knows nothing, but is one
With nature, and feeds on other food.
Go now, Lord Mortimer. Go here and there.
And wandering in the sun, bear witness to
The way the son of Edward Longshanks has
Avenged his friend.

MORTIMER

Speaking of Daniel Gaveston, your friend
At five o'clock when England's king turned tiger
He was still alive in Killingworth wood.
And if, when my friends began to speak
You had not drowned out their words with drums
If you had not allowed too little trust
Too much passion and too quick anger to
Becloud your mind, your darling Gaveston
Would still be living.
(*Goes out*)

EDWARD

If Gaveston's body is found, see to it
That he is given fitting burial.
But don't go looking for him; he was the kind
Of man who strays into the woods; the bushes
Close behind him, the grasses spring
Back into place, until a thicket holds
Him fast.

And now we'll wipe off this day's sweat
And eat and rest until we're called upon
To cleanse this realm of the last vestiges
Of civil war.
For I will not set foot again in London
Or sleep in any bed but a soldier's cot
Until I have engulfed that rabble as
The sea engulfs a drop of rain.
Come, Spencer.

THREE O'CLOCK IN THE MORNING

Soft wind.

ANNE (*alone*)
Since Edward, heedless of my tears and earnest pleas
Has driven me to cold-hearted Mortimer
I'll put on widow's weeds. Four times I let him
Spit on my hair. But now I'd rather stand
Bald-headed beneath the sky. The fifth time
Is different. The wind and sky are different
And different too is the breath of my lips.
To London!
(*Mortimer has entered*)
MORTIMER
Better not, my lady.
London cooks watery soup for such as we.
ANNE
Where is your army, Earl Mortimer?
MORTIMER
My army
Lies murdered between the willows and the quarry.
A sluggish swamp has also swallowed many.
Where is your husband, my lady?
ANNE
With the dead Gaveston.

MORTIMER

And you, the sister of the King of France?

ANNE

At the crossroads between London and Scotland.
On Killingworth Day he bade me
Raise troops in Scotland.

MORTIMER

Me he bade
Wander as a living witness
To Killingworth Day.
He has struck seven heads from the hydra. Let him
Find seven times seven when he wakes.
A prisoner to battle and encampment
He'll never extricate himself from this war
For his exterminated Gaveston.

ANNE

He slighted his wife before the eyes of all—

MORTIMER

And exploited his kingdom like a pimp—

ANNE

And bound me fast and sent me away—

MORTIMER

And gutted the land as a hunter guts his kill—

ANNE

Strike him, Mortimer!

MORTIMER

Because he kicked you like a mangy dog—

ANNE

Because he kicked me like a worthless dog—

MORTIMER

You who were a queen—

ANNE

Who was an innocent child
Ignorant of the world and men—

MORTIMER

Sink your teeth into him!

ANNE

I will be a she-wolf
Raging through the forest with bared fangs.

I will not rest
Until earth covers Edward, long extinct
Edward Gloucester, my sometime husband.
Covers him. Earth.
(*She throws three handfuls of earth behind her*)
I will incite the wretched forest-dwellers
Myself tainted with the guile of a wicked world and people
Ranging like a she-wolf, mounted by wolves
Drenched by the rain of exile
Hardened by foreign winds.

MORTIMER
Earth on Edward of England!

ANNE
Earth on Edward Gloucester!

MORTIMER
To Scotland!

ANNE
Ah, Mortimer! A war is set in motion
That will plunge this island into the ocean.

After four years of war King Edward is still in the field. Landing of Queen Anne. The Battle of Harwich (September 23, 1324).

CAMP AT HARWICH

Edward, Spencer, Baldock.

EDWARD
  Thus after treason and four years of war
  Edward of England triumphed with his friends.
  (*Enter a herald with a message*)
SPENCER
  News, my lord?
EDWARD (*tearing up the message*)
  No, do you know of any?
SPENCER
  No.
EDWARD
  That's strange. I'd heard of a great slaughter
  And cleansing throughout the kingdom.
BALDOCK
  If I am not mistaken,
  That was four years ago, my lord.
EDWARD
  Four good years. There's relish in a life
  Of camp and battle. Horses are a good thing.
  Wind clears the lungs, and even if the skin
  Shrivels and the hair falls, rain washes
  The kidneys, and it's all better
  Than London.

BALDOCK
I'd rather be complaining about London
In London.

EDWARD
Have you still got those lists?

SPENCER
Yes, my lord.

EDWARD
We should like to hear them. Read them, Spencer.
(*Spencer reads the list of executed Peers*)
It seems to me one name is missing. Mortimer.
Have you put up placards promising reward
To the man who brings him in?

SPENCER
We have, Sire, and renewed them every year.
(*Enter a second herald*)

HERALD
There have been rumors that ship after ship
Is coming from the north.

EDWARD
That doesn't mean a thing. It's herring fishers
That come down from the north.
(*The herald goes out*)
As for the other names there listed
They were still barking a few years ago.
But now they neither bark nor bite.

BALDOCK (*to Spencer*)
He believes nothing. He's gone into a decline.
His only wish is to forget whatever
Is said to him.

EDWARD
But where are the Scottish troops?
You're always hearing about troops. False rumors.
But still no sign of those Scottish troops
The Queen was sent to raise four years ago.
(*Enter soldiers*)

FIRST SOLDIER
The army, tried by four years of campaigning
Since it destroyed as many Peers as rats

Now short of food, footwear and clothing
Asks of King Edward, son of Edward Longshanks
Father of England's army, to let them eat
Thames eels again before the year is out.

SOLDIERS

Hurrah for King Edward!

SECOND SOLDIER

Our wives want babies. We wouldn't mention it
Except this war may never end, because the King
Swore he would never sleep in a bed again
Until the enemy was brought to heel.

FIRST SOLDIER

And now that quite a few have gone off home
Because of pregnant wives, or so they said
Or wills or beer concessions, we'd like to know
Whether or not the King is planning to go
To London.

THIRD SOLDIER

Are you going to London, Sire?

FOURTH SOLDIER

Or what is he planning to do?

EDWARD

To wage war on the herons of the air, or
On fishes more quickly multiplying than killed
Monday on the great Leviathan, and Thursday on the vultures
Of Wales. But now I mean to eat.

SPENCER

The meager fare has made the King
A little feverish. Begone.
(*Spencer and Baldock push the soldiers out*)

EDWARD

Bring me something to drink, Baldock.
(*Baldock goes out*)

SPENCER

They won't be back.
You really won't go to London, Sire?
(*Enter third herald*)

HERALD

My lord, armed men have been seen in Harwich forest.

EDWARD
  Let them be. They are the guards
  Of the Welsh merchants.
  (*He sits down to eat*)
  Have ships been sighted?
HERALD
  Yes, Sire.
EDWARD
  Are villages burning in the north?
HERALD
  Yes, Sire.
EDWARD
  That's the Queen coming with the Scottish troops
  To help us.
SPENCER
  I doubt it.
EDWARD
  I will not have you watch me while I eat.
  (*Spencer and the third herald go out*)
EDWARD (*alone*)
  What grieves me most is knowing that my son
  Edward was lured to siding with their wickedness.
  (*Enter Spencer*)
SPENCER
  Fly, Sire! There isn't time to eat.
  Shall I summon your army to battle?
EDWARD
  No. Edward knows his army has gone home.
SPENCER
  You won't fight Roger Mortimer?
EDWARD
  God help me! He's like a fish in water.
  (*Goes out with Spencer and soldiers. Behind the scenes, the sound of camp being raised, battle, flight*)
  (*Enter Mortimer, Anne, young Edward, troops*)
ANNE
  The God of kings confers success in battle
  On those who fight for justice. Since we
  Have proved successful, hence just, thanks be

To Him who guides the stars for Our benefit.
We have come in arms to this part of Our island
To stop a breed of men more abject than
The rest from knotting strength with strength, and ravaging
England, bled with its own swords that slaughter
English bodies. As the most loathsome case
Of the seduced King Edward clearly shows—

MORTIMER

My lady, if you want to be a soldier
Don't show your passion in your speeches.
This island's face has changed; the Queen of England
Has landed today with her son.
(*Enter Rice ap Howell*)

RICE AP HOWELL

Edward has fled. By all forsaken, he
Has boarded a light vessel. The wind's for Ireland.

MORTIMER

Let the wind drown him or leave him in the lurch.
And now, my lords, since we possess this kingdom
From the Channel to the Irish Sea
Raise up young Edward on a shield
And swear allegiance to him. Show
The soldiers their Regent!
(*Young Edward is carried out. All go out except Mortimer and the Queen*)

ANNE

At last he has his Scottish troops
At last his she-dog comes and springs at him.
There's nothing left of him but a few half-eaten
Scraps and a ragged camp bed, while my body
Is coming almost virginally to life.

MORTIMER

We must dispatch troops to the south.
And you must be in London tomorrow night.
There's still no word about the Irish fleet.
I hope they get here. You must be tired?

ANNE

You have work to do?

MORTIMER
I must make England safe for you.

ANNE
Ah, Mortimer, there's less enjoyment than I thought
In tasting the fruit of this victory. It's stale
In my mouth, it's watery. It's not
Really amusing.

MORTIMER
You mean because of Edward?

ANNE
Edward? I don't know him any more. There's his smell
Here in the tent.
It was better in the Scottish hills
Than in these swampy lowlands. What
Will you offer me now, Mortimer?

MORTIMER
You're surfeited. Your bloated flesh
Is dreaming of London.
(*Enter Baldock with the drink*)
Who are you, fellow?

BALDOCK
King Edward's Baldock. Bringing him his drink.

MORTIMER (*taking the drink from him*)
Hang him!

BALDOCK
I wouldn't advise you to do that, my lord.
Not that I wouldn't gladly die; it's the
Most earthly fate and doesn't take long. But
My mother in Ireland wouldn't like it, my lord.
Leaving the tent to get some water for him—
Ah, between fortune and calamity
There isn't time for a sip of water—I loved him well.
And now, returning to his tent
I must regretfully betray him. For you see
You won't catch him without me, for I
Alone have access to his heart. Besides
You wouldn't know him, Madam, nor would his mother
Nor his innocent son;

For time and life have changed him very much.

MORTIMER

Good. Bring him to us!

BALDOCK

The Bible tells us how it's done.
When your men come in with manacles and straps
I'll go to him and say: Dear lord
Calm yourself, Sire, here's a towel for you.
The man I give the towel to will be he.

NEAR HARWICH

KENT (*alone*)

He fled at the first gust of wind. He's sick.
Why was I so unbrotherly as to take
Up arms against you? Sitting in your tent
On their honeymoon, that tainted pair
Is plotting against your life. God rain down vengeance
On my accursed head.
As sure as water will not flow uphill
Injustice won't endure. But justice will.

The arrest of King Edward in the flour loft of the
Abbey of Neath (October 19, 1324).

ABBEY OF NEATH

Edward, Spencer, the Bishop.

BISHOP

My lord, don't be distrustful or afraid.
Forget you wronged me. That was long ago.
The times have greatly changed; in storms like this
What are you and I but pilgrims to
Our Lady of Shipwreck?

EDWARD

Father, the heart of any man would falter
Pierced by the sight of what my flesh has come to.
Indeed, the times have changed.

BISHOP

Since you prefer to hide from hostile eyes
Here in this flour loft, take at least this pillow.

EDWARD

No need of pillows, Bishop. Leave the soldier
His cot.
(*Enter Baldock*)
Who's there?

BALDOCK

King Edward's Baldock.

EDWARD

Our only friend. What comfort to a hunted man
When a brother seeks him out in his hiding place.

Share Our water, eat Our bread and salt.

BALDOCK

The moon has changed three times since last I saw you
In the camp at Harwich.

SPENCER

What's new in London?

BALDOCK

They say that everything is topsy-turvy.

EDWARD

Come, Spencer. Baldock, come. Sit down with me
Test the philosophy you sucked
From those breasts of illustrious wisdom
Plato and Aristotle. Ah, Spencer
Since words are crude and only stand between
Heart and heart, and understanding fails us
There's nothing left amid such deafness but bodily
Contact between men. And even that is very
Little. All is vanity.
(*Enter a monk*)

MONK

Father, another ship has put into the harbor.

BISHOP

When?

MONK

A few minutes ago.

EDWARD

What are you talking about?

BISHOP

Nothing, Sire.
(*To Spencer*)
Did anyone see you come here?

SPENCER

No one.

BISHOP

Are you expecting someone else?

SPENCER

No, no one.

MONK

The ship has docked.

BALDOCK

> Tell me, King Edward, why, when Roger Mortimer
> Was in your hands, on Killingworth Day
> You chose to spare him?
> (*Edward is silent*)
> Today you'd have had a fair wind for Ireland.
> In Ireland, you'd be safe.

SPENCER

> First the wind left us in the lurch, then nearly
> Drowned us.

EDWARD

> Mortimer! Why speak of Mortimer?
> A bloody man. Oh, Bishop, I'm tired of suffering
> And violence. Let me rest my head in your lap.
> I wish I might never open my eyes again.

BALDOCK

> What's that sound?

SPENCER

> Nothing. The snowstorm.

BALDOCK

> I thought it was the crowing of a cock.
> I must have been mistaken.

SPENCER

> Open your eyes, my lord! Baldock, this drowsiness
> Is a bad sign. We are betrayed already.
> (*Enter Rice ap Howell with soldiers*)

SOLDIER

> I'll wager all of Wales it's them.

BALDOCK (*to himself*)

> See how he sits there hoping to escape
> Unseen from murderous hands
> As if protected by a screen of flies.

RICE AP HOWELL

> In the name of England. Which of you is the King?

SPENCER

> There's no king here.

BALDOCK (*goes to Edward*)

> Here, take this towel, my lord.
> Your forehead's bathed in sweat.

RICE AP HOWELL
Take him. It's this one.
(*Edward is led out by soldiers. He looks at Baldock*)
BALDOCK (*in tears*)
My mother in Ireland wants bread to eat.
Forgive me, my lord.

Imprisoned in Shrewsbury Castle, King Edward refuses to abdicate.

SHREWSBURY

The Bishop of Coventry, now Archbishop of Winchester, and Rice ap Howell.

BISHOP
    After succeeding to his father Edward
    He had his happy day with a man
    Named Gaveston
    Who baptized me in slops
    In a dark lane behind Westminster Abbey.
    Then, by reason of a blunder, he swore
    An insane oath and turned into a tiger.
    A little later, with many others, the Queen
    Who for a time had dearly loved him, forsook him.
    We met again a few years later. Shipwrecked
    Tainted with vice and blood, he was entrusted
    To my protection at the Abbey of Neath.
    Today I am Archbishop of Winchester
    Successor to a man whom he beheaded
    And I have been commissioned to demand
    His crown from him.
RICE AP HOWELL
    He has refused all food and drink since he
    Was taken captive. Mind how you speak to him.
    Appeal not to his mind, appeal to his heart.
BISHOP
    When from my lips you hear these words: "By your

Leave, Sire, I will recite the formula"—
Come close with several others to witness
Edward the Second's abdication. For
I mean to draw it from him like a
Bad tooth, unnoticed and therefore without pain.
(*Enter Edward*)

RICE AP HOWELL
He's always talking. Listen and say nothing.
Talking is better than thinking. Bear in mind
That he warms himself with words. You see, he's chilled.
Will you not eat, my lord? Why do you refuse
To eat?
(*Edward is silent. Rice ap Howell goes out*)

EDWARD
The wounded stag
Runs to an herb that closes up his wounds.
But when a tiger's flesh is pierced, he tears
Himself with savage claws.
Often it seems to me that all is change.
But then when I remember I'm a king
It seems to me I should avenge myself
For the wrong that Anne and Mortimer have done me
Though once our power's gone, we kings are no
More than sharp shadows on a sunny day.
Indeed, I think that much is vanity.
The barons rule, and still I'm called the King
And my unfaithful Queen—who once repelled me
With her doglike devotion, and has proved
So base that love, instead of being a natural
Growth like her hair, is a mere thing, changing
Amid change—is sullying my marriage bed
While trouble stands beside me at my elbow
And misery holds me and I bleed
To death from so much sudden change.
But then I say to myself, if only I
Could have a roof above me!

BISHOP
The Lord paints those He loves with grief and pallor.
Would it please Your Majesty to unburden
Your heart to me?

EDWARD

I extorted taxes from the fishermen
Of Yarmouth when they were starving.

BISHOP

What else weighs on your heart?

EDWARD

All through the torrid August of thirteen fifteen
I kept my Queen in London. Out of caprice.

BISHOP

What else weighs on your heart?

EDWARD

I spared Roger Mortimer. Out of perversity.

BISHOP

What else weighs on your heart?

EDWARD

I whipped my dog Truly till he bled. Out of pride.

BISHOP

What else weighs on your heart?

EDWARD

Nothing.

BISHOP

Not unnatural vice? Or murder?

EDWARD

Nothing.
Oh savage misery of man's condition!
Tell me, Father, must I give up the crown
And make the evil Mortimer a king?

BISHOP

You are mistaken, Sire. You are being asked
Most deferentially to cede the crown
To young Prince Edward.

EDWARD

Nevertheless it is for Mortimer
And not for Edward, who's only a poor lamb
Between two wolves, who will be at his throat
Before you know it.

BISHOP

God will protect the child in London
And many say your abdication would be
Good for your son—and for you too.

EDWARD
>   Why do they tell a man such lies when he's
>   So weak he can hardly keep his lids from drooping?
>   Never mind my weakness. Out with it. You're doing this
>   Because you want England's royal vine to perish
>   And Edward's name to be missing from the chronicles.

BISHOP
>   My lord, you must have suffered cruelly these
>   Last years to be so stubbornly obsessed
>   With human baseness. Now that you have opened
>   Your heart to me, my son, come rest your head
>   In my lap again and listen to me. Edward
>   (*Edward lays his head in the Bishop's lap*)
>   Put off your crown. Your heart will be relieved.

EDWARD (*takes off his crown. Then*)
>   Let me just wear it one more day. Stay with
>   Me until nightfall. I will fast
>   And cry: O sun! Keep shining
>   Don't let the black moon seize upon this England!
>   O ebb and flow, stand still upon the shore!
>   Stand still, O moon, and all the seasons, stand!
>   And let me remain king of this fair England!
>   For a day like this is so quickly done.
>   (*He puts the crown on again*)
>   Inhuman creatures, nursed on tiger's milk
>   Are lusting for the downfall of their king.
>   Beasts in Westminster Abbey, look this way!
>   I cannot get it off, my hair comes with it
>   They have grown together. Oh, it has been
>   So light a burden to me all these years
>   No heavier than the crown of a maple tree
>   Gentle and always very light to bear.
>   And now thin blood and scraps of skin, the black
>   Blood of Edward, the Weakling, the Poor, the Prey
>   Of Tigers, will stick to it forever.

BISHOP
>   Calm yourself. All that's green discharge from
>   A tortured body, delusion, the howling of the
>   Wind on a rainy night. Now bare your breast.

I lay my hand upon your heart. It beats
More quietly, because my hand is real.

EDWARD

If it and all this were reality
The earth would open and engulf us both.
But since it doesn't open, and consequently
All this is dream, illusion, unrelated
To normal everyday reality
I will take off my crown . . .

BISHOP

Yes! Tear it off! It's not your flesh!

EDWARD

Certain that this cannot be real, because
I'm bound to wake up in Westminster Castle
In London, after thirteen years of war
That ended well.
I, according to the Carnarvon baptismal records
Edward King of England, son of Edward Longshanks.

BISHOP

You're sweating, Sire. You must eat. I'll
Remove it from your sight! But quickly now!

EDWARD

Must we hurry? Here, take it. Grab it!
But better hold it in a cloth. It's wet.
Quick! Quick! It's almost nightfall. Go! Tell them
How Edward in Shrewsbury was disinclined to eat
Snowstorms with wolves and changed his crown for shelter
In winter, which was not far off.

BISHOP

By your leave then, I will recite
The formula: I Thomas
Archbishop of Winchester, ask you
Edward of England, second of that name
Son of Edward Longshanks: Do you agree
To abdicate the crown and to renounce
All right and claim thereto?
(*Rice ap Howell and others have entered*)

EDWARD

No! No! No! You liars! You thieves! Can you measure

The ocean with your little measuring cup?
Have I gone too near the brink? Have I said
Too much? Have you come this time without a storm?
Have you changed your clothes again, Bishop?
Winchester, years ago I had one face
Of yours cut off, but faces of that kind
Have an annoying way of multiplying—
Like fleas, as a certain Mortimer once put it.
Or can it be that when I washed you in
The gutter, you lost your face, which would explain
Why I didn't see it when I laid my head
In your lap. Yes, Bishop, the things of this earth
Do not endure.

BISHOP

Don't delude yourself! Your hand may be too good
To touch my face, but all the same, believe me
My face is real.

EDWARD

Go quickly! Night is falling. Tell the Peers
Edward will soon be dead. Less haste would be
More seemly. And say he gave you leave
Not to mourn very much when his death knell rings
But bade you kneel and say: He's better off now.
And say: He asked us, because of his madness
Not to believe him if he said anything
That sounded like surrender of the crown.
Three times he answered: "No."

BISHOP

My lord, it shall be as you have said.
For our part, our only motive is concern
For Mother England. After ransacking
London for two whole days to find a man
Who didn't hate you, they found none but me.
And with that, Sire, we will take our leave.
(*Goes out with the others, except Rice ap Howell*)

EDWARD

Come now, Rice ap Howell, get me some food.
For Edward is now going to eat.
(*He sits down and eats*)

Now that I haven't abdicated, I know
The next thing they bring me will be my death.
(*Enter Berkeley with a letter*)

RICE AP HOWELL
What have you brought us, Berkeley?

EDWARD
We know.
Excuse us for eating, Berkeley.
Come, Berkeley
Plunge your message into my naked heart.

BERKELEY
My lord, do you really think that Berkeley
Would stain his hands with murder?

RICE AP HOWELL
It's an order from Westminster
Relieving me of my charge.

EDWARD
And who is to guard me now? You, Berkeley?

BERKELEY
That is the order.

EDWARD (*taking the letter*)
From Mortimer, whose name is written here.
(*He tears up the letter*)
May his body be torn like this paper.

BERKELEY
We must leave at once for Berkeley, Sire.

EDWARD
Wherever you wish. All places are alike.
And any ground is fit to be buried in.

BERKELEY
Sire, do you think that Berkeley's cruel?

EDWARD
I don't know.

From 1324 to 1326 the captive King Edward is passed from hand to hand.

SHREWSBURY

RICE AP HOWELL (*alone*)
  His condition wrung my heart.
  That is why Berkeley had to
  Drag him away.
  (*Enter Kent*)
KENT
  In London they say the King has abdicated.
RICE AP HOWELL
  Lies.
KENT
  Mortimer says so.
RICE AP HOWELL
  He's lying. Three times, I heard him, the King
  Said no.
KENT
  Where is my brother?
RICE AP HOWELL
  Berkeley took him to his castle two weeks ago.
KENT
  In London they think he's here with you.
RICE AP HOWELL
  Berkeley had orders signed by Mortimer.
KENT
  It's strange that no one's seen the King
  Face to face, and strange that no one's heard him

Speak for himself, and strange that he speaks only
Through Mortimer's mouth.

RICE AP HOWELL

Yes, very strange.

KENT

To Berkeley then I'll ride and sift
Falsehood from truth from Edward's lips.

The Queen laughs at the emptiness of the world.

WESTMINSTER

The Queen, Mortimer, the two Gurney brothers.

MORTIMER
Did Berkeley hand him over willingly?

ELDER GURNEY
No.

ANNE (*aside*)
Here in Westminster, amid these tapestries
It reeks of butchered roosters. In the Scottish air
Your step was lighter.

MORTIMER (*speaking with the Gurneys*)
You see, this Berkeley was a man with milk
In his bones, and tears came easy to him.
He couldn't even watch somebody having
A tooth pulled without fainting on you. May the earth
Rest lightly on him. You're not that kind?

ELDER GURNEY
Oh, no, my lord, we're not like that.

ANNE
Business! Business! The smell of too much
History within the walls of
Westminster. Won't the skin of your hands
Peel in the lye of London? They are the hands
Of a scribe.

MORTIMER
Where is your prisoner?

YOUNGER GURNEY
North-east-west-south of Berkeley, my lord.

MORTIMER
You see, there are some people that fresh air
Can't hurt. Tell me, have you some knowledge of
Geography? Could you show England to
A man who didn't know it very well?
Up and down and back and forth?

ELDER GURNEY
You mean to keep him moving?

MORTIMER
Especially in places without people or sunlight.

ELDER GURNEY
Most certainly, my lord, we are your men.

ANNE
Ale! Ale! Jonah sat down and waited
For Nineveh to pass away as promised.
Only God was busy somewhere else and
Nineveh didn't pass away. But I
Have eaten well. I'm full of food, and my
Capacity is greater than when I
Was growing. Tell me, Mortimer, do you
Still remember your metaphysics?

MORTIMER
Of course there are some people
Who talk too freely.

YOUNGER GURNEY
We're not that kind.

MORTIMER
Have you ever read a chronicle?

ELDER GURNEY
No. No.

MORTIMER
Good. You may go.
(*The two Gurneys go out*)
We're holding an old wolf by the ear. If he
Escapes, he'll turn on both of us.

ANNE
Do you sleep badly? Do you see white shapes?

Often? It's bed sheets, Mortimer, that's all.
It's just your stomach.

MORTIMER

If his name is even mentioned, the Commons
Burst into tears.

ANNE

The man you seem to be speaking of is silent.

MORTIMER

Since he's so stubborn and refuses to speak
We must outlie our lie with lies.

ANNE

Business! Business! Here in Westminster the days
Are too slow for my liking. And too many.

MORTIMER

The murder of a spouse comes after parricide
In the catechism.

ANNE

You have an indulgence.

MORTIMER

Anne, with your legs parted and your eyes closed
Grasping at everything, you're insatiable.
You eat in your sleep, and in your sleep you say
Things that will kill me.

ANNE

You think I'm sleeping, then? How will you wake me?

MORTIMER

With the bells of Westminster, and bared fangs.
For in the teeth of those godless Peers
You must crown your son at once.

ANNE

Not my son, I beg you!
Not this child suckled on she-wolf's milk
Dragged on her wanderings through the swamps and hills
Of gloomy Scotland. Not this child
Who has too much night on his eyelids to look up in innocence.
I will not have him
Entangled in your savage net!

MORTIMER

Hoisting a small burden from the

Primeval muck, I, though already my strength is
Failing, cannot help but see the human weeds
That cling to my load. More and more of them
Struggling upwards, I feel new weight
At every step. And clutching the knees
Of the last, another last. Human ropes.
And manning the tackle, drawing all
These human ropes over the pulleys, breathless:
Myself.

ANNE

Name the faces of your human weeds.
My husband Edward? My son Edward?

MORTIMER

You.

ANNE

I often used to fear that the arms with which
I held a man erect might weaken and fail me.
And now that age has mingled the blood of my veins
With weariness, nothing is left but
A crude machine of outstretched arms, an empty
Mechanism of clutching. Roger Mortimer
I am old and tired.

(*Enter young Edward*)

MORTIMER

Hook up your dress, Anne. Don't let your son
Look on that tear-stained flesh.

YOUNG EDWARD

Mother, remove this stranger from Our sight.
We wish to chat with you.

ANNE

Earl Mortimer is your mother's mainstay, child.

YOUNG EDWARD

I wish some news of my father Edward.

ANNE

Child, should your mother let a dangerous
Decision depend on your words, tell me, would
You go to the Tower with her if the color
Of your answer so disposed the dice?

(*Young Edward is silent*)

MORTIMER
Edward, you show a wise reserve.
EDWARD
Mother, you shouldn't drink so much.
(*Anne laughs. Young Edward goes out*)
MORTIMER
Why are you laughing?
(*Anne is silent*)
Let's crown this boy as quickly as we can.
The things we do will have a different look
Once a king's name is signed to them.
ANNE
Whatever has happened, or will happen—
Whether heaven forgives it or not—
I've tasted your blood and will not leave you
Till everything collapses.
Meanwhile, write, sign, give orders
As you see fit. My seal is yours.
(*She laughs*)
MORTIMER
Why are you laughing yet a second time?
ANNE
I'm laughing at the emptiness of the world.

A ROAD

KENT (*alone*)
Berkeley is dead and Edward's disappeared.
And Mortimer, more brazen than ever, is saying in London
That Edward, in Berkeley's hearing, renounced the crown.
And Berkeley's dead and cannot speak. The outlook
For Edward Longshanks's sons is very dim.
A while ago there were signs of brightening. The Commons
Were growing restive, demanding to be told
The truth about the prisoner's whereabouts,
People were speaking of "poor Edward," the Welsh
Were muttering against the butcher Mortimer.

But now it seems that only the crows
And ravens know where Edward is.
And I had hopes my repentance hadn't come too late!
Who's that poor fellow surrounded by pikes and lances?
(*Enter Edward, the two Gurneys, soldiers*)

YOUNGER GURNEY

Heigh! Who's there?

ELDER GURNEY

Keep an eye on him, it's Kent, his brother!

EDWARD

O noble brother, help me, set me free!

ELDER GURNEY

Part them! Quick, take the prisoner away!

KENT

Just let me ask him one little question.

YOUNGER GURNEY

Stop his mouth!

ELDER GURNEY

Push him into the ditch!
(*Edward is taken away*)

KENT (*alone*)

Edward! Did you abdicate? Edward! Edward!
Oh, God!
They're dragging the King of England like a calf.

December 3, 1325: The powerful Earl Roger Mortimer is hard-pressed by the Peers because of the King's disappearance.

WESTMINSTER

Mortimer, the Queen, Bishop, Rice ap Howell.

BISHOP
My lord, a rumor is growing like a cancer
That Edward has not abdicated.

MORTIMER
At Berkeley, in the hearing of Robert Berkeley
The second Edward freely abdicated.

BISHOP
At Shrewsbury, in my hearing, Edward plainly
Shouted: No.

RICE AP HOWELL
And often in my presence.

BISHOP
It would be useful to have Berkeley
Testify under oath, before the Commons how
And in whose presence Edward renounced the crown.

MORTIMER
I've just had news about Lord Berkeley.
He's on his way to London now.

RICE AP HOWELL
And where's the King?

MORTIMER
At Berkeley. Where else would he be?

Too much knowledge, Rice ap Howell, spoils
The appetite. Since I gave up reading
And knowledge, I've been sleeping better.
My digestion's better too.

RICE AP HOWELL

But where is Edward?

MORTIMER

I have no knowledge of your Edward, whom
I neither love nor hate nor dream about.
If you have inquiries to make about him, go
To Berkeley, don't come to me! You yourself
Winchester, have been against him.

BISHOP

The Church has favored whom God favored.

MORTIMER

And whom did God favor?

BISHOP

The winner, Mortimer.

(*Enter Kent with young Edward*)

KENT

They say my brother is no longer
In Shrewsbury.

MORTIMER

Your brother is at Berkeley, Edmund.

KENT

They say he's not at Berkeley either.

MORTIMER

Since Harwich, rumors have been growing
Like mushrooms in the rain.

ANNE

Come to your mother, child.

MORTIMER

How is my honored Lord of Kent?

KENT

Well, Lord Mortimer. And you, my lady?

ANNE

Well, Kent. These are good times for me, and I'm
Quite satisfied. Last week I went
Fishing in Tynemouth.

MORTIMER
   There was a time when lots of fishing in Tynemouth
   Would have been highly beneficial to
   A certain man.
ANNE
   Come, Kent, and fish with me next week in Tynemouth.
MORTIMER (*aside*)
   You eat too much, Anne, and you don't chew.
ANNE
   I eat and drink and love with you.
BISHOP
 ˙ What were you saying about Berkeley, my lord?
MORTIMER (*to Kent*)
   You have been missed in London these last three weeks.
KENT
   I've been riding through this ravaged country
   Attentive to traces of my brother's passage.
YOUNG EDWARD
   Mother, don't tell me to take the crown.
   I won't.
ANNE
   You should be glad. The Peers demand it.
MORTIMER
   All London wants it.
YOUNG EDWARD
   Just let me talk with my father first.
   Then I'll do it.
KENT
   Well spoken, Ned.
ANNE
   Brother, you know that is not possible.
YOUNG EDWARD
   Is he dead?
KENT
   They're saying all sorts of things in London.
   Mortimer, you must know.
MORTIMER
   Must I? In Little Street, in broad daylight
   Five sharks were seen entering a tavern.

They had some ale, then, slightly tipsy
Knelt in Westminster Abbey.
(*Laughter*)

KENT

They must have prayed for Berkeley's soul.

MORTIMER

Inconstant Edmund! Now you wish him well?
You who were the cause of his arrest?

KENT

The more cause now to make amends.

YOUNG EDWARD

Very true!

KENT

Take my advice, Ned, don't let them persuade you
To take the crown from your father's head.

YOUNG EDWARD

I don't wish to.

RICE AP HOWELL

Nor would he wish you to, Edward.

MORTIMER (*picks up young Edward and carries him to the
Queen*)

My lady, will you kindly tell your son
That England tolerates no oppostion.

YOUNG EDWARD

Help, Uncle Kent! Mortimer's going to hurt me.

KENT

You keep your hand off England's royal blood!

BISHOP

Do you really mean to crown him in all this confusion?

MORTIMER

In accordance with the law.

RICE AP HOWELL

In accordance with your wishes.

BISHOP

In the name of the law, I ask you then
In the presence of his son, wife, brother:
Has he abdicated?

MORTIMER

Yes.

BISHOP
Your witness?

MORTIMER
Robert Berkeley.

KENT
Who is dead.

RICE AP HOWELL
Berkeley's dead?

KENT
Has been for seven days.

RICE AP HOWELL
Didn't you say that you had news today
That he was on his way to London?

BISHOP
Mortimer, since your witness passed away
Some seven days ago—or was it two?—
I'll ride with your permission to Berkeley
And ascertain the truth.

KENT
In Berkeley you'll find blood upon the floor
You will not find the King.

RICE AP HOWELL
Didn't you say the King was at Berkeley?

MORTIMER
I thought so. We've been pressed for time.
The revels in Wales have been keeping us busy.
In due time, once we get a breathing spell
These things will clear up of their own accord.

BISHOP
Then your first witness, Berkeley, cannot speak
And your second witness, Edward, has disappeared?

MORTIMER
Even if I have to search the whole of England
I'll track that witness down.

KENT
In that case, Mortimer, search your army first.
I saw my brother surrounded by pikes and lances
Being driven down the road by knaves.

BISHOP

Did your brother speak to you?

RICE AP HOWELL

You're pale, my lord.

KENT

His mouth

Was bandaged. But what do you think, Archbishop

That mouth would have testified?

MORTIMER

You say he didn't abdicate? You lie.

I invoke martial law. Off with his head.

YOUNG EDWARD

He is my uncle, my lord. I won't allow it.

MORTIMER

My lord, he is your enemy. I demand it.

KENT

Do you need my head too, butcher Mortimer?

Where is the head of Edward Longshanks's

Elder son?

BISHOP

He's not at Berkeley, and not in Shrewsbury.

Where is he today, Roger Mortimer?

YOUNG EDWARD

Mother, don't let him kill Uncle Kent!

ANNE

Don't turn to me, child! I can't say a word.

KENT

Why ask the murderer where his victim is?

Look in the Thames, look in the Scottish pines

If you want to find the man who had no place

To hide, because his teeth held back that one

Word, Yes, you need so badly.

RICE AP HOWELL

Where is he now, Roger Mortimer?

ARCHBISHOP

Has he abdicated?

MORTIMER

Convene the Commons on the eleventh

Of February. Then Edward will in person
Confirm his abdication. As for me
Reaping suspicion where I sowed gratitude
Ready to submit my heart and every
Hour I've spent in Westminster to God's
Inspection, I give back my trust into
Your hands, my Queen; I will return to my books, my
Only true friends, which many years ago
I exchanged for the horrors of war and the world's disfavor.
But now, before you and the Peers, I
Charge Edmund Kent, the son of Edward Longshanks
With high treason and demand his head.

BISHOP

You're going too far.

MORTIMER

The decision rests with you, my lady.

ANNE

This is my decision:
Edmund Kent, you are banished from London.

KENT (*to Mortimer*)

You will pay me back in full for this.
Kent will be glad to leave Westminster Castle
Where he was born, now taken over by
A lecherous woman and a bull.

ANNE

Earl Mortimer, you still are Lord Protector.

BISHOP

And I will summon the Commons on the eleventh
Of February. Then the naked truth
Will be made patent by poor Edward's mouth.
(*All go out except Mortimer*)

MORTIMER (*alone, admits the two Gurneys*)

You must teach your man to say yes
To every question. Grind it into him.
And be in London on the eleventh.
I leave you a free hand. He must say yes.

After fourteen years of absence, King Edward sees
London again.

NEAR LONDON

Edward, the two Gurneys.

ELDER GURNEY
  Why these dark looks, my lord?
EDWARD
  Always at nightfall, ever since you've been
  With me, you've marched me overland. Where now?
  Don't go so fast. I'm weak because you never
  Give me anything to eat. My hair is falling.
  And the smell of my own body makes my head swim.
YOUNGER GURNEY
  Then you're in good spirits, Sire?
EDWARD
  Yes.
ELDER GURNEY
  We're coming to a big city now.
  Will you be glad to see the Eel?
EDWARD
  Yes.
YOUNGER GURNEY
  Aren't those willows, Sire?
EDWARD
  Yes.
ELDER GURNEY
  The Eel doesn't care for unwashed visitors.
  Here's a gutter. Won't you sit down? We'll shave you.

EDWARD
  Not with gutter water!
YOUNGER GURNEY
  You say you wish to be shaved with gutter water?
  (*They shave him with the gutter water*)
ELDER GURNEY
  The nights are getting shorter.
YOUNGER GURNEY
  Tomorrow's the eleventh of February.
ELDER GURNEY
  Wasn't it a man named Gaveston
  Who brought you to this trouble?
EDWARD
  Yes, I remember that Gaveston very well.
YOUNGER GURNEY
  Hold still!
ELDER GURNEY
  Will you do everything you're told to do?
EDWARD
  Yes. Is this London?
YOUNGER GURNEY
  This is the city of London, Sire.

February 11th, 1326.

Soldiers and mob outside Westminster Castle.

FIRST MAN
> The eleventh of February is going to be a big day in the history of England.

SECOND
> A man could freeze his toes off on a night like this.

THIRD
> And still another seven hours to wait.

SECOND
> I wonder if Ned's inside by now.

FIRST
> They must pass here to enter Parliament.

SECOND
> Look. There's light again in the castle.

THIRD
> Do you think the Eel will bring him round?

FIRST
> I'll bet one silver shilling on the Eel.

SECOND
> And I'll bet two on Ned.

FIRST
> What's your name?

SECOND
> Smith. And yours?

FIRST
> Baldock.

THIRD
> It's bound to snow by morning.

WESTMINSTER

Edward, disguised; the two Gurneys.

ELDER GURNEY
  You'll be seeing the Eel soon. Are you glad?
EDWARD
  Yes. Who's the Eel?
YOUNGER GURNEY
  You'll find out soon enough.
  (The two Gurneys go out. Enter Mortimer)
MORTIMER
  This sweaty marketplace of London has
  Brought things to such a pass that my head
  Depends, as it were, on these few minutes, on
  The Yes or No of this humiliated man.
  He's very weak. I'll draw a Yes
  Out of him like a tooth.
  (He removes Edward's disguise)
EDWARD
  Is this Westminster, and are you the Eel?
MORTIMER
  That's what they call me. It's a harmless beast.
  You must be tired. You'll eat and drink
  And take a bath. Does that appeal to you?
EDWARD
  Yes.
MORTIMER
  And choose a young friend.
  (Edward looks at him)
  You will be carried into Parliament
  And there you will inform the Peers that you
  Have abdicated.
EDWARD
  Come closer, Mortimer.
  You may be seated. But state your business briefly
  For Our health is shaken.

MORTIMER *(aside)*
  He's playing it sharp. Antaeus-like, he draws
  Strength from the soil of Westminster.
  (Aloud)
  Brevity is the salt in watery soup. I'm here
  To discuss your answer to this question. Will
  You abdicate in favor of your son Edward?

EDWARD
  After thirteen years of absence from Westminster
  After long campaigns and the thorny practice of
  Command, the exigencies of the flesh
  Have brought me to a sobering concern
  With the make-up and decay of my own body.

MORTIMER
  I understand you.
  Night marches, disillusionment with human
  Affairs, make a man thoughtful. But tell me now
  After the hardship you speak of, which you have borne
  Patiently, and in view of your enfeebled
  Health, is it still your intention to
  Continue in office?

EDWARD
  Our plans make no provision for it.

MORTIMER
  Then you consent?

EDWARD
  Our plans make no provision for it. The substance
  Of these last days is growing clear. Edward
  Whose end, inevitable but not frightening, is
  Approaching, knows himself. He has no longing
  For death, but relishes the utility
  Of shrinking annihilation. Death is a
  Small price for Edward, who is poor Edward
  No longer, to pay for what pleasure he can
  Gain at the Strangler's expense. Come, Mortimer.
  If that is how things stand, do it yourself!

MORTIMER
  You show a gross preoccupation with
  Yourself, while I who lost all taste for power

Long ago, bear the crunching weight of this
Island, which one plain, everyday word from you
Can save from civil war. I may be blunt
Of feeling, but certain things I know.
Perhaps I wasn't born to be a king
But fair and just I am, or if you prefer
Not even that, but only the
Crude stammering mouth of poor old England
Commanding you, but also begging you
To abdicate.

EDWARD

Don't importune Us with your threadbare claims.
And yet, in this hour of my body's transfiguration
I lust to feel your hands around my throat.

MORTIMER

You're a good fighter. As a connoisseur
Of rhetoric, who has earned the nickname of
The Eel, I value your exquisite taste.
And yet in this dull business, so late at night
I'm obliged to ask you for a succinct answer.
(Edward is silent)
Don't stop your ears! Do you want the heaviness
Of the human tongue, a moment's whim
And ultimately misunderstanding, to plunge
England into the ocean? Speak!
(Edward is silent)
At noon today, before the Commons, will
You abdicate?
(Edward is silent)
Then you won't abdicate?
You refuse?

EDWARD

Though Edward has more complicated things
Than you, busy Mortimer, can dream of
To settle while time races, nevertheless
So long as he remains in this world
He will not presume
To say anything whatever of your affairs
Which strike him as more and more dreary as his distance

From them increases.
And so he cannot answer No or Yes.
From this time on, his lips are motionless.

WESTMINSTER

MORTIMER (*alone*)
   As long as he draws breath, it can come out.
   Since the fierce wind has not torn off
   His foolish mantle, and the smiling sun
   Can't lure it from him, let it rot with him.
   A strip of paper, carefully prepared
   Odorless, proving nothing, will provoke
   The incident.
   Since he won't give me a Yes or No
   I will answer him in the same style.
   "Eduardum occidere nolite timere bonum est."
   I drop the comma, leaving them free to read:
   "To kill Edward fear, not good it is,"
   Or, depending on the state of their innocence
   And the fullness or emptiness of their stomachs
   "To kill Edward fear not, good it is."
   I'll send it as it is, without the comma:
   "To kill Edward fear not good it is."
   And now: beneath Our feet, England
   And above Us God, who's very old. I'll go
   Before the Peers myself, my only witness.
   Lightborn, come in.
   (*Enter Lightborn*)
   If by dawn the prisoner has still learned nothing
   He's beyond saving.

THE CESSPIT OF THE TOWER

The two Gurneys.

ELDER GURNEY
  He hasn't stopped talking once tonight.
YOUNGER GURNEY
  It's hard
  To believe. This king refuses to crack. We've
  Done all we can to wear him down; our drum
  Starts up whenever he tries to sleep, he's standing
  Up to his knees in slime. All the privies in
  The Tower drain into that pit. And he won't say Yes.
ELDER GURNEY
  It is strange, brother. A while ago
  I barely opened the trapdoor to throw
  Him meat, and nearly suffocated from
  The stench.
YOUNGER GURNEY
  He's taking more than we could. And he's singing.
  When you raise the trapdoor, you can hear
  Him singing.
ELDER GURNEY
  Maybe he's making up psalms
  Because spring is coming. Open up.
  We'll ask him again.
ELDER GURNEY
  How about it, Ned? Is it Yes?
YOUNGER GURNEY
  No answer.
  (*Lightborn has entered*)
ELDER GURNEY
  He hasn't cracked yet.
  (*Lightborn hands over his letter*)
YOUNGER GURNEY
  What's this? I can't make head or tail or it.
  "To kill Edward fear not good it is."

ELDER GURNEY
"To kill Edward fear not." That's what it says.
YOUNGER GURNEY
Give the sign.
(*Lightborn gives the sign*)
ELDER GURNEY
There's the key and there's the pit.
Carry out your orders. Is there anything else you need?
LIGHTBORN
A table. A featherbed.
YOUNGER GURNEY
Here's a light for down below.
(*The two Gurneys go out. Lightborn opens the trap*)
EDWARD
This hole they've put me in is the cesspit.
For seven hours now the dung of London
Has dropped on me. But London's foulness
Hardens my limbs. Already they're as hard
As cedar wood. The stench of droppings doubles
My stature. The good sound of the drum
Keeps me awake for all my weakness
So that my death may find me not unconscious
But wide awake.
Who's that? What's that light? What do you want?
LIGHTBORN
To comfort you.
EDWARD
You're going to kill me.
LIGHTBORN
Why is Your Highness so distrustful?
Come out, brother.
EDWARD
Your look says death and nothing else.
LIGHTBORN
I'm not without sins, but not heartless either.
Just come and lie down.
EDWARD
Howell had pity. Berkeley was less kindly
But didn't stain his hand. Old Gurney's heart
Is like a block hewn from the Caucasus.

The younger is still harder. And Mortimer
Who sent you is solid ice.

LIGHTBORN

You haven't slept. You're tired, Sire. Lie
Down on this bed and rest a while.

EDWARD

The rain was good. Not eating made me full. But
The darkness was the best. All
Were irresolute, many were reserved, but
Those who betrayed me were the best. Therefore let
The dark be dark and the unclean unclean.
Praise hunger, praise mistreatment, praise
The darkness.

LIGHTBORN

Sleep, Sire.

EDWARD

There's something buzzing in my ear. It whispers:
If I sleep now, I'll never wake.
It's anticipation that makes me tremble so.
But my eyes won't open. They're stuck.
So tell me what you've come for.

LIGHTBORN

For this.
(*He smothers him*)

WESTMINSTER

MORTIMER (*alone*)

Eleventh day of February, dawn for me.
The rest of them are dwarfs beside me.
They tremble at my name. They wouldn't dare
To implicate me in this death.
Let them come and try.
(*Enter the Queen*)

ANNE

Ah, Mortimer, my son has had report

Of his father's death. Already hailed
As King, he's on his way here, and he knows that
We are the murderers.

MORTIMER

What matter if he knows? He's
Only a child, so frail that a raindrop
Would knock him down.

ANNE

Yet he has gone to Parliament to rouse
The Peers to help him. Peers and populace
Have been waiting since the matins bell to see
The Edward you've been promising them. He's been wringing
His hands and tearing his hair and swearing
To be avenged on both of us.

MORTIMER

Do I
Look like a man who hasn't long to live?

ANNE

Ah, Mortimer, we're going under. Look
He's coming, and they with him!
(*Enter young Edward, Bishop, Rice ap Howell, Peers*)

YOUNG EDWARD

Murderer!

MORTIMER

What are you saying, child?!

YOUNG EDWARD

Don't imagine that your words still frighten me.

ANNE

Edward!

YOUNG EDWARD

Stand aside, Mother!
If you had loved him half as well as I
You couldn't bear his death so patiently.

BISHOP

Why don't you answer My Lord the King?

RICE AP HOWELL

This is the hour
When Edward was to speak to Parliament.

A PEER
And at this hour
King Edward's lips are silent.

MORTIMER
Where is the man who dares
To implicate me in this death?

YOUNG EDWARD
Here.

MORTIMER
Your witness?

YOUNG EDWARD
My father's voice in me.

MORTIMER
Have you no other witnesses?

EDWARD
My witnesses are those who are not here.

BISHOP
The Earl of Kent.

RICE AP HOWELL
Berkeley.

THE PEER
The Gurney brothers.

BISHOP
A man by the name of Lightborn, seen
In the Tower.

ANNE
Enough.

BISHOP
Who was carrying a paper in your writing.
(*The Peers examine the paper*)

RICE AP HOWELL
Yes, it's ambiguous. The comma is missing.

BISHOP
Deliberately.

RICE AP HOWELL
Perhaps. But it doesn't say that anyone
Issued an order to dispatch the King.

YOUNG EDWARD
Ah, Mortimer, you know you killed him.

And so shall you be killed
To show the world that your too guileful guile
Whereby a king died in a cesspit
Was too much guile for God.

MORTIMER

If I understand you right, you are accusing
Me of Edward the Second's murder. Sometimes
The truth becomes implausible, and one
Can never tell which side that buffalo
The State, will roll on. Morality is on
The side where it doesn't roll. The buffalo
Has rolled and come to rest on me. If I
Had proofs, what good would my proofs do me? When
A State decides to call a man a murderer
That man does best to consider himself as such
Even if his hand's as white as Scotland's snow.
Therefore I have nothing to say.

BISHOP

Ignore the wriggling of the Eel.

MORTIMER

Take my seal. France is spewing squadron
On squadron at our island. Our Norman armies
Are rotting. Banish me to Normandy
As governor. Or captain. Or recruiting
Sergeant. Or tax collector. Have you any-
One else who with his naked arm can lash
Armies against the enemy? Send me as a
Soldier while others do the lashing. But don't
Fling me down headlong between dinner and mouthwiping
Because a cub that's lost his jackal father
Is yapping for blood. Do you really think this is
The moment to look into Edward the Second's
Death? Do you want this island, cleansed
Of one murder, to be washed away
In a sea of blood? You need me.
Your silence can be heard as far as Ireland.
Have you got a new language between your teeth
Since yesterday? If your hands aren't stained with blood
It only means they're not stained yet. Dispatching

A man so coldly smacks of morality.

ANNE

For my sake, son, spare Mortimer's life.
(*Young Edward is silent*)
Be silent, then. I never taught you to talk.

MORTIMER

Stand aside, Madam. I would rather die
Than beg a milk-faced boy for my life.

YOUNG EDWARD

Hang him!

MORTIMER

There's a wheel, my boy, and the strumpet Fortune
Runs it. It takes you upward. Upward
And upward. You hold tight. Upward.
Then comes a point, the highest. There you see that
It's not a ladder. It carries you back down.
Because, as we all know, a wheel is round.
Now tell me, when this happens to a man, does
He fall with the wheel, or does he let go? The question's
Amusing. Get the full taste of it!

YOUNG EDWARD

Take him away.
(*Mortimer is led away*)

ANNE

Don't bring the blood of Roger Mortimer on yourself.

YOUNG EDWARD

Those words, Mother, show that you may well
Have brought upon yourself my father's blood.
For you are linked to Mortimer, and I fear
Are under equal suspicion of his death.
We send you to the Tower for questioning.

ANNE

It wasn't with your mother's milk that you
Sucked up your gravelly wit, Edward the Third.
Much traveled, more than most, and not from any
Liking for change, I've always seen injustice
Nourish its own, rewarding every conquest
Of conscience with success. With me
Even wrongdoing comes to grief.

You tell me a man has died today, someone
Of whom your face reminds me dimly.
Great suffering he brought me, and I forgot him
(My way of forgiving him, if you like)
Dismissed his voice, his face entirely.
So much the better for him.
And now his son is sending me to the Tower.
It will be as good as any other place.
You have the excuse that you, a child,
Have looked into such hard and lifeless things.
But what do you know of this world, in which
There is nothing more inhuman than cold
Judgment and righteousness?
(*Anne goes out*)

YOUNG EDWARD
For us it still remains to give
His body a fitting burial.

BISHOP
Thus none of those who in Westminster Abbey
Attended that man's coronation will
Witness his funeral. For Edward the Second
Not knowing, or so it seems, which of his enemies
Remembered him, not knowing what breed of men
Dwelt in the light above his head; not knowing
The color of the leaves, or the season
Or the position of the constellations, died
Forgetful of himself
In misery.   .

YOUNG EDWARD (*as all kneel*)
May God grant them remission in this hour
Lest Our whole line be burdened with their sin.
And may God grant to Us
That Our line shall not have drawn corruption
From Our mother's womb.

The Wedding

Translators: Martin and Rose Kastner

CHARACTERS

THE BRIDE'S FATHER

THE BRIDEGROOM'S MOTHER

THE BRIDE

THE BRIDE'S SISTER

THE BRIDEGROOM

HIS FRIEND

THE WIFE

HER HUSBAND

THE YOUNG MAN

A whitewashed room with a large rectangular table in the middle. Above it a red Japanese lantern. Nine plain roomy armchairs. Along the wall, right, chaise longue; left, a cupboard. In between, French doors hung with portieres. In the rear, left, a small smoking table with two easy chairs. On the left side a door, on the right, a window. The table, chairs, and cupboard are of plain unstained wood. It is evening. The Japanese lantern is lit. The wedding guests are seated around the table, eating.

MOTHER (*bringing in a platter*) Here comes the codfish.
  (*Mutterings of approval*)
FATHER That reminds me of a story.
BRIDE Eat, Father! You always forget to eat.
FATHER First my story. Your late uncle—at my confirmation when he . . . but that's another story—well, we were all of us eating fish when suddenly he gags, those damn bones, you've got to be very careful; anyway, he gags and starts flapping his arms and legs.
MOTHER Take the tail, Jacob.
FATHER Flapping and turning as blue as a carp and knocks over a wineglass and scares everybody out of their wits. We thumped him on the back, gave him a good going over, and he, he threw up all over the table. We couldn't go on with our dinner—we were delighted, we ate it outside later on all by ourselves, after all it was my confirmation—anyhow, all over the table, and when we had him afloat again he said in his deep cheery voice

—he had a fine bass and sang in the choral society, that's another great story, anyhow, he said—

MOTHER   Well, how's the fish? Why doesn't anybody say anything?

FATHER   Delicious! So he said—

MOTHER   You haven't even tasted it!

FATHER   All right, now I'm going to eat. So he said—

MOTHER   Have some more, Jacob.

GROOM   Mother, Father's telling a story.

FATHER   Thank you. Anyway, the codfish, oh yes, he said: Children, I almost choked to death. The food was ruined . . .

(*Laughter*)

GROOM   That's a good one!

YOUNG MAN   He's a wonderful storyteller.

BRIDE'S SISTER   But I don't think I'll eat any more fish.

GROOM   Geese never eat fish. They're vegetarians.

WIFE   I suppose that lamp never got finished?

BRIDE   Ina, you don't use a knife with fish!

HUSBAND   Lamps are in bad taste. It's very nice like this.

SISTER   This is much more romantic.

WIFE   But it leaves us without a lamp.

FRIEND   The light's just right for codfish!

YOUNG MAN (*to sister*)   Do you think so? Are you romantically inclined?

SISTER   Oh, yes. I'm crazy about Heine. He has such an adorable profile.

FATHER   He died of tabes.

YOUNG MAN   Terrible disease!

FATHER   One of old Weber's uncle's brothers had it. It was frightful to hear him talk about it. You couldn't get to sleep afterwards. He told me, for instance . . .

BRIDE   Oh, Father, it's so indecent.

FATHER   What?

BRIDE   Tabes!

MOTHER   How's the fish, Jacob?

WIFE   And tonight we'll all want to sleep. Won't we?

FRIEND (*to groom*)   Prost, old-timer!

GROOM   Prost, everybody!

(*All clink glasses*)

SISTER (*to young man, in a half-whisper*)   At a time like *this?*

YOUNG MAN   Do you think it's out of place? (*They go on whispering*)

WIFE   It smells so good here!

FRIEND   Simply intoxicating!

MOTHER   The groom donated half a bottle of cologne.

YOUNG MAN   Smells marvelous. (*Goes on chatting with the young girl*)

WIFE   Is it true that you made all the furniture yourselves, even the cupboard?

BRIDE   Everything. My husband designed it, made the drawings, bought the lumber, planed it, everything, and then he glued it, simply everything, and it doesn't look bad at all.

FRIEND   It looks splendid. When did you find the time?

GROOM   Evenings, at noon, sometimes at noon, but mostly in the morning.

BRIDE   He got up at five every morning. And worked.

FATHER   It's a fine piece of work. I kept telling them, I'll give you the furniture, too. But he wouldn't hear of it. Just like Johannes Segmüller. He had . . .

BRIDE   He just had to do it all himself. We'll show you the other pieces later.

WIFE   But will it stand up?

BRIDE   It'll outlast us all. We know exactly what went into it. He even made the glue himself.

GROOM   You can't rely on that junk you get in stores.

HUSBAND   It's a great idea. That way it's really part of you. And you take better care of it. (*To wife*) I wish you'd made our things.

WIFE   Naturally me, not you! That's him all over.

HUSBAND   You know I didn't mean it that way.

FATHER   That story about Johannes Segmüller was really funny.

BRIDE   I never see anything funny in your stories!

SISTER   Don't be horrid, Maria!

GROOM   I think he tells them very well.

FRIEND   Splendidly. Especially the way you deliver the punchline.

BRIDE   They're always so long.

GROOM   Nonsense!

FRIEND   They're pithy! Clear! Well rounded!

WIFE   And we have all the time in the world.

MOTHER (*comes in*)   Now comes the dessert.

FATHER   I can make it short. A few words; six, maybe seven sentences, no more . . .

FRIEND   That smells positively ambrosian.

MOTHER   It's pudding with whipped cream.

FRIEND   I'm just about stuffed.

MOTHER   Take *that* piece, Jacob, Go easy on the whipped cream, I'm a bit short. Well, everybody dig in!

SISTER   I'm crazy about whipped cream.

YOUNG MAN   Really?

SISTER   Yes, you have to fill your whole mouth with it. It's like not having any teeth.

GROOM   More cream, Father?

FATHER   Easy, easy! Johannes Segmüller used to say . . .

BRIDE   Mother, the cream is delicious. You must give me the recipe.

GROOM   She'll never be the cook you are, Mother.

MOTHER   It's got three eggs in it.

BRIDE   Naturally if you put in all those ingredients!

SISTER   But you've got to. Otherwise it's no good.

WIFE   Especially the eggs!

FRIEND (*guffaws to the point of gagging*)   Eggs, hahaha, eggs, that's hahaha, rich . . . eggs are rich, marvelous; otherwise, hahaha, otherwise it's no good, hahaha, that's really marvelous . . . hahaha. (*When no one joins in, he stops rather abruptly and starts eating hastily*)

GROOM (*slapping him on the back*)   What's the matter with you?

SISTER   Well, eggs *are* good.

FRIEND (*starts in again*)   Very good! Marvelous! Can't say a word against eggs!

FATHER   Oh yes, eggs. Your late mother once gave me one to take with me on a trip. "Is it hard-boiled?" I ask her. "Hard as a rock," says she. I believe her and pack it up. I'd no sooner . . .

BRIDE   Father, the whipped cream, please!

FATHER   Here. No sooner . . .

WIFE (*mischievously*)   Did you make the bed too?

GROOM Yes, genuine walnut!

BRIDE It looks all right!

SISTER A little wide, I think.

WIFE. That's what happens when you make it yourself.

HUSBAND You haven't even seen it . . .

FATHER I had a very good bed for you. An heirloom. An antique, worth money. And really solid.

FRIEND In those days, they knew how to make things.

YOUNG MAN People were different then.

FATHER Different people, different beds, as Fritz Forst used to say. He was a card. One time he came into church just as the minister . . .

MOTHER (*comes in*) Here comes the pastry! Maria, help me carry the wine.

GROOM To flush it all down.

FATHER Wait a minute, there's a story about toilets I have to tell first. When flush toilets were introduced . . .

GROOM First have some of that wine, Father. It'll keep your tongue moist.

(*Wine is served*)

FRIEND Look at the color of that wine. Superb! And what a bouquet!

MOTHER What are you two kids gabbing about?

SISTER (*starts*) Us? Oh, nothing. He was only saying . . .

HUSBAND (*to young man*) Why do you keep stomping on my toes? Do you think I'm a piano pedal?

YOUNG MAN I'm sorry, I thought . . .

HUSBAND Yes, you thought . . . thinking is all very well—but not with your feet!

MOTHER Pass your glass, Jacob.

WIFE Why don't you drink instead of making clever remarks? Big brain! You usually drink like a fish.

(*Silence*)

FRIEND You were telling us about that heirloom before you were interrupted.

FATHER Oh yes, the bed. Thank you, thank you very much. You know, Maria, more than one member of our family died in that bed.

GROOM Let's drink to the living instead. Prost, Father!

EVERYONE   Prost!

HUSBAND (*standing up*)   My dear friends! As I hold this glass aloft . . .

WIFE   If you must hold something, hold your tongue!

(*Husband sits down*)

FRIEND   Why don't you make your speech? Your charming wife was only joking.

WIFE   He can't take a joke.

HUSBAND   I forget what I was going to say. (*Drinks*)

(*Young man stands*)

WIFE   Psst!

MOTHER   Jacob, button your vest. That's not nice.

(*At this moment church bells begin to ring*)

SISTER   The bells, Mr. Mildner! Now you've got to make a speech!

FRIEND   Listen! Isn't that beautiful! So solemn and holy!

SISTER (*to groom, who is still eating*)   Psst!

BRIDE   Let him finish his food.

YOUNG MAN (*standing very straight*)   When two young people—an innocent maiden and a man who has weathered life's stormy seas—enter into matrimony, they say the angels in heaven rejoice! When the young bride (*Turns to the bride*) looks back at the carefree days of her childhood a gentle sadness may steal over her, for now she is stepping out into life, turbulent life (*Bride sobs*) at the side of a man, who, to be sure, has built a home with his own hands, in this case literally, with a view to sharing his joys and sorrows with his heart's choice. Let us drink, then, to these noble young people, who will belong to each other tonight for the first time (*Wife giggles*) and then for all eternity. And now in their honor let us sing Liszt's "It Is a Wondrous Thing." (*He starts singing, but stops short and sits down when no one joins him. Silence*)

FRIEND (*sotto voce*)   Nobody knows it, but the speech went well.

SISTER   Marvelous! What a speech! Just like a book!

HUSBAND   Page 85, "Speeches for Wedding Receptions." He memorized it word for word.

WIFE   You ought to be ashamed of yourself!

HUSBAND   Me?

WIFE   Yes, you!

FRIEND Excellent wine.

(*The bells have stopped ringing. They all relax*)

FATHER Oh yes, I was going to tell you the story about the bed.

BRIDE We've heard it before!

FATHER About how your Great-Uncle August died?

BRIDE Yes, we have.

GROOM How *did* your Great-Uncle August die?

FATHER That's the last straw. First you ruin my story about the eggs, then the one about toilets, that was a good one, too; then the one about Forst, not to mention the one about Johannes Segmüller, which I admit was a bit too long, but not more than ten minutes or so; anyway, maybe later . . . Well—

MOTHER Fill the glasses, Jacob!

FATHER Uncle August died of dropsy!

HUSBAND Prost!

FATHER Prost! Dropsy. First it was only his foot; well, no, the toes, actually; then up to the knee; then it spread faster than it takes to make babies; then everything turned black. His stomach was all bloated, though they kept draining it . . .

HUSBAND Prost!

FATHER Prost, prost! . . . draining it, but it was too late. Then his heart started acting up, and he went downhill fast. There he was lying in the bed I was going to give you, moaning like an elephant, and looking like one too, I mean his legs! In his last agony, his sister, your grandmother, said to him—it was coming on morning, the room was turning gray, incidentally, I think the curtains are still there, well, she said to him: August, do you want the priest? But he doesn't answer, just looks up at the ceiling, which he'd been doing for the past seven weeks because he couldn't lie on his side any more—then he says: It's mostly my foot. And he groans again. But Mother wouldn't give up; in her opinion it was his soul that mattered; so a little while later she said: Well, August, do you want the priest? Uncle doesn't even listen and Father, who was there too, says: Let him be; he's in pain. Father was the soft one. But she wouldn't let go, on account of his soul; they're a stubborn lot: August, she says again, it's on account of your immortal soul. The way Father told it later, Uncle looked over to his left where they were standing—he had to squint to see them, and says

something which I can't repeat here. It was a bit salty, but then Uncle was a salty man. No, I really can't. But the story . . . I guess I'll have to say it or the story won't make sense. He said: Kiss my . . . well, you know what. After he said that, and as you can imagine it took quite an effort to say it, he died. And that's the gospel truth. We still have the bed up in the attic. Come to think of it, I'll get it ready for you. You can pick it up if you ever want it. (*Drinks*)
(*Silence*)

SISTER   I don't feel like drinking any more.

FRIEND   Don't take it like that. Well, prost! It's a very good story, that's all.

BRIDE (*to groom, whispering*)   Really, he might have spared us that vulgar drivel.

GROOM   Let him have his fun!

YOUNG MAN   I like what you've done with the light.

MOTHER   Jacob, stop cutting your pastry!

FATHER   Couldn't we have a look at your furniture?

BRIDE   Why not?

FRIEND   Very practical, those extra-wide chairs. Room enough for two.

WIFE   The legs are kind of thin!

YOUNG MAN   Thin legs are elegant!

WIFE   Where'd you hear that?

MOTHER   Jacob, can't you eat your pastry without a knife?

WIFE (*gets up, walks around*)   This is the chaise longue . . . it's wide enough, but the upholstery at the head isn't very comfortable. Oh well, as long as it's homemade . . .

BRIDE (*stands up*)   The cupboard is pretty though, isn't it? Look at that inlay! I don't know; some people don't seem to have any feeling for these things. They plunk down their money and pick up a piece of furniture just as if it were—well, a piece of furniture, without any soul or anything, just to have a piece of furniture. These are really *our* things because our sweat and love went into them, and we made them all ourselves.

HUSBAND (*to wife*)   Hey, come over here and sit down!

WIFE   Why? I want to see the inside!

HUSBAND   You don't go looking in other people's cupboards!

WIFE   I just thought . . . but you always know better. Oh, all right.

It's just that from the outside it isn't very impressive. Nobody goes in for inlays any more. Now they make them with glass doors and curtains. But it might be all right on the inside. That's what I wanted to see.

HUSBAND   Never mind, just sit down!

WIFE   Don't take that tone with me! You drank too much again. I'll have to water down your drinks. You can't take it.

GROOM   Do look inside if you'd like to. I'm flattered that you're interested. Here's the key. Maria, open the door!

BRIDE   I don't know if . . . is this the right key? It doesn't turn.

GROOM   Here, you'll just have to learn how to do it. I put the lock in myself. (*He tries key*) Damn! Christ! (*Furious*) Sonofabitch!

BRIDE   See, you can't open it either.

GROOM   I can't understand it. Maybe the lock's broken.

WIFE   Never mind; maybe it's not so hot on the inside either. It must be quite a bother getting the lock open on this cupboard. That's *one* trouble with your cupboard!

HUSBAND   (*threateningly*)   I said sit down! That's enough out of you!

SISTER   No, let's not sit down; let's dance!

YOUNG MAN   Yes, let's! We'll move the table out of the way.

GROOM   Good idea! But what about music?

FRIEND   I can play the guitar. It's out in the hall. (*He goes to get it. Others get up too. Father and husband go to the left and sit down. They smoke. Groom and young man lift table and move it to the right*)

YOUNG MAN   Easy does it!

GROOM   Don't worry. It can take a little rough treatment. (*Bangs it down, bending one leg*) All right, let's dance!

YOUNG MAN   Now you've done it! The leg's broken. You should have put it down more gently.

BRIDE   What's broken?

GROOM   Oh, nothing important! Come on, let's dance!

BRIDE   Why couldn't you be more careful!

WIFE   Think of all the sweat that went into it. But maybe good glue would have been better!

GROOM   What a sharp tongue you have! May I have this dance?

WIFE   Oughtn't you to dance the first one with your wife?

GROOM   Of course. Maria, let's dance!

BRIDE   No, I should like to dance with Mr. Mildner.

SISTER   Who will *I* dance with?

BRIDE (*to husband*)   Aren't you dancing?

HUSBAND   No, my wife would give me an earful.

SISTER   But you've got to. I don't want to be a wallflower.

HUSBAND   It's not really fair when I don't want to. (*Stands up and offers her his arm*)

FRIEND (*sits on chaise longue with guitar*)   I know a waltz. (*Starts to play. Three couples dance: groom with wife; bride with young man; sister with husband*)

WIFE   Faster! Faster! Like a merry-go-round! (*They twirl rather fast, then stop*) That was elegant! Not a bad dancer. (*She plumps down on the chaise longue. A cracking sound is heard. Wife and friend jump up*)

FRIEND   Something cracked.

WIFE   Something must be broken, and it's all my fault!

GROOM   Oh, don't worry; I can fix it.

WIFE   Yes, you know all about furniture. That's the main thing.

BRIDE   I guess it was too fast for you, to make you collapse like that.

WIFE   Yes, that husband of yours really moves!

SISTER   Didn't you enjoy it?

HUSBAND   Today I enjoyed it. Oh yes.

WIFE   You should be more careful, with your heart trouble.

HUSBAND   Are you worried?

WIFE   It's always me that pays for it.

GROOM   Maybe we ought to sit down.

BRIDE (*to friend*)   You play beautifully.

FRIEND   Because I was watching you dance!

GROOM   Don't be silly! Let's all sit down. How did *you* like it?

YOUNG MAN   I loved it, but can't we dance some more?

GROOM   No.

FATHER   Isn't there any more wine? It helps the conversation.

GROOM   Let's put the table back first. (*Young man helps him*) But this time be careful. (*Mother brings the wine. All sit down, pushing the chairs against the wall*)

WIFE   How about a song? I'd love to hear you sing.

FRIEND   I don't sing very well.

GROOM   It doesn't matter. Sing anything, we need some enter-
tainment.
WIFE   My husband sings sometimes. He plays the guitar too.
YOUNG MAN   Come on, play something.
WIFE   Here's the guitar.
HUSBAND   I've forgotten how.
SISTER   Please play!
HUSBAND   Suppose I get stuck . . .
WIFE   You always do.
SISTER   Just one!
HUSBAND   Maybe I remember one.
WIFE   He used to devote all his time to playing. But he gave it
up when we got married. Now he devotes all his time to boring
me. He used to know a lot of songs but he forgot most of them,
and then he'd get stuck halfway through, as if he had amnesia.
He ended up remembering only one song. You can sing it for
us now!
HUSBAND   All right, I will. (*Strums a few chords and begins to sing
briskly*)

Hear ye! the ghost of Liebenau
Had quite a . . .

(*Stops*) Had quite a . . . I don't remember . . . Now I've forgotten
that one too . . . It was my last song . . .
WIFE   Amnesia!
GROOM   Never mind. I can't sing a note.
YOUNG MAN   Then let's have some more dancing.
FRIEND   Yes, let's! Now I'd like to dance too. You must know
some waltz. The A-major chord with the seventh. It's my turn,
Madame Maria.
WIFE   I've had enough.
GROOM   Then let's watch.
FATHER   Maria's a fine dancer.
(*Bride and friend dance*)
HUSBAND (*strumming the guitar*)   A-major. That's it.
FRIEND (*passionately*)   You're a great dancer. Faster.
GROOM   Just don't fall down!
WIFE (*to groom*)   Never catch me dancing like that.
SISTER   *Could* you?

WIFE   Depends on the man.

FRIEND (*stopping*)   It really gets you. Here's your wife. She's an elegant dancer. But now I need a drink.

FATHER   Shouldn't we move back to the table? This way you can't talk at all.

GROOM   Right. Sit down everybody. (*Whispers to bride*) Or would you rather go on dancing?

BRIDE   Now we'll change places. (*To friend*) You sit here! (*To wife*) Would you mind sitting over there? (*Wife takes seat next to groom*) Father, you sit at the head.

GROOM (*opens bottles*)   Now let's drink! Happy days!

YOUNG MAN   In your own home!

FRIEND   Built with your own hands!

FATHER   Prost! You had wine once, Maria, when you were only knee-high to a grasshopper. Your grandfather got a kick out of it. He wanted you to dance, but all you did was fall asleep.

WIFE   In that case you'd better not drink tonight, eh?

HUSBAND   I've never seen anyone dance so well!

FRIEND   Now I'm in good spirits. It was a little stiff before—but wonderful just the same. (*Gets up*) Hey! What was that? (*Looks at chair*) I got stuck on something.

GROOM   Did you hurt yourself?

FRIEND   Just a splinter.

GROOM   No harm done.

FRIEND   Not to the chair, maybe. But these were my best pants.

GROOM   You put them on in my honor?

FRIEND   Yes, but now I'm going to sing.

GROOM   You don't have to if you don't want to.

FRIEND (*picks up guitar*)   I want to.

GROOM   I mean, if you're upset . . .

FRIEND   I'm not upset.

GROOM   About your pants . . .

FRIEND   Consider it payment for the dance.

FATHER   There is such a thing as providence. Forst said so too.

FRIEND (*sings "Ballad of Chastity in Major"*)
Locked fast by their deep desire—
Mine! he thought. His heart beat fast.
Darkness fanned their passion's fire
And she sighed: Alone at last.
Then he kissed her forehead lightly—

She's no slut for hire nightly
Hers is not a purple past.

Oh, sweet game of hands exploring!
She felt faint, weak at the knee!
Make him bold, Lord! they're imploring
Mad with longing, she and he.
Then she kissed his forehead lightly.
She's no slut for hire nightly
Unschooled in love's ways is she.

Since he would not desecrate her
He went out and found a whore.
There he learned to puke, and later
All the body's bawdy lore.
Sweet oblivion entices.
But, though not averse to vices
Now, he vowed, he would stay pure.

Now to quench the roaring fire
He'd unleashed unwittingly
She'd picked a guy to satisfy her—
No shy, shrinking violet, he.
(Spread her on the stairs and banged her
Laughing at propriety.)
And, since she's no blushing virgin
She submits without much urging
Craving more incessantly.

Now they praise all God's creation
Grateful that He heard them pray
"Lead us not into temptation"
On that misty night in May.
He a bigot, she a strumpet
Righteously their vows they trumpet
All that filth just doesn't pay.
(*Wife giggles*)

GROOM   I know that song. It's one of your best. (*To wife*) Like it?
Hold on, I'll get more wine.

FRIEND   Yes, it's a good song. Especially the ending. (*To bride*)
How did you like it?

BRIDE   I'm not sure I understood it.

WIFE   It doesn't apply to you, of course.

FATHER (*uneasy*)   Where can Ina be?

BRIDE   How should I know?

GROOM   Mildner's gone too. Why was he invited anyway?

BRIDE   He's the janitor's son.

GROOM   A common servant.

BRIDE   They must have stepped outside.

FATHER   It's just as well. Then they didn't hear the song. But you'd better take a look, Maria.

WIFE   Maybe *they* understood it!

HUSBAND   Well anyway, your mother's in the kitchen too.

GROOM   Yes, she's making mousse.

BRIDE (*under her breath, to groom*)   That was filthy.

GROOM   After the way you danced with him.

BRIDE   I'm mortified.

FROOM   Because of the dance?

BRIDE   No, because of the people you make friends with! (*Goes out*)

FRIEND   Now I feel really great. After a few drinks I feel like God Almighty.

GROOM   You mean after a few drinks God Almighty feels like a shipping clerk.

FRIEND (*nettled, laughs*)   Very good. You're not usually so clever.

HUSBAND   That calls to mind a joke. One day the good Lord decided to go for a stroll incognito. But he forgot to put on a tie, so they recognized him and threw him in the loony bin.

FRIEND   You didn't tell it right. You missed the point.

FATHER   That was a good one. But Josef Schmidt really landed in a loony bin. It happened like this . . .

(*Bride, sister, young man return*)

SISTER   We were helping Mother with the mousse.

GROOM   That's all right. We're having a good time telling jokes.

YOUNG MAN   That's going to be some mousse.

WIFE   Is it made on the stove?

SISTER   No. *We never* make mousse on the stove.

WIFE   I only thought you'd say mousse was made on the stove because you're both so red in the face! (*Laughing, throws herself into a chair. It cracks*) Oh! (*Leaps up*)

FRIEND Something break?

WIFE I'm afraid that chair . . .

GROOM Nonsense. You could dance on that chair. I used 1¼ -inch dowels.

WIFE I don't dare sit on it. I'll sit on the chaise longue.

SISTER That's where you were before. One of the legs is loose.

FRIEND (*feels around her chair*) There really is something wrong here, and this time it's not a splinter. But you'd better mind your clothes just the same.

GROOM (*walking over*) That's the chair I had trouble with. I ran out of dowels. I didn't realize it was that chair or I'd have asked you to take another one.

BRIDE Then it would have been the *other* chair!

HUSBAND There's a chair available over here.

(*Silence*)

MOTHER Here's the mousse! And the spiced wine!

FRIEND Aaah, spiced wine! (*Stretches*) It was only the arm. And nothing was torn. Let's have a drink. (*The armrest falls off*)

GROOM Now it's getting cozy. Prost!

OTHERS Prost!

GROOM (*to mother*) Your health, Mother!

MOTHER Yes, but don't spill anything on your nice vest. There's a spot on it already.

FATHER Speaking of chairs . . . Rosenberg and Company used to have such low chairs for the customers that when you sat in them your knees were level with your head. It got the customer so demoralized that Rosenberg made a fortune. He bought himself a bigger house and fancier furniture, but he always kept those chairs. He'd point to them lovingly and say, I started out with this simple furniture and I'll never forget it, lest God punish me for my pride.

WIFE I didn't mean to break the chairs. It wasn't my fault.

HUSBAND Nobody said a word.

WIFE That's just it. Now *I'm* to blame.

FRIEND I detect a note of discord. Should I sing something?

GROOM If you're not too tired.

FRIEND Why should I be?

GROOM All that dancing and drinking. You do have stomach trouble.

274   **The Wedding**

FRIEND   I have no stomach trouble.
GROOM   You're always taking bicarbonate.
FRIEND   That doesn't mean I'm sick.
GROOM   I'm just concerned about your health.
FRIEND   Thanks a lot. But I'm not tired.
    (*Pause*)
YOUNG MAN   Did you see that play *Baal*?
HUSBAND   Yes. It's unadulterated filth.
YOUNG MAN   Very powerful, though.
HUSBAND   Powerful filth, then. Even worse than weak filth. Should it be excused just because someone has a talent for it? You shouldn't be seeing that kind of thing.
    (*Silence*)
FATHER   The way those modern writers drag family life into the gutter. When it's the most precious thing we Germans possess.
FRIEND   You said a mouthful.
    (*Pause*)
GROOM   All right, let's have merriment! I don't get married every day. Have a drink and relax. I for one am going to take my jacket off. (*He takes it off*)
    (*Pause*)
FRIEND   Have you got cards? We could play rummy.
GROOM   There are cards in the cupboard.
WIFE   Which doesn't open.
FRIEND   Maybe a chisel would do it.
BRIDE   You can't mean that?
FRIEND   You'll have to open it sooner or later . . .
BRIDE   But not today.
GROOM   To get the cards.
FRIEND (*brutally*)   All right, then tell us what else there is to do around here!
WIFE   We can look at the rest of the furniture.
GROOM   That's an idea. Follow me.
    (*They all stand*)
SISTER   I'd rather stay here.
BRIDE   By yourself? Oh no.
SISTER   Why not?
BRIDE   Because there are limits.
SISTER   Then I'll tell you. I didn't want to get up because the chair's broken.

BRIDE   Why did you break it?

SISTER   It just came apart.

FRIEND (*feels the chair*)   If you're very careful and sit very still nothing will happen.

FATHER   Maybe we should look at the rest of the furniture.

FRIEND (*whispers to wife*)   The table's still in one piece.

GROOM   There's nothing special about the other things.

WIFE   If only they hold up.

GROOM   Come on, Maria.

BRIDE (*remains seated*)   I'll be right there. You go ahead.
  (*They all leave through center door*)

WIFE (*to friend, as they leave*)   The groom's taken off his jacket.

FRIEND   What rudeness. Now anything goes.
  (*Bride sits at the table, sobbing*)

GROOM (*entering*)   I have to get the flashlight. There's something wrong with the wiring.

BRIDE   Why couldn't you let an electrician install it?

GROOM   What's wrong with you? Your sister could have behaved a little better too.

BRIDE   And your friend?

GROOM   That's no way to dance if you want people to respect you.

BRIDE   What about Mildner? That speech about the innocent maiden was no accident! I turned red and everybody noticed. The way he kept staring at me. And then that song that didn't come off. He was getting back at me for something.

GROOM   And then the smutty ballad. He probably figured he could get away with it with someone like you.

BRIDE   He's your friend, remember! And what do you mean, someone like me!

GROOM   How can we get rid of them? All they do is eat, drink, smoke and blabber, and they don't budge! After all, it's our party.

BRIDE   Some party!

GROOM   Don't be like that. As soon as they leave . . .

BRIDE   They've spoiled everything.

GROOM   I wish we were alone. Here they come.

BRIDE   I don't want them to leave! It'll be worse after they go.

GROOM (*putting on jacket hurriedly*)   It's a bit chilly in here.
  (*Others appear in doorway*)

FATHER   We had to wait in the kitchen. The lights in the bedroom didn't work.

FRIEND   I hope we're not intruding?

(*Wife laughs hysterically*)

HUSBAND   What is it now?

WIFE   It's all too funny!

HUSBAND   What's funny?

WIFE   Everything! Just everything! The broken chairs! Their new home! The conversation! (*Laughs uncontrollably*)

BRIDE   Emmi!

WIFE   Everything collapses! (*Sinks laughing into a chair; it collapses*) Even this! Now I'll have to sit on the floor!

FRIEND   (*joining in her laughter*)   Well, I'll be! We should have brought camp chairs.

HUSBAND   (*grabs wife*)   You're out of your mind! The way you carry on, all the furniture will collapse; you can't blame the furniture for that! (*To groom*) I'm sorry.

FRIEND   Let's just sit anywhere. Who cares as long as we have fun.

(*They sit down*)

SISTER   Too bad there was no light. The bed is really beautiful.

WIFE   Yes, the lights don't work either.

BRIDE   Won't you get some more wine, Jacob?

GROOM   It's in the cellar. Give me the key.

BRIDE   Just a moment.

(*Both leave*)

WIFE   There's a peculiar smell in here.

FRIEND   Yes, I didn't notice it before.

SISTER   I don't smell anything.

WIFE   I know—it's the glue!

FRIEND   That's what they did with the cologne I gave them! A whole half-bottle!

WIFE   But there's no denying it now, the glue smell is coming through.

(*Bride returns*)

FATHER   You're a lovely sight standing there in the doorway. You always were a lovely sight, even when you were little. But now you're really blooming.

WIFE   Her dress is well made.

BRIDE   Thank goodness, I don't need any subterfuges.

WIFE   What's that supposed to mean?

BRIDE   If the shoe fits . . .

WIFE   People who live in glass houses shouldn't throw stones.

BRIDE   Who's living in glass houses?

WIFE   Your dress is so well made it completely hides the fact that you're . . .

FRIEND   Prost! That's good wine.

BRIDE (*sobbing*)   That's, that's . . .

HUSBAND   Now what?

GROOM (*returning*)   Here's the wine. What's wrong?

SISTER   No manners!

WIFE   Who has no manners?

FATHER   Come, come, let's all relax. Prost!

GROOM (*to sister*)   You mustn't insult our guests.

SISTER   But it's all right for the guests to insult your wife!

WIFE   I didn't say a word!

HUSBAND   You did! You were rude.

WIFE (*angrily*)   I was only telling the truth!

GROOM   The truth about what?

WIFE   Who do you think you're kidding?

HUSBAND (*bending down*)   I'm warning you.

WIFE   When a woman's pregnant, she's pregnant!
(*Husband wrenches a leg off the table and throws it at wife; hits a vase on the cupboard instead. Wife cries out*)

GROOM (*to sister, angrily*)   That was your vase!

SISTER   Yes, and it couldn't have meant much to you if you stuck it up there!

GROOM   I have no time to answer you because this also happens to be my table. (*Checks to see if it will still stand*)

HUSBAND (*pacing back and forth in agitation*)   Now I've punished her and that makes *me* the bully. That's how it's always been: she's the martyr and I'm the bully. For seven years I've taken it. But who made me this way? I was too worn out from working to support her to be able to hit her. When I'm feeling good, she always has a pain. She counts the pennies when I take a drink, but when I try to keep track of the money she bursts into tears. Once she made me throw out my favorite picture—she didn't like it because it gave me pleasure. Then she hauled it down from the attic and hung it in her room. She was happy when I saw it there. "I suppose it's good enough for me," she said. And she felt sorry for herself for having to make do with my castaways. I got mad and took it back, and then she cried because I'd deprived her of even that little joy. "Not even that," she'd say, speaking of things we simply couldn't afford. That's the way she is; that's the way they all are. From the very first day of marriage you cease to be an animal working for a mistress—you're a human being working for an animal. They make such a mess of you that in the end you deserve everything you get.

(*Pause*)

GROOM (*with an effort*) More wine, anybody? It's only nine o'clock.

FRIEND There are no more chairs.

YOUNG MAN We could dance.

FRIEND I've had enough of that.

GROOM You seemed to be enjoying it before!

FRIEND That was before the splinter.

GROOM Oh! (*Laughs*) Is that why you've been standing around so quietly?

FRIEND It wasn't my chair, was it?

GROOM No, it used to be mine. It's not a chair any more.

FRIEND Then I guess we might as well leave! (*Goes out*)

YOUNG MAN Thanks for everything. It was very nice. But first I must put on my coat.

WIFE You can take me home!

HUSBAND (*had left; returns with wife's things*) Now I must apologize again for having such a wife.

GROOM No need to.

WIFE I'm afraid to go home.

HUSBAND That's *your* revenge. But the party's over now. Back to real life. (*Takes her arm*) Let's go. (*Leaves with wife, who is silent and subdued*)

GROOM Now that they've gorged themselves, they walk off and leave us with the evening only half over.

BRIDE A minute ago you couldn't wait for them to leave! You're so inconsistent! And of course you don't love me either.

FRIEND (*returning with hat on, viciously*)   That stink is more than
I can take.

GROOM   What stink?

FRIEND   That glue that didn't hold. You've got some nerve, inviting people to a dump like this.

GROOM   Then I suppose I should apologize because I didn't like
your filthy song and you broke my chair.

FRIEND   Perhaps you'd better wait for Uncle Dropsy's old bed
after all! Pleasant dreams! (*Leaves*)

GROOM   Go to hell!

FATHER   We'd better go too. We'll talk about the furniture later;
the bed is yours if you want it, of course. I've always thought
it was best to tell stories that have nothing to do with present
company. People can't be left to their own devices. Come
along, Ina.

SISTER   Too bad our lovely evening had to end like this. After all,
it's only once in a lifetime. Then, as Hans says, life takes over.

BRIDE   You certainly did your part. And since when have you
been calling Mr. Mildner "Hans"?

YOUNG MAN   Thanks again. For me it's been a lovely evening.
(*They leave*)

GROOM   Thank God and the devil they've finally gone!

BRIDE   Spreading our disgrace all over town. How mortifying!
Tomorrow everybody will know, and they'll laugh themselves
sick. They'll stand at their windows and laugh as we go by.
They'll look around at us in church and start thinking about the
furniture, the lights that didn't work, the mousse that didn't
quite make it, and worst of all, the bride who was pregnant. And
I was going to say the baby was premature!

GROOM   What about the furniture? And the five months of hard
work? Does that mean nothing to you? Why did they laugh
themselves sick over that smut that they only dared to sing
because you danced with them like it was a whorehouse till our
best chairs were smashed. That was your girl friend!

BRIDE   But your friend did the singing! The hell with your furniture! You didn't even stain it, because you said: "The looks
don't matter as long as it's strong and comfortable"! We waste
five months waiting for you to finish the stuff, until there's no

hiding my condition! Look at that junk! Rickety crap! In that case, what did we get married for?

GROOM   Well, they've all gone home and this is our wedding night. This is it!

(*Pause. He paces back and forth. She stands at the window, right*)

BRIDE   Why did you have to make a mockery of it all by dancing the first dance with that awful woman that I didn't really know until tonight and considered my friend. Oh, the shame of it!

GROOM   Because of what she was saying about the furniture.

BRIDE   And you were trying to change her mind. That makes it better!

(*Pause*)

GROOM   People get nasty whenever you do something they don't do. Especially when it's something they wish they *had* done. Then they get back at you. Of course, not one of them is capable of making a stick of furniture, let alone designing or cutting it. One little flaw, like bad glue, and they all jump on you. Let's forget the whole thing. (*Goes to cupboard and tries to open it*)

BRIDE   They'll never let you forget it. And I'll never forgive you! (*Sobs*)

GROOM   Because of the glue?

BRIDE   God will punish you for making fun of me!

GROOM   He's started already. Damn that lock!—Well, it doesn't matter any more. (*He forces the door. It cracks*)

BRIDE   Just because the lock was broken you didn't have to break the door too!

GROOM   I wanted to get my house jacket, and now you can clean this place up! How much longer do I have to wade around in this pigsty?

(*Bride stands up, starts tidying*)

GROOM (*in house jacket, beside cupboard; counts his money*)   And it certainly cost a pretty penny. We really didn't need to bring up that extra wine.

BRIDE   The table's wobbly. Two of the legs are gone.

GROOM   The food! The spiced wine! And now the repairs!

BRIDE   The chairs, the cupboard, the chaise longue!

GROOM   Those damn bastards!

BRIDE   And *your* furniture!

GROOM   Our own little home!

BRIDE   You know what you've got!

GROOM   And you take better care of it!

BRIDE (*sits down, holding her face in her hand*)   It's so humiliating!

GROOM   Do you have to do the cleaning up in your wedding dress? Now that'll be spoiled too. Look, a wine stain.

BRIDE   You look measly in that jacket. Your face is different too; it looks mean.

GROOM   And you look old when you cry!

BRIDE   Nothing is sacred any more!

GROOM   This is our wedding night!

(*Pause. Then groom goes to the table*)

GROOM   They polished off everything. The tablecloth got more than I did. Empty bottles, but plenty left in the glasses. We'd better start economizing right now.

BRIDE   What do you think you're doing?

GROOM   Finishing the leftover wine . . . look, a full glass!

BRIDE   I'm not in the mood.

GROOM   After all it is our wedding night.

(*Bride takes glass, looks aside, drinks*)

GROOM   Although I can't very well drink to your chastity, since you're five months gone . . .

BRIDE   How low can you get? You've outdone yourself! Whose fault is it? You were after it like a billy goat!

GROOM (*unperturbed*)   Yet now the night is at hand when, under the gaze of our family, within our very own four walls . . . (*Bride laughs bitterly*) we are to multiply! A sacred event, so to speak.

BRIDE   You're some talker!

GROOM   And so I drink to your health, my dear wife, and to a happy life for both of us.

(*They drink*)

BRIDE   Some of those things you said were wrong but it's true that this is a day of celebration and when you celebrate things are apt to get out of hand.

GROOM   It could have been a lot worse.

BRIDE   With that friend of yours!

GROOM   And those relatives of yours!

BRIDE   Do we have to fight all the time?

GROOM   Not on our wedding night.
(*They keep drinking*)
BRIDE   Wedding night! (*Chokes; laughs wildly*) That's a laugh!
Some wedding night!
GROOM   All the same, why not? Prost!
BRIDE   That song was really filthy. (*Giggles*) "And he banged her
. . ." That's a man for you. "Spread her on the stairs . . ."
GROOM (*jumping to his feet*)   And those stories your father told!
BRIDE   And my sister out in the hall! Enough to make you die
laughing!
GROOM   And that broad practically falling on the floor.
BRIDE   And the way they gaped when the cupboard door didn't
open!
GROOM   At least they couldn't see what was inside!
BRIDE   I'm glad they're gone.
GROOM   All it gets you is a racket and a mess.
BRIDE   Two's company.
GROOM   Alone at last.
BRIDE   That jacket looks terrible.
GROOM   So does that dress. (*Rips it down the front*)
BRIDE   Now you've ruined it.
GROOM   It doesn't matter. (*Kisses her*)
BRIDE   You're so wild.
GROOM   And you're adorable. Your white breasts!
BRIDE   Oh, darling . . . you're hurting me . . .
GROOM (*pulls her to the door, opens it; doorknob comes off in his
hand*)   There goes the doorknob! Ha ha ha! That's too much!
(*Throws knob at lantern which goes out and falls to the floor*) Come
on!
BRIDE   But the bed! Ha ha ha!
GROOM   What about it?
BRIDE   It's going to collapse too!
GROOM   Who cares? (*Drags her out. Darkness. Sound of bed collaps-
ing*)

The Beggar,
or the Dead Dog

Translator: Peter Hertz

CHARACTERS

THE EMPEROR
THE BEGGAR
SOLDIERS

A gate. To the right of it squats the beggar, an immense ragged fellow with a white forehead. He has a small hurdy-gurdy that he keeps hidden under his rags. It is early in the morning. A cannon shot is fired. The Emperor enters, escorted by soldiers; his hair is long and reddish, uncovered. He is clothed in purple wool. Bells are ringing.

EMPEROR   Just as I am setting out to celebrate the conquest of my greatest enemy, just as the whole country is mingling my name with black incense, a beggar is sitting at my gate, stinking of misery. Yet in between great events, it is only fitting that I should speak with nothingness. (*The soldiers step back*) Wretch, do you know why the bells are ringing?

BEGGAR   Yes. My dog has died.

EMPEROR   Was that impudence?

BEGGAR   No. It was old age. He held out to the last. Why, I thought, do his legs tremble so? He had rested his forepaws on my chest. We lay that way all night, even when it grew cold. But by dawn he had long been dead, and I rolled him off me. Now I cannot go home, for he is starting to decay, and stinks.

EMPEROR   Why don't you throw him out?

BEGGAR   That's no concern of yours. Your chest is as hollow as a drain hole; you ask foolish questions. Everyone asks foolish questions. Why all this questioning?

EMPEROR   Nevertheless, I shall ask another: Who brings you food? For if no one brought you food, you'd have to go away. Carcasses are not allowed to rot here nor may any scream be heard.

BEGGAR   Am I screaming?

EMPEROR   Now you yourself have asked a question, though there's a mockery in it that I don't understand.

BEGGAR   I don't know, and it concerns me.

EMPEROR   I'm not listening to you. But tell me who brings you food?

BEGGAR   Sometimes there's a boy, begotten by an angel while his mother was picking potatoes.

EMPEROR   Have you no sons?

BEGGAR   They've gone away.

EMPEROR   Like the army of the Emperor Ta Li, that was buried in the desert sand?

BEGGAR   He marched through the desert and his men said: It is too far; go back, Ta Li. And each time he said: This country must be conquered. They marched every day, until their shoes wore out; then their skin went to shreds and they continued on their knees. One day the whirlwind caught a camel alongside the marchers. It died before their eyes. One day they came to an oasis and said: Our home is like this. And then the Emperor's little son fell into a cistern and drowned. They mourned seven days, their grief was inexhaustible. One day they saw their horses die. One day their women were unable to go on. One day the wind and the sand came and the sand covered them and then it was all over and quiet again, and the country was theirs, and I've forgotten its name.

EMPEROR   Where did you hear that? It's all wrong. It was entirely different.

BEGGAR   When he became so strong that I was like a child to him, I crawled away, for I will let no one impose his rule on me.

EMPEROR   What are you talking about?

BEGGAR   Clouds rushed by. Toward midnight stars broke through. Then it grew still.

EMPEROR   Do the clouds make a sound?

BEGGAR   Some died in the filthy huts by the river, which overflowed last week, but they couldn't force their way through.

EMPEROR   You know so much: don't you ever sleep?

BEGGAR   When I lie back on the stones, the child that was born begins to cry. And then the wind begins to blow again.

EMPEROR   Last night the stars were shining bright and clear, no one died by the river, no child was born, there was no wind here.

BEGGAR   Then you must be blind and deaf and ignorant. Or deliberately malicious.

(*Pause*)

EMPEROR   What do you do with yourself? I've never seen you before. Where were you hatched?

BEGGAR   I noticed today that the corn is poor this year, because there's been no rain. A dark, warm wind has been blowing from the fields.

EMPEROR   That is true. The corn is not doing well.

BEGGAR   It was like this thirty-eight years ago. The corn was wilting in the sun, and just before it perished, torrential rains began to fall and rats appeared that ravaged all the other crops. Then they went into the villages and gnawed at the people. That food killed them.

EMPEROR   I know nothing of that. Perhaps you made it up just like the rest. History says nothing of it.

BEGGAR   There is no history.

EMPEROR   And Alexander? And Caesar? And Napoleon?

BEGGAR   Stories! Who is this Napoleon you speak of?

EMPEROR   The man who conquered half the world and was destroyed by overconfidence!

BEGGAR   Only two can believe that. He and the world. It's not true. In reality Napoleon was a man who rowed in a galley and had such a thick head that everyone said: We can't row, because there's too little room for our elbows. When the ship sank because they didn't row, he pumped his head full of air and stayed alive, he alone, and because he was in chains, he had to go on rowing, though from down there he couldn't see where he was going, and all were drowned. Then he shook his head at the world and because it was too heavy, it fell off.

EMPEROR   I've never heard anything so silly. You have greatly disappointed me with that story. At least the others were well told. But tell me what you think of the Emperor?

BEGGAR   There is no Emperor. Only the people believe there is one and only one man believes it's he. Then, when too many war chariots have been built and the drummers have learned to drum, there's a war and they look for an enemy.

EMPEROR   But now the Emperor has defeated his enemy.

BEGGAR   He has killed, not defeated him. One idiot has killed another.

EMPEROR (*laboriously*)   It was a mighty enemy, take my word for it.

BEGGAR   There's a man who puts stones in my rice. That is *my* enemy. He boasted of the strength in his hand. But he died of cancer, and as they were closing the coffin, the lid came down on his hand, and no one noticed, and as they carried the coffin away, his hand stuck out, empty, bare, helpless.

EMPEROR   Don't you ever get bored, lying here like this?

BEGGAR   A while ago some clouds were floating down the sky, endlessly. I watch them. They never stop.

EMPEROR   There are no clouds in the sky. You're raving. That's as clear as the sun.

BEGGAR   There is no sun.

EMPEROR   You may even be dangerous, paranoid, insane.

BEGGAR   It was a good dog, no ordinary dog. He deserves the best. He even brought me meat, and at night he slept in my rags. One day there was a great clamor in the city, everyone had something against me, because I never give anyone anything worth mentioning, and soldiers even came marching up. But the dog drove them off.

EMPEROR   Why are you telling me this?

BEGGAR   Because I think you're stupid.

EMPEROR   What else do you think of me?

BEGGAR   You have a weak voice, so you are timid; you ask too many questions, so you are servile; you try to set traps for me, so you lack confidence even in what is most certain; you don't believe me and yet you listen to me, so you are a weak man; and finally you believe that the whole world revolves around you, whereas there are far more important people, me for example. Moreover, you are blind, deaf, and ignorant. I am not yet acquainted with your other vices.

EMPEROR   It looks bad. Don't you see any virtues in me?

BEGGAR   You talk quietly, so you are humble; you ask a lot of questions, so you are thirsty for knowledge; you test everything, so you are skeptical; you listen to supposed lies, so you are indulgent; you believe that everything revolves around you, so you are no worse than everyone else and your beliefs are no more foolish than theirs. Moreover, you are not confused by too much vision, do not bother with what does not concern you, nor let knowledge prevent you from acting. You know your other virtues better than I or anyone else.

EMPEROR   You are clever.

BEGGAR   All flattery deserves a reward. But I won't pay you now for what you have paid me.

EMPEROR   I reward all services rendered me.

BEGGAR   That goes without saying; the fact that you expect approval shows you have a commonplace soul.

EMPEROR   I bear you no ill will. Is that, too, commonplace?

BEGGAR   Yes. For you can do nothing to injure me.

EMPEROR   I can have you thrown into a dungeon.

BEGGAR   Is it cool there?

EMPEROR   No sun can enter.

BEGGAR   There is no sun. Your memory must be poor.

EMPEROR   I can also have you killed.

BEGGAR   Then it will cease to rain on my head, my vermin will run away, my stomach will calm down, and I shall have the greatest peace I have ever enjoyed.

(*A runner enters and speaks in a soft voice to the Emperor*)

EMPEROR   Say I won't be long. (*Runner goes out*) I'll do nothing of the sort to you. I'll think about what to do.

BEGGAR   You mustn't tell anyone that. Or conclusions will be drawn when we see your deeds.

EMPEROR   I don't believe people despise me.

BEGGAR   Before me they all bow down. But I don't let it affect me. Only the insistent ones annoy me with their chatter and their questions.

EMPEROR   Do I annoy you?

BEGGAR   That is the silliest question you have asked me. You are an impudent fellow! You have no respect for a man's inviolability. You don't know solitude, so you want approval from a stranger like me. You are dependent on the respect of every man.

EMPEROR   I rule the people. That is why they respect me.

BEGGAR   The rein thinks it rules the horse, the beak of the swallow thinks it leads the way, and the crown of a palm tree thinks it draws the tree after it into the sky.

EMPEROR   You are a wicked man. I would have you exterminated, except that I couldn't help thinking I did it out of injured pride. (*Beggar pulls out his hurdy-gurdy and plays. A man goes by quickly, bowing as he does so*)

BEGGAR (*putting his hurdy-gurdy away*)   That man has a wife who steals from him. At night she bends over him to take his money. Sometimes he wakes up and sees her over him. Then he thinks she loves him so much that she can bear it no longer and must look at him. And so he forgives her the little deceits that he discovers.

EMPEROR   Are you at it again? There's not a word of truth in it.

BEGGAR   You may go now. You are growing vulgar.

EMPEROR   This is unbelievable.

(*Beggar plays on his hurdy-gurdy*)

Is the audience over?

BEGGAR   Now they all see the sky more beautiful and the earth more fruitful, because of that bit of music, and they prolong their lives and forgive themselves and their neighbors, because of that bit of melody.

EMPEROR   Tell me at least why you can't bear the sight of me and yet have told me so much?

BEGGAR (*casually*)   Because you were not too proud to listen to my chatter, which I needed only to forget my dead dog.

EMPEROR   I am going now. You have spoiled the most beautiful day of my life. I should not have stopped. Nothing can come of sympathy. The one thing you've got is your courage, that you dare talk to me like this. And for that I have kept everyone waiting! (*He goes out, the soldiers escorting him. The bells ring again*)

BEGGAR (*it becomes apparent that he is blind*)   Now he has gone. It must be morning because the air is so warm. The boy won't come today. There's a celebration in the city. That idiot just now was going there too. Now I shall have to think about my dog again.

He Drives Out A Devil

Translators: Martin and Rose Kastner

CHARACTERS

THE GIRL
THE YOUNG MAN
THE MOTHER
THE FATHER
THE PRIEST

THE WATCHMAN
THE TEACHER
THE MAYOR
FARMERS

One-story farmhouse with a very large red tile roof. There is a bench in front of the house. An evening in August.

1

Young man and girl sitting on bench.

YOUNG MAN Nice evening!
GIRL There's a dance at the Red Bull. Did you hear the music?
YOUNG MAN Yes; they've got two horns.
GIRL Mother won't let me go.
YOUNG MAN Why not?
GIRL She says it's dangerous.
YOUNG MAN Yes, a girl has to be careful.
GIRL Right now you can hear the music even here. That's the wind.
YOUNG MAN Maybe it's going to storm. It was hot today.
GIRL I think the stars will be out soon. Then I'll have to look after the cows.
YOUNG MAN They're lucky.
GIRL Why?
YOUNG MAN Because you look after them.
GIRL Yes, aren't they lucky?
YOUNG MAN You never look after me!
GIRL 'Cause I don't have to.
YOUNG MAN 'Cause you don't want to.
GIRL I don't think it's going to storm.

YOUNG MAN   If it is you'll have to get out of bed.

GIRL   And go to the good room. Where Mother says her prayers.

YOUNG MAN   Instead of praying in bed.

GIRL   Now I've got to look after the cows.

YOUNG MAN   I don't see any stars yet.

GIRL   I can see that.

(*Pause*)

YOUNG MAN   What does that mean?

GIRL   Something.

YOUNG MAN   You have to tell me.

GIRL   I don't have to anything.

YOUNG MAN   Going to tell me?

GIRL   Not if you're so stupid!

YOUNG MAN   I'll make you pay for that.

GIRL   You make me laugh!

YOUNG MAN (*trying to kiss her*)   Let's see you laugh now!

GIRL   You didn't even touch my lips!

YOUNG MAN   That's what you think!

GIRL   Do you think you really kissed me?

YOUNG MAN   You ought to know.

GIRL   Is it too dark for you?

YOUNG MAN   Yes, I'm really scared.

GIRL   Take your arm away. It's bothering me.

YOUNG MAN   It's your arm.

GIRL   I mean *that* one!

YOUNG MAN   You can have it!

GIRL   I'm going to look after the cows now.

YOUNG MAN   Have you got feet too?

GIRL   And then I'll go to bed.

YOUNG MAN   With your feet?

GIRL   Is that supposed to mean something?

YOUNG MAN   What?

GIRL   Those things you say.

YOUNG MAN   Search me. Look, the stars!

GIRL   Do you have to look after the cows too?

YOUNG MAN   I think you're pulling my leg.

GIRL   If I pull your leg, will music come out?

YOUNG MAN   It's too late in the day to figure that one out.

GIRL   I guess I've thrown you off.

YOUNG MAN   Was I ever on?
GIRL   Now you've spoiled it all.
YOUNG MAN   But I didn't say a thing.
GIRL   Do you think that was clever?
YOUNG MAN   Well, then I'll play a different tune.
GIRL   Just in time because here comes Mother.

2

Mother enters.

MOTHER   Good evening, Jake.
YOUNG MAN   Good evening.
MOTHER   Have you looked after the cows?
GIRL   There's plenty of time.
MOTHER   Meaning: you had no time to spare.
GIRL   Why not? (*She gets up*)
YOUNG MAN   We've been talking about the cows the whole time.
MOTHER   Because they were so much on her mind.
YOUNG MAN   She says she's to go look after the cows!
MOTHER   But doesn't budge.
YOUNG MAN   That's the way girls are.
GIRL   You've had so much experience.
YOUNG MAN   Anybody can see that.
MOTHER   You shouldn't be out so late.
GIRL   I worked all day.
YOUNG MAN   She's right about that.
MOTHER   You two sure stick up for each other.
YOUNG MAN   Because she's right.
MOTHER   They'll soon be ringing for prayers.
GIRL   I guess I can stay out till then.
MOTHER   You'll have to be in by then.
YOUNG MAN   Why?
MOTHER   Because it's the right thing.
YOUNG MAN   But it's nicer outside . . .
MOTHER   That's why she's got to come in.
GIRL   Yes, it's dangerous outside.

MOTHER   What would you know about that? Don't talk silly. You know nothing.

YOUNG MAN   But she's right.

MOTHER   What, again?

YOUNG MAN   It's been known to happen.

MOTHER   Nothing happens. Go look after the cows.

GIRL   It's much too early.

MOTHER   What do you mean, much too early? It's almost dark.

YOUNG MAN   But we can still see each other.

MOTHER   You won't be able to see the cows.

GIRL   You can see the donkeys though.

MOTHER   Don't take it amiss, Jake, she is so young.

YOUNG MAN   Yes, that's how they are at that age.

GIRL   You think you're so smart.

FATHER'S VOICE   Wife!

MOTHER   He's hollering for me! Now we really have to go in. Good night, Jake.

YOUNG MAN   Good night. Can't she stay a little longer?

GIRL   No, I'm going.

YOUNG MAN   Just until the stars come out?

MOTHER   Get on with the cows! (*Leaves*)

YOUNG MAN   Why don't you want to stay?

GIRL   Because.

YOUNG MAN   She would have let you.

GIRL   Only because I didn't want to.

YOUNG MAN   Is that why you didn't want to?

GIRL   That's what you think.

YOUNG MAN   I don't think anything.

GIRL   I'm going now.

YOUNG MAN   Or you'll get a licking.

GIRL   You been listening?

YOUNG MAN   Sure, I hear those whacks.

GIRL   You ought to be ashamed of yourself.

YOUNG MAN   No, it's fun.

GIRL   You're disgusting.

YOUNG MAN   You like it, though.

GIRL   Where do you get such ideas?

YOUNG MAN   Why are they always against it?

GIRL   Against what?

YOUNG MAN   Against us being together.
GIRL   Come off it.
YOUNG MAN   Do *you* think it's wrong?
GIRL   Me? No.
YOUNG MAN   See!
GIRL   But my parents do.
YOUNG MAN   Why?
GIRL   Because they don't really know me.
YOUNG MAN   Do you know yourself?
GIRL   Yes. And you too.
YOUNG MAN   You know such nice people.
GIRL   I'm going in now.
YOUNG MAN   Are you tired?
GIRL   Maybe I am.
YOUNG MAN   Then I'll carry you in.
GIRL   You'd collapse.
YOUNG MAN   (*grabs her*)   I would, would I?
GIRL   Stop, suppose they see us.
YOUNG MAN   Sure, they'll see us.
GIRL   Let me go!
YOUNG MAN   First a kiss.
GIRL   My mother!
YOUNG MAN   Won't like it. (*Puts her down*)
GIRL   That wasn't nice.
YOUNG MAN   It was too. You kiss all right.
GIRL   But now I'm going.
YOUNG MAN   So long!
GIRL   Now that you've satisfied your lust.
YOUNG MAN   Do you want me to stay?
GIRL   I didn't say that!
YOUNG MAN   The stars are out now.
GIRL   I'm going to look after the cows.
YOUNG MAN   It's not going to storm tonight.
GIRL   Do you mind?
YOUNG MAN   Yes. There's a crack in your wall.
GIRL   What of it?
YOUNG MAN   Nothing. It's perfect.
GIRL   How you talk!
YOUNG MAN   When there's a storm.

GIRL   Then what?

YOUNG MAN   I can see you.

GIRL   Can't you see me now?

YOUNG MAN   Not in your shift.

GIRL   And you can when there's a storm?

YOUNG MAN   Yes, saying your prayers.

GIRL   Have you peeked?

YOUNG MAN   Wouldn't you like to know?

GIRL   You haven't seen a thing.

YOUNG MAN   Oh no. Except your shift is patched in the upper right-hand corner.

GIRL   That's not true.

YOUNG MAN   Want me to show you?

GIRL   What else do you know?

YOUNG MAN   You sleep above the cowshed, don't you?

GIRL   Did you see that through the crack too?

YOUNG MAN   You haven't slept there long, have you?

GIRL   How do you know?

YOUNG MAN   I've seen worse lookers.

GIRL   Stop talking silly.

YOUNG MAN   Yes, I've seen worse lookers.

GIRL   And you saw them too?

YOUNG MAN   Yes, you're not bad at all.

GIRL   And you're just showing off.

YOUNG MAN   Sure I'm showing off. But you're nicely shaped in front.

GIRL   Phoo, that's dirty.

YOUNG MAN   Is it dirty to be nicely shaped in front and not flat as a pancake?

FATHER (*calls from inside*)   Anna!

(*Girl starts with fright. Young man puts his arm around her. They listen*)

GIRL   Let me go. I was scared.

YOUNG MAN   You might get scared again.

GIRL   I've got to go now. I haven't any more excuses.

YOUNG MAN   Because the stars are out?

GIRL   Yes. And because he's calling.

YOUNG MAN   You won't see the stars if you lay your head down here.

GIRL   But I won't lay my head there.
YOUNG MAN   Why not? Afraid I'll bite you?
GIRL   Just for a minute.
YOUNG MAN   All right.
GIRL   I bet they can see us.
YOUNG MAN   But it's pitch-dark.
GIRL   But you must take your hand away.
YOUNG MAN   Which one?
GIRL   This one and that one. You can't do that.
YOUNG MAN   Sure I can.
GIRL   I've got to go now.
YOUNG MAN   Your body is so soft.
GIRL   You're hurting me.
YOUNG MAN   Can you see me?
GIRL   Only when I look up.
YOUNG MAN   You mean your eyes are shut?
GIRL   Don't!
YOUNG MAN   Does *that* hurt too?
GIRL   Let go of me! Please!
YOUNG MAN   You're so warm.
GIRL   But your hands are cold.
YOUNG MAN   They'll soon be warm.
GIRL   Watch out! (*They jump apart*)
YOUNG MAN   God damn it! (*Steps behind the house*)

3

Father appears.

FATHER   Anna? What's the matter?
GIRL   Is that you, Father?
FATHER   What are you doing out there?
GIRL   Nothing. I've just been sitting here for a spell.
FATHER   Oh, you're sitting here for a spell.
GIRL   Yes, I'm tired.
FATHER   All by yourself?
GIRL   Yes. No one ever comes to see us.

FATHER   Oh, no one ever comes to see us?

GIRL   Do you want me to look after the cows now?

FATHER   Yes, damn it, look after the cows now! (*Hits her*) I'll
teach you to mess around with boys in the middle of the night
and ruin your good name!
(*Girl crying, goes out rear. Father follows her out*)

YOUNG MAN   Well, now she's in for it! Now she'll be ready for the
other thing. (*Goes out. Bells pealing*)

4

Candlelight in the room.

MOTHER (*sticks her head out the window*)   It's a lovely evening. You
can smell Böswald's wheat all the way up here. The wind is
nice. (*While pulling her head back*) A day like this isn't too easy
on a body. I'm glad the night has come. (*Her head disappears.
The light is put out. Cassiopeia is visible over the roof.*)

5

Young man appears with a ladder. He moves quietly.

YOUNG MAN   Lights are out. Here I go. I'll comfort her. It's really
fun when they're bawling. Then they really let go. The old
folks are right. (*He places ladder to the left against the front wall
of the house which is not visible to the audience*) Outside here you
might be spotted. This way nobody has to worry. (*Climbs up.
On top*) Hey, what's wrong?

GIRL'S VOICE   For God's sake! What if they see you?

YOUNG MAN'S VOICE   Then open the window all the way!

GIRL'S VOICE   You can't come in!

YOUNG MAN'S VOICE   Is that what your old man said?

GIRL'S VOICE   Don't be so fresh!

YOUNG MAN'S VOICE   There, they can't see me now!
(*Silence. Wind. And the creaking of a bed*)

6

Father approaches below from right. Listens.

FATHER   Damn nuisance! In the middle of the night! (*Notices ladder*) Well, well! Look at that! (*Takes ladder away*) We'll see about that. (*Fetches a club, returns. Walks off to the right. Sound of footsteps on stairs. Sharp cry followed by commotion*)
FATHER'S VOICE   Open up! God damn it! Dirty bitch!

7

Young man and girl climb onto the roof by the skylight, which they shut from the outside.

YOUNG MAN   Shshsh!
GIRL   He'll kill me!
YOUNG MAN   Shut up!
  (*Pause*)
GIRL   He'll find us.
YOUNG MAN   If you don't shut up!
  (*Sound of a door being smashed*)
GIRL   He's breaking down the door.
YOUNG MAN   Dammit, he'll hear us.
GIRL   Now he's looking for us. Wait, he's going down again. What must he be thinking?
YOUNG MAN   He's going back to bed.
GIRL   He's taken the ladder away. He's not going back to bed.
YOUNG MAN   I guess he's looking for you.
GIRL   Why did I come out here with you?
YOUNG MAN   You could have stayed inside.
GIRL   Nothing would have happened.
YOUNG MAN   Now we're in trouble.
GIRL   Should I go back in?

YOUNG MAN   Won't be much fun by yourself.

GIRL   But if he asks where I was?

YOUNG MAN   In the outhouse!

GIRL   If only I hadn't let you in!

YOUNG MAN   Cut it out! All right, now we're in trouble. But we had fun before.

GIRL   He'll throw me out.

YOUNG MAN   No he won't. It would ruin his reputation. But they'll rib me.

GIRL   You only think of yourself.

YOUNG MAN   If only you hadn't hung your shifts on the clothesline.

GIRL   Then you didn't look through the crack in the wall?

YOUNG MAN   Hadn't you better go in?

GIRL   You want to get rid of me? I'm afraid!

YOUNG MAN   Yes, and out here you can watch the stars. Shhh!

8

Father appears, mumbling to himself. Looks up left front.

FATHER   Anna! If I wake up my wife the whole town will know. Holy Jesus, she must be around somewhere. Why else would he climb in? And I was on the stairs. (*He goes out right, mumbling*)

YOUNG MAN   Now's your chance.

GIRL   I guess my body isn't soft any more?

YOUNG MAN   Better think of getting back inside, or he'll beat you to a pulp.

GIRL   I wish I'd never come up here.

YOUNG MAN   Me too.

(*Girl starts for the skylight*)

YOUNG MAN   Stop, somebody's coming! If you make a sound I'll bash your teeth in!

GIRL   The priest!

9

Priest and night watchman.

PRIEST   Did you see anybody tonight?

WATCHMAN   Nobody so far. You can't see inside the houses, you know.

PRIEST   That's true. That's why they're such hotbeds of lewdness!

WATCHMAN   Yes, they make more babies in there than anywhere else.

PRIEST   It's such a lovely night, I decided to go for a walk. It's much nicer outside. It gets pretty close in the house.

WATCHMAN   I thought it was going to storm tonight, but it cleared up nice.

PRIEST   The wind has chased the clouds away. It's a bright night.

WATCHMAN   It's getting brighter by the minute. It's the stars.

PRIEST   That's Cassiopeia over there! Like a big "W." Can you see it?

WATCHMAN   Yes. It's beautiful.

PRIEST   What are you looking at? It's over there.

WATCHMAN   Father!

PRIEST   Yes.

WATCHMAN   Up there! Somebody's sitting up there.

PRIEST   Where?

WATCHMAN   Up on Frick's roof.

PRIEST   You're right. There are two of them.

WATCHMAN   Let's go up closer. (*They move closer*)

PRIEST   Different sexes! Scandalous!

WATCHMAN   Now I've seen everything.

PRIEST   Now they're even doing it on rooftops.

WATCHMAN   Maybe it was too close for them downstairs.

PRIEST   It's Anna!

WATCHMAN   Maybe they're looking at Cassiopeia too.

PRIEST   Stop joking! This is dreadful. Hey, who is it up there?
(*Silence*)

WATCHMAN   They think we won't see them if they keep still. Or they can't think of anything to say.

PRIEST   But it is Anna. Can't you hear me up there?

TEACHER'S VOICE   What's going on?

PRIEST   Come over here! This is disgraceful!

TEACHER (*appears with the mayor*)   What's got into you? Feel like a game of cards?

PRIEST   Look up on the roof!

TEACHER   Well, I'll be . . . They've got a fine view up there.

MAYOR   Say—that's something! What can they be doing up there?

WATCHMAN   Probably waiting for us. They don't seem to hear us.

PRIEST   Go get Frick.

TEACHER   Let him enjoy the sight, too.

MAYOR   His new weathervane!

WATCHMAN   A stork's nest! (*Knocks*)

PEASANTS (*gathering*)   Good evening, Father. Look, up on Frick's roof!—That's something!—They can't hear anything—They're too high up! (*Laughter*)

FATHER (*comes out of the house*)   What's going on. A fire?
(*Peasants roar with laughter*)

TEACHER   No, there's no fire.

FATHER   What's going on?
(*Laughter*)

MAYOR   Nothing. We're just happy.

FATHER   Damnation! Speak up!
(*Laughter*)

PRIEST   It's a sin the way you conduct your household!

FATHER   I don't know what you're talking about.
(*Laughter*)

WATCHMAN   The devil has taken your daughter!

FATHER   Where in the devil's name is she?

WATCHMAN   He's sitting right beside her on your roof!
(*Roars of laughter*)

Lux in Tenebris

Translators: Martin and Rose Kastner

CHARACTERS

PADUK

MRS. HOGGE

THE REPORTER

THE CHAPLAIN

THE ASSISTANT

PEOPLE

MRS. HOGGE'S GIRLS

A street in the red-light district. On the right and in the background brothels with red glass doors surmounted by red lanterns. The street runs upstage where it turns left at a right angle. On the left a large canvas tent having in front an opening covered with a flap that blows in the breeze. Outside this opening, to the right, a table and chair. At some distance from the tent and surrounding it, a board fence. On the tent a large sign, reading: "Let there be light! Mass education!" A spotlight on the roof of the tent throws a chalky white light on the whole street.

1

Night. Paduk, a red-haired man, is sitting at the table with a cash register. People are buying tickets.

PADUK   Soft chancre: one mark. Gonorrhea: one-sixty. Syphilis: two-fifty. Don't push!

A MAN   When does the lecture start?

PADUK   In three minutes.

A WOMAN   Is it wax models?

PADUK   Here's your change: forty pfennigs. Then you don't want syphilis?

THE WOMAN   Is it wax models, or . . .

PADUK   Wax models and specimens in alcohol.

THE WOMAN   Then I'll take syphilis too.

PADUK   Two-fifty.

A MAN   Gonorrhea.

PADUK   Right. Here you are.

A WOMAN   Syphilis, please. No, just syphilis. That's the scariest, isn't it?

PADUK   Can't have syphilis by itself. Lecture starts with gonorrhea. So it's gonorrhea.

A WOMAN (*standing in line*)   My sister was so upset she couldn't sleep all night.

ANOTHER WOMAN   I thought I might as well have a look. I usually go to the movies on Thursdays.

FIRST WOMAN   The street alone is worth the money.

PADUK   Step up! Have your money ready! Gonorrhea, one mark; soft chancre, one-sixty; syphilis, two-fifty.

A MAN   Gonorrhea.

PADUK   One mark. That's only fifty pfennigs!

THE MAN   That's all I'm paying.

PADUK   Then you don't get in. Next!

THE MAN   We'll see about that. You want me to catch all these terrible diseases because I only have half a mark?

PADUK (*to the next person*)   Syphilis, two-fifty. Right.

THE MAN   You mean I don't get a ticket?

PADUK   No.

THE MAN   What about my health? My wife! My kids!

PADUK   What about my investment! My expenses! My taxes! The lecture! Beat it or I'll call the cops!

(*The man, cursing, goes out right*)

A WOMAN   He's soused to the gills.

SECOND WOMAN   I wonder where he's going.

THIRD WOMAN   Looked as if he'd decided to get even.

FIRST WOMAN   You said it. He's going across the street.

THE MAN (*entering the brothel, right*)   Damn bastards!

PADUK   With half a mark? Fat chance! Gonorrhea, one mark. The lecture is about to start. The rest of you ladies and gentlemen, kindly wait half an hour. We're open all night. (*Gets up and draws curtain. Several people are left standing on the left; they are joined by newcomers. From inside the tent, unintelligible sounds in a steady monotone.*)

2

REPORTER (*to Paduk*)   I'm Schmidt of *The News*. Got a moment
to spare?
PADUK   You're from the press? Of course.
REPORTER   Business seems to be booming.
PADUK   We're sold out.
REPORTER   That's very encouraging. Very encouraging, indeed.
PADUK   I think so too.
REPORTER   I mean because it's for such a worthy cause.
PADUK   You're so right.
REPORTER   What exactly does your exhibit consist of?
PADUK   My exhibit portrays the disastrous effects of venereal
disease. A warning against prostitution which is contaminating
our society. A fervent appeal to the infected to undergo treat-
ment before the poison destroys them body and soul.
REPORTER   Is this an advertisement for some doctor?
PADUK   My dear fellow! I have but one motivation: love for my
fellowmen. Just think of the thousands of sufferers!
(*Reporter writes this down*)
PADUK   The countless victims of prostitution who, in a moment
of weakness, perhaps induced by alcohol, stagger into the arms
of disease-ridden whores.
REPORTER   I see you're an idealist. What made you decide to work
for the good of your fellowmen?
PADUK   For years I have been investigating the vice and corruption of the big city. They destroy the soul and undermine the
body, paving the way for prostitution, liquor and crime.
REPORTER   And crime. You have a marvelous command of the
language. Are you aware of that? You sound as if you'd been
a newspaperman for years. Did you go to college?
PADUK   No, I just finished public school. My poor parents
couldn't afford to train me for a lucrative profession.
REPORTER   That's very well put. Can you tell me something about
your childhood and early development? Your exhibit has
aroused such widespread interest.

PADUK   My life is as clear as daylight. I am a believer in clarity. I am also a self-made man. My father was a small shopkeeper whose drinking brought misery on his family. My mother was bedridden all her life. In a word my childhood was filled with poverty, privation and humiliation.

REPORTER   And so at an early age you acquired a profound understanding of the suffering in our midst?

PADUK   Exactly.

REPORTER   And you found the root of all evil in prostitution?

PADUK   Absolutely.

REPORTER   Is that why you picked this particular street?

PADUK   Obviously. Fight the enemy in his own backyard. The people who frequent these dens of iniquity must be induced to study the consequences of vice right here. I will not rest until the last of these unfortunates has turned his back on these hotbeds of depravity.

REPORTER   It's a pleasure to hear you speak. Is your exhibition only open at night?

PADUK   Yes. For the same reason.

REPORTER   You sacrifice all your evenings?

PADUK   I'm used to it.

REPORTER   May I ask how you came to develop this subtle form of attack? It seems to me that such an idea can spring only from intense hatred.

PADUK   What do you mean?

REPORTER   Was it something you read, or had you some model to inspire you? Was it some experience . . . perhaps a revelation?

PADUK   You might call it a revelation.

REPORTER   Of what kind?

PADUK   It came to me that these people pay money to have their health destroyed. Wouldn't it be far better to give them, in return for their money, at least a chance of preserving their health?

REPORTER   Then it was mainly financial considerations . . .

PADUK   (taken aback)   Not at all. What gave you that idea? It was a question of morality. It's ignorance that drives these poor souls to destruction—ignorance of the danger. We must show them what these pleasure establishments do to them. Then the whorehouses will go broke and the people will be saved.

REPORTER But you do charge admission. Is that for educational reasons?

PADUK Certainly. People only appreciate what they pay for. Here they get syphilis for two-fifty. Over there, it's at least five, not counting drinks.

REPORTER (*snickers*) But then it's the real thing over there.

PADUK This is a very serious subject, sir.

REPORTER Forgive me. And what has been the reaction to your lectures?

PADUK They're sold out every night.

REPORTER I mean, what is the audience reaction?

PADUK Couldn't be better. Some faint, others throw up.

REPORTER Excellent.

PADUK And those places across the street are deserted. Up for rent.

REPORTER How do you know?

PADUK My beam spotlights anyone who goes in. There hasn't been a soul. Besides, you can tell by the piano playing when there's anyone there to be led astray.

REPORTER Then you can actually gauge your success. A most ingenious idea! But didn't you run into difficulties in carrying it out?

PADUK It's the same with anything new. I had trouble with the city, especially since I operate at night.

REPORTER But the city provided the site?

PADUK That's true.

REPORTER And the money was donated by anonymous private philanthropists?

PADUK That's right. But now the lecture's over.

REPORTER I have enough, thank you. You'll see it in the paper tomorrow. *I adore the newspapers!*

PADUK It's been a pleasure. Would you care to attend the next demonstration?

REPORTER Thank you, no. I have a distaste for such things.

PADUK Perhaps, then, you'd like to wait till the next show starts. I make a little speech.

REPORTER I'd most certainly like to hear that, yes. You are an outstanding speaker.

3

People leave the tent and disperse.

MEMBERS OF THE CROWD   I feel sick.—I had to throw up. Good thing they had pails.—I tell you, it's just as revolting as coming out of a cat house.

MAN (*waiting in line*)   Is it worth it?

MAN COMING OUT   Absolutely. Especially the syphilis exhibit. It's great.

A CHAPLAIN (*to Paduk*)   May I introduce myself? I'm Father Benkler, chairman of the Young Catholic Workers' Association. We are considering a visit to your institute.

PADUK   All are welcome here.

CHAPLAIN (*the young workers have lined up behind him*)   May I inquire whether there is a special rate?

PADUK   Not usually. But didn't you say "Young Workers' Association"?

CHAPLAIN   Quite so.

PADUK   Catholic?

CHAPLAIN   Yes, Catholic.

PADUK   In your case we'll make an exception. How many of you are there?

CHAPLAIN   Only half our members are here, unfortunately. Ah, yes. Seventy-three.

PADUK   You can have a whole lecture to yourselves. For you it'll be one hundred marks.

CHAPLAIN   Does that include everything?

PADUK   Certainly. Gonorrhea, soft chancre, and syphilis.

CHAPLAIN   Here you are. A hundred marks.

PADUK   But no singing.

CHAPLAIN   Of course not.

PADUK (*jocularly*)   We wouldn't want to interfere with people's sleep.

CHAPLAIN   But surely there are no dwellings in this district.

PADUK   What about the houses across the way? I'd say they've been sleeping a good deal since I started up.

CHAPLAIN   Oh, I see! Excellent, excellent. No, we won't do any singing.

PADUK   Do recommend me to your friends. (*Takes the young workers inside; comes back out.*) You gentlemen will have to be patient for another fifteen minutes, that's all it will take this time. (*To reporter*) Perhaps you could come by tomorrow night.

REPORTER   Certainly. Thank you. (*Leaves*)

PADUK   (*left alone*)   Things are quieting down. Nobody comes after midnight. And I have to stick around, damn it. All because of that spotlight . . . (*Looks up*) That light is perfect. (*Walks over to fence*) Not a sound. Bankrupt! The bed is dry. The stream's been diverted. And how quiet they are! It'll be a long time before they start playing the piano again.

4

Mrs. Hogge appears in the red door, right.

MRS. HOGGE   Paduk!

PADUK   Huh?

MRS. HOGGE   (*moves out to the street*)   Got a moment?

PADUK   Of course. The lecture's on.

MRS. HOGGE   Business good?

PADUK   Sold out.

MRS. HOGGE   Paduk!

PADUK   *Mr.* Paduk!

MRS. HOGGE   Oh, pardon me. *Mr.* Paduk. I thought we were old friends.

PADUK   (*muttering*)   Not so's I remember.

MRS. HOGGE   An old customer.

PADUK   (*glances over his shoulder*)   What do you want? Haven't you anything to do?

MRS. HOGGE   It's cleaning day. But I wanted to apologize for that little misunderstanding in our house the other day.

PADUK   (*distant*)   Oh, don't bother.

MRS. HOGGE   We treated you badly.

PADUK   You do me too much honor.

MRS HOGGE   In a large organization, these things sometimes happen . . .

PADUK   Is it still so large?

MRS HOGGE   Now you're being sarcastic.

PADUK   I thought I'd be doing you a favor if I cut down your organization a little so you could take better care of your customers.

MRS. HOGGE   But you really didn't have any money.

PADUK   True. So I thought I'd better make some.

MRS. HOGGE   But this is *our* money.

PADUK   But *this* is come by honestly.

MRS. HOGGE   What do you mean, "honestly"? You're taking the bread out of our mouths.

PADUK   You still have the wine, though, all to yourselves.

MRS. HOGGE   What about my poor girls?

PADUK   They're only poor because they're your girls.

MRS. HOGGE   You're very hard on an old woman. I wanted you to know how sorry I was that you were thrown out.

PADUK   I was sorry too. But unlike you, I did something about it.

MRS. HOGGE   You used to be one of our best customers.

PADUK   That didn't prevent you from throwing me out the one time I was broke.

MRS. HOGGE   Now tell me, what's this all about? Showing all these shameful things! As if that would help people to mend their ways!

PADUK   You know very well that isn't the reason. I was only looking for a way to light up the street. To throw some light on your disgraceful business!

MRS. HOGGE   So it's nothing but revenge, just an excuse to put up (*She looks up*) a spotlight. That's why you cooked up the whole shooting match? All on account of the spotlight? The petitions? The philanthropists? The exhibition?

PADUK   That's right. I couldn't very well stand here all by myself holding up a light bulb. All for your benefit. I can't afford it. It was you who called my attention to the fact that a man needs money.

MRS. HOGGE   You're really despicable!

PADUK   You flatter me. I simply had a good idea—a blessing to thousands!

MRS. HOGGE   We know you like a book!

PADUK   Yes, I suppose I did call attention to myself.

MRS. HOGGE   Torturing the girls so they'd come running to me half naked and screaming, never paying, a rowdy, the worst of the lot, a crook, kicked out because of the way he carried on, kicked out of our house.

PADUK   Risen from the dead, straight up to heaven on the third day. Creator of a welfare service! A champion of morality! A capitalist!

MRS. HOGGE   Pig! Scum! Filthy bastard! (*Goes back into brothel, right*)

5

PADUK (*goes back to table*)   Old tart! Ignorant slut! Just because the Young Workers' Association honored *me* with their patronage this time! Pure jealousy!

MAN (*from the left, where he has been waiting in line*)   What was that all about?

PADUK   Any business of yours?

MAN   I'm with the city. It might be interesting to find out just what you were discussing.

PADUK   Only the ravings of a vulgar person; we pioneers of morality expect such abuse.

MAN   All the same I'll have the matter investigated. There's other people's money in this thing! (*Leaves abruptly*)

PADUK (*stares after him*)   Damn his big ears! This could be unpleasant . . . well, there's still my "marvelous command of the language," as that fool put it. And tomorrow the paper will carry my life story. Sure. Complete with heartrending details. Hm. Still, maybe something more could be done to clear up any last doubts about the civic importance of my work!

6

The performance has ended; the young workers stream out.

PADUK (*to chaplain*)   How did you like it?

CHAPLAIN   Excellent . . . that is . . . why, it's hell on earth!

PADUK   So it is. Pure hell. And most of it comes from prostitution. Father, with your permission I'd like to get something off my chest. As you know, when the heart is full . . . (*He disappears into the tent for a moment; returns followed by his assistant, who places two jars filled with formaldehyde on the table. The young workers haven't moved. Those in line move closer, from the left. The street also comes to life as Paduk starts speaking; girls in dark street clothes leave the brothels singly or in groups of two and three. Some creep up to the fence; others stroll across the street, giggling. In the end they all look silently over the fence*)

PADUK   My dear young friends! You have seen the fruits of vice, the dread diseases that result from prostitution. It is no accident that this institution—dedicated to moral uplift—was established in this precise location. It's an expression of solemn protest! (*He notices the girls behind the fence and clambers up on the table, holding up the two jars with specimens in alcohol*) My dear young friends, our quarrel is not with the poor unfortunates who live in those houses, but with the houses themselves; with the very spirit of those houses! I do not condemn these unfortunate young women who spend their lives in slavery, compelled to sell their God-given bodies without collecting a penny! (*Addressing himself more and more to the girls*) Only a brute would do that. They are the victims. They are more wretched than the lowest beast of burden, more wretched than any convict, more wretched than the sick and dying! What about their immortal souls and their rotting bodies? They are forced to submit to every perversion and depravity; and because they must satisfy every bestial lust they become infected with incurable diseases. (*He brandishes the jar in his left hand*) These lips ravaged by disease once sang hymns in church, just as you do.

This head pitted with festering sores was once caressed by a mother's hand. On this breast (*Picks up a wax model*) eroded by pus, a cross once rested, as it does on yours. And when these eyes (*Picks up another wax model*), these drained, wasted eyes first opened, they delighted a parent's heart even as yours did. Never forget that! Think of it when temptation beckons and the devil seduces you. There may still be time; you may be lucky; perhaps it is not too late. Therefore, give thanks. Never forget this! Do not commit fresh injustice. (*Steps down*)

CHAPLAIN   Well said! Spoken like one of God's chosen. My deepest thanks.

PADUK (*holding the jars*)   Please, Father; I was only doing my duty. (*Chaplain presses Paduk's hand, which Paduk must first disengage, then leaves with the young workers*)

PADUK   No more performances tonight. Time to clean up. (*Goes inside*)

7

The people leave; the girls disappear into the houses.

PADUK (*comes out, followed by his assistant*)   Any tips?

ASSISTANT   Yes, a few marks.

PADUK   Hand it over.

ASSISTANT   But it's mine.

PADUK   The hell it is. I pay you a salary.

ASSISTANT   Then you can rattle off your own drivel from now on! It's all yours—stink and all!

PADUK   You're free to leave.

ASSISTANT   O.K. But this time I'm really leaving. This time you're mistaken. It's the end. The money you pay me won't even buy one night's pleasure. And the displays turn my stomach. I'm through.

PADUK   Do you really mean it?

ASSISTANT   Now you've decided to give in. No, sir! Not this time. I'm getting my things. You can look after that crap yourself. (*Throws the money on the table*)

PADUK   Keep the money. I was only joking. Don't get so excited.
ASSISTANT   No, this time I'm through. For good. Besides, I never
get any respect around here. (*Goes inside*)
PADUK   Damn it. Everything's gone wrong. And I've never
spoken so well. Now I know how the apostles felt at Pentecost.
Today His spirit was on me. But like all women, Fortune loves
a fool. (*Sits down*) And now this waiting around. And I'm raven-
ous. But who can keep food down in a place like this. I'm having
nightmares as it is. And the time it'll take to teach a new one
those Latin names! Torture! And that fellow from City Hall.
The ass! The fink! (*Snaps around as though struck by lightning.
Several men stand at the brothel door, right. They have rung the
bell*)
FIRST MAN   Hell, why is the joint closed?
SECOND MAN   As if the light weren't bad enough! That goddam
searchlight!
THIRD MAN   Open up! Gone on strike? (*Door opens; they enter*)
PADUK   What are they doing over there? (*Walks over to the
fence*) The first ones in more than two weeks! (*More men follow
and enter other doors*)

8

*Paduk goes back to the table, shaking his head. Pulls out cash box and
starts counting his money.*

MRS. HOGGE (*emerges from door, right; crosses street and listens. Walks
quietly through gate; stands behind Paduk*)   Satisfied, Mr.
Paduk?
PADUK (*startled, angry*)   What is this! Get out!
MRS. HOGGE   Take it easy, Mr. Paduk. Our customers are begin-
ning to come back.
PADUK   Hm, I haven't heard any music yet!
MRS. HOGGE   We don't play for just anyone. The first ones back
are the five-mark boys. The others'll come later.
PADUK   *You* ought to know.

MRS. HOGGE   See here, Mr. Paduk, how about a chair?

PADUK   Anything else?

MRS. HOGGE   No. You stand to gain by it.

PADUK (*locks the cash box*)   After the way you insulted me not ten minutes ago . . .

MRS. HOGGE   A few things have happened since then. A few, I said.

PADUK   I haven't noticed anything

MRS. HOGGE   First of all, our customers are coming back. That's one for me. Then, there's the speech you made.

PADUK   That's one for me. You've caught on.

MRS. HOGGE   You haven't. You haven't caught on at all. Your speech was rubbish.

PADUK   Rubbish, you say?

MRS. HOGGE   Yes. From our point of view. Not from the chaplain's. But from yours and mine.

PADUK   Not bad. Amusing, in fact. (*Brings a chair*) Here's a chair. Would you care to explain?

MRS. HOGGE   Sure. Thank you. (*Sits down*) The fact is I'm grateful. Besides, I wanted to apologize for that misunderstanding a while ago.

PADUK   You were talking about my speech.

MRS. HOGGE   Now if I caught the gist of your speech, you were saying that we suck the girls' blood. A fine phrase but not entirely true. When you talked so movingly about ravaged lips that once sang in church choirs, you might just as well have mentioned the booze they drank except it would have been less effective. And that bit about the heads caressed by mothers' hands—as often as not they were being battered by the less publicized fists of a pimp. But why go into that? You ought to know. You've been a student of ours long enough. Obviously, we have to show a profit. And normally we do better than you by a long shot.

PADUK   You speak well! It's a pleasure listening to you. But what about my speech being rubbish? That's the part you got the chair for.

MRS. HOGGE   It's not going to make you very happy. I'll give it to you little by little. First let me say a word about your prospects for the future: you're making money now because the novelty hasn't worn off. People flock to your exhibits because they've never seen anything like them unless they've paid the high price of seeing them on their own flesh. But since nobody will come back twice—you can bet your life on that—the party will soon be over. Two weeks after you've folded we'll be back on top. I have about 6,000 customers. We've started a campaign that's already persuaded a great number of them to stay away from your disgusting exhibits, which are in bad taste anyway because they appeal to the worst in people: cowardice and hypocrisy. The rest of them—the ones we can't keep away— are people who enjoy watching you degrade life's greatest joys —the joys of love, including married love. But even those will be back at our establishment two weeks after visiting you. Because of you our income has dropped considerably, but this can happen only once. And visitors to our establishment always come back.

(*Silence*)

PADUK (*sits across from her at his table perspiring heavily*)   None of this has any connection with my speech.

MRS. HOGGE   It does, though. As far as I can see, your business consists in exploiting the diseases brought on by prostitution. That will hurt prostitution as long as you're able to spread your information. Then it's over and we prosper as before. But in your speech you set out to destroy the source of infection— namely prostitution. Which is the very foundation your business is built on—like a house on a rock. In short: I don't care if you enlighten the men about venereal disease. That doesn't affect us in the least. But if you enlighten my girls, you kill prostitution and with it the source of infection—and yourself as well! (*Triumphant, but apprehensive*) That's what you did today when you sent those girls running to me in tears. Now you tell me: was that speech rubbish, or wasn't it?

(*Silence. Paduk breathes heavily. Mrs. Hogge wipes her forehead with her handkerchief*)

PADUK (*trying to sound casual*)   All right. Now what? (*Silence*) Spoken like a scholar.

MRS. HOGGE   I've had the benefit of higher education.

PADUK   All right. I got carried away, just the way you did a while ago. But what now?

MRS. HOGGE (*sigh of relief*)   Now you're talking! And here's my thank-you for the chair: a piece of advice. Close down this joint and invest the money you've made in our place.

PADUK (*rising*)   What do you mean?

MRS. HOGGE   Exactly what I say!

PADUK   What about my reputation? And the city officials who got me the site? And the story in the paper?

MRS. HOGGE   Minor inconveniences! Afterwards—success!

PADUK   I can't do it. Not with my reputation. I've already thought of everything you said. But it won't work.

MRS. HOGGE   What about your reputation? If you keep this up I'll be ruined—and so will you! I won't just sit by while it happens. You're forcing me to tell the world what your motives really are. Then see how far your reputation will get you!

PADUK   That doesn't sound bad! But what about my beautiful scheme! And the way you treated me . . .

MRS. HOGGE   Carmen could treat you that way when you were a nobody without a penny. But now you're part owner you can do whatever you like with her. Have you seen her latest pictures?

PADUK   No, I've been out of touch.

MRS. HOGGE (*pulls photos from her bosom and shows them*)   Here's Carmen, sideways and from the back. Here's Ludmilla—really fetching—full face. In the nude. Those eyes! Those breasts! That mouth! That gorgeous face!

PADUK (*squaring his shoulders*)   All right. I'll inspect your establishment. (*Puts cash box under his arm*) I don't expect anyone else tonight. Besides, Lind is here. Oh, hell . . . Lind, stay another fifteen minutes; I've got some business to attend to.

ASSISTANT'S VOICE (*inside the tent*)   Not another second!

PADUK (*to himself*)   This place is on the down-grade anyhow. (*Walks away, right, behind Mrs. Hogge. Both disappear behind the red door. Inside, a piano begins to play immediately. A girl cries out. Sound of dancing*)
(*It turns dark. Silence*)

9

PADUK (*entering from right, somewhat dishevelled, cash box under his arm*)   Let that damn fool investigate all he likes. I'll give him the information myself. (*Stops at the table*) Lind! Now where are you?

ASSISTANT (*crawling out*)   Mr. Paduk?

PADUK   Have you decided to stay?

ASSISTANT   Only on condition that . . .

PADUK   You can go. You're fired! (*Choking with triumph*) Get out or I'll throw you out! Bloodsucker! Scum! Depraved no-good!

ASSISTANT   You'll pay for that. I'll expose your past!

PADUK   Go right ahead! Tell them I'm the owner of a cat house! Tell them I make a hundred marks a day. Go on, tell everybody who still has something between his legs. Now beat it!

ASSISTANT (*leaves*)   Bastard!

PADUK (*hums the same tune the piano played*)   We could build business (*Climbs on the table and removes sign*) by showing educational films. No problem getting a license for that. Then we'd use our influence in higher circles to put through a law making private intercourse a criminal offense and abortion punishable by death. It would do wonders for business. Well, that's that. It's the ideas that count. (*He removes the sign from the entrance. Looks around, grins*) In two weeks' time business will be back in shape. Today, the first customers started turning up again. (*Switches off the spotlight; strolls humming to the right and disappears behind the red door, carrying the cash box. Piano music and the stomping of dancing feet*)

The Catch

Translators: Martin and Rose Kastner

CHARACTERS

THE FISHERMAN

HIS WIFE

FIRST MAN

SECOND MAN

SIX FISHERMEN

BEGGAR

BEGGARWOMAN

Inside a fisherman's shack. On the left side of the back wall a window hung with cheap muslin drapes; to the right, almost center, a large fourposter with a canopy. To the right of the bed a heavy square wooden door. In the center of the room a huge wooden table; against the left wall, a leather sofa with a fishnet thrown over it.

Night. In the bed, the fisherman's wife tosses in her sleep.

WIFE (*talking in her sleep*) Tom! . . . Tom! . . . Don't, Tom . . . (*She wakes with a start and sits*) Must be way past midnight, and no sign of him . . . Didn't catch a thing all day and now he's out boozing it up . . . Oh . . . (*Lies back*) oah . . . (*Falls asleep*)
(*Silence; then pounding on the door*)

FISHERMAN'S VOICE (*outside*) Hey! Open up!

WIFE (*waking with a start*) Tom! (*Jumps out of bed. Snatching a burning candle, she opens the door; draws back, startled. Two men propping her husband between them enter the shack*)

FISHERMAN (*angry*) How come . . . the door doesn't open . . . when I get home!

WIFE (*throwing something on*) I was asleep.

FISHERMAN Door's always gotta be open, damn it. How's a man supposed to get in?

WIFE But I was sleeping.

FISHERMAN From now on the door stays open! See? (*Makes his way unsteadily to the table*)

FIRST MAN He's had one too many, missus. But we made it all right between the three of us.

WIFE   Is that you, Munken? So he's full as a herring barrel, but *his* barrels are empty.

FISHERMAN   Don't say that. I get my best ideas when I've had a few nips.

WIFE   That'll sure keep our bellies full.

FISHERMAN   When you're drunk you never feel hungry—see?

SECOND MAN   You better hit the sack!

FISHERMAN   He's good and drunk. He'll fall asleep soon as he sits down. Walks as crooked as a yawl in a stiff wester. He'll have some coffee with me.

WIFE   Do I have to get the stove going at this time of night?

FIRST MAN   Not for me.

FISHERMAN   Expect me to wait till morning? Get into that kitchen, and make it hot.

WIFE (*going off, right*)   One of these days I hope you croak on that booze.

FIRST MAN   It's no picnic for her.

FISHERMAN   No picnic for anybody. Christ, I'm sleepy. Woman!

WIFE (*returning*)   Are you hollering again?

FISHERMAN   Wash me!

WIFE   At this time of night?

FISHERMAN   Wa-ash! When I shut my eyes the sky's all rosy-red . . . like in heaven, except I gotta belch.

(*Wife douses his head; he almost dozes off*)

SECOND MAN (*grinning*)   She's fresh out of bed.

FIRST MAN   I can see that.

SECOND MAN   Makes them look like tousled cats.

FIRST MAN   She sure ain't skinny.

SECOND MAN   That dumb bastard.

FISHERMAN   Hell! I left my pipe back there. Get it, woman!

WIFE   In my night-shift?

FIRST MAN   Guess one of us could go back.

SECOND MAN   Guess he could.

FIRST MAN   Want me to go?

SECOND MAN (*to wife*)   You oughtn't to go there at this time of night.

FIRST MAN   It would make their eyes pop!

SECOND MAN   I'll run over.

FIRST MAN   I was just about to go. (*Neither moves*)

WIFE   They'd laugh me out of town.

SECOND MAN   Then one of us'll go.

FIRST MAN   One of us could make it in no time.

SECOND MAN   It's only a little way.

FIRST MAN   No need to go over there in your night-shift on his account.

SECOND MAN   I won't have it.

FIRST MAN   Yeah, he'll scoot right over. We can't let you.

FISHERMAN   But be back in time for the coffee, Jürgen.

SECOND MAN   You bet. (*Leaves reluctantly*)

WIFE   You can wait for the coffee. It's almost boiling.

FIRST MAN   Thanks, but I'm not cold.

WIFE   Do you good just the same.

FIRST MAN   My eyes are all right, too.

WIFE   Then you just better shut them.

FIRST MAN   The light's pretty bad.

WIFE   He's almost asleep.

FIRST MAN   He's really drunk.

WIFE   He's a pig.

FIRST MAN   That's no way for a man to come home.

WIFE   That's the way he always comes home.

FIRST MAN   But you look fine . . .

WIFE   I've only my shift on . . .

FIRST MAN   That doesn't matter.

FISHERMAN   (*starting*) Get a move on! Water's too cold . . . Where's that coffee? . . . What doesn't matter?

WIFE   That the water's cold.

FISHERMAN   Get going! Stupid cow!

WIFE   Jürgen went instead of me.

FIRST MAN   I wanted to stay.

(*Wife laughs, leaves*)

FISHERMAN   Crabbing again 'cause she's got to go out. Treats me like a dog. Lazy as they come. Tramps, the whole lot of them.

FIRST MAN   Better be on my way!

FISHERMAN   Haven't you had enough to drink?

FIRST MAN   I'm dizzy.

FISHERMAN   Sit down!

FIRST MAN   I'd fall asleep.

FISHERMAN   Just can't take it, either of you. Too much tomcatting. Weakens you. Doesn't bother me though. I can stand anything.

FIRST MAN (*goes to right, stands in doorway*)   Must have been nice and warm in that bed?

WIFE   No fun getting up!

FIRST MAN   Half naked.

WIFE   For that old boozer.

FIRST MAN   And those cold tiles in the kitchen!

WIFE   It's a tough life.

FIRST MAN   Under your warm feet.

WIFE   Why are you men always getting soused?

FIRST MAN   I got no wife—that's why I do it.

WIFE   And suppose you had one?

FIRST MAN   Everything would be different.

WIFE   That's what they all say.

FIRST MAN   I'm not like that. And I'm not drunk either.

WIFE   Could you still manage to hold this pan for me?

FIRST MAN   I'm not that drunk. (*Goes into the kitchen*)

FISHERMAN (*raising his head from table*)   Head's like a beehive. Merry-go-round. Goddam candle . . . Munken! He's pissed again. Swills it like water . . . Where did that guy disappear to? Oho! Goshamighty, got to . . . got to sober up. Up you go! Atten-SHUN! Column right! March! (*Goes over to pail, left*) Head . . . DOWN! Dive! (*Plunges head in pail*) Brrrr! (*In the kitchen, a pan clatters to the floor*) Hey! What's goin' on! (*Walks to right and listens, head bent and dripping; then staggers back to left*) Hey, woman!

WIFE (*appearing a bit too promptly*)   Now what? What is it this time?

FISHERMAN   Your apron! Quick! (*Stamps his foot impatiently*)

WIFE   Where have you been putting your head? That was the dirty dishwater.

FISHERMAN   Well, it cleared my head. Apron!

WIFE (*takes an apron from a hook on the wall and wipes him dry*) Munken, mind it doesn't boil over!

FISHERMAN   There, and now get a move on! Coffee! Is it going to take all night? Or won't it boil without a kick in the ass? (*Ties apron around her waist*) Look how she runs around. Want me to get the preacher? Now get going! (*Gives her a kick as she*

goes out to the right; he sits at the table, brooding) It won't boil
over. That guy's stewed to the eyeballs. And that bitch half
naked. I'm falling asleep anyway. Sleep! Whether she gives in
or not. Sleep. When the lights go out, the roaches start crawling. And in my own house! If I kick him out and bolt the door,
the bolt will come open. If I don't let them do it here she'll run
off and do it behind my back. Christ! Goddam tramps! Best to
sleep.

WIFE (*entering with coffee*)   Here. Drink!

FIRST MAN (*behind her*)   Mmm, that hits the spot. (*They drink their
coffee*)

FISHERMAN   Sit down! There! You! Get the net.

WIFE   What do you want with the net?

FISHERMAN (*pounds the table*)   Get it!

FIRST MAN   In the middle of the night?

WIFE (*bringing him the net*)   You're going fishing now?

FISHERMAN   Yeah, fishing—ha ha ha!

WIFE   Didn't catch a thing all day! Boozing, that's all you did!

FISHERMAN (*triumphantly*)   Booze gives me my best ideas. When
I drink I catch fish. Mend that net!

WIFE   At this time of night? (*She starts mending it*)

FISHERMAN (*pounds the table*)   At this time of night!

FIRST MAN   That's no good. This is no time for anything but
sleep. Aren't you sleepy?

FISHERMAN   Booze always makes a man sleepy. You finished?

FIRST MAN   They're still at it over there.

FISHERMAN   It's Midsummer Night.

FIRST MAN   They ought to be in bed.

WIFE   Like decent folk.

FISHERMAN   Like us! When you sink down and let go—Woman!
Here's another hole—and you're sinking, heavy as an anchor
. . . lazy bitch! . . . full up, not a thought in your head, and you
don't give a damn . . . You finished?

FIRST MAN (*getting up*)   My head's getting heavy too. Thanks for
the coffee. Sleep tight. (*He leaves*)

WIFE   Night, Munken. Thanks for bringing this no-good drunk
home!

FISHERMAN (*pounds the table*)   Clear the table!

WIFE   Tomorrow's time enough.

FISHERMAN   Slut! Get into that kitchen! Clear off! Wash those dishes!

WIFE (*picking up candle*)   Wah, I'm asleep on my feet.

FISHERMAN   Leave the candle here! Get going! (*She leaves*) Playing footsie under the table . . . Mud in your eye! Sonofabitch'll pay for that coffee. Found out that legs are connected with thighs and so on, steady hand, keep going and you'll find the promised land! Wish you luck! (*He gets up, picks up the net, and fastens it to the canopy. Next he takes a heavy rock anchor and rolls it onto the foot end of the bed. The action here must not be too specific. At one point he clambers onto the bed. He mumbles to himself all the while*) There, that'll do it, and over here, and now . . . Enjoy yourselves, my friends! Fornicators! . . . Boozers! Trying to outsmart me . . . young alley cats . . . (*Steps down from bed*) Now I'll dunk my head again, and then to sleep . . . (*Goes out unsteadily*)

(*The two men come in*)

FIRST MAN   Let's go home together. Two are stronger than one.

SECOND MAN   I got his pipe and you got your way.

FIRST MAN   Coffee's all gone.

SECOND MAN   It wasn't very nice of you to drink my coffee while I was running around in the middle of the night so you could stay here.

FIRST MAN   You weren't very anxious to go.

SECOND MAN   I fell down twice.

FIRST MAN   You shouldn't have drunk so much.

SECOND MAN   Or I shouldn't have gone.

FIRST MAN   You're too young.

SECOND MAN   That's why I went. I figured an old man doesn't have what it takes.

FIRST MAN   Let's go. There's nobody here.

SECOND MAN   I want to say good-bye.

FIRST MAN   You can just leave the pipe here.

SECOND MAN   But I can't say good-bye here!

FIRST MAN   You'll only be in the way. They want to be alone.

SECOND MAN   They haven't gone to bed yet.

FIRST MAN   Man and wife!

SECOND MAN   Well, I've had enough. You're doing too much fishing in my boat.

FIRST MAN   I don't know what you mean!

SECOND MAN   I'll spell it out: I've got my eye on her too.

FIRST MAN   On who?

SECOND MAN   Don't get me mad, Munken.

FIRST MAN   Shame on you—a young pup like you!

SECOND MAN   And an old man like you!

FIRST MAN   She's faithful.

SECOND MAN   Where?

FIRST MAN   In her heart.

SECOND MAN   But we like her legs.

FIRST MAN   Don't talk like that. It's not decent.

SECOND MAN   I just want my turn.

FIRST MAN   I'll tell Mack.

SECOND MAN   And I'll knock your block off!

FIRST MAN   Just try!

SECOND MAN   Coward!

FIRST MAN   Blowhard!

SECOND MAN   Sonofabitch!

FIRST MAN   Snotnose! (*They fight*)

FISHERMAN (*walks in, his hair falling forward and dripping*)
What's going on here? Lousy drunken bums! In my house! I'd
throw you out if I wasn't so damn tired. (*They stop scuffling*)

FIRST MAN   He started it.

SECOND MAN   Damn liar!

(*Fisherman lies down on the sofa*)

FIRST MAN   Come on outside!

SECOND MAN   Any time!

FIRST MAN   Night, Mack.

SECOND MAN   Asleep already? Now we'll see who makes it.

(*Both leave. Silence. In the distance, sound of the sea*)

WIFE (*in the doorway*)   Hey you! Asleep again! (*Stretches*)

FISHERMAN (*half asleep*)   Shut that window! Damn music.

WIFE (*closes window*)   Why are you sleeping on the sofa?

FISHERMAN   Shut . . . up! . . .

WIFE   Too lazy to take off his pants! What a pig! He's stretching!
He's falling asleep! He'll never wake up now. And we've got
the bed. He must be out of his mind! It's his own fault. What
does he take me for—an animal? (*Sits down on the bed*) It's two
o'clock. It'll be light by four. But he won't get up before eleven.

But then people will see the door. The others go fishing.
They're different. Aren't I entitled to anything? Now he's
asleep! (*Picks up the candle and puts it in the window*) Where can
he be? Maybe he's dozed off. He wasn't all that sober either.
Here he comes. Listen to that racket! God Almighty! Just listen
to it. (*Sound of scuffling and heavy breathing. She looks out the
window, cries out*) Oh God, it's Jürgen! They're fighting! Dear
Lord Jesus, help me! Our Father who art in . . . Thank God!
He's got him! (*She cries out again!*)

FIRST MAN (*rushes to the window and leans in*) Hi there . . .

WIFE   What do you want?

FIRST MAN   That's a dumb question.

WIFE   I think I am entitled to ask what you're doing in my
window.

FIRST MAN   Why did you put that light there?

WIFE   So you'd know he was asleep.

FIRST MAN   You said you'd put the candle there as soon as he was
asleep.

WIFE And now he's asleep.

FIRST MAN   I'm coming in.

WIFE   I didn't say that.

FIRST MAN   Then why did you want me to know?

WIFE   Because you said you were afraid he'd beat me.

FIRST MAN   Well, didn't he?

WIFE   Why should he?

FIRST MAN   Because you went into the kitchen like that.

WIFE   He was too sloshed.

FIRST MAN   Then why did you put the candle in the window?

WIFE   Hurry up then. Somebody'll see you.

FIRST MAN (*climbs in*)   Well, I'll be . . . Women! Try and figure
them out! (*He takes the candle*)

WIFE   What happened to the other one?

FIRST MAN   He got a good clout.

WIFE   And now?

FIRST MAN   He's happy.

WIFE   I hope you didn't hurt him.

FIRST MAN   Hmmm . . .

WIFE   Come over here. There's plenty of room.

FIRST MAN (*looks around with the candle*)   Just a minute.

WIFE   He's on the sofa.

FIRST MAN   Hadn't we better go outside?

WIFE   No, they'd see us. Now what are you doing?

FIRST MAN (*shines the candle on fisherman's face*)   You think he's asleep?

WIFE   Of course. Look out, you'll wake him.

FIRST MAN   Let's go outside.

WIFE   Don't you like it here?

FIRST MAN   I like you!

WIFE   Can you find your way?

FIRST MAN   Sure can.

WIFE   Then put out the candle? (*Trembling*) It'll have to do for tomorrow morning.

FIRST MAN (*puts out the candle; gropes his way over*)   He's out cold.

WIFE   On the sofa!

FIRST MAN   Instead of his bed! Is that your knee?

WIFE   Yes. Watch out! Sit over here.

FIRST MAN   He's out cold.

WIFE   He's like an animal.

FIRST MAN   Is that your hand?

WIFE   Why does he get so drunk?

FIRST MAN   So I have to lug him home!

WIFE   And I have to get out of bed!

FIRST MAN   Was it warm?

WIFE   I waited for him.

FIRST MAN   In your night-shift . . .

WIFE   Didn't catch a thing all day.

FIRST MAN   We could put out his night lines, hmm?

WIFE   He's a pig, that's what he is.

FIRST MAN (*breathing more heavily; so does she*)   Is that your breast?

WIFE   Don't!

FIRST MAN   Does it hurt?

WIFE   Don't do that!

FIRST MAN   You put the light in the window.

WIFE   But you mustn't—do that.

FIRST MAN   Like it says in the sixth commandment.

WIFE   You don't smell of booze.

FIRST MAN   I'm decent.

WIFE   Let go my knee.

FIRST MAN   You'll be more comfortable that way.

WIFE   Ouch!

FIRST MAN   Take it off!

WIFE   You do it.

FIRST MAN   There. That's better.

WIFE   No, don't!

FIRST MAN   Stop fidgeting.

(*The rock anchor tumbles off with a loud crash. Wife gives a smothered scream; first man swears; then both lie very still*)

FISHERMAN (*raising head*)   Hey! The sky's fallen! You'll pay for this. Waking me up! (*Gets up, lights the candle*) Didn't use the candle very long. Pigs. (*To the bed*) Cheers, Munken! Are you there? Are you good and drunk? That's fine! Did it boil over? Hahahaha! Pigs! . . . What a catch! A gift from heaven. The Lord rewardeth the righteous even while he sleepeth . . . Munken. (*Goes to the window*)

FIRST MAN (*tossing and cursing*)   God damn it! It's a net!

FISHERMAN   So you figured it out! No use struggling! The net'll hold. She mended it. And I didn't catch a thing today. Too sleepy. (*Drums on the windowsill*) Fresh fish! Hey, fellows! Over here! Look at this! I've caught something! Sweet Jesus, I've caught something!

VOICES   You gone off your rocker?—What's up?

FISHERMAN   Fresh fish! Fresh fish!

VOICES   Drunk as a lord.

FISHERMAN   Over here! Fresh fish!

FIRST MAN   What the devil! It's your disgrace.

FISHERMAN   It *was* my disgrace, Munken! Fresh fish! Fresh fish! (*Goes to door*)

OTHER FISHERMEN (*crowding in*)   What's up?—Why all the racket?—Had a baby?

FISHERMAN   Something's happened. I've caught some fish.

OTHER FISHERMEN (*craning their necks*)   Here?—A minute ago you were high as a kite.

FISHERMAN   I was too drunk to go out. I did my fishing right here!

OTHER FISHERMEN   He's flipped his lid!—Where's his wife? You can talk sense to her.

FISHERMAN   My wife's gone. I'm so drunk I think she's turned into a fish. Do you hear that wind? It is our Lord who cometh in the raging tempest. He said to me: Go forth, and you shall have a fine catch!

OTHER FISHERMEN   Pour water on his head.—He's delirious.

FISHERMAN (*moves aside to let them see what he was hiding; shouting*)   Fresh fish! Fresh fish!

OTHER FISHERMEN (*pushing forward*)   Is she dead? Is it a corpse? —There's another one. There's two of them—Is it a corpse? (*They burst out laughing*) It's his wife and Munken!

FIRST MAN (*inside the net*)   Damn you, take this thing off! Damn you . . . at least put a blanket over us!

OTHER FISHERMEN (*laughing uproariously*)   It's habit, said the woman to the eel as she pulled off his skin—Do unto others as you would have them do unto you, said the bride to the groom on their wedding night—That's a cozy spot you've got yourself into, boy—Nice and soft down there? Was it hard getting in there?

FISHERMAN   I bet it's worth a bucket of booze to him to get out.

FIRST MAN   Sure, a whole bucket, you old devil; but first, a blanket!

FISHERMAN (*to one of the others*)   Get the liquor, pal, before he changes his mind. Pick up these fish, boys, and dump 'em in the bay, boys—that'll cool 'em off. Take that pole, carry them carefully, carry them reverently, sing a hymn. You don't see a sight like this every day.

OTHER FISHERMEN (*fasten the net to a pole and carry the two off with loud laughter*)   Make yourselves light, children! Don't twist and turn!—Hold still a while?—If you come back you'll be better off than a fart, a fart never comes back.

FISHERMAN   Nice fish! Pretty fish! Big fat wriggling fish! Throw them back, I don't want 'em. Set them free. But it was a rare catch. Now you're all invited to the wake. My wife passed away, she was a good soul. Drink up, the drinks are on the boyfriend! Enjoy my misery. Keep me company and drive away my sorrow.

(*The fishermen sit down. A bucket full of liquor is brought in. Some play cards; others start to sing*)

FISHERMAN (*lights candles*)   These candles in the cups are vigil lights. Don't blow them out when you laugh. This is a house of mourning, so turn your heads when you throw up. These glasses come from the inn; my wife's dead and I don't know where she keeps the glasses.

(*Wind, the fishermen sing*)

FIRST FISHERMAN   Wind's coming up. Getting cold. Drink, that'll keep you warm.

SECOND FISHERMAN   Thought I'd split a gut laughing. Watching them squirm wasn't half as good as the way they lay still, pretending it wasn't them and looking the other way. Hahaha!

FISHERMAN   Please, let's not have laughter in a house of mourning! Can't you drink quietly? Can't you see I'm trying to pass out?

THIRD FISHERMAN   She really was a good woman. She kept you going. She washed you and combed you, and took your beatings.

FIRST FISHERMAN   Hear how the wind is blowing!

FOURTH FISHERMAN   Drink up! What's the wind to *you*?

THIRD FISHERMAN   She looked mighty good in that shift, I'll say that.

SECOND FISHERMAN   It was her shroud!

FIRST FISHERMAN   The way she held it together at the top and cuddled up to Munken so you couldn't see anything. That was your fault, Mack.

FOURTH FISHERMAN   This started out good, but now it's getting gloomy in spite of the booze.

(*The fifth and sixth fishermen come back*)

FIFTH FISHERMAN   They made a real big splash.

SIXTH FISHERMAN   Serves them right.

FIFTH FISHERMAN   Right in your bed! What crust!

SIXTH FISHERMAN   The way they hollered!

FIFTH FISHERMAN   Why doesn't somebody say something? This is like a funeral.

SIXTH FISHERMAN   The liquor is here and the woman's gone.

FISHERMAN   Sit down and shut your faces. My wife is dead! There's a wind blowing up and when it stops she'll be gone forever. She was a good wife. God takes the best. Listen to that wind. Drink up; let's just say my wife drowned in the wind.

SECOND FISHERMAN   Don't let it get you down. It was all stupid.

FOURTH FISHERMAN   She shouldn't have done it in your bed.

FISHERMAN   God has punished me. I drank too much. She was

my best wife. The wind came up and she went down with the boat. Drink up and tell a Rosary for her soul. Hail Mary, full of grace, the Lord is with thee. Eternal rest give to her, O Lord. (*He prays alone*)

FIFTH FISHERMAN   That doesn't make sense. It's blasphemy.

SIXTH FISHERMAN   He's drunk.

THIRD FISHERMAN   Enough is enough, said the man as he beat his wife to death.

SECOND FISHERMAN   You should have been in that bed. There's only room for one man.

FOURTH FISHERMAN   Or you should have given her a good beating. This way it's a disgrace.

THIRD FISHERMAN   It's indecent.

FISHERMAN   Not decent? You're indecent! The Lord has punished me and you make fun of me! Who lost his wife? I'm a sinner, a drunk, a lousy good-for-nothing but now the Lord has punished me, and nobody has a right to laugh at me!

OTHER FISHERMEN (*getting up*)   He's out of his head.—Let's go. Take the liquor.—Poor woman! Serves the drunk right!—She can do as good as him any time.

FISHERMAN   That's blasphemy! Where's the man that's suffered like me? Ye of little faith, you have no shame! I'm grieved to the bottom of my soul. (*Takes a drink*)

OTHER FISHERMEN   Get the bucket and let's go back to the inn. —He's out of his head.

FISHERMAN (*getting up and throwing arms around bucket*)   This is a wake and you're the guests. Now you're drunk and you're saying evil things. You ought to be worrying about your miserable souls.

OTHER FISHERMEN (*trying to take the bucket*)   Let go, you old bastard!—Let go or we'll break your neck!

FISHERMAN   Lechery was written all over your faces when you looked at those pigs. You were drooling with envy as you carried them out! You're the bastards! You're depraved!

OTHER FISHERMEN (*crowding toward the door*)   God help us! He's stark raving mad.—He's crazy, he dreamt the whole thing. Gives me the shivers. No more drinks for me.—Leave him lay with his candles. Maybe God will perform a miracle and he'll drown in that bucket. (*They leave*)

(*Fisherman blows out all but three candles. Kicks the chairs out of the way. Stares straight ahead*)

SECOND MAN (*appearing in window, left*) Hey!

FISHERMAN (*startled; turns*) Who's that? Oh, it's you. Come on in. My wife's dead.

SECOND MAN (*climbs in. His face is bloody*) Are you drunk?

FISHERMAN Do you hear that wind? She got drowned.

SECOND MAN When?

FISHERMAN A little while ago.

SECOND MAN How do you know?

FISHERMAN The Lord woke me up. There was my wife in bed, dead. She looked like a fish. Have a drink with me. I'm so lonely.

SECOND MAN I don't get it. It's kind of spooky in here. Is this your booze?

FISHERMAN Yes. Have a drink. It's a present from her boyfriend.

SECOND MAN Did she have a boyfriend?

FISHERMAN Lots of them. But only the last one gave me liquor.

SECOND MAN How long have you been sitting here by yourself?

FISHERMAN Not long. Some people were here. They laughed and then they left. They saw my disgrace and now they're spreading it all over.

SECOND MAN I feel funny in here. I'm getting out.

FISHERMAN How come your face is bloody? Somebody hit you too?

SECOND MAN I had a bad fall. I was drunk.

FISHERMAN You're my only friend, because you've had troubles too. The Lord Himself has seen fit to punish me. I'd have given him my heart and said: Take it. But he took my wife that I loved even more. Now I'll drink and rot. It's all his fault.

SECOND MAN When did it happen?

FISHERMAN Just now. And if the Lord says to me at the end of my days: You're rotten to the core; where should I put you? I'll answer: Put me in hell, so I can be with my wife.

BEGGAR (*in doorway; behind him beggarwoman*) Come on.—Is this where the liquor is? They said you could get liquor here.

FISHERMAN Come on in and sit down. This is a wake. My wife's dead. I'm happy that you honor me with your presence.

BEGGAR (*as he and the beggarwoman sit down*) She must have been a good woman?

FISHERMAN   Always speak well of the dead. Drink up!

BEGGARWOMAN   Outside the wind is blowing. But it's warm in here.

BEGGAR   Good liquor. It's sad, when you lose a wife.

FISHERMAN   You're left all alone. But they're beasts, all of them. (*Bangs the table*) Beasts! The idea of the net came to me when I stuck my head in the pail. I looked up at the stars and I thought: This will help.

BEGGAR   You speak like one possessed by the spirit. It's very moving. (*Keeps drinking*)
(*During the next scene the beggars move to the sofa, left. Occasional giggling and murmuring*)

FIRST MAN (*from the doorway, right; dripping wet*)   Say, can I have a drink of my booze?

FISHERMAN (*as though having a vision*)   I stood in the doorway just like that myself after I stuck my head in the pail.

FIRST MAN   Right. But you had no business getting so drunk!

FISHERMAN   You can come in, but you'll have to keep quiet. I'm not mad any more. Did you dry in the wind my wife drowned in? Sit down and have a drink. All is vanity! (*Talks with an effort; he is very drunk*)
(*First man steps up to the table*)

SECOND MAN (*gets up. They glare at each other*)   Don't you dare sit here!

FIRST MAN (*uncertainly*)   I've got to talk to him.

SECOND MAN (*steps forward unsteadily*)   You want a punch in the nose? You bastard!

FIRST MAN (*drinks*)   I'm sober now.

SECOND MAN (*sits down heavily*)   And I'm going to knock your block off. Tomorrow.

FIRST MAN   I've got to tell him something. (*Drinks*)

SECOND MAN   He's talking about God. What happened?

FIRST MAN   Something happened. (*Drinks*)

SECOND MAN   It's not exactly cosy here.

FIRST MAN   Who's that back there?

SECOND MAN   The mourners.

FISHERMAN (*thickly*)   God has punished me. God has fished me out of the booze. Can you hear that wind? That's the wind I was out in.

FIRST MAN   They have no shame.

SECOND MAN   That's because of your liquor!

FIRST MAN   His wife's out there in the dark and doesn't dare come home. In this wind! He must be pretty angry.

SECOND MAN   He's sure tanked up.

FIRST MAN (*to fisherman*)   We're sinners, all of us.

FISHERMAN (*embraces him*)   Now she's drowned, and I'm alone without anybody.

FIRST MAN (*drinks*)   You've got to take her back. (*He keeps drinking. Fisherman rests his head on the table*)   I have five kids. You've got to take her back. (*To the second man, who has slipped under the table*) You tell him! He's dead drunk. My heart is so heavy. (*Bursts into tears*) You've got to take her back. Everybody saw us. I'm so miserable.

FISHERMAN   We're alone. All alone. Listen to that wind! (*Silence. The wind*)

WIFE (*Dripping wet, net across her shoulders, in the doorway*)   Is he still angry?

FIRST MAN   He's asleep. (*Walks toward her unsteadily, tries to embrace her. She pushes him away*) I put in a good word for you.

WIFE   Get out of here. (*Throws the net on the floor*)

FIRST MAN   You've had a rough time . . .

WIFE   Go on home! (*Pushes him to the door; turns, drags the second man to the door*) Pigs! All of you. Get out of here!

FISHERMAN (*gets up with an effort*)   They're all beasts. Say a Mass for her soul. Beasts . . . Wind . . . Soul . . .(*Fisherman sits down, falls asleep. Both men, completely drunk, leave together*)

WIFE (*closes window. Pours the liquor out of the bucket, mops the floor with it. Sees the beggar and beggarwoman*)   Who's this scum?

BEGGAR   Poor people!

WIFE   Get out! Have you no shame?

BEGGARWOMAN   It's cold outside! And the wind!

WIFE (*chases them out with broom*)   Get out of here! (*Sweeping; talking half to the fisherman*) What did you have to get so drunk for? Want me to put on coffee? (*He doesn't answer*) They were going to throw the net in the well, those swine. (*Looks at him*) He's asleep. (*She puts out the candles, carries him to bed on her back*)

Notes and Variants

BAAL

Texts by Brecht

Prologue to the 1918 Version

LAST WILL

The subject of this play is the very ordinary story of a man who sings a hymn to summer in a tavern without selecting his audience —together with the consequences of summer, schnapps and song. The man is not a particularly modern poet. Baal has not been ill-favored by Nature. He belongs to the period of the play's performance. Remember Socrates and Verlaine, with their lamentable skulls. Attention actors who love extremes, except when they can get by with mediocrity: Baal is neither a specially comic character nor a specially tragic one. Like all animals he is serious. As for the play, the author has thought hard and managed to find a message in it: it sets out to prove that you can have your cake if you are prepared to pay for it. And even if you aren't. So long as you pay. . . . The play is the story neither of a single incident nor of many, but of a life. Originally it was called *Baal eats! Baal dances!! Baal is transfigured!!!*

> The prologue to the 1919 version is the same, with the addition after "ill-favored by Nature," of the sentence: "It should be realized that he led an entirely blameless life until after his thirtieth year."[GW *Schriften zum Theater*, p. 954.]

Prologue to the 1926 Version

This dramatic biography by Bertolt Brecht shows the life story of the man Baal as it took place in the first part of this century. You see before you Baal the abnormality trying to come to terms with the twentieth-century world. Baal the relative man, Baal the passive genius, the whole phenomenon of Baal from his first appearance among civilized beings up to his horrific end, with his unprecedented consumption of ladies of high degree, in his dealings with his fellow humans. This creature's life was one of sensational immorality. In the stage version it has been considerably toned down. The performance begins with Baal's first appearance as a poet among civilized beings in the year 1904. As a preliminary you will see Baal in the round from several aspects and hear from his own lips how he used to perform his famous Chorale of the Great Baal, accompanied on his unique invention, the Authentic Tin-stringed Banjo.

[*Ibid.*, pp. 954–55.]

The Model for Baal

The dramatic biography called *Baal* treats of the life of a man who really existed. This was a certain Josef K., whom I heard about from people who retained clear memories of the man's person and the commotion created by his activities. K. was the illegitimate son of a washerwoman. He soon made a bad name for himself. Though without formal education of any sort he is said to have been able to impress the most highly educated people by his extraordinarily well-informed talk. A friend told me that the idiosyncrasy of his movements (when taking a cigarette, when seating himself on a chair, and so on) made such a mark on a number of (mainly) young people that they imitated him. His carefree way of life, however, led him to sink ever deeper, particularly since he never lifted a finger himself but shamelessly took advantage of every opportunity offered him. A number of shady episodes were laid at his door, including a girl's suicide. He was a trained mechanic, though so far as we know he never worked. When A. became too hot for him he went off on protracted wanderings with a down-at-heel doctor, returning to A. in about 1911. There his friend was killed in an affray with knives in a tavern on the Lauterlech, almost certainly by K. himself. At all events he then disappeared with remarkable suddenness from A., and is supposed to have died miserably in the Black Forest.

["Das Urbild Baals," from *Die Szene*, Berlin, January 1926, reprinted in GW *Schriften zum Theater*, p. 955. Elisabeth Hauptmann's "Notizen über Brechts Arbeit 1926" on p. 241 of the *Sinn und Form* special Brecht issue of 1957, cites her diary for January 18: "Wrote the 'Model for Baal' for *Die Szene* in the form of a newspaper report. The model for Baal, the 'antisocial' man, is an Augsburg mechanic." This has not prevented commentators from taking at their face value both the report and Brecht's claim to have written it.]

Bad Baal the Antisocial Man

but that is what makes bad baal the antisocial man great
that the report of his enemy
describing him with my voice is
permeated by his
accusing me that i
a delighted onlooker
while he was exploiting the exploiters
and making use of the users
started treating him more harshly
as soon as he spurned my own rules
but that is his offense
and why he is called antisocial
because in making reasonable demands on him
the perfect state would appear like an exploiter.

["Baal," from Dieter Schmidt (ed.): *Baal. Der böse Baal der asoziale*, Suhrkamp, 1968, p. 90. This poem, which is not included in GW, is part of the material relating to the Baal *Lehrstücke* project discussed on pp. 349-350 below.]

On Looking Through My First Plays [ii]

Baal is a play which could present all kinds of difficulties to those who have not learned to think dialectically. No doubt they will see it as a glorification of unrelieved egotism and nothing more. Yet here is an individual standing out against the demands and discouragements of a world whose form of production is designed for exploitation rather than usefulness. We cannot tell how Baal would react to having his talents employed; what he is resisting is their misuse. Baal's art of life is subject to the same fate as any other art under capitalism: it is attacked. He is antisocial, but in an antisocial society.

Twenty years after completing *Baal* I was preoccupied with an idea (for an opera) related to the same basic theme. There is a carved wooden Chinese figure, two or three inches high and sold in thousands, representing the fat little god of happiness, contentedly stretching himself. This god was to arrive from the East after a great war and enter the devastated cities, trying to persuade people to fight for their personal happiness and well-being. He acquires followers of various sorts, and becomes subject to persecution by the authorities when some of them start proclaiming that the peasants ought to be given land, the workers to take over the factories and the workers' and peasants' children to seize the schools. He is arrested and condemned to death. And now the executioners practice their arts on the little god of happiness. But when they hand him poison he just smacks his lips; when they cut his head off he at once grows a new one; when they hang him from the gallows he starts an irresistibly lively dance, etc., etc. *Humanity's urge for happiness can never be entirely killed.*

For the present edition of *Baal* the original version of the first and last scenes has been restored. Otherwise I have left the play as it was, not having the strength to alter it. I admit (and advise you): this play is lacking in wisdom.

["Bei Durchsicht meiner ersten Stücke." Foreword to *Stücke I*, all editions but the first. GW *Schriften zum Theater* pp. 947–48. For a more accurate view of the revisions to the first and last scenes, see p. 351 below.]

Editorial Note

For the following note and for the writings by Brecht quoted in it the editors have drawn gratefully and extensively on the two volumes of "materials" edited by Dieter Schmidt—*Baal. Drei Fassungen* and *Baal. Der böse Baal der asoziale. Texte, Varianten und Materialien*, published by Suhrkamp-Verlag in 1966 and 1968, respectively ("edition suhrkamp," numbers 170 and 248).

1. General

Brecht's first play was not written in four days and for a bet, as has sometimes been alleged, but developed from a paper which he read in the spring of 1918 to Professor Arthur Kutscher's theater seminar at Munich University. His subject was Hanns Johst, the expressionist novelist and playwright who later wrote the Nazi play *Schlageter* and at the end of 1933 became president of the (purged) Prussian Academy. Brecht undertook to write a "counter-play" to Johst's *Der Einsame* (The Lonely One), an emotionalized account of the life of the nineteenth-century dramatist Christian Dietrich Grabbe, which the Munich Kammerspiele were presenting. A first draft was complete by mid-May, and a month later he could write to his lifelong friend Caspar Neher that:

> My play:
> Baal eats! Baal dances!! Baal is transfigured!!!
> What's Baal up to?
>
> 24 scenes
>
> is ready and typed—a substantial tome. I hope to get somewhere with it.

He revised the play in the spring of 1919, after his military service and the writing of the earliest draft of *Drums in the Night*. That was the version first submitted to publishers and theater managements, but Brecht appears to have decided that it was too long—there were twenty-nine scenes—and too wild, and before its publication he overhauled it yet a third time, jettisoning about one third of the 1919 text. Publication should have taken place some time in the second half of 1920, but the original publishers were by then already in trouble with the censorship over other books, and only a few copies for Brecht's own use were ever printed. The rights were transferred to another firm (Kiepenheuer of Potsdam) who brought the book out two years later at the time of the première of *Drums in the Night*, virtually unchanged apart from the addition of the first woodcutters' scene.

This first published version was the play as we now have it, apart from the first and last scenes. It was republished in 1953 in the first volume of Brecht's collected *Stücke;* then in 1955 scene 1 was given its present form (including the two poems supposedly quoted from the Munich expressionist periodical *Revolution*, which are in fact Georg Heym's "Der Baum" and "Vorbereitung" by the then East German Minister of Culture, Johannes R. Becher), while Brecht restored the final scene which he deleted from the proofs in 1920. What Brecht says in his own note of 1954 is not precisely right, since neither of these scenes is in its original form. But clearly he was content to leave it as an early work.

In the later 1920's he felt otherwise. The version which he himself staged at the Deutsches Theater in February 1926 (a single afternoon performance by the "Junge Bühne"—and *Baal's* only performance in Berlin to this day) was a largely new, much shorter play called *Life Story of the Man Baal*. As will be seen below, it retained only eleven of the published scenes, which were altered so as to set Baal in the emergent technological society of the first decade of the century. They were stripped of much of their original lyricism and given an "epic" framework by means of titles to each scene. Brecht wanted this text to appear as an appendix to the *Stücke* edition of the 1950's, but it remained unpublished until 1966. Its only other known performances were in Vienna in 1926 (with a prologue by Hofmannsthal) and in Kassel the year after.

Around 1930—the dates and also the intended arrangement of
the fragmentary typescript are uncertain—he planned a number
of linked *Lehrstücke* (or didactic playlets) about the character he
now called *Bad Baal the Antisocial Man*. Here he thought of
making Baal appear in various guises—
  guest/whore/judge/dealer (bulls)/engineer (only concerned
  with experiment)/suppliant—in need of help (exploiting
  other people's wish to be exploited)/nature-lover/dema-
  gogue/worker (strikebreaker)/mother/historian/soldier/lover
  (baker's apprentice scene from "breadshop")/as priest/as civil
  servant/the 2 coats
—but apart from a reception where Baal is guest and the Baal
Chorale is sung this plan has very little to do with the play. The
writing is deadpan, with strange word order and virtually no
punctuation apart from full stops. Brecht's aphoristic *alter ego*
Herr Keuner appears, and the only *Baal* character apart from Baal
himself is Lupu. Some idea of the style can be got from the
beginning of "Bad Baal the Antisocial Man and the Two Coats,"
which is one of the few complete episodes.

BAAL   all night i have been going in increasing cold through the
forests towards where they get darker. the evening was icy. the
night was icier and a crowd of stars disappeared in a whitish
fog towards morning. today the bushes occupy the least space
of the entire year. whatever is soft freezes. whatever is hard
breaks.
THE LEFT HAND CHORUS   the best thing is
                    the cold comes before the warmth
                    everything makes itself as small
                    as it can. everything is
                    so sparingly silent only
                    thinking becomes im-
                    practicable and then
                    comes the warmth
THE POOR MAN   it is cold. i have no coat. i'm freezing. perhaps
that grand gentleman can tell me what i can do against the cold.
good day sir . . .

In 1938 Brecht again looked at the play with a view to the
Malik-Verlag collected edition of his work (which was never completed). "A pity," he then noted: "it was always a torso, and on

top of that it underwent a number of operations . . . Its meaning almost disappeared. Baal the provocateur, the admirer of things as they are, who believes in living life to the full, other people's lives as well as his own. His 'do what amuses you' would be very rewarding if properly handled. Wonder if I could find the time." That is, aside from the *Lehrstücke* plan, which was still on the agenda. A few months later he seems to have written that off, to judge from a diary note of March 4, 1939:

> Today I finally realized why I never managed to turn out those little *Lehrstücke* about the adventures of "Bad Baal the Antisocial Man." Antisocial people aren't important. The really antisocial people are the owners of the means of production and other sources of life, and they are only antisocial as such. There are also their helpers and their helpers' helpers, of course, but again only as such. It is *the* gospel of humanity's enemies that there are such things as antisocial instincts, antisocial personalities and so on.

He also came to feel that he had made a mistake in seeing socialism as a matter of social order rather than of productivity, which may have been another reason underlying his more sympathetic judgement of Baal at the end of his life.

2. The Versions of 1918, 1919, and 1920-22 (first published version)

Numbers in square brackets refer to the scene order of the final text (pp. 1-58 in this volume), other numbers to that of the particular script under discussion.

Though *Baal* at first appears to have little structure, so that Brecht could change scenes around, or add or delete them without greatly affecting the play's character, there are nine basic scenes which recur in the same order in every version, together with four others* which are cut only in the 1926 text. They are: [1] (the opening party scene), [2] (Baal and Johannes), [3] (the first tavern scene), [4 i] (Baal and Johanna, after the seduction), [4 iii] (first scene with Sophie), [6]* (second ditto), [7] (Night Spot scene),

[8]* (Baal and Ekart), [15] (Baal reading a poem to Ekart, who speaks of his girl), [17]* (Baal reads "Death in the Woods"), [18] (last tavern scene, with the murder of Ekart), [20]* (the two policemen), and [21] (the death scene in the forest hut). Accordingly we shall start by describing the more significant changes in these scenes, from one version to another up to 1922.

[1] In the first two versions it is a grand party: full evening dress. The host and other guests are not named; the host's wife is not mentioned. Unspecified poems by August Stramm, Novotny, and A. Skram are read; Baal, who is a clerk in the host's office, calls the last drivel. The servants try to throw him out, but he fights them off, saying "I'll show you who's master."

The 1922 version is virtually the same as the final text, less the character of Pschierer and everything between the first remark of the Young Man and the last remark of the Young Lady. The scene ends, after Piller's last jibe, with Johannes asking Baal if he may visit him and Emilie saying, "I'm sorry for him."

[2] Baal's speeches are longer than in the final version, but the scene is not essentially changed.

[3] In 1918 it is a bourgeois bar. Baal reads the "Ballad of Evelyn Roe" (now in Brecht's collected poems), is applauded and introduces Johannes and "Mr. Ekart, a brilliant composer who is passing through." He insults the bourgeois, who fail to pay for his drinks; he refuses to join Ekart on his wanderings because Marie the waitress, who is in love with him, cannot come too. Johannes leads him away.

In 1919 this becomes the tavern with an audience of teamsters to whom he sings "Orge's song." Johannes brings Johanna; Emmi arrives, identified by Baal as "wife of my office boss" and described as *well-dressed, nervous, rather domineering.* It is virtually the final version.

[4 i] Essentially the final version, though in 1918 Johanna is called Anna. Instead of asking Baal if he still loves her she asks, "Do you love me?" *in a small voice, breathlessly.*

[4 iii] Sophie Dechant in 1918 appears dressed in white. She is an actress, on her way to play (presumably Hebbel's) Judith. Much of the final version is there—Baal calling her a white cloud, her reference to Baal's ugliness, her virginity, her declaration that she loves him—up to the point where Baal's mother comes in,

accusing him of having whores in his room. He says Sophie is to be his wife, and asks her if she will. A piano is playing all the time, off.

In 1919 the scene has been largely rewritten. Sophie ceases to be an actress and takes her eventual form. Baal still says she is to be his wife, but no longer asks her.

By 1922 the mother is cut out of the play. Baal's long opening speech, which originally introduced another scene with his mother (see below) is added to this one. Johannes makes his brief appearance. Sophie's name is changed to Barger, and there is no mention of her becoming Baal's wife. Instead of the piano there is intermittently a beggar's hurdy-gurdy playing *Tristan*.

[6] In 1918 it is "Night," with no place given. Sophie says they are penniless, and wants to go back to the stage. Baal says he will go on the stage: in a night spot. He sings the verse which later introduces 4 (ii).

In 1919 the scene is rewritten. It is a bedroom in the summer, and several phrases of the dialogue survive into the final version. It is now Baal who says, "Do you realize we've got no money?" The night spot is not mentioned.

In 1922 there is no song and the scene is set out of doors in May, as we have it.

[7] In 1918 there is an unnamed compère instead of Mjurk. There is no Lupu and no mention of the agreement about schnapps. The dialogue is differently phrased, but the only major differences from the ultimate version are (1) the eruption of a group of young artists, who tell Baal: "Your latest poem in the *Phoebus* is good, but too affectedly simple—Princess Ebing's taking an interest in you. She's hot stuff. Lucky fellow!"; (2) the song which Baal sings, dressed in tails and a child's sailor hat, which goes roughly:

> If a woman's hips are ample
> Then I want her in the hay
> Skirt and stockings all a-rumple
> (Cheerfully)—for that's my way.
>
> If the woman bites in pleasure
> Then I wipe it clean with hay

My mouth and her lap together
(Thoroughly)—for that's my way.

If the woman goes on loving
When I feel too tired to play
I just smile and go off waving
(Amiably)—for that's my way.

The 1919 version is textually the same, except for the replacement of "Compère" by "Nigger John" throughout. For Nigger John, see below.

In 1922 Mjurk, Lupu, and the final song made their appearance. There is a typescript of the song dated January 21, 1920.

[8] Basically the same in all versions.

[15] 1918 and 1919 (slightly lengthened) versions show Ekart talking about his pale-faced girl as an experience of the past; Baal goes to sleep while he is talking about her. The poem which Baal recites to him is not "The Drowned Girl" (as in the 1922 text) but "The Song of the Cloud in the Night" (in the collected poems).

[17] In 1918 the scene is set outside a country tavern. The text is almost word for word the same as in the final version, apart from some slight variations in the poem "Death in the Woods," until what is now the end of the scene. Thereupon Baal says, "I'll go and get one" (i.e., a woman) and breaks into the dance which has started inside the tavern. There is almost a fight with the man whose partner Baal pulls away from him, then Baal suddenly crumples and leaves.

In 1919 the setting becomes "Maple Tree in the Wind," and the dance episode is detached to make a separate short scene, which Brecht dropped in the third version.

[18] The 1918 and 1919 versions are almost identical apart from the absence of Johannes from the former and certain differences in the arrangement of the verses. Baal here arrives on the top of his form, having sold a book of his poems to a publisher. "I want meat! What's your name, kids, and what's your price? I'm as choosy as a vicar. But watch what I can do. I'll pay for everything!" He orders champagne (in the final version an allusion to this is left after the third verse of the Ballad) and, with Luise on his knee (who does not yet look like Sophie), sings an obscene,

blasphemous and largely untranslatable song about the Virgin. Watzmann, whose character was even then unexplained, sings in lieu of "There are plenty of trees you can turn to":

> When the hatred and venom he's swallowed
> Are more than his gullet can take
> He may well draw a knife from his pocket
> And languidly sever his neck.

Both verses come from the poem "Orges Antwort" in Brecht's *Hauspostille.* At the end of the scene, before Baal attacks Ekart, Ekart tries to get Luise off his lap, saying, "Oh, rubbish! Gentlemen! Let's drink to fair shares between brothers!"

There is a draft of January 1920, showing the waitress with Sophie's features and Baal a wreck, as in the 1922 text, which also substitutes the new dialogue between Baal and Ekart at the end.

[20] The dialogue between the two policemen is little changed. In 1918 and 1919 three other professions are attributed to Baal: gardener, city clerk and journalist. Those of merry-go-round owner, woodcutter and millionairess's lover only appear in the 1922 version.

[21] This scene has remained essentially unchanged from the 1918 version, apart from Baal's last speech, which both there and in 1919 runs:

> Dear God. Gone. (*Groans*) It's not so simple. My God, it's not so simple. If only I. One. Two. Three. Four. Five. Six. Not much help. Dear God. *Dear* God. (*Feverishly*) Mother! Send Ekart away! Oh, Mary! The sky's so damned near. Almost touch it. My heart's thumping out of me. One. Two. Three. Four. (*Whimpers, then all of a sudden, loudly*) I can't. I won't. It's stifling here. (*Quite distinctly*) It must be clear outside. I want to. (*Raising himself with difficulty*) Baal, I want to go out. (*Sharply*) I'm not a rat. (*He tumbles off the bed, and falls*) Hell. Dear God! As far as the door! (*He crawls to the threshold*) Stars . . . hm. (*He crawls out*)

In the 1922 version the five invocations of God and one of Mary are replaced by the three invocations of "Dear Baal."

OTHER SCENES

Seven further scenes were cut or telescoped with others when Brecht revised the play in 1919. Two of these represent a loss to the narrative: scene 9, which shows Baal arrested on Corpus Christi because he is drunkenly outraged by the cutting of young trees for the procession, and scene 11, where a theater review which he has written is rejected by the manager of his newspaper, and the editor then sacks him. The main points of the other five scenes (which elaborate the affairs with Emmi and Johanna, show him being visited in prison by his mother, and later forcing an unnamed girl to sell herself for him) are incorporated in or anticipated by other changes.

There are three new long scenes in the 1919 revision, and five others of which two appear in this version only. The long ones are [10] the scene over the body of the dead woodcutter Teddy, [13] the Bolleboll-Gougou scene and [9] Baal's pretence of buying bulls. The two scenes subsequently cut are scene 8, immediately following the first Sophie scene, where the barman Nigger John offers Baal (in a top hat) a job in his night spot; and scene 19, preceding the "Death in the Woods" scene, where Baal, Ekart, and a new girl called Anna try to get a night's lodging. A man opens his window and says that Anna can come in his room and the others can sleep in the hay.

ANNA I'm so frightened. I don't want to be alone.
BAAL You won't be alone.

The man says he can offer them bread and milk soup. "The young lady gets the cream, hahaha."

ANNA I must do whatever you want, but I'm sure it's not right.
BAAL Nonsense. Warmth is right and soup is right. Don't make a fuss. You've been a burden so far; now you can make yourself useful.

The other new scenes are [12], where Baal and Ekart abandon the pregnant Sophie; an early version of [11], with Baal and Ekart in a hut in the winter; and the very short [14], in the leafy thicket by the river, where Baal says, "I don't care for women any more . . ."

In the 1922 text the position of all these new scenes is changed relatively to the basic framework. Four more are added, of which [4 ii], where the two sisters visit Baal's room, is the most substantial. [5] with the drunken tramp restores the point of one of the scenes cut in 1919. [16] is the scene with Ekart's pale, red-haired woman, now very much part of the present. [19] is Baal's brief passage across the stage "Longitude 10° East of Greenwich." Nine scenes are cut, including the two 1919 additions mentioned above and the detached (quarrel at the dance) episode of [17]. The others are two scenes with Baal's mother, who is thus eliminated from the play (one, originally scene 4, showing her reprimanding her son for his drunkenness, the other preceding the last tavern scene and showing her on her deathbed); a scene following the night spot episode, with Baal arrested by the police in a café; the next scene after that, with Baal in prison being reasoned with by a clergyman:

CLERGYMAN   You're sinking deeper all the time.

BAAL   Thanks to my immense weight. But I enjoy it. I'm going down. Aren't I? But I'm doing all right, aren't I? Am I going off course? Am I a coward? Am I trying to stave off the consequences? Am I scared of you? Death and I are friends. Hardship's my whore. I'm more humble than you.

CLERGYMAN   You're too light to go under. You cheerful bankrupt.

BAAL   Sometimes I'm like a diver whose cables and breathing tubes have been cut, going for a walk all alone in the depths.

CLERGYMAN   Nothing is so terrible as loneliness. Nobody is alone with us. We are all brothers.

BAAL   Being alone has so far been my strength. I don't want a second man in my skin.

Finally two short scenes are deleted near the end of the play: one with a moralizing Baal interrupting lovers on a park bench, the other between [20] and [21], where Baal, on the run at night, tries vainly to get a peasant girl to walk with him.

3. Life Story of the Man Baal (1926)

This later typescript is published in the first of Dieter Schmidt's volumes, and is subtitled "Dramatic Biography by Bertolt Brecht. (Stage adaptation of 'Baal')." It consists of the nine basic scenes in shortened and largely rewritten form, plus [12] and [19], and a new short scene only found in this version (scene 9 below). All except scenes 1 and 9 are given titles. Some of the names are spelled differently. The play begins with seven verses of the Chorale (verses 1, 2, 4, and the last four) sung by Baal, who then leaves the stage.

Scene 1, Room with dining table.
Enter Mäch, Emilie Mäch, Johannes Schmidt, Dr. Piller, Baal.

MÄCH (*while Baal stands eating at the buffet*) I think I may claim to have been the first to foresee your path to those heights of fame for which born geniuses are predestined. Genius has always suffered persecution; as it listens in its unworldly way to higher voices it is brought down to the cold realities of the world. I would like to think that my salon had been the first to welcome you before the distinction of the Kleist Prize snatches you away from us. Will you have a glass of wine? . . .

Johannes says that Baal sings his poems to the taxi drivers.

MÄCH   Fantastic.
EMILIE

> With the cynical charm of airy poems
> Leaving an orange bitterness on the palate
> Straight off the ice! Meanwhile with an eye on
> Black Malayan hair! O tobacco opiate!

> Is that really by you?

JOHANNES   That's Herr Baal's. They generally give him three glasses of kirsch for each song. And one glass for a look at the special instrument he invented, which he says posterity will know as Baal's Authentic Tin-Stringed Banjo.

MÄCH Fantastic.

JOHANNES It's in a tavern at a freight station.

EMILIE I suppose you've read a great deal?

MÄCH Just let him eat in peace for the moment. Let him recover. Art's hard work too, you know. Help yourself to brandy, Hennessy, it's all there.

EMILIE You live in a garage?

BAAL 64a Holzstrasse.

MÄCH Fantastic. Weren't you a mechanic?

EMILIE

In wind-crazed hovels of Nanking paper
O you bitterness of the world's joys
When the moon, that mild white animal
Falls out of colder skies!

—these two stanzas being from Brecht's own poem "On Effort" (in the Hauspostille). Apart from one remark of Baal's, who announces: "In the year 1904 Joseph Mäch gives Baal a light for his cigar," the last two thirds of the scene is close to our version from after the last remark of the Young Lady (on p. 7) to the end. Then the Servant is cut (as in 1922) and after Johannes has asked if he may visit Baal, Emilie says: "I don't know. I like him. He needs looking after." Then a new closing speech from Baal:

It's raining. At the time of the Flood they all went into the ark. All the animals, by agreement. The only time the creatures of this world have ever agreed about anything. They really all did come. But the ichthyosaurus didn't. Everybody said he should get on board, but he was very busy just then. Noah himself warned him the Flood was coming. But he quietly said, "I don't believe it." He was universally unpopular when he drowned. Ah yes, they all said, the ichthyosaurus won't be coming. He was the oldest beast of them all, well qualified by his great experience to say whether such a thing as a Flood was or was not feasible. It's very possible that if a similar situation ever arises I shan't get on board either.

BAAL'S UNHESITATING ABUSE OF DIVINE GIFTS

Scene 2. Garage.

The tone is drier, but it is essentially a condensed version of the Baal-Johannes scene as we have it, except that it ends with Baal saying not "*you* should keep away from it" but "I think you should bring her to me."

BAAL ABUSES HIS POWER OVER A WOMAN

Scene 3. Tavern.

Baal, Eckart, a tart. Taxi drivers at the bar.

ECKART   I'm on the move. I've had just about enough of this town. Last night I slept with this lady and realized that I'm too grown up for that sort of thing. My advice is to hang all ovaries on the hook once and for all. I'm for freedom of movement till one's forty-five. Plato says the same, if I'm not mistaken.

BAAL   Where are you going?

ECKART   The South of France, I think. Apart from anything else they seem to have a different type of town there. The plan is different, to start with, because there's enough light and that guarantees order. Are you coming?

BAAL   Got any money?

ECKART   Up to a point.

BAAL   Enough for a train?

ECKART   Enough for feet.

BAAL   When are you off?

ECKART   Today. I'm leaving this tavern at eleven-thirty.

BAAL   How come?

ECKART   I've got a photo of Marseilles. Three dingy ellipses. Are you coming?

BAAL   Possibly. I don't know yet.

A version of the scene as we have it then begins with Baal's account of Mäch's party and then Johannes's entrance. Johanna

however is now fifteen: two years younger. It is not specified what
ballad Baal sings. Eckart having already made his appeal does not
make it again, but before singing, Baal says:

> . . . Today, my friends, I was made an offer which no doubt
> has erotic motives. Kirsch, Luise. The man in question is
> about to move off. He's just smoking his last cigar and drink-
> ing his last kirsch. I'm probably going to say "Not yet."
> Drink up, Emilie. Obviously I'm in the market for counter-
> offers. I imagine that poses a problem for you, Emilie.
> EMILIE I don't know what's the matter with you today . . .

After the driver Horgauer has kissed Emilie the ending is wholly
changed. The taxi drivers applaud and Johanna tells Baal he
should be ashamed of himself, as in our version. Then Emilie tells
Johanna:

> Don't pay any attention to me. I've been criticized for not
> having enough temperament for this kind of place. But per-
> haps I've shown that my dirtiness has been underestimated.
> ECKART Check!
> BAAL Emmi, you haven't paid either. You can relax. It's over
> now. Forget it.
> ECKART I'm going.
> BAAL Where?
> ECKART South of France. Are you coming too?
> BAAL Can't you put it off?
> ECKART No, I don't want to do that. Are you coming or not?
> BAAL No.

64A HOLZSTRASSE

Scene 4. Garage.

A condensed conflation of scenes [4 i] and [4 ii]. The tone of
Baal's dialogue with Johanna is drier. She has no remorse, and is
only concerned about getting dressed. The Porter's Wife irrupts
after Baal's "Give me a kiss," and berates him in much the same
shocked words as the landlady of [4 ii]. Then back to the finish
of [4 i], with Baal saying:

Off home with you! Tell Johnny Schmidt we just came in for
five minutes because it was raining.

JOHANNA Tell Johnny Schmidt it was raining. (*Goes out*)

BAAL Johanna! There she goes.

—and no music.

TWO YEARS LATER: BAAL DISCOVERS A (TO HIM) NEW KIND OF
LOVE

Scene 5. Garage.

*On the wall a drawing of the female anatomy. Baal arrives with
Miss Barger.*

BAAL My workshop.

BARGER Excuse me, but I'm going back down.

BAAL You can't just do that.

BARGER They'll find me here. There was a man who followed
us when you came up and spoke to me outside.

BAAL Nobody'll find you here.

BARGER Out there you told me you were a photographer.

BAAL That's what I said out there, wasn't it?

BARGER Then I'm going.

BAAL There was something particular I wanted to ask you.

BARGER No.

BAAL What are you scared of all of a sudden?

BARGER I'm not the least bit scared.

BAAL Oh. That's a drawing I did to help make matters clear.
If you don't like it we'll take it down. But you see I know
you inside and out; there's no mystery. There! (*He scratches
out the drawing with his knife*)

BARGER Holy Mother of God! (*Screams*)

BAAL What are you screaming about? Don't make such a
noise. They'll hear you next door. Is it the knife? (*Picks up
a bottle*) Nothing left in there. No air left either. As for the
meat! The meat's pathetic. It's not meat at all, just skin and
a couple of fibers. I don't call that meat. Altogether this
planet's a washout. A piece of impertinence. All fixed up for

the tourists. With mountains. But there aren't any mountains. That's what the valleys are for. Stuff the one into the other and the stupid planet's flat again. There, now you've stopped.

BARGER   Shall I stay with you?

BAAL   What?

BARGER   Your drawing's very ugly. But you look discontented. Me too. When I was fourteen the butcher next door wouldn't even let me sweep the snow off his pavement because I was too ugly. Lately men have taken to turning round and looking at me in the street; what I've got won't last long; I think I ought to make use of it. I don't think it has to be a man in a smart hat. But it's no good having something that isn't made use of.

BAAL   Now could that surprising way of talking be because she's scared of death?

BARGER   Scared of death? Have you had ideas of that sort?

BAAL   Don't get up. I don't like you. (*Smokes*) Get your voice in operation again. It was a great moment. I'm abandoning hope. Seven years in this room, eighteen months' constant abstention from food, washing out my mind with unadulterated consumption of alcohol. Never in my life having done the least little thing, I'm on the verge of entering new territory. This place of mine is all worn out. Mostly by systematic overestimation of everything, I suppose. I can see them saying that at the time of my death table and wall had been utterly worn away. And I still have to resolve the permanent problem of my life: the devising of an evil deed.

BARGER   It isn't easy, but I'm sure I can understand you if I really try.

BAAL   I give up. You talk now. I wouldn't want people to say I neglected anything. You've got a woman's face. In your case a man could probably cause seven pounds of misfortune, where with most women he couldn't even cause two. How old are you?

BARGER   Twenty-four in June.

BAAL   How many men have you had in your life? (*Barger says nothing*) Then you've got that behind you. Any family?

BARGER   Yes, a mother.

BAAL   Is she old?

BARGER   She's sixty.
BAAL   Then she's used to evil.
BARGER   They oughtn't to blame me. I can't support myself.
BAAL   You'll learn.
BARGER   You're asking an awful lot. You're so ugly it's terrify-
ing. What's your name?
BAAL   Baal.

BAAL EARNS MONEY FOR THE LAST TIME.

Scene 6. The Prickly Pear night spot.

This is scene [7], still the "Small filthy café," with the difference
that the parts of the Soubrette and her accompanist have been
considerably written up, that the text of Baal's song is not given,
and that when Baal escapes through the toilet window it is (according to the accompanist) to go to the Black Forest, where a
postcard from Eckart at the beginning of the scene has asked him
to join him.

BAAL ABANDONS THE MOTHER OF HIS UNBORN CHILD

Scene 7. Sky and evening.

This is approximately [12], but without reference to Baal's taking
Eckart's women, or having been in prison, and without the two
men's wrestling at the end of the scene. It is all shorter, and it
appears to come as a surprise to Baal that Sophie is pregnant:
BAAL   Pregnant? That's the last straw. What do you think
you're up to? And now I suppose I'll have you hanging round
my neck?
ECKART   On principle I don't interfere in your exceedingly
shabby human relationships. But at least when a third party
is present they should be conducted with some semblance of
fairness.
BAAL   Are you going to abandon me on her account? That'd
be just like you. She can clear out. She's becoming a real
bitch. I'm as patient as a lamb. But I can't change my skin.
SOPHIE   You see, Baal, I didn't need to tell you before. It's been

slower than I thought, mostly because you didn't like me all that much. I'm in the fourth month.

ECKART   She's showing some vestige of common sense. Once again: I refuse to let my feelings get involved, but I'll wait here till it's all settled.

Sophie then starts begging them to stay, for an hour, for half an hour. She tells Baal: "Oh yes, it's a beautiful evening, and you like it. But you won't like it when you have to die without another soul there." "Yes, I will, " says Baal. And as Sophie shouts that they are degenerate beasts Baal says to Eckart, "I absolutely insist that you and I leave now."

IN THE YEARS 1907–10 WE FIND BAAL AND ECKART TRAMPING ACROSS SOUTH GERMANY.

Scene 8. Countryside. Morning. Wind.

Baal, Eckart

BAAL   The wind's getting up again. It's the only thing you get free in this country, but all it does now is touch my skin. It isn't strong enough for my ears these days. Your fugue hasn't made much progress either.

ECKART   The sounds my fugue is based on are no worse than most. As for the mathematics of it, it's more mathematical than the wind. The landscape keeps getting more mathematical. It's humanity's only prospect. There's already a corrugated iron barn over there; tomorrow there'll be a steel-framed building. The big cities are spreading their standardized limbs across the old landscape. Between all those tall buildings the wind will be measurable.

BAAL   We're the last people to see the flat plain. In forty-nine years the word "forest" won't be needed. Wood will cease to be used. Mankind will disappear too, if it comes to that. But to stick to our own lifetime, by the time your big cities are built you'll be delirious. Instead of those tall constructions you'll see rats.

ECKART   By then it will take entire typhoons to make you hear the slightest noise.

BAAL   My friend, even without a skin I want to live. You're really an evil man. Both of us are. Unfortunately. Here's a poem I've written.

He then reads "The Drowned Girl," as in [15], after which:

ECKART   You don't seem to have lost much of your power.
BAAL   Everything there is to say about life on this planet could be expressed in a single sentence of average length. That sentence I shall some time or other formulate, certainly before I die.

Scene 9. Countryside.

Night. Baal asleep. Eckart looking at him.

ECKART   This man Baal worries me. He's not light enough any more. I'm an objective kind of man. It would be simple enough to pick up a piece of chalk and establish the graph of his life on the next wall. When I think about it, the only thing that keeps me is the fact that if anything his character's getting harder. All the same, I'm the last man to want to witness the enfeeblement that's bound to accompany his decline and death. I'm not a vindictive character. He's been keeping a very sharp eye on me lately. It's difficult to tell if he's really asleep now, for instance. There are no fields left for him to graze down. It's starting to rain again; I'd better cover him up.

IN THE YEAR 1911 BAAL SUCCUMBS TO HIS PREDESTINED DISPOSITION TO MURDER.

Scene 10. Tavern.

Autumn evening. Eckart, Emilie Mäch and Johann Schmidt in black.

This is essentially [18], with the difference that the waitress is Sophie and that Emilie is present, with a good deal to say. Watzmann is cut, his verse about "When the hatred and venom" from

the 1919 version being now sung in an undertone by Emilie. There
are no other verses apart from those of the "Ballad of the Adventurers" sung by Baal.

It starts with Johann asking, "When's Baal coming?" Then
Eckart:

> It's become increasingly clear to me in these last few years
> that great times are in store for us. The countryside is going
> to ruin. I've seen photographs of buildings on Manhattan
> Island which indicate a vast power in the human race. Hav-
> ing reached a high point of insensitivity, mankind is setting
> to work to create an age of happiness. The years in question
> will be limited in number; what matters is to be there. For
> a few weeks I've felt myself becoming increasingly restless.
>
> EMILIE   When's Baal coming?

They discuss who has any money to pay for drinks. Emilie's
husband has died. They discuss Baal, before his entrance, somewhat as in [18]. Emilie says she has "come to see the golden boy
eight years later . . . You know, I'd feel there was something
missing if he didn't somehow or other go completely to pieces,"
and asks Eckart if he is abandoning him. Eckart says: "Yes, it's
already written on my face. It's obvious to everybody. Only he
doesn't realize it yet. Although I keep telling him. As I will again
today, just watch," then breaks off as Baal arrives.

The first exchanges are much as in [18], but Baal then asks the
waitress, "Is that you, Sophie?" Johann answers:

> Yes, that's her all right. How are you? I'm doing very nicely.
> It's a very good atmosphere here. Beer.
>
> SOPHIE   Beer.

After Eckart's outburst, where he says he is going back to the
forests, Baal says, "Are you off again? I don't believe it, you know.
I feel perfectly well myself." Eckart then tells the story of the man
who thought he was well, as told by the Beggar in the Bolleboll-
Gougou scene [13], up to the final "Did he get well?" (here asked
by Baal). "No."

Johann(es) makes none of his long melancholy speeches, but

when for the second time he says, "It really is a very good atmosphere here," he adds, "Like in the old days." Emilie thereupon sings her verse, and Baal turns to Eckart:

> That girl Johanna Schreiber was with us then.
> EMILIE Oh, the one who killed herself. She's still stuck in a culvert somewhere. They never found her. He's got a wife now, and a nice little coal business.
> JOHANN Brandy.
> SOPHIE Brandy.
> EMILIE Have I changed much? I wasn't too bad after you'd finished with me. I don't imagine you're pleased to hear that. For a time I couldn't take any drinks that hadn't been mixed eight times over. My late husband got me off wood alcohol by hitting me.
> BAAL Nothing doing.
> EMILIE Give me a cigar.
> SOPHIE Cigar.
> EMILIE Give me the strongest schnapps; it's all right. And I'll go to bed with any of you that knows his business. Technique: that's what I'm interested in. What are you looking at now?

She claims to have drunk more than any of them. Baal replies: "You were never drunk, you had amazing control of yourself, you never were worth anything. That girl back there, for instance, who was very close to me once, is absolutely used up. She was a first-class phenomenon on this planet." As Emilie weeps, Baal sits by her and makes a formal declaration:

> . . . If you for your part still have some inclination towards my body, then I, being unaccustomed ever in my life to let any sort of offer go by, would now like to say this to you: my outward circumstances will make me incline towards you in six years at the most, by which time you will have achieved a total age of forty years.

He smashes the light and sings, and the murder of Eckart follows much as in [18].

BAAL ON THE RUN. IO DEGREES EAST OF GREENWICH.

Scene 11.

Almost identical with [19].

BAAL DIES WRETCHEDLY AMONG WOODCUTTERS IN THE
YEAR 1912.

Scene 12. Night, rain, woodcutters playing cards.

Baal on a dirty bed.

This is considerably cut, but otherwise very close to [21]. The
main difference is that as the last woodcutter is leaving, after
wiping Baal's forehead, Baal calls him closer and says:

> . . . I agree. [Ich bin einverstanden]
> MAN   What with?
> BAAL   With everything.
> MAN   But it's all over now.
> BAAL   That was excellent.
> MAN   Off we go, then.
> BAAL   Hey, give me the book.
> MAN   But you haven't any light.

In Baal's final speech there is no "Dear God" and no "Dear Baal."
He calls for Eckart, not for his mother, and his last words are "It's
better in the doorway. Man! Trunks. Wind. Leaves. Stars. Hm."

DRUMS IN THE NIGHT

Texts by Brecht

BALLAD OF THE DEAD SOLDIER

(Sung by Glubb at the beginning of Act 4 of *Drums in the Night*)

And when the war reached its fifth spring
with no hint of a pause for breath
the soldier did the obvious thing
and died a hero's death.

The war, it appeared, was far from done.
The Kaiser said, "It's a crime.
To think my soldier's dead and gone
before the proper time."

The summer spread over the makeshift graves.
The soldier lay ignored
until one night there came an offi-
cial army medical board.

The board went out to the cemetery
with consecrated spade
and dug up what was left of him
and put him on parade.

The doctors sorted out what they'd found
and kept what they thought would serve
and made their report: "He's physically sound.
He's simply lost his nerve."

Straightway they took the soldier off.
The night was soft and warm.

You could tip your helmet back and see
the stars they see at home.

They filled him up with a fiery schnapps
to bring him back to life
then shoved two nurses into his arms
and his half-naked wife.

The soldier was stinking with decay
so a priest goes on before
to give him incense on his way
that he may stink no more.

In front the band with oompah-pah
intones a rousing march.
The soldier does like the handbook says
and flicks his legs from his arse.

Their arms about him, keeping pace
two kind first-aid men go
in case he falls in the shit on his face
for that would never do.

They paint his shroud with the black-white-red
of the old imperial flag
with so much color it covers up
that bloody spattered rag.

Up front a gent in a morning suit
and stuffed-out shirt marched too:
a German determined to do his dut-
y as Germans always do.

So see them now as, oompah-pah
along the roads they go
and the soldier goes whirling along with them
like a flake in the driving snow.

The dogs cry out and the horses prance.
The rats squeal on the land.
They're damned if they're going to belong to France:
it's more than flesh can stand.

And when they pass through a village all
the women are moved to tears.
The party salutes; the moon shines full.
The whole lot give three cheers.

With oompah-pah and cheerio
and wife and dog and priest
and, among them all, the soldier himself
like some poor drunken beast.

And when they pass through a village perhaps
it happens he disappears
for such a crowd comes to join the chaps
with oompah and three cheers. . . .

In all that dancing, yelling crowd
he disappears from view.
You can only see him from overhead
which only stars can do.

The stars won't always be up there.
The dawn is turning red.
But the soldier goes off to a hero's death
just like the handbook said.

In memory of Christian Grumbeis, infantryman, born on April
11, 1897, died in Holy Week 1918 at Karazin (Southern Russia). Peace to his ashes! He had what it takes.

> [Appendix to the 1922 edition. Now in the "Hauspostille"
> section of Brecht's collected poems, dated 1918, less the dedica-
> tory note, with "fourth" for "fifth" in the first line, and under
> the title "Legend of the Dead Soldier."]

Note for the Stage

At Caspar Neher's suggestion this play was performed in Munich with the following scenery. Pasteboard screens some six feet high represented the walls of the rooms, with the big city painted in childish style behind them. Every time Kragler appeared the moon glowed red a few seconds beforehand. Sounds were thinly hinted. In the last act the Marseillaise was performed on a gramophone. The third act can be left out if it fails to work fluently and musically and to liven up the tempo. It is a good idea to put up one or two posters in the auditorium bearing phrases such as "Stop that romantic gaping."

> [GW *Stücke*, p. 70. In all previous editions the words "At Caspar Neher's suggestion" were absent and a second phrase "Everybody is best off in his own skin" included at the end.]

Note to the Script of the Berlin Production (1922)

A small stage, consisting of wood and pasteboard. Thin flats, only partly painted. Doors, windows, walls all have a makeshift air. Similarly although the great revolutionary operation steadily grows in power offstage it makes only a thin, ghostlike effect in the auditorium. The persons nevertheless must be extremely real and the acting naïve. The auditorium contains posters with phrases from the play such as "Everybody is best off in his own skin" and "The Lord's eye maketh the cattle fat" and "Stop that romantic gaping."

> [Unpublished. Brecht-Archive typescript no. 2122 and 1569. This production was in December 1922.]

Preface to *Drums in the Night*

1. CONVERSATION WITH GEORGE GROSZ

What the bourgeoisie hold against proletarians is their bad complexion. I fancy that what made you, George Grosz, an enemy of the bourgeois was their physiognomy. It's fairly common knowledge that war is currently being waged between the proletariat and the bourgeoisie. To judge by the arguments on both sides, it isn't a war that depends on divergences of taste; but those arguments are deceptive and unconvincing, and above all nobody ever pays them the slightest attention. The bourgeoisie commit injustices, but then injustices are committed on all sides. You and I, George Grosz, are against injustice (like everybody else). But we would be less against it if it could be committed by the proletariat. I mean to say: it can't be injustice that "forced you to take up your brushes." And if it were, then you'd be a counter-revolutionary, and I would shoot you and erect you a monument. I don't believe, Grosz, that overwhelming compassion for the exploited or anger against the exploiter one day filled you with an irresistible desire to get something about this down on paper. I think drawing was something you enjoyed, and people's physiognomies were so many pretexts for it. I imagine you becoming aware one day of a sudden overwhelming love for a particular type of face as a marvelous opportunity for you to amuse yourself. It was *The Face of the Ruling Class* [*Das Gesicht der herrschenden Klasse*, one of Grosz's early albums]. I'm not underrating your enjoyment of protest, which was what no doubt moved you to expose as swine the very people who saw themselves as the élite of the human race —and necessarily had to be since none but an élite could be permitted such swinish behavior. In the Protestant sense there wasn't any truth worth revealing in reducing a proletarian type to his basic pattern. Proletarians have no call to be other than they are. In the immense effort it costs them just to keep alive they spontaneously adopted their most genuine basic form. Any kind of frills were out of the question. In appearing better than he really was, that type of bourgeois was doing business, but proletarians don't do business at all. Art nowadays is in the same position as you: the type you adore as subject-matter you are bound to detest as a member of the public. Politically you regard the bourgeoisie as your enemy not because you are a proletarian but because you are an artist. Your political position (which unlike you I treat as secondary, you see) is a position in relation to the public, not in relation to your subject-matter. I have gone through the same process as you, just as seriously though with nothing like the same success. Let me refer you to a play of mine which greatly displeased those who share your political opinions: the little comedy called *Drums in the Night.*

2. *DRUMS IN THE NIGHT*'S SUCCESS WITH THE BOURGEOISIE

This play was performed on some fifty bourgeois stages. Its success, which was considerable, simply proved that I had come to the wrong address. I was totally dissatisfied at this: why, I could not immediately say. I just had an uncomfortable sensation. I had a vague idea that the people who were so wildly anxious to shake my hand were just the lot I would have liked to hit on the head, not in this play perhaps but in general. My condition was like that of a man who has fired a gun at people he dislikes, and finds these same people coming and giving three cheers for him: inadvertently he has been firing off loaves of bread. When I then consulted the papers to find out what had happened I found that the chief element of my success lay in the furious attacks launched by the aesthetically reactionary press. So there were still those who complained of the loaves!

The whole thing was an aesthetic business of which I understood nothing. In any other period I might have been able to understand something about it, but at this particular moment, with New York being built and Moscow being destroyed, and both processes seeming likely to concern the whole world, aesthetics were wholly irrelevant. The bourgeois theater, equally incapable of performing the oldest plays or the most modern, imagined that its continued existence was merely a question of styles. Like a foundering ship, the sinking theater concerned itself with the possibly very difficult but basically unimportant question whether it was better to sink to the left or to the right. And the crew criticized the band, which in its confusion kept on playing "Nearer, my God, to Thee," meaning the God who is on the side of the big battalions. To avoid dreadful misunderstandings I should point out that this image for the decline of the theater may perhaps be inappropriate, for the reason that the theater was a lot more expensive than an old steamship and worth a lot less, and that those who went down in her by no means suffered any loss but quite the reverse. Moreover a brief bout of introspection was enough to convince audience and artists alike that the theater was bound to go under; and those shrieks of desperation were paid for by the theaters out of what they made by selling advertising space in the programs.

I have always regarded myself as a man who, given a few drinks and cigars, can equip himself to turn out a literary work such as careful reflection will lead him to think desirable. The only thing is that I'm not sure what will happen if I give my abilities their head. Of course, I am not now speaking of aesthetic results. *Drums in the Night* is an admirable instance of the weakness of the human will. I wrote it to make money. But although, amazingly enough, I really did make money I would be deceiving you if I said that my pains had been rewarded with success. A number of people managed to hand me money for them; but I managed to write a political play.

3. THE LOVE STORY

In view of the fact that my choice of subject for the play was decided on speculative and financial grounds, it is perhaps of public interest that I should have specifically decided that a love story was called for. Writing this play was a really serious business undertaking, which was precisely what made me able to understand the needs of the paying public. (The experiences embodied in the play, in other words, were avarice and writing.) I was accordingly quite ready to supply the love story, but what I found interesting about it above all was of course the property aspect. The character of Kragler, who struck me as a typical hero of our time, reduced it to that. He wanted a particular woman, and the only course open to him psychologically if he didn't get her was that of a man who fails to get a house that he used to, or wishes to, possess. The causes of his desire struck me as not worth going into. I didn't in fact make the woman particularly desirable. She commands a certain run-of-the-mill sensuality, which can hardly be termed strong since it gets satisfied without further ado, and indeed without reference to the object or partner. The entire sexual motivation remains makeshift and ordinary. You or I would call it innocuous. It is not that powerful, almost revolutionary call for physical satisfaction which arises when a woman needs somebody to sleep with her and has to put up with whatever man she can get. To Anna Balicke a man is not an article for use but a cheap luxury. In bourgeois society the erotic sphere is exhausted. Literature reflects this by the fact that sex no longer gives rise to associations. In fact the strongest erotic life nowadays is probably to be found in that primitive literature (which occurs in the form of certain notoriously efficacious words and) which ordinary people wield with naïve virtuosity. Clearly the significance of their refusal to use vulgar words in front of women is that such words can be relied on to be thoroughly effective.

Today the tragic potentialities of a love relationship consist in the couple's failing to find a room. Unfortunately it is difficult to find out whether today's conditions also applied yesterday, as one can hardly ask one's father about his sex life. But at least today one can clearly establish the attraction of vulgar words relating to sex and its organs. Enjoyment of dirty words largely depends on their guaranteed obscenity. Indeed there are times when enjoyment of sex depends on its guaranteed obscenity. This romantic factor comes into play when Miss Balicke lusts after Kragler's obscene ignominiousness. The bourgeoisie will see it as a triumph of the ideal. In my view not even such depressing considerations as these will deprive the love story in question of its charm.

It may also be that real sexual enjoyment is now only to be got from venereal diseases. Here is a marketplace for our feelings where there is still some activity going on. One of these venereal diseases is pregnancy. Murk, whose rootlessness is due to the woman's indifference—a very common pestilence that can truly be compared with those in the Bible, goes and infects her with a child. His conduct is moral: in occupying her troubled mind he improves his economic standing. But morality is there to prevent miscalculations. And the woman behaves immorally. She thinks she will get more from that atmosphere of obscene sexuality: from lying with Kragler when in a pregnant condition.

4. 1918: THE KRAGLERS' REVOLUTION

When the play proved successful what succeeded was the love story and the use of drums offstage. (At the same time I'm prepared to admit that a certain fresh and personal quality and a fairly unrestrained penchant for putting things in a poetical way counted in my favor.) My interest in the revolution whose job it was to serve as background was about as great as the interest felt in Vesuvius by a man who wants to boil a kettle on it. Moreover my kettle seemed to me a very large affair compared with the volcano in question. It truly wasn't my fault that the play ended up by giving something like a picture of the first German revolution and, even more, a picture of this particular revolutionary. This revolution followed after a war which originated in a nervous breakdown on the part of the diplomats and was finished off by a nervous breakdown of the military. The bourgeoisie waged it with particular force. Wars have been waged before now for sillier reasons than the annexation of the coal and iron-ore districts of Briey. That famous dagger which the proletariat thrust into the army's back (the legend of which went on buzzing a long while in the heads of the Fascists and the Communists) would, if successful, have struck a region the army had long since abandoned; defeated, it was withdrawing. That was where the Kraglers came in. They made a revolution because their country, which some of them hadn't seen for four years, had changed. The Kraglers were rigidly conservative. Thanks to the sudden disappearance from all government positions of that part of the bourgeoisie which was aware that it was the bourgeoisie, the part which wasn't (i.e., the

Social-Democrats) was put in the embarrassing situation of having
to fill them. These men were revolutionaries in the sense that
miners in an insecure pit are mining engineers. The problem for
the Kraglers was how to become bourgeois. Most people treated
them as revolutionaries, and on the stage indeed I found that
Kragler gave a very revolutionary impression. Above all he gave
the impression of being a proletarian. Of course the military had
been proletarianized. Their complexion was not what it used to
be. Factories had always been like barracks, and now it could be
seen that they had similar effects. For a while the true revolutionaries could deprecate the play, since they took Kragler to be a
proletarian and had learned what good heroes such proletarians
make. They could also oppose it on the grounds that they took
Kragler to be a bourgeois and didn't want a hero like that. For
there wasn't any doubt about his being a hero. Today, however,
they could no longer deny that it is a thoroughly political play. An
object-lesson such as one seldom gets. What they had before them
was that disastrous type of Social-Democrat, in his heroic incarna-
tion at that. It was difficult to identify him as a bourgeois, either
on the stage or in real life. The revolution had undeniably been
lost. This was the type that had made it. What mattered most was
to learn how to identify him. He had made it, and here he was.
Here, in an ordinary romantic love story with no particular depth
to it, was this Social-Democrat, this fake proletarian, this catas-
trophic revolutionary who sabotaged the revolution, who was
more bitterly fought by Lenin than the bourgeois proper, and
who so evaded even Lenin's grasp that before the Russian Revolution it was scarcely possible to identify him to the masses so that
they could be warned. This then was Kragler, this revolutionary
whom sympathy converted back into a property-owner, who
wept and nagged and, as soon as he got what he had been lacking,
went home. As for the proletarians, they were not shown the play.

[GW *Schriften zum Theater*, p. 960 ff.
Written after Brecht's move to Berlin.]

Notes of Conversations about *Drums in the Night*

[. . .]

BRECHT   Ten years since I wrote it. The whole business pretty strange to me now. What I saw was important. Possibly a lot there that I failed to see. Total impression a wrong one. Kragler = drama of the individual. But impossible to depict the German revolution as drama of the individual. I see him coming back after the war. He finds home devastated, no place for him. You're shown what happened to the fellow. But not shown, e.g., that the fellow is first-rate material; not shown him in any situation where the revolution can make use of him; not shown how the revolution fails to do this. The way Lenin would have seen him: out of reach for four years, but submitted to increasing revolutionary tension. If he would have ratted nonetheless, then play bad. That isn't what happens, though.

PISCATOR   That would make sense if there'd been nobody capable of showing. But you had Liebknecht, Luxemburg . . . When the troops came back from the war the line was all of a sudden "Take part in the Workers' and Soldiers' Councils!" Play needs changes. The man was a prisoner. Doesn't alter the position. Battle for the newspaper offices. Everyone knew the proletarian slogans. Only a half-wit could avoid them. Can Kragler remain so ignorant and apart? Then he's an individual case, not a typical worker. Didn't act as a blackleg either. No feeling either for or against the revolution . . . That's as close as one can get to him. There lies the tragedy, but it didn't originate with Kragler. The tragedy about Kragler . . .

BRECHT   He's not tragic.

PISCATOR   The world around him's supposed to seem tragic. The tragedy is that the German revolution is a failure, that people aren't faced with a challenge.

BRECHT   Tragic or not tragic, from the point of view of the revolution it's wrong that no approach was made to the man.

PISCATOR   Establish the crux. The man turns up as an ex-prisoner. Chance is the decisive factor in the situation. He's always having to circumvent chance incidents.

STERNBERG   The 1918 revolution must be present in the background. I'd say that now we've got a militant Red organization, the German Communist Party, we're too apt to project everything back to the 1918 period, which is something Brecht has instinctively avoided doing. The slogan "Convert the war into a civil war!" only dates from the beginning of the revolution. This was one thing in Russia, where they already started trying to convert a war into a civil war in 1905, and another in Germany, where social-democracy was a force. (New number of *Klassenkampf* today: Ebert wanted to save the monarchy as late as November 9: the leader of social-democracy!) That's how things were in 1918 when the troops came home. So and so many million workers were then in the same sociological situation. They had the same program as the majority Socialists: let's hope we get in. There must have been a tremendous preponderance of pacifist forces to detach a worker from the revolution.

BRECHT   Needs every possible force to get his girl back.

STERNBERG   The girl's running away isn't an occasion for making a revolution. But suppose you were a German worker who had been flung into the war and badly misused, and had heard one side's slogans, then you would have to be a lot more positive in your attitude to the revolution. In the days of the Spartacists there were 8 million workers coming back from the war and 2 percent who joined in.

PISCATOR   Projecting back is something we do with Shakespeare as well as with Brecht. Seeing things in a present-day light.

BRECHT   But not modernizing a 1918 play.

PISCATOR   You mustn't forget, though, that you're now seeing what you failed to see then. Today's angle on the subject is a new one. Not a question of seeing further; that's not possible. The new viewpoints are different and must be brought into use too. Piscator came back to Berlin at the beginning of January. Factories all striking, workers all parading with enormous signs along Unter den Linden. More workers coming the other way with signs saying "Liebknecht, Luxemburg," both groups grabbing each other's signs. Fighting, till somebody shoots. All the workers on the streets. Everywhere small parties of people arguing.

BRECHT   Make him just a historian. Kragler was part of the general movement. Hearing different advice from all directions: "You must save the revolution—You must carry on the revolution

—You must pull back, reconstruct—Bourgeois republic's the pattern now—etc." He is simply raw material. And on the third day? He goes home. He counts how much money he's got in his pocket, and goes home.

PISCATOR   That'd be an exceptionally calculated reaction.

BRECHT   An Ebert man, who really does reckon that private life's more important.

PISCATOR   In that case the line has got to be drawn very clearly. He must connect up with the subject if he's to be dramatic. As it stands, the play is felt poetically. Brecht saw the man splitting away from the movement rather than the movement itself. Brecht today is looking back at the revolution scientifically; in those days he was a poet.

BRECHT   All the same, Kragler does notice one or two things. He's been told he must go along, he's faced with the choice of going along, he doesn't go along, he has an extremely bad conscience, he feels he's a stinker, that it's a cheap drama. It ends with him saying, "I'm a stinker, and the stinker goes home."

STERNBERG   That's the crux. Piscator's right.

BRECHT   He turns against the revolution, rejects it; he's for romanticism. (The Russian Revolution classic, the German not.)

PISCATOR   You may say I look at the revolution romantically, but Liebknecht and Luxemburg didn't.

STERNBERG   What he said agrees with Piscator's view. He's a chance instance. Finds the revolution romantic.

BRECHT   Bunk, according to a lot of people.

[. . .]

PISCATOR   What are they sitting at home for? Kragler because he realizes the revolution's bunk; many others because they're disillusioned.

BRECHT   They're still Kraglers. All those you saw were Kraglers. The only kind who weren't Kraglers, the genuine revolutionaries around Rosa Luxemburg and Karl Liebknecht, were the chaps with their eyes open, and they weren't typical. Typical were types like Kragler. He was my revolutionary.

STERNBERG   This is where you really need film to show how they came to be the majority.

BRECHT   And to get their way.

[. . .]

STERNBERG   [. . .] I can picture Kragler today sitting in the

KPD: a proper Communist. A simple type. He's no longer typical today. He's once again subject to the law of decreasing wages, no longer views the revolution as bunk. A type who has undergone a change.

BRECHT   In effect: a man sits there, in this year of grace 1928, talking about 1918. Not at all the same conversation as in 1918. (What with all conversation becoming increasingly political.) In those days he thought about nothing but the woman.

PISCATOR   It's still an isolated case of one individual's drama. Observed by somebody who had nothing to do with the movement.

BRECHT   One can't say that. He'd just as much to do as those million others.

STERNBERG   We're taking one man and showing what they were all like in 1918.

[. . .]

PISCATOR   Why does the play have to be performed?

BRECHT   To show why these people went home, why the revolution came to nothing. Historical enlightenment. The stumbling block was a type who really existed.

PISCATOR   In the hope of showing how revolution can lead to something.

> [*Schriften zum Theater 2*, p. 272 ff., shortened as indicated. Not in GW. This conversation, dated November 18, 1928, was followed by another six days later.]

On Looking Through My First Plays [i]

Of all my early plays the comedy *Drums in the Night* is the most double-edged. Here was a case where revolting against a contemptible literary convention almost amounted to contempt for a great social revolt. A "normal" (i.e., conventional) approach to this story about the returning soldier who joins the revolution because his girl has got engaged to somebody else would either have given the girl back to him or have denied her to him for good; either way it would have left him taking part in the revolution. In *Drums in the Night* Kragler, the soldier, gets his girl back, albeit "damaged," and puts the revolution behind him. It seems just about the shabbiest possible solution, particularly as there is a faint suspicion of approval on the part of the author.

Today I realize that my spirit of contradiction—I'm suppressing my wish to insert the word "youthful" as I hope I still have it at my disposal in full strength—led me close to the limits of absurdity.

The "human predicament" drama of those days, with its unrealistic pseudo-solutions, was uncongenial to the student of science. It set up a highly improbable and undoubtedly ineffectual collective of "good" people who were supposed to put a final stop to war —that complicated phenomenon whose roots lie deep in the social fabric—chiefly by moral condemnation. I knew next to nothing definite about the Russian Revolution, but my own modest experience as a medical orderly in the winter of 1918 was enough to make me think that a totally new and momentous force had appeared on the scene: the revolutionary proletariat.

It seems that my knowledge was not enough to make me realize the full seriousness of the proletarian rising in the winter of 1918–19, only to show me how unseriously my obstreperous "hero" took part in it. The initiative in this fight was taken by the proletarians; he cashed in. They didn't have to lose property to make them rebel; he got restitution. They were prepared to look after his interests; he betrayed theirs. They were the tragic figures, he the comic. All this, I realized on reading the play, had been perfectly evident to me, but I could not manage to make the audience see the revolution any differently from my "hero" Kragler, and he saw it as something romantic. The technique of alienation was not yet open to me.

Reading Acts 3, 4, and 5 of *Drums in the Night* I felt such dissatisfaction that I thought of suppressing the play. The only thing that stopped me from erecting a small funeral pyre was the feeling that literature is part of history, and that history ought not to be falsified, also a sense that my present opinions and capacities would be of less value without some knowledge of my previous ones—that is, presuming that there has been any improvement. Nor is suppressing enough; what's false must be set right.

Admittedly I could not do much. The character of Kragler, the soldier, the *petit-bourgeois*, I couldn't touch. My comparative approval of his conduct had also to be preserved. Anyway even the workers always find it easier to understand the *petit-bourgeois* who defends his own interests (however sordid these may be, and even if he is defending them against the workers) than the man who joins them for romantic reasons or out of a sense of guilt. However, I cautiously reinforced the other side. I gave the gin mill owner Glubb a nephew, a young worker who fell as a revolutionary during the November fighting. Though he could only be glimpsed in outline, somewhat filled in, however, thanks to the gin mill owner's scruples, this worker provided a kind of counterpart to the soldier Kragler.

The reader or spectator has then to be relied on to change his attitude to the play's hero, unassisted by appropriate alienations, from sympathy to a certain antipathy.

[From "Bei Durchsicht meiner ersten Stücke" in GW *Schriften zum Theater*. pp. 945–47. Dated March 1954.]

Editorial Note

The original version of this play was written in the spring of 1919. A title page exists headed *"The Dying Ghost* or *Spartacus"*, but no script has so far been found. The Brecht Archive has only the typescript of the version used for the Deutsches Theater production of December 1922, three months after the Munich première. The earliest known text is that published by Drei-Masken Verlag in Munich in 1922, which was also reissued twice by Propyläen-Verlag (i.e., Ullstein) in Berlin during the second half of the 1920's. Brecht used it for the first volume of his collected *Stücke* in 1953, with the extensive revisions outlined in his own retrospective note. This revised text was printed, with minor amendments, in the *Gesammelte Werke* of 1967 and is the basis of the present translation.

Three main versions are thus accessible: the 1922 publication, the script of December 1922, and the final text of 1953. The first describes the play as a "Drama," the other two as "Comedy." In the second the prostitute Augusta is for some reason called Carmen, though Augusta remains a nickname. At some earlier point the Bar in Act 4 seems to have been called "The Red Raisin": hence the nickname given to one of the waiter brothers in the final version. The confusion in the timing of the action (which is said to take place in November, though the Spartacist revolt and the battle for the Berlin newspaper offices actually occurred in January) was not cleared up until 1967, when a note appeared in GW saying, "The action of the play now takes place in January 1919." The most serious divergences between the different versions, however, occur in Acts 3, 4, and 5, and they represent a seemingly permanent dissatisfaction on Brecht's part with the second half of the play.

This is already on record in his diaries of 1920, even before our earliest version. "I have rewritten the beginning of Act 3 of *Drums*," he noted on August 3rd, "and the second (optional) ending to Act 4. . . . I've done four versions of Act 4 and three of Act

5. I've now got two endings, one comic, one tragic." A little later
he is "dictating *Drums in the Night*. The third act is in the main
good; the fourth a bastard, an abortion. . ." Twenty-five pages later
he is still at it:

> nagging away at *Drums in the Night*. I'm drilling rock, and the
> drills are breaking. It's terribly hard to make this fourth act
> follow grandly and simply after the first three, at the same time
> carrying on the external tension of the third, which works
> pretty well, and bringing the internal transformation (in 15 min-
> utes) forcefully home. What's more, the play's strong, healthy,
> untragic ending, which it had from the outset and for the sake
> of which it was written, is the only possible ending; anything
> else is too easy a way out, a weakly synthetic concession to
> romanticism. Here is a man apparently at an emotional climax,
> making a complete volteface; he tosses all pathos aside, tells his
> followers and admirers to stuff it, then goes home with the
> woman for whose sake he got involved in this extremely dan-
> gerous mess. Bed as final curtain. To hell with ideas, to hell with
> duty!

The contrast between this view of the play and the author's ver-
dicts of 1928 and 1954 needs no stressing. Moreover even by 1922
he had become less certain of the effectiveness of the third act,
which seems to have gone badly at the première.

The detailed notes that follow show what passages Brecht cut
or changed when he reviewed the 1922 text in the early 1950's. One
or two minor amendments apart, the whole of the 1922 version can
be reconstructed from it. The script used by the Deutsches Theater is different yet again, particularly where Acts 4 and 5 are
concerned. This would be too complicated to analyze in full, but
an account of the more substantial changes follows the extracts
from the 1922 version. It will be found to shed light on one or two
obscurities, notably the characters of Glubb and Laar.

1. Variant Material from the 1922 Published Text

The text of the 1922 version may be reconstituted by substituting
the words following the equal sign (=) for the words preceding it.

Brief passages before the equal sign are quoted in full; longer passages are indicated by first and last words separated by a dash.

In Acts 3, 4, and 5 extensive sections were rewritten for the final version. Here the original versions are given in full even though they occasionally contain unaltered bits of text which may have been displaced into a different context or else require a slightly different translation because of changes in the surrounding material.

The marginal symbol (o) in the text of the play (pp. 59–106) indicates where such variants occur.

ACT I

68   downtown. But = downtown. The revolutionary action seems to be localized in the slums. But

ACT II

84   *The "Internationale"—outside) = A slowly swelling sound of stamping feet outside. Shouting. Whistling. Singing. Drumming. The shouting and stamping continue)*

district and stinking = district and whistling into the cafés. Stinking

hide, because = hide? And drums out in the street? Because

ACT III

88   Newspaper District = Slums

But your . . . = But your wife?

There are knives. = Christ, there's sleep. There's schnapps. There's tobacco. There are knives.

liquor = tobacco

Let's get going. = Let's go down there.

They're—district. = Down there they'll be swimming in schnapps tonight.

89   Cannon. = Listen to that drumming.

On Friedrichstrasse! = In our neighborhood!

Do you—*hand*) Bang, bang! = Feeling dizzy?
SECOND   Knocks the wind out of you, doesn't it?
FIRST

newspaper district has = slums have

90   And look at him now! = And take a look at that! Now it's drunk but it used to have buttoned shoes and push a floozie around the dance floor with the best of them. Well, take it from me, right now it's feeling cold and doesn't know exactly what to do. It mustn't be left lying here.

about him = about it

linen? Is = linen? Is it that drunken bundle? Is

That will—scores. = And that will be the man who's scared shitless. I've known him since he was a boy.
MANKE   To the dogs and to Glubb's bar, that's where he'll go. If he's lucky, they'll stand him up against the wall.
BABUSCH   He'll settle for the bar. Or he'll call them all together and if you hear a hubbub in the newspaper district toward morning and something drumming in the night, that'll be him.

ANNA   I can't =
ANNA   I can't.
MURK   Can't you see me?
ANNA   Yes.

91   four years. ANNA I can't. = four years.
MURK (*sobering up*)   The linen has been bought and the apartment has been rented. And where are you going?
MANKE   Do you hear what the skunk is saying? Where is she going? We'll tell you: to the filthy little houses, that's where

we're going. You know. Where you slip in all the vomit on the stairs. To the dingy black garrets where the wind whistles through.

ANNA   That's where I'm going.

MANKE   We won't go under. Into the old beds, the rain comes in, and how can you expect to get warm with the wind whistling through. Maybe it's worse there. That's the place for you. There you can disappear. Those are the houses they're drumming in today. They're crammed full of bundles like this, without a shirt, and the whole thing will take maybe twenty, thirty years, the last years on this earth, you don't count them, and yet your soul feels more at home there than anywhere else.

MURK   Father and mother are making arrangements for the wedding.

ANNA   I can't do it.

91   But the man has come who has = But the man has come who has waited four years.

MURK   Who has no clean shirt on his body . . .

MANKE   And his skin is like a crocodile's.

MURK   And you didn't recognize him, the way he looked.

MANKE   But she still had her lily when he came.

ANNA   The man has come who has

newspaper district is = slums are

Friedrichstadt? And nothing = the slums, into darkness, into nothingness?

ANNA   Yes. Into nothingness.

MURK   It's all schnapps fumes. A dime novel. Last year's snow.

ANNA   That's all . . .

MANKE   Right, that's all it is. Now she knows: she's headed for nothingness.

MURK   And nothing

Nothing—thing"? = Nothing? Not even the lily? And when no wind reaches you any more, and when you've floated downstream and out of sight, you won't think of the "other thing" any more?

And you—animal. =
MURK   And we finished him off. Completely.
ANNA   And they beat him like an animal.

MURK   He's done for! ANNA   And he's done for! =
MURK   And he was done for! Absolutely finished!
ANNA   And he was done for!

92   she gone?—The Ride = she gone? Into the wind, and I'm so drunk. I can't see my hands and she runs out on me.
BABUSCH   I've suddenly seen the light, man. So that's the pond we're fishing in. The Ride

son. = son. Now this spooky pond business is getting deadly serious.

newspaper district = slums

And now = Take it home, do something for your immortal soul. And now

MANKE (calls—revolution is =
MANKE (drags Murk to his feet, spreads both arms wide, grandly): The slums are

ACT IV
93   (A Dawn Will Come) = (The Schnapps Dance)

93-   Lazarus.—(He removes = Lazarus
94   BABUSCH (at the window)   Has a soldier been here?
GLUBB (pouring schnapps)   No, he hasn't been here.
BABUSCH (over his shoulder)   He hasn't been here.
GLUBB   Is one expected here?
(Babusch shrugs his shoulders)
GLUBB   Should I give him a message?
BABUSCH (looks at Anna, who shakes her head)   No, we'll be back.
(Both go out)
MANKE   If they requisition something, it's schnapps, if they share something, it's a bed, and if they produce something, it's babies. Good God! If you had schnapps inside you, sonny boy, and those pale- faces and trembling knees (He acts it out) and your nose in the air where it was raining, raining

bullets, sonny boy, and a gun in your hand and a tight feeling in your fingers, my boy.

BULLTROTTER   Freedom! Space! Air! (*He removes*

94   *"Internationale" = "Marseillaise"*

tremolo. Freedom! = tremolo. The bourgeois!

BULLTROTTER (*throws a newspaper at him*)   Where there's a horse, there's horseshit. (*They throw newspapers at each other*) Freedom!

MANKE   Freedom!

AUGUSTA   Why = AUGUSTA   Oh, so that's the kind you are? Why

"Couldn't you—know how! [Not in 1922 text.]

94-   BULLTROTTER   That's—MANKE   Prisoner? =
95   BULLTROTTER   Riots! Strikes! Revolution!

AUGUSTA   Christ Almighty, where are they going?

GLUBB   To the newspaper offices! They're the readers! (*He closes the window*)

BULLTROTTER   But what's that wind?

AUGUSTA   Christ Almighty, who's that standing in the doorway?

(*Kragler is in doorway, swaying as though drunk, rocking on the balls of his feet*)

BULLTROTTER   What a coincidence! He's got an artillery uniform on.

MANKE   Odd-looking outfit. Are you going to lay an egg?

AUGUSTA   Who are you, coming with the cannon like that?

KRAGLER (*with a malignant grin*)   Nobody.

AUGUSTA (*drying him*)   The water's running down his neck.

MANKE (*crossing over to him*)   Then what have you been up to, boy? I know a guilty face when I see one. Some kind of trouble in a gin mill, eh?

AUGUSTA   You been running as fast as all that?

MARIE   They took away his girl he'd been waiting four years for. They drove to the Piccadilly Bar, he ran the whole way to the Piccadilly Bar behind the cab.

THE DRUNK   Like a calf? So there's a story?!

AUGUSTA   Is it romantic?
KRAGLER   I don't know any story.
BULLTROTTER   Are you in it? Do you belong with him?
MARIE   I only ran out with him.
MANKE   Why do you run like a calf?
THE DRUNK   You got the trots?
KRAGLER   No, I haven't got the trots.
THE DRUNK   Well now, is there a story?
BULLTROTTER   What do you mean, story?
THE DRUNK   Or maybe a gospel? Give him some schnapps, let him smoke, then he can tell it. (*The door is closed. Kragler stands against the wall. The others smoke and stare at his mouth. Glubb wipes glasses*)
THE DRUNK   Keep the door closed. It's only the wind, brother, but it's barred. It's barred.
KRAGLER (*boasting with bitter humor*)   I was in Africa . . . Lot of sun down there. We shot niggers, man, and . . . so on. We paved roads too. We went down in cattle cars.
MANKE   Prisoner?

95   And meanwhile—*the table*) [Not in 1922 text.]
95-   (*Kragler—the others*) [End of Act IV] =
99   KRAGLER   Sure, Africa. (*Silence*) The sun dried up your head like a fig, our brains were like figs, we shot niggers, always in the belly, and worked on the roads, and I had a fly in my head, friends, and no brains left, and they kept hitting me on the head.
BULLTROTTER   That story's true to life. A good yarn. Have another drink! What happened before that?
KRAGLER   Before? I was lying in a mudhole. Like a corpse in putrid water. We pumped water. We stared at time. It didn't pass. Then we stared at the sky, a patch like an umbrella, always dark as a puddle, but the water was coming out our ears anyway, because the ditch was always full. (*He drinks*)
GLUBB   You fellows certainly knew how to take it easy.
AUGUSTA   Tell us about Africa! About Africa!
KRAGLER   Well, it never passed, all we could do was stink. We were fighting for our country, the stones and the other thing,

and I fought for the sky and the earth and the water and—
everything.

MARIE   Andry! His name is Andry.

KRAGLER   Andry! My name's Andry. It used to be Andry.
Thick green trees in the air, I've seen that. But not during
the four years.

GLUBB   You didn't see them. What of it?

KRAGLER   I fought, and now and then somebody was killed,
and I had a fly in my head, a fly, it was my wife, only she
wasn't my wife yet, she was innocent, and (*Drinks*) and then
came Africa.

BULLTROTTER   (*smiling broadly*)   And the ass down there,
what's the ass like?

KRAGLER   It was an island or something. Never a letter and the
nights were cold. (*Opening his eyes wide*) All you people have
to do is throw cats off a wall! (*He drinks*)

MARIE   How long did it last? How long?

KRAGLER   Three years. Three years is more than a thousand
days. They held us under water, see, like cats in leather bags,
they don't want to die. (*Counting on his fingers*) I might have
died on the second day or the tenth, or the twentieth or the
fortieth . . . But there was Anna, standing morning after
morning behind the barracks, among the dogs.

THE DRUNK   And you didn't desert?

KRAGLER   (*more calmly*)   The third time I deserted I was all
right and I sang when things got too bad, I was all right and
I was alive. (*He sits down and speaks more and more slowly and
laboriously, drinking a good deal. Now he pauses and says very
calmly*) Don't get the idea I was grasping or anything like
that and that I thought she went to the barracks in the morning and didn't do anything else. I'd thought out a plan, a way
of getting her used to me again, because I'd turned into a
ghost. That's a fact. (*He drinks. The sound of wind. The drunk
groans with suspense*)

KRAGLER   (*calmly*)   She wasn't home when I got there.

GLUBB   No, she wasn't. She really wasn't.

BULLTROTTER   So?

THE DRUNK   Was she gone? Where was she?

KRAGLER   The schnapps was all drunk up and the niggers were dead and the umbrella had collapsed and the fly, the fly had flown away. (*Looks into space*) I fought for him. He sent schnapps for the bulls and he sent the umbrella, and he let the fly live, so we wouldn't get fed up. (*Points a finger as if he could see him*) And now he's running around in the sun, that other fellow. And now he's lying in bed and you people take your hats off when he comes around, and he's skinning you alive, and my wife's lying in his bed.

BULLTROTTER (*with newspaper*)   Somebody swiped her, eh?

GLUBB   They swiped my bicycle.

MANKE (*running his hand over his neck*)   You're mighty patient, son.

AUGUSTA   And you didn't strangle her like a cat?

MARIE   They went off with her. And he just ran along behind them.

KRAGLER (*drinking*)   I went cold when they said that, my mind was a blank. And even now my pulse is normal when I think of it; you can feel it. (*Holds out his hand, drinks with the other*) I went looking for her and she knew me too, though my face used to be like peaches and cream, and she said something to me. Give me back my glass.

THE DRUNK   Go on! What did she say?

KRAGLER   Well, she said (*He drinks*) it's all over.

(*Silence. He is still absently feeling his pulse*)

GLUBB   Nothing time won't heal.

THE DRUNK   What did you do?

KRAGLER   You go right on drinking. I'm leaving. You go on, I'm not here any more. Dance and swill and croak when the time comes. (*He gets noisy*) Take me, for instance, I've got Africa in my blood, a lousy sickness. A fly in my head, a horsefly, dance away, give me schnapps, you don't know the whole story. Turn up the nickelodeon, one day you'll know the rest.

MANKE   You've had a rough time. Drink away, boy!

BULLTROTTER   Drink yourself blind. He feels like a corpse, he's dead, but he doesn't know it. Last week in Merseburg we ran this story . . .

THE DRUNK   Is she still alive? (*Has started the nickelodeon*) It's not possible.

KRAGLER (*hums the tune, grabs Augusta, hops around with her*)
Forward march! And keep marching!

GLUBB   Don't break my glasses, soldier.

MARIE   He's drunk now. He feels better.

KRAGLER (*upstage, being given schnapps by Augusta*)   Does he
feel better? Hasn't he any flesh, is he made of paper? Console
yourself, brother; say: It's not possible. Can you hear it,
Brother Brandykeg, can you hear the wind? Step lively,
Sister Prostitute! Step lively, Brother Red! I say unto you:
don't wait. What's a pig before the Lord! It's nothing. Drink
yourselves blind, never mind about the pig, then you won't
notice.

GLUBB   Why are you shouting so?

KRAGLER   Who's paying for this? Who's making the music? All
this music! I've got my fly! Just give me schnapps, it'll drown
itself. Can you abolish the army or God? Can you abolish
suffering and the torments that men have taught the devil?
You can't abolish them, but you can drink. You can drink
schnapps and sleep even on the sidewalk. All things must
serve those that sleep, remember that, it's in the Catechism,
you've got to believe it. So drink and shut the door, and don't
let the wind in, the wind is shivering too. Shut the door and
bolt it! Don't let the ghosts in. They're cold.

GLUBB   Ah, Brother Soldier, you've suffered a slight injustice.

KRAGLER   Did you say injustice, Brother Red? What a funny
word! Injustice! Make yourselves comfortable on this star.
It's cold here and kind of dark, Mr. Red, and there's no time
for injustice, the world is too old for better days and schnapps
is cheaper, and Heaven's already rented out, my friends.
(*Goes upstage humming, puts coins in the nickelodeon which each
time plays very rapidly and briefly*)

BULLTROTTER (*has been drinking in silence*)   What can you say
to that? Cuffs! Cuffs!

MANKE (*stands up*)   But your wife's looking for you, man!

KRAGLER (*dancing alone*)   Trot! Trot! Double-quick march!
(*Sings in an undertone*)

A dog went to the kitchen
To find a bone to chew.

MANKE (*smoking*)   Now he's hopping around with his horsefly.

AUGUSTA   Having a good smoke?

GLUBB   See here, you people are only supposed to drink schnapps.

MANKE   But we're smoking too.

THE DRUNK   Sure, you're the revolutionary. We know you and your speeches. They poured your schnapps down the toilet, you were selling schnapps.

GLUBB (*still busy with the glasses, coldly*)   I had more under the floorboards. And it's not because the schnapps was gone but because there are human hands that pour it down the toilet.

KRAGLER (*blinking, and as though waking her up*)   Anna! Anna!

BULLTROTTER (*crowing*)   Cuffs! You should have swiped some cuffs, boy!

GLUBB   I was standing out in the yard, it was night. It was raining, I looked around, that's probably when it came to me. And now I'm for drinking, and when I drink I'll sing the chorales.

KRAGLER

The cook picked up his chopper
And chopped the dog in two.

MARIE   What should we do? We're nobodies. A lot of people say we should go to the newspaper district, that's where things are happening. But what *is* happening in the newspaper district?

KRAGLER   A cab is driving to the Piccadilly Bar.

AUGUSTA   Is she in it?

KRAGLER   She's in it.

MANKE   Your wife must be looking for you, man.

THE DRUNK (*has climbed up on the table and is looking out at the city in the night*)   Just go on drinking!

LAAR   They were only pine trees, small pine trees . . .

GLUBB   The stone is opening its mouth.

LAAR   You see, there was this guy who happened to have some money on him.

BULLTROTTER   And you sold them, you beast!

(*Laar goes to rear*)

GLUBB (*to Kragler who is much calmer*)   Keep drinking! Some people out there are drumming and now they've even started shooting. You can hear it plainly. If you people will only shut up a minute. They're shooting for your benefit. Yes, heaven and hell are making a revolution, man, and you shouldn't even be drinking schnapps. You've suffered a slight injustice. Accept it and swallow it. Hold still when they skin you, soldier, or your skin will fall apart, and it's the only one you've got. (*Puts a glass down behind him, calmly*) To the machine guns, all of you!

SEVERAL   To the newspaper district!

GLUBB   Sure, you should put out a newspaper.

KRAGLER   It's a long way to the Piccadilly Bar.

MANKE (*with a stogie between his teeth, takes off his jacket*)   That's going too far; no need for anybody to let himself be kicked in the stomach.

GLUBB (*sees the man standing there in his shirt sleeves*)   Sure, put on clean shirts over your rotten skin, so nobody notices it. Are stories something to eat? Oh well, a slight injustice. Eat salad, drink kirsch! (*Starts the nickelodeon*) Yes, you're kind of drowned in brandy, they've pushed you around with rifle butts, they slaughtered you with cannon and sabers, and swindled you and spat on you a little.

AUGUSTA   You cowards let us starve and say Amen. A glass of schnapps! (*Tumult, shouts "Hell," "No"*) Yes, look at me. I'm a lousy whore and I've had a lousy time. Just look at me: my name is Augusta.

GLUBB   Yes, and you've got syphilis.

WOMAN SELLING NEWSPAPERS (*upstage*)   Papers! Spartacus in newspaper district! Red Rosa addresses open-air meeting in Tierpark! State of siege! Revolution!

BULLTROTTER   Give us a paper! That's something for us.

THE WOMAN (*shrilly*)   Mob riots! Where's the army? Here you are, soldier. Only twenty pfennigs.

KRAGLER   Are they shooting again? (*Bends down*) Is it a joke? On to the barricades with this ghost! (*Stands firmly, takes a deep breath*) Ending it all is better than schnapps. It's no joke. To vanish is better than to sleep.

BULLTROTTER (*jumps onto the table*)   I was at Jutland. That was no picnic, either.

(*Glubb closes the glass cabinet, wipes his hands*)

MANKE   Let's go, Augusta! With my shield or without it!

BULLTROTTER   And what about your distillery, liquor-dealer?

GLUBB   The rats will live in it.

KRAGLER (*on a chair, tinkers with the lamp, an antediluvian relic*)   They're shooting again, my friends. Winners in the morning or drowned cats on the asphalt.

THE OTHERS (*shout*)   Winners in the morning, Andry!

KRAGLER (*puts out the lamp*)   Or drowned cats!

MANKE   Forward, Augusta!

THE DRUNK (*pointing at Marie*)

Sinful Sadie was good as gold
She sheltered him through tears and cold.

KRAGLER (*slipping down*)   I'm a corpse, it's all yours! (*Angrily*) All right, come to my heart. To the newspapers, all of us! (*The others follow him*)

THE DRUNK (*last in line*)   Wash me, Lord, and make me white. Wash me, make me as white as the snow.

(*Laar staggers to the nickelodeon, takes the drum, and, playing drumrolls, staggers after the others*)

ACT V

100   You'd better go home—*the houses*) = They stormed the barracks after two o'clock.

ANNA   He won't be coming any more.

BABUSCH   Now they're marching to the newspaper district. Yes, you'd better go home.

ANNA   I can't any more.

BABUSCH   The last time, around four o'clock, it seemed to me as if he had given up, he was swimming hard, but he couldn't surface.

ANNA   What's the use, I waited four years with his picture. Then I took another man. I was afraid at night.

BABUSCH   I'm out of cigars. Aren't you ever going home?

ANNA   It's so late in the year and the moon is so red! Like in a dream. I sit here on a stone and the moon's red and it's late in the year.

BABUSCH   They're drumming again down there. They're ripping up newspapers and throwing them into puddles, they're screaming at machine guns and shooting in each other's ears. They think they're making a new world. There comes another bunch of them.

ANNA   It's him!

(*A great turbulence invades the streets as the group approaches. The sound of shooting from all directions*)

ANNA   The streets wake up when they come. Fever is dropping through the roofs. The houses are getting restless. I'm going to tell him now!

BABUSCH   I'll stop your mouth!

ANNA   I'm not an animal. I'm going to scream.

BABUSCH   That's the fever, and I'm out of cigars.

(*Glubb, Laar, the drunk, the two prostitutes, and Andry Kragler emerge from between the houses*)

101   (*Silence*) But you—in your ear. = (*Silence*) But mustn't you go? You haven't got a cap and it's cold. I've got to whisper something in your ear. Now I don't remember. I suppose it's not to be.

fiancée = wife

Isn't she = She's

102   *down*) And now = *down*)

GLUBB   She's made of earth, too, boy, look at her down under.

AUGUSTA   And now

FIRST   They've—(*They are gone*) =

FIRST   Now they're in the newspaper district.

SECOND   And the artillery is pulling up.

FIRST   Things are going to be different now.

SECOND   It's all too little and too late.

FIRST   There's a lot of them coming.

SECOND   Much too late.

(*They are gone, but upstage many pass by marching to the newspaper district*)

today. = today. Has he still got his hand in his pants pocket?

103   It only—Wedding. = And of course, the unflattering light. (*Looks
at the sky*)
AUGUSTA   They're marching, they're shouting, they're beck-
oning.

faded—But = faded, and it's the unflattering light that makes you
look as if your hair had fallen out. All in all, you look kind of pale
and wrung out. And your fingers are black, let's see them. But

air) Yes, = *air*) Hell, I've only known you for four hours. Yes,

eleven o'clock = then

ANNA   Where's the subway, somebody? =
ANNA   Is it seven o'clock?
KRAGLER   Come here to me, Anna.
ANNA   Where's the subway, somebody?

103-   Anna.—ask me. = Anna.
104   ANNA   Are you coming around?
GLUBB   Wouldn't you rather have a slug of whiskey?
KRAGLER   Here to me!
ANNA   Is it because of the Catechism?
KRAGLER   Anna.
AUGUSTA   Aren't you a soldier, son?
ANNA   Are you whistling for me again?
GLUBB   You've got to milk the cow while she's warm.
MANKE   In your artillery uniform, man?
KRAGLER   My voice is gone from shouting, but I've still got my
knife, you!
(*Glubb posts himself in front of Anna, the enormous shadows of
the marchers in the background fall across the buildings, and
snatches of the "Marseillaise" are borne on the wind*)
GLUBB   Well, she looks like vomited milk, it's disagreeable.
(*Kragler is silent*) Some of us would have liked another drink
of whiskey, but you were against it. Some of us would have
liked to lie in a bed one more time, but you had no bed and
it was the same way with smoking stogies. Too bad. (*Kragler
is silent*)

GLUBB Won't you come with us part of the way, Brother Soldier?

(*Kragler is silent*)

MANKE Why is he staring in that funny way? Is he laying an egg again?

ANNA Aren't you going, Andry?

MANKE For God's sake, man, take that hand out of your pocket.

ANNA You may go, Andry. Go on.

AUGUSTA Now he'll be lighting his pipe.

ANNA Go, go! I never want to see you again, your face is black, go away, I'm glad.

KRAGLER Throw stones at me, here I stand. I'll give you the shirt off my back, but I won't hold out my neck to the knife.

THE DRUNK Heavenly blazing assholes!

AUGUSTA But but but what . . . what about the newspapers?

(*Kragler shakes his head. Augusta gives a horse laugh*)

GLUBB The Eternal Womanly is leading him aloft.

KRAGLER (*looking at her*) Come, Anna.

GLUBB Couldn't you just jump in the river and take a bath?

KRAGLER I'm freezing cold.

AUGUSTA (*upstage*) Only a few of them are left now, they're running faster, and now they're disappearing. On to the newspapers, all of you, to the newspapers!

GLUBB (*to Anna*) Can't *you* get this wild animal down to the newspaper district?

KRAGLER It's no use. You can't drag me to the newspaper district in my shirt sleeves. I'm through with being a lamb. Every man is best off in his own skin. (*Takes his pipe once more from his pants pocket*)

GLUBB Haven't you any pity for these people?

KRAGLER So help me God, stone me. What kind of a face is that, Anna? Do I have to justify myself to you too? They've poured your kirsch down the toilet, but I've got my wife back. Anna, come!

GLUBB They can give me half a dozen kirsch factories, I'll spit in their face for their kirsch, I'll rip out their guts for their kirsch, I'll burn down their houses for two kegs of kirsch and smoke while they burn.

KRAGLER   Anna! (*To Glubb*) You'll go to the wall, smoking. I
can see you standing against the wall before dawn, can't you
see him, how gray and glassy he looks standing against the
wall? Can't you smell something about him? What's to become of you all? Go home!
(*Augusta laughs*)

GLUBB   Oh, they'll get small wounds in their throats or chests,
everything in good order, they'll get tags with numbers
fastened on their chests when they're stiff, not like drowned
cats, more like people who've suffered a slight injustice.

KRAGLER   Stop it!

GLUBB   Rather contemptible, don't you think?

KRAGLER   They'll shoot a bull's-eye in your chest. How'll your
chest be then?

GLUBB (*looks at him coldly*)   The rats will live in it.
(*A dolled-up woman comes across the bridge*)

AUGUSTA   Coming from the newspaper district?

THE WOMAN   Indeed, I am.

MANKE   Are they fighting down there? How is it going?

THE WOMAN   Nobody knows—no.

AUGUSTA   Have they taken the newspaper buildings?

THE WOMAN   (*raises her arm, shouting is heard in the distance*)
Is that the soldier the Friedrichstadt people are waiting for?

AUGUSTA   Oh, are they waiting?

THE WOMAN   Yes, many are going to be rubbed out today.
(*Hurries off*)

AUGUSTA   D'you hear? They're attacking now.

KRAGLER   Anna.

AUGUSTA   Now would you care to oblige, sir?

KRAGLER (*to Anna*)   Why are you looking at me like that, damn
it?

104   Get going! = The Devil!

You're another stinker. = Stinker!

closing in on Mosse's. = attacking.

105   don't give a damn. = love you.

MANKE Throw = MANKE Now they're exploding like fish.
(*Pointing at Anna*) Throw

AUGUSTA—Anna! =
   AUGUSTA God help anybody who's there!
   KRAGLER Anna!

rear) Christ, = *rear*) Artillery! Christ,

Sure. You've = Sure, the moon is turning pale and you've

morning. But = morning. The night is passing like black smoke.
But

106   Half-baked Spartacist = Half-decayed Lover

Every—Skin = A Man's Justification of Himself." "The Stake in
the Flesh, or A Tiger in the Dawn."

in it) Drunken = *in it. But the man goes to the woman and goes
home*) Drunken

It's cold. = It's getting cold early this year.

(*They walk* = (*Like a little flag, the first red appears above in the
smoky-gray dawning sky. They walk*

2. Deutsches Theater Acting Version, 1922

A copy of the Deutsches Theater Typescript is in the Brecht Archive in Berlin. It is annotated in pencil (not by Brecht) with a full cast list, a sketch plan of the stage arrangement for Act I and other production details, and was presumably used for the production of December 20, 1922. This was directed by Otto Falckenberg, who had also directed the Munich première three months earlier. Kragler was played by Alexander Granach, Glubb by Heinrich George, Babusch by Paul Graetz, Anna by Blandine Ebinger.

The introductory note, which differs from that to the 1923 edition, has been given above on p. 372. The Piccadilly Bar becomes the Grünes Haus (though at one point it has been changed back in pencil). Augusta becomes Carmen; she is sometimes alluded to as Augusta, and then objects, presumably because the name is not fancy enough. Kragler on his first entry is described as "a short, thickset man," and there is no reference to his old blue uniform. Otherwise the main changes in the first two acts are confined to cuts.

There is also a long cut at the start of Act 3, which now begins with Anna's entry. The stage direction for this begins: *Clouds racing by. The street runs from upstage left to downstage right. From the left come...* The street leads over a bridge, not along a barracks wall. The rest of the act is virtually unchanged.

Act 4 starts thus:

Glubb, a pale, desiccated individual with a little red goatee, sings "The Ballad of the Dead Soldier" to guitar accompaniment. Two drunks—a farmer and a dark man, both intoxicated—stare at his fingers. Manke the waiter, a tall fellow, is dancing with Carmen, a blowzy creature. A small square man called Bulltrotter is reading the paper. The drunks keep on laughing.

BULLTROTTER   When the landlord's drunk and singing like a primadonna, till the glasses rattle, then everything's cock-eyed. Look at that tart dancing with a shark like that between her legs: how the hell is a fellow to digest his paper? You see your ass through it. A godforsaken bar in the back of beyond, where the waiter shuffles around the dance-floor looking like a shark and the landlord serves him, when he isn't singing chorales.

BULLTROTTER (*putting his feet on the table*)   The revolution's on the way! Freedom's here!

GLUBB   You're spoiling my marble that's made of wood. (*Goes on singing.*)

THE DRUNK (*to Laar*)   Scum and Lazarus. I'm scum, you're Lazarus. Heavenly assholes and bits of string. None of them know a goddam thing.

MANKE   When they grab something it's schnapps, when they share something it's a bed, and when they produce something it's babies. Augusta, come across my knee and pour some brandy into me!

BULLTROTTER   That's all talk. Pure grand opera. Where are you saying all that? In a schnapps bar!

MANKE   Where there's a horse there's horse shit. That's the way, Augusta.

CARMEN   Make up your mind. It's Carmen, or you can dance by yourself. Vulgar beast!

MANKE   Right, Augusta, they're practicing the "Marseillaise," in four parts with tremolo. Those bourgeois. Well done, landlord.

THE DRUNK   Bourgeois. (*Coming forward*) The bourgeois is a necessity, just like the men's room. If it weren't for those two institutions public life would be immoral.

BULLTROTTER   Change the record. Shut up, landlord! I saw those guys before. And they've got a look in their eye, pals, or rather landlord, just like before going over the top. You know what I mean?

MANKE   I've got an idea. When they had some schnapps in

them, my boy, with those pale faces in the air where it was
raining, raining bullets, dear man. And guns in their hands
and a tight feeling in their fingers, my boy!

BULLTROTTER   That's how they look, that's how they looked
just now, just a minute or two ago.

It then continues much as before up to Kragler's entrance, which
is slightly different in that the rumble of guns is not heard, and
no reference is made to his artillery tunic. His account of his
experiences in Africa is also very much as in the 1922 edition (see
pp. 392–394 above), up to where the nickelodeon plays and he
begins dancing with Carmen/Augusta. Then comes an expanded
version of Laar's cryptic remarks about the pine trees (which in
both other texts are put later):

GLUBB   Quiet: the farmer's got something to say, the stone is
going to speak. Watch out! He's always opening his mouth;
now he's made it.

LAAR   But I had land and animals and a forest, simply pine
trees, little pine trees.

GLUBB   (*excitedly watching him*) Listen to the stone speaking,
he's speaking now.

LAAR   Nowadays I'm drunk all the time. There was a fellow
who just happened to have some money on him, see?
(*Silence. Kragler sits by the nickelodeon, which has stopped playing. Carmen has her arm round him*)

BULLTROTTER   And you sold, you beast?

LAAR   Yes, I did. I didn't want to deliver, and I thought . . .
I thought I'd sell instead. It's just a lot of paper, and I handed
over my land and my animals, that's right, for paper and
some schnapps in my gullet. The wife and kids are living like
pigs. I live here. We're peaceable folk and we get on; the
music plays and the schnapps flows and we say, "Yes, yes,
Amen." A small schnapps, please.

GLUBB   A small schnapps, please!

MANKE   Can't you get your land back?

GLUBB   They'll get the whole damn lot—
Wife, land and all you've got.
Let them swallow it . . . etc.

BULLTROTTER   What a world!

CARMEN   It isn't possible.

THE DRUNK   Looks as though it is, pal, so close your eyes. Close your hand, pal.

GLUBB   Isn't it possible? Isn't he flesh and blood? Is he just paper? . . .

Glubb's song "They'll get the whole damn lot" recurs below. (The songs or jingles in the other two texts are omitted.) Glubb also has more to say about his particular motive for joining the revolutionaries. After the Drunk's remark in the 1922 edition (p. 396 above), he says:

> Don't insult me. Don't insult anyone, pal. Yes, they poured my schnapps away, just two little barrels; I'd more under the floorboards but it went down the drain because of a regulation on a bit of paper. Mind my words. Since that day I have[n't] slept properly, not because the schnapps went but because of the human hands that poured it down the drain. Because that's when I decided the world was all wrong.

Needless to say there is no hint of this (not even by the Drunk) in the 1953 text, where Glubb is relatively silent. Glubb is also given a verse speech, more or less in lieu of his two longer speeches (p. 397). He *climbs on a chair:*

You who have drowned in schnapps—
You whose skin is covered in rashes—
You whom they thrust back with bayonets—
You whom they gave guns and swords to and turned into murderers—
You who have always been beaten and spat upon—
You who were never loved
Come here and see, your hour is here
And you shall enter into the kingdom!

Then, as the bullets whistle and the woman selling newspapers appears with her headlines about the Spartacists, it is he rather than Kragler who leads them all into the street:

GLUBB   Just keep calm. Come along, all of you, link arms. Join all the others and face up to the soldiers and just let them

shoot. And the story will be told wherever there are people
who have forgotten their own . . .

These changes in the character and weight of the role persist
throughout the next act, and may of course be connected with the
powerful talents of Heinrich George, the actor in question. There
is none of the disillusioned cynicism of the other versions.

In Act 5 the opening stage direction is again changed:

> *A street corner in the slums. Autumn night. Big red moon. Left, the
> low pale wall of a house. In the right background a wide wooden
> bridge, rising towards the rear. Sitting on a stone, left, Anna, who
> is still wearing her light-colored dress. Babusch is walking up and
> down. The wind is blowing. Distant shots and shouting are heard.
> Rapid tempo.*

The start of the act is basically as in the other two versions, though
it is somewhat expanded both before and after Kragler's entry.
Then, when Anna has told him she is expecting a child, his next
stage direction (*Teeters . . . as if learning how to walk*) is made to
run on:

> *Then turns and looks around at Anna. Anna sits on the stone and
> looks up at him with as loving a look as she can muster, while he
> groans and shuts his eyes and draws a deep breath. Manke and the
> drunk approach from the bridge. Glubb squats there, waiting. Be-
> hind them Marie slowly comes nearer)*

Kragler's attack on Anna with clods of earth is again expanded,
mainly with additional rhetoric that represents no change of substance. An extra stage direction describes the scene as the men
hold Kragler down and Babusch crosses the battlefield (p. 102):

> *(At this point Marie is standing protectively in front of Anna, with
> her arms round her. Glubb has stood up by the bridge. Laar is sitting
> in the roadway, picking dirt out of his hair. Manke is holding
> Kragler by the collar . . .)*

Babusch's ensuing speech is likewise expanded, and concludes:

> It isn't a vast idea. The nights are chilly in November. You're
> out to liberate the world, by all means do so, it's an excellent
> thing; but tell the woman you want no part of her. Tell her to

go home if she can. Don't give us any purple passages, no more speeches, it's a small and perfectly simple human situation.

The emphasis on the "idea" is peculiar to this version. The two men are cut, with their conversation about how the attack on the newspaper offices is going. Then from Carmen/Augusta's appeal to Kragler to come down there (p. 102), to his final refusal with the speech beginning, "Throw stones at me" (p. 103, 401) there is an entirely new section, enlarging on the "idea." Thus:

BABUSCH   Say yes or no. If you don't, you're a coward.

GLUBB   Tell her, Andry. Try to think what you want. Don't tell her all that quickly. It's as well to say yes or no. Have you got your idea inside you? It needn't be in the catechism. Tell her. She'll go away, she's not bad-looking.

THE DRUNK   I'll marry her, let's have her. Because none of them know a goddam thing.

BABUSCH   They don't. Know a thing, I mean. That is, men don't. Dogs do.

GLUBB   Don't listen to him, Andry. Watch the woman. He's making fun, he has rotten teeth. Watch the woman. Andry! Have you still got your idea? You have to sense it in your throat.

MANKE   What's this nonsense? He said, "To the newspaper buildings"; he's going to the newspaper buildings. Why is he hanging around with his hands in his pockets, trying to get out of it? Come along!

CARMEN (*on the bridge*)   They're coming! Stop quarreling. They're coming, lots of them, the streets are black with them, as if they'd gone rotten.

BABUSCH   *He's* got one, Kragler, I'm quite sure. I know the story of his schnapps. But you haven't, though you did have. You've got a gullet full of phrases.

GLUBB   Andry, it's only the devil, but best say yes or no.
    (*The others start concentrating on events offstage, where it seems that masses of people are approaching with drumming and shouts*).

BABUSCH   Don't let them make a hero of you, Kragler. If it's what you want it isn't so tragic. Do whatever you really want. Everybody is best off in his own skin.

[There is a blank space in the typescript here.]

MANKE (*over his shoulder*)   Why doesn't he say something? Has
he fallen on his face?

CARMEN   More and more of them are coming, and they're all
going to the newspaper offices. Come along! Isn't it settled?

GLUBB (*somewhat hoarsely*)   And I'd like to know why *you* don't
say something. Are you so feeble? It's irritating, your not
saying anything. Here we are, charging through the streets
like bulls and finding nothing, and you're not with us. God
has tossed you your woman, half torn to pieces and with a
body full of strange fruit, all you have to do is step over her;
are you stuck? I tell you, if you're pure a hundred women
won't be able to touch you. They're less than an idea, they
only mislead you. The swine poured my schnapps in the
gutter; it made my head go wrong, and no wonder. They can
give me a hundred schnapps factories instead of those two
small barrels of mine, and I'll still spit in their faces for the
schnapps that was washed away and will never come back.
I'll tear out their guts for that schnapps. I'll burn down their
houses for that schnapps that went down the drain. I'm telling you, Andry, the idea is what matters.

KRAGLER (*angry and obstinate*)   No, it isn't.

BABUSCH   Bravo! No, it isn't! When a woman's going to pieces
it isn't the idea what matters.

GLUBB   Well? Are you going to stay back here?
(*Offstage crowds are marching by. The wind brings snatches of
the "Marseillaise" and military band music*)
(*Kragler is silent*)

In all this concluding section of the play Anna now is given
nothing to say, nor is there any mention of Kragler's knife as in
the 1922 edition. His "throw stones at me" speech ends, "It's a
waste of time, believe me, it's nickelodeon stuff and you're all
drunk and that way you're going to hell."

GLUBB   Andry, it's not a waste of time. God forbid you should
think so. There's a thin red flame shooting sharply out of the
human breast and scorching the world.

KRAGLER   What for?

GLUBB   At the innermost heart of the world, racing at the
speed of our planet—a man blown like a leaf, lonely, ice-cold
and without a home, a man who goes on strike and the world
falls apart.

BABUSCH   Don't let yourself be bamboozled; he's got a pigeon's
egg in his head. His talk is all newspaper articles, his ideas
are grand opera. Go to bed. Don't be drunk. Mind the cold
wind—it's November 9th—and go home.

KRAGLER   I was drunk, I'm sober now. It's a waste of time.

GLUBB   Heaven and hell are full of revolution, and you're going
to bed! Smash your head against the bridge! Jump in the
water and float with the ice; but don't go home!

BABUSCH   You haven't any coat and it's freezing, Andry.
November nights are cold, and it's nearly morning. Four
years is a long time. Take your woman with you.

GLUBB   Let her lie, let the woman lie. Let her lie where she's
lying on the stones. She's like grass in the wind, she's not
there any more and she doesn't know where she belongs. In
four times four years her face will have faded, and we'll all
be dead by then and wondering where to go next.

BULLTROTTER   The whole lot have gone past, just about. We're
last, and you're still hanging back.

CARMEN   They're last, and they're still hanging back.

GLUBB   And we're hanging back. He'll never let her lie, the
world will roll on, and they'll let the schnapps go down the
gutter and nothing'll ever change. Andry, come with us.
We're setting off into the dark, into our most crucial hour.
Don't abandon us. What can we do with the schnapps in our
heads if there are so few of us? What will the beast do if we're
beaten? I've known you for only four hours, yet in that time
whole skies full of stars have floated away and kingdoms have
surrendered. I've known you for four ages; oh, don't disap-
point me.

(*Silence*)

Why do I have to stand here on a street corner in the dark
after all these years, for them to shoot me tomorrow? Wrestling with you for your soul, and my hands not strong
enough? Look: none of these people are any help to me.

KRAGLER (*calmly*)   We all know a lot of unfortunates go under, and if it's in our power we give a hand. But I'm almost done for myself and have to fight for dear life. My girl is with child.

GLUBB   Is that all you have to say?

CARMEN   Coward! Coward! He's shaking like a jelly because he heard shots. He's not coming with us, don't worry, he's going to take cover. In her body, which has already got something in it.

KRAGLER (*calmly*)   Don't you think it takes rather more to go home now and tell the hyenas, "I want no part of it," and say to the sharks as they swim around under the red moon hunting for corpses, "I've got some procreating to do"? More than to run along after the lot of you, yelling something I don't believe in?

THE DRUNK   Look at the old blood-orange! Sh! Quiet! Don't shoot, look at the sky!

KRAGLER   Go home too. All a man has to do is what he wants. Because a man mustn't do what other people want. And I want to go home. That's all I wanted. I ought to know. (*Very calm*) I can't go on.

(*Silence*)

GLUBB   I don't know what to say to you. There's nothing in my mouth that would fit you.

KRAGLER   They poured your schnapps into the shit, brandy-seller, and they turned your farm into paper, Laar. But I've got my woman back.

After Glubb's "Haven't you any pity for these people?" etc. (p. 401) (his following remarks having been transposed as above) they move more or less straight on as in the 1922 edition to Carmen/Augusta's, "Then it was all a lot of lies? Africa and all that?" and to an extended version of Manke's "He was yelling like a stockbroker." Right up to the attack on Anna by Laar and Manke (p. 105), the only substantial differences lie in Anna's silence and the absence of any clue as to how the fighting is going. This is given only when the shooting starts after Glubb has extricated Anna. The final section, which follows, is a good deal longer, but the changes are unimportant until everybody begins moving to the bridge. Then:

GLUBB   If he wants to go, let him. Don't stop him. Let him get into bed, we're fighting for him. Let them all do as they want, don't press them. He shouted for us, he went with us. There are so many of us, let him feel tired. We've got the room, we can accommodate lots of them. Admit him too, he still belongs to us.

KRAGLER (*laughs raucously*)   You people almost drowned at first with weeping at my story, and now you want to drag me down to the newspapers to get shot. Just because you've stuffed your heads with newspapers and novelettes, because you can't get grand opera out of your system. I barely managed to get my own wife; am I now supposed to liberate all yours? Free my neck so I can hang a hurdy-gurdy around it? And I just washed my shirt in your tears. Ha ha ha ha! My flesh is to rot in the gutter so their ideas can win out? Are you drunk?

CARMEN   What kind of nonsense is he talking? Come on! They've retreated. We'll still be in time for the attack!

BULLTROTTER   It's about time, damn you!

GLUBB (*with simplicity and grandeur*)   Tonight everybody must be out on the street. Tonight it will happen. Come with me, we've got to stick together now. Take each other by the hand and run for all you're worth. It's over there!
(*They run up the slope and vanish over the bridge. Glubb can still be heard, singing*):

They'll get the whole damn lot—
Wife, land and all you've got.
Let them swallow it
They'll get no benefit
The kingdom must be ours.

BABUSCH (*flaps along after him*)   There'll be heavy gunfire over Berlin in a quarter of an hour's time.
(*Exit across the bridge*)

KRAGLER (*piqued*)   All right, go off to your newspaper buildings. Knock yourselves out! If you won't let a man help you.
(*He throws dirt after them. Anna tries to come to him, but he thrusts her off and doesn't look her in the eyes*)

ANNA   Andry! (*He has sat down*) I must go home, Andry. I'm
not going to have one. I'm not going to have a baby.

Kragler's long last speech, which follows, is basically the same as
in the other two versions, including the anomalous mention of "so
early in the year." Among the passages added are "The shouting
and that red moon they hoisted over the newspaper buildings: all
of it's to swindle the people!" and

> Am I a baritone? Ha ha ha! Were you aiming to wash your
> dirty faces with tears once again? Did you want a swollen
> pregnant body floating down to the dam under the red
> moon? Was I myself to die in the newspaper buildings for
> you? Every night? Did you want to have a good cry? Well,
> I'm going to bed. Would you like to help them? Rip the
> phrases from their throats! (*Drumbeat*) Wash your own shirt!
> (*Drumbeat*) Hang, hang yourselves if you don't get ahead!

Finally, in lieu of "Drunken foolishness!" comes "You can all stick
it up your ass. I'm the lover."

IN THE JUNGLE OF CITIES

Texts by Brecht

Three Early Notes

(1) The play is set in an unreal, chilly Chicago. Shlink wears a long dirty yellow costume down to his ankles, picturesquely blackened hair and a black tuft on his chin.

George Garga is like A. Rimbaud in appearance. He is essentially a German translation into American from the French.

(2) Towards the end of *Jungle:*
Everything performed in front of a cyclorama. At the back all the actors not immediately involved sit in a dusty light, following the script. When Jane Garga dies she drops hers, and so on.

(3) A play.
Chicago.
The lumber dealer Shlink, a Malay (Wegener's type), fights a war of annihilation with the younger George Garga (Granach's type), in the course of which both reveal their most extreme human characteristics. By means of an appearance of passivity the man Shlink slashes through the ties binding young George Garga to the world around him and makes him fight a desperate war of liberation against the steadily thickening jungle of Shlink's intrigues against him. Shlink's lumber business and Garga's family are among those annihilated. Increasingly isolated, more and more tightly entangled, the two go into the woods to fight it out. In the final conflict, which is fought with utter dedication, George Garga regains solid ground; he breaks off the fight (which was the man Shlink's final sensation) and takes over his lumber business in the great city of Chicago.

The events dealt with are concrete ones: the fight for the lum-

ber business, the family, a marriage, the fight for personal freedom. There are not many characters, no walk-on parts.

> [From Bertolt Brecht: *Im Dickicht der Städte.* Erstfassung und
> Materialien. Edited by Gisela E. Bahr. Suhrkamp, Frankfurt,
> 1968, pp. 134, 136-7. Paul Wegener and Alexander Granach
> were prominent German actors of the time.]

Program Note to the 1922 Text

The judicial proceedings to clarify the *Jane Garga murder mystery*
led to the unmasking of one of those *sinister affairs in Chinatown*
in Chicago which are so irresponsibly exploited by the press. A
Malayan lumber merchant's fishing expedition in a lending library,
the almost total *ruination* of an immigrant *family* of French descent, the *mysterious lynching of the Malay.*

The play before you provides a possibly somewhat rough piece
of theatrical carpentry whose raw material would certainly interest a wider public. There are a fair number of gaps in it. It omits
even points which the proceedings cleared up, such as the
Malayan murderer's crimes, thanks to which he regained possession of his *lumber business donated to the Salvation Army,* and
which characterized his flight into the yellow swamps with
George Garga as an act of fear of the *lynch law of the respectable
population.* Others remained obscure, and will no doubt always
remain so. The *fate of Mae Garga,* her whereabouts, her motives
for abandoning a family she had cared for for many years, have
never been cleared up.

The present stage text is primarily intended to make theatrical
material of *certain remarkable incidents* whose originals in real life
appear to have taken place in the gloomy September of 1914 in
Chicago's Chinatown and whose consequences will no doubt be
recalled from the newspapers. Accordingly only extracts are
given of the few conversations that concern us here (for this
unusual and most horrific story reposes only on a small number
of conversations, whose substance was difficult and expensive to
get at). They consist, making allowance for some clarifications and
improbabilities such as are *inevitable* to the drama and for a perhaps over-*romantic embroidery* of the events due to stage require-

ments, simply in the most important sentences uttered here at a specific point on the globe's surface at specific moments in *the history of mankind.*

> [*Ibid.*, pp. 9-10. Brecht instructed that the italicized words should be shouted from behind the curtain before the start of the play, in imitation of newspaper sellers' cries.]

Synopsis (incomplete)

i. A Malay called C. Shlink appears in the life of George Garga and for no known reason starts a fight. He tries Garga out to establish his fighting qualities, then starts by annihilating his economic existence.

ii. George Garga fights back.

iii. Shlink gives up his property so as to fight on equal terms. He thereby arouses the interest of Marie Garga, his enemy's sister.

iv. Garga abandons his family so as not to be hampered in the fight. Shlink moves into the vacant space.

v. Garga has vanished. Shlink has summoned up his reserves.

vi. Garga reappears, determined to exploit Shlink's fighting mood to further his own and his sister's objectives.

vii. Shlink is ready to follow out Garga's instructions.

viii. Garga tries to dig in behind his family. This results in the Garga family's total liquidation. Garga himself disappears provisionally into prison, but not unprovided with weapons.

> [*Ibid.*, p. 137, with the suggested date 1923-4.]

A Statement

At one or two points in my play *Jungle*, a character quotes verses by Rimbaud and Verlaine. In the script these passages are marked as quotations by means of quotation marks. Apparently the stage has no technique by which to express quotation marks. If it had, then a considerable number of other favorite works would become possibly more palatable for literary scholars but pretty intolerable for the audience. In view of the difficulty of their craft, those currently concerned with the manufacture of plays are unlikely, I fear, to have time either now or in the next ten years to sit back and think about such matters. Interested parties from the world of scholarship are accordingly invited to ring back in eleven years or so. (It can be divulged here and now that if the drama is to progress at all it will progress surely and serenely over the dead bodies of the scholars.)

> ["Eine Feststellung," from GW *Schriften zum Theater*, p. 969. This appeared in the *Berliner Börsen-Courier* of November 4, 1924, after an article by Herwarth Walden in *Die Republik* of October 31 complaining of Brecht's borrowings. There were statements under the same heading by the Rimbaud translator Hans Jacob, siding with Walden, and by Herbert Ihering, pooh-poohing such revelations.]

Prologue to *Jungle*

What was new was a type of man who conducted a fight without enmity but with hitherto unheard-of (i.e., undepicted) methods, together with his attitude to the family, to marriage, to his fellow humans in general, and much else—probably too much. That wasn't, however, what people regard as new. The sort of thing they regard as new is the machine, in other words something they can use without having made it or being able to understand it. In literature the last thing to strike them as new is the idea, say, that a husband ought not to treat his wife as a doll, or that marriage is dangerous, or that a cart driver can be just as tragic as a more highly placed individual, indeed more so in that he doesn't know his way around so well.

To those with this culinary outlook formal novelty lies exclusively in the packaging. Since we were served up in the oldest possible packaging we were not new enough. "Valencia" with jazz is new. It's not particularly new without. Jazz itself is, of course, new.

> ["Neu und alt" from GW *Schriften zum Theater*, p. 67. About 1926.]

Program Note for the Heidelberg Production

1

In the Jungle of Cities has turned out to be such a difficult proposi-
tion for the audience that only the most courageous theaters have
been prepared to tackle it. Indeed nobody should be surprised if
the audience rejects the play entirely. The play rests on certain
assumptions, which is always troublesome and the reason why the
usual playbill avoids it. The following notes about these assumptions will be of little or no help.

2

The behavior of our contemporaries, as frequently though by no
means fully expressed in the newspapers, is no longer to be ex-
plained by old motives (largely borrowed from literature). An
increasing number of police reports attribute no "motive" to the
criminal. That being so, it ought not to surprise you if the newer
plays show certain types of person in certain situations behaving
differently from what you expected, or if your guesses as to the
motives for a particular piece of behavior turn out to be wrong.
*This is a world, and a kind of drama, where the philosopher can pick
his way better than the psychologist.*

3

In the theater as elsewhere, the bourgeoisie, having wasted a
hundred years staging fights between men merely over women,
is not going to have much time left for fights over more serious
matters before it finds itself forced, in the theater as elsewhere, to
concentrate on the most serious of all contemporary fights, the
class struggle. An idealized fight such as can be seen in the play
In the Jungle of Cities is at present only to be found in the theater.
For the real thing you will have to wait fifty years.

4

In the meantime I am sure you see that I still need to defend the
simple basic conception of the play *In the Jungle of Cities*. This is
that pure sport might involve two men in a fight which transforms

them and their economic circumstances to the point of unrecognizability. The passion for sport is here being classed with all the other passions already at the theater's disposal. No doubt it will take at least five decades of continuous practice on at least two continents before this passion is put on an emotional par with those great and tragic passions liable to produce triumphs and catastrophes on the grand scale. What I mean is: there are catastrophes today whose motive is sport even though it cannot be recognized as such. Besides this continuous practice there will have to be an end to those other, less pure motives for fighting which still preponderate, such as the urge to own women or means of production or objects of exploitation: motives, in short, that *can* come to an end since they can simply be organized away.

5

The territory used for fighting in this play is probably unfamiliar. For the territory so used consists in certain complexes of ideas such as a young man like George Garga holds about the family, about marriage or about his own honor. His opponent uses these complexes of ideas in order to damage him. Moreover each combatant stimulates such thoughts in the other as must destroy him; he shoots burning arrows into his head. I can't explain this way of fighting more clearly than that.

6

My choice of an American setting is not, as has frequently been suggested, the result of a romantic disposition. I could just as well have picked Berlin, except that then the audience, instead of saying, "That character's acting strangely, strikingly, peculiarly," would simply have said, "It's a very exceptional Berliner who behaves like that." Using a background (American) which naturally suited my characters, covering them rather than showing them up, seemed the easiest way of drawing attention to the odd behavior of widely representative contemporary human types. In a German setting these same types would have been romantic; they would have contrasted with their setting, not with a romantic audience. In practical terms I would be satisfied if theaters pro-

jected America photographically on the backcloth and were content to imply Shlink's Asiatic origin by means of a plain yellow
make-up, generally allowing him to behave like an Asiatic, in
other words like a European. That would keep at least *one* major
mystery out of the play.

> ["Für das Programmheft der Heidelberger Aufführung,"
> July 24, 1928, from GW *Schriften zum Theater*, p. 969.]

On Looking Through My First Plays [iii]

My memories of writing the play *In the Jungle of Cities* are far
from clear, but at least I remember the desires and ideas with
which I was seized. One factor was my having seen a production
of Schiller's *The Robbers*: one of those bad performances whose
very poverty emphasizes the outline of a good play, so that the
writer's high aims are brought out by the failure to fulfill them.
In *The Robbers* there is a most furious, destructive and desperate
fight over a bourgeois inheritance, using partly non-bourgeois
means. What interested me about this fight was its fury, and
because it was a time (the early 1920's) when I appreciated sport,
and boxing in particular, as one of the "great mythical diversions
of the giant cities on the other side of the herring pond," I wanted
my new play to show the conclusion of a "fight for fighting's
sake," a fight with no object except to decide who is "the best
man." I ought to add that at that time I had in mind a strange
historical conception, a history of mankind seen through incidents
on the mass scale and of specific historical significance, a history
of continually new and different modes of behavior, observable
here and there on our planet.

My play was meant to deal with this pure enjoyment of
fighting. Even while working on the first draft I noticed how
singularly difficult it was to bring about a meaningful fight—
which meant, according to the views which I then held, a fight
that proved something—and keep it going. Gradually it turned
into a play about the difficulty of bringing such a fight about. The
main characters had recourse to one measure after another in their

effort to come to blows. The family of one of the fighters was
thrown into the battle, as was his place of work and so on and so
forth. The other fighter's property was likewise "thrown in"—
and with that I was unconsciously moving very close to the real
struggle which was then taking place, though only idealized by
me: the class struggle. In the end it dawned on the fighters that
their fight was mere shadow-boxing; even as enemies they could
not make contact. A vague realization emerged: that under ad-
vanced capitalism fighting for fighting's sake is only a wild distor-
tion of competition for competition's sake. The play's dialectic is
of a purely idealistic kind.

At the same time one or two seemingly quite formal wishes
were involved. In Berlin I had seen Jessner's production of *Othello*
with Fritz Kortner and Hofer at the then State Theater on the
Gendarmenmarkt, and had been impressed by one of its technical
aspects: the lighting. Jessner had used intersecting spotlights to
create a peculiar dusty light which strongly emphasized the
figures; they moved about in it like figures by Rembrandt. Other
impressions also played a part: my reading of Rimbaud's *Une
saison en enfer* and of J. V. Jensen's Chicago novel *The Wheel.* Also
the reading of a collection of letters whose name I forget; they had
a chilly, conclusive tone almost like that of a will. The influence
of the outskirts of Augsburg should also be mentioned. I often
used to go to the annual autumn *Plärrer,* a fair with sideshows on
the so-called Small Parade Ground, with music from a number of
merry-go-rounds and with panoramas showing such naïve art as
"The Shooting of the Anarchist Ferrer in Madrid" or "Nero
Watching While Rome Burns" or "The Lions of Bavaria Storm-
ing the Earthworks at Düppel" or "Flight of Charles the Bold
after the Battle of Murten." I remember Charles the Bold's horse.
He had huge frightened eyes, as if aware of the historical situation.
I wrote the play very largely out of doors while walking. An alley
of Spanish chestnuts ran parallel with the old city moat past my
father's house; beyond it were the wall and the remnants of the
fortifications. The chestnuts were shedding their yellow leaves.
The paper I wrote on was thin typing paper, folded in four to fit
inside my leather notebook. I made concoctions of words like
strong drinks, entire scenes out of words whose texture and color
were specifically designed to make an impression on the senses.

Cherrystone, revolver, pantspocket, paper god: concoctions of
that kind. At the same time I was, of course, working on the story,
on the characters, on my views of human conduct and its effectiveness. I may be slightly overstressing the formal side, but I wanted
to show what a complex business such writing is and how one
thing merges into the other: how the shape arises from the
material and in turn molds it. Both before and later I worked in
a different way and on different principles, and the resulting plays
were simpler and more materialistic, but there too a considerable
formal element was absorbed by the material as they took shape.

[From "Bei Durchsicht meiner ersten Stücke," in GW *Schriften zum
Theater*, pp. 949-50. Dated March 1954. Brecht reviewed a pro-
duction of *The Robbers* at the Augsburg municipal theater on October
23, 1920. Leopold Jessner's Berlin production of *Othello* with Fritz
Kortner, Johanna Hofer, Albert Steinrück, and Rudolf Forster had its
première on November 11, 1921; it must have been one of the first plays
that he saw in Berlin. For a note on Brecht's debt to Rimbaud and
Jensen, see p. 435 below. The collection of letters, so Dr. Reinhold
Grimm has suggested, may be a volume called *Knabenbriefe* edited by
Charlotte Westermann and published in Düsseldorf in 1908.]

Editorial Note

This is based, with grateful acknowledgments, on the texts and information given in the volume of "materials" edited by Gisela E. Bahr under the title *Im Dickicht der Städte, Erstfassung und Materialien* and published by Suhrkamp-Verlag in 1968 ("edition suhrkamp" number 246).

1. General

A diary note of September 11, 1921, shows Brecht just before his visit to Berlin, wondering why "nobody has yet described the big city as a jungle."

> Where are its heroes, its colonizers, its victims? The hostility of the big city, its malicious stony consistence, its Babylonian confusion of language: in short, its poetry has not yet been created.

As he was then fresh from reading Jensen's *The Wheel* and Sinclair's *The Jungle*, both of which are set in Chicago, this cannot be taken too literally, but it relates nonetheless to the first draft of the play, on which he embarked about this time.

In the Jungle, as it was then called, had its première on May 9, 1923. The typescript (of which two versions exist in the Brecht Archive) had by then already been considerably modified, to judge from the evidence of the two heavily amended scripts used by the director Erich Engel (and left by him to the East German Academy of Arts) and of the printed program. Thus there are sixteen scenes in the typescript, but the program says it is a "Drama in 10 Scenes." It evidently began with the shouted headlines from the Program Note (p. 416 above), and lasted over three hours. At the first Berlin performance, which took place on Octo-

ber 29, 1924, at the Deutsches Theater, again under Engel's direction, it was renamed *Jungle*, with the subtitle "Decline of a
Family," and prefaced by the present prologue. Essentially, however, it seems to have been a cut version of the same play.

The revised *In the Jungle of Cities*, virtually in its final form, was
published by Ullstein (Propyläen-Verlag) in the spring of 1927 and
given its first performance under Carl Ebert's direction in Darm-
stadt that December. There are eleven scenes (though misnum-
bering makes it look as if there were only ten); their titles have
been made apparently more precise with exact dates and times;
stage and lighting directions are less atmospheric; some names
and characters are altered, notably those of Skinny and Manky;
there are fewer references to the jungle and more to the fight; a
generally more urban, American, technological flavor is given,
not least by the illustrations at the end of the book, which show
"typical cities and people of the first decades of the century."
There are also some major alterations in the story; the murder of
Jane is dispensed with; the illegal reselling of Shlink's timber is
new, and the lynchers who come for him in the end are no longer
individuals he has wronged but citizens responding to a denuncia-
tion made by Garga before he goes to jail and left smoldering
under Shlink like a kind of time bomb.

In the 1950's a few very small changes were made when the play
was republished in Brecht's collected *Stücke*. Among them are the
substitution of "Schönes" (or "my beautiful") for Manky's odd
English term of endearment "nice," and the cutting of the dedication to Brecht's first wife, Marianne.

2. The 1922 Version

The following is a scene-by-scene comparison of the typescript
(corrected version) of *In the Jungle* (1922) and the published text
of *In the Jungle of Cities* (1927). Arabic scene numbers refer to the
former, Roman to the latter.

1. *Lending Library.* (Fairly close to I.)
Described as "*Brown. Wet tobacco leaves. Soapy-green sliding windows, steps. Low. Lots of paper.*" Shlink (who had originally been conceived as a Chinese) wears a "*long dirty yellow soutane.*" According to Engel's script he "speaks quickly, but with large slow gestures, never giving anything away. Broad, powerful back." Moti Gui, who was renamed Skinny in the 1927 text, "has a rather asthmatic snuffle. Rhythmic speech due to pauses for breath. Halfbreed, run-down, agog for sensations." Worm, who then had no other name, is "bald, syphilitic. Saddle-shaped nose, wide-set eyes. Genial." Baboon, likewise, "A pimp. Dressed in greasy black. Occasionally imitates Shlink."

The references to Jensen and Rimbaud early in the scene are new in 1927. In 1922 Garga at one point recommends "Noa! Noa! A good, first-rate book, written in blood on leather . . ." and Brecht evidently considered inserting a quotation from this work of Gauguin's to follow Shlink's first reference to Tahiti.

By 1927 pounds had become dollars and schnapps whiskey. Garga's references to prostitution and Shlink's declarations that he is opening the fight against him and will shake his foundations are all new.

2. *In the Quarry.* (Cut.)
This dialogue between Garga and the Green Man is given in full at the end of the present notes. It was cut from the 1927 version, and probably also from the two earlier productions as, although it is in Engel's and Erwin Faber's (the Munich Garga's) scripts, the Green Man is not named on the 1923 program.

3. *Shlink's Office.* (Cut and slightly transposed to form II.)
Described as "*Brown, like an open sluice-gate.*" In lieu of the opening exchange with Worm, Shlink soliloquizes:

> Smooth, round, full, that's me. It's all so little effort, it all comes easy to me. How easily I digest! (*Silence*) For ten years there's been no difficulty in living like this. Comfortable, well dug in, avoiding any kind of friction. Now I've begun to take easiness for granted, and I'm fed up with everything.

Marie enters in white. As Garga puts on his new linen behind the screen he exclaims, "White linen! That means adventures. White muslin. For daydreaming about horses in." He makes his remark about Shlink having stripped his skin (now on p. 117) immediately after emerging from behind the screen, thus confirming the relation between the two leitmotivs of skin and linen.

The resale of Broost and Company's timber is all new in 1927. In the 1922 text the sacking of Moti Gui (= Skinny) is more elaborate. Baboon is not in this scene at all (nor are his remarks re Papua and toi cha), so that when Shlink tells Marie "he loves you" he is referring to Moti Gui—altogether a more pathetic and less comic character in this version. He tries to woo Marie by telling her that she gives off a smell like a horse; hence Garga's remark at the end of the scene, which remains, a little bafflingly, in the 1927 text. In a sub-episode labeled "The Auction" and cut in the second of Engel's scripts, Marie is inspected "like a horse" and has been put up for auction when the Salvation Army arrive. Her closing lines to the scene are new.

4. *The Family Sacrificed.* (III is much the same, but plus the episode with Worm and subsequent references to it.)

The setting is an "*Attic with light-colored wallpaper. Ivory people. Dark circular table. John, Mae, Mankyboddle seated around it.*" Mankyboddle, sometimes called Manky for short in this version, is altogether more prominent and more emphatically an old sea dog than in 1927. A very early note referring to Marie's suitor as "(Kutteldaddeldu)" suggests that both name and character may derive from Joachim Ringelnatz's comic seaman of that name.

More is made in 1922 of the tension between the Garga parents, also of George Garga's drinking. "This is a city," says John before George's entrance, "people live in holes like this; my brother ran around in the jungle—the deserter. George has got his blood." It is new in 1927 that George should bring money and hand it to Mae. The episode with Worm is already in two of the 1923 stage scripts.

In one of these when John and Manky reappear before Shlink's entrance they sing a verse of the "Ballad of the Woman and the Soldier" (subsequently used in *Mother Courage*). In the other they sing "Fifteen men on the dead man's chest" from *Treasure Island.* It has been suggested that they did so in the Munich production.

5. *In the Coal Yards*. (Replaced by IV "Chinese Hotel," which was evidently written for the 1923 production.)

In the first half Marie, who has been bringing food to Shlink as he heaves coal, declares her love for him and is rejected. The second is a long battle of words between him and Garga, ending with the latter's refusal to go to Tahiti. In the background "the thunder of awakening Chicago."

The 1923 "Chinese Hotel" scene is largely the same as in the 1927 text, the chief addition in the latter being Baboon's opening remarks about Shlink's activities.

6. *In the Sack*. (Cut and partly rewritten to form V, the second "Chinese Hotel" scene.)

"*Schnapps saloon in the Coal Bar. Divided by sacking, though not completely.*" The division is in effect as in V. Garga is lying on the bed "psalmodizing"; Manky is sitting drinking in the saloon. There are even more Rimbaud quotations or imitations than in 1927, and an introductory episode where Worm and Moti Gui/ Skinny report to Garga and the latter humiliates Moti Gui by throwing a coin into the dishwater and getting him to fish it out with his teeth. In the 1927 text Skinny is not in this scene.

Marie and Garga have more to say about their parents' plight. Shlink announces that he has bought back his house. Garga tells Shlink that he is beginning to feel at home in his skin; then when he tries to cadge a drink Shlink says he can't buy his skin with money. The general gist of the scene remains the same, though it is new in 1927 that Shlink should hand over the proceeds of the Broost lumber sale and then be treated as "overdrawn."

7. *Mankyboddle's Attic*. (Cut from 1927 text.)

"*Greenish wallpaper.*" A short scene between Manky and Marie. Her desperate efforts to love him have been too much for both. She denounces him and goes out, leaving him muttering, "Nice! Christ, what a hysterical cow you are! Nice!"

Manky is rum-sodden and nautical in this scene. Thus:

MARIE   You puff away at your stogie and lie in bed with your clothes on. Why don't you take your pants off?
MANKY   I got the habit on the *Anaqueen*, see?

The scene is in Engel's script, but has evidently not been worked on and is deleted from the list of scenes there.

8. *At the Gargas'.* (Telescoped with scene 10 to form VII.)
  "Attic. Sacking. Whitewash. Circular table. Midday meal." About five sixths of the scene is cut in the 1927 version, and there is a good deal of cutting already in the 1923 stage scripts. About a third of scene 10 (q.v.) is tacked on to what remains.

The evidence of prosperity in the Gargas' room—the new clothes and furniture and John's opening speech—are absent from the 1922 version, which begins with a desultory mealtime conversation in which Manky is prominent. He also plays the accordion, and later joins John in a song taken (unacknowledged) from Kipling's *The Light That Failed*:

> There were three friends that buried the fourth,
> The mould in his mouth and the dust in his eyes,
> And they went south and east and north—
> The strong man fights but the sick man dies.
>
> There were three friends that spoke of the dead—
> The strong man fights but the sick man dies—
> "And would he were here with us now," they said,
> "The sun in our face and the wind in our eyes."

In 1927 Manky is named in the opening stage direction, but has nothing to say.

Between Shlink's entry and Jane's description of the wedding about 130 lines are cut. Shlink announces that Marie has left Manky, then the landlord appears demanding the rent and complaining of the accordion. Shlink produces the title deeds to some southern cotton fields and hands them to Garga, thus saving the family. A reference by Garga to the "chalky light" is changed in 1927 to "a cold light."

The mention of the Broost lumber swindle and of Garga's intention to go to jail is new in 1927.

The scene ends with Mae's disappearance and the entry of the waiter with John's farewell drink.

9. *Woods.* (VI.)
  "Low trees with faded brown leaves. Whitish mist." Taken over almost unchanged in 1927, but transposed to precede the foregoing

scene. The word "jungle" is used instead of "bushes" at the point where Shlink speaks of Marie being like a [rabid] bitch.

10. *Garga's Attic.* (Telescoped with 8 to form VII.)
"*Yellow wallpaper. Watercolor. Evening drips down the panes like dishwater.*" Most of the rest of VII after the waiter's exit is from the beginning of this scene: i.e., Marie's attempt to give John Garga money. Garga's reappearance, however, and his writing of the note to the newspaper (the police in 1927) are new.

In 1922 Shlink arrives after Marie's exit, and accuses Garga of raising money in a bar on his cotton-field deeds. In fact Jane was responsible, but Garga is prepared to take the blame and go to prison. He threatens Shlink with a knife; Shlink challenges him to plunge it into his breast.

11. *Bar.* (Transposed and cut to form IX.)
Scene VIII in the 1927 text is entirely new. IX, called "Bar in Chinatown" in 1927, was renamed "Bar across the Street from the Prison" in the 1953 *Stücke* volume. In 1922 the setting is not described. The characters named include the Yellow Gentleman (not listed in the 1923 program)—he tells the G. Wishu story—and Moti Gui (Skinny).

After the Wishu story the Pug-nosed Man asks, "Do you believe in God?"

THE YELLOW GENTLEMAN   No. By no means. Not in any sense. Absolutely not. I'm an anti-Semite.

Otherwise, apart from the absence of Baboon's opening remarks (new in 1927), the beginning of the scene up to Garga's entrance is much as in the final version. Garga, however, appears alone, without witnesses. The arrangement of his dialogues with Jane and with Marie is rather different, though their substance is much the same. Jane, on going off with Baboon, leaves the possibility of returning to Garga open. The Salvation Army man's attempted suicide is put at the end of the scene.

Garga's speech about the fight, the ring and the knockout is new in 1927. Shlink's entrance at the end of IX is taken over in very shortened form from scene 12, below.

12. *Garga's Attic.* (A few lines taken into IX; otherwise cut.)
"*Night. Flying shouts from below. The partition seems to be rocking. A ship.*" Three quarters of the scene is Shlink and Garga. Garga looks out of the window and sees "Black linen hanging on the balcony. No wind." Shlink thinks the shouting is getting louder.

> GARGA   They're looking for you. (*Silence*) They're going to lynch us. They might . . . They might lynch us. They've been lynching today. Niggers strung up like dirty linen. I heard on the Milwaukee Bridge that they were looking for you—you.

Shlink again calls it "the white howling." (*His* lynching party, however, is only organized in scene 14.)
They leave together to go "down to the marshes." Then Jane and Baboon appear and occupy the rest of the scene. She is drunk, and he makes her write a note to Garga saying she is coming to him.

13. *In the Jungle.* (Telescoped with scenes 14 and 15, with a good deal of transposition, to form X.)
"*Brown. Golden.*" The scene is confined to Shlink and Garga, who begin by speaking of their enmity, somewhat as at the start of X but at greater length. Shlink then gives Garga Jane's note.
In Engel's stage scripts the scene is cut and partly incorporated in 15.

14. *Bar in the Jungle.* (Almost entirely cut.)
No description of setting. Characters are the Bear, the Chair, the Ape, the Preacher, joined shortly by Garga and Moti Gui. The first three are not listed in the 1923 program, but the stage scripts suggest that Chair and Ape are identical with Worm and Baboon.
Bear reads in his paper that a woman's body has been found in the marshes. Garga on entering speaks of his enmity with the Malay. Asked if it is a business matter he says, "A physical affair. You must help me, because we've all been molded from the same earth. Is this our country or not?"

> THE OTHERS   It's our country! He shall hang! They're our trees.

Garga works them up into a lynching party. "Are you free?" he calls after them. "Come down into the dark arena. Your knife in your hand, bare in the cold blackness. . . . Are you free? Your mistress, freedom, is sailing on the ships!"

15. *Hut in the Jungle.* (See 13. Most of X derives from this scene.)
Again Shlink and Garga talking about their fight. "Yes," says Shlink. "You wanted it to end, but I wanted a fight, Garga." He offers to lend him a horse to escape on. Then shows him the books of the lumber business, where Garga finds as the final entry: "Twenty pounds for strangling Jane Garga in the yellow swamps." Garga's speech on p. 158 beginning, "Shlink! I've been listening to you now for three weeks . . ." is new in the 1927 edition, which also adds Garga's "New York" after Shlink's "Tahiti?", thus altering the direction of Garga's Rimbaud quotation. The words "in the eyes of God" are cut where Garga, just before his exit, says that it is not important to be the stronger man.
Marie enters in black gauze. *"A whitish light appears around her."* Shlink's auto-obituary ("I, Wang Yen," etc.) on taking the poison is new in 1927. In 1922 the lynching party (the five characters of scene 14) propose to rape Marie, and drag her off.

16. *Shlink's Office.* (Largely rewritten as XI.)
In 1922 John says, "Forward against the jungle," merely, "of the city!" being added in 1927. Garga is off to the south to till the soil, not to New York. The play ends with a longer speech by Garga, finishing up: "It was the best time. The chaos is used up; it dismissed me without a blessing. Maybe work will be a consolation. It's certainly very late. I feel abandoned." Then Moti Gui's voice, off: "East wind!" Garga remains alone, grinning.

3. Scene 2 from the 1922 Version

IN THE QUARRY

White chalk slope. Morning. The rumbling of the Pacific trains, off.
People shouting.

George Garga. The Green Man.

GARGA (*ragged, in shirt and trousers, hands in pockets*)   An average
morning. Anything strike you, sir?
GREEN MAN   Let's go and have another drink.
GARGA   What's that noise?
GREEN MAN   The trains to Illinois.
GARGA   Yes. As usual.
GREEN MAN   Aren't you working in a shop any longer, sir?
GARGA   It's my time off.
GREEN MAN   Let's have a drink.
GARGA   No, no.
GREEN MAN   How's the seamstress?
    (*Garga whistles*)
GREEN MAN   Is she off too?
GARGA   The clouds! Like soiled swans! Do you enjoy having a
boot put in your face?
GREEN MAN   No.
GARGA   What can we do about it?
    (*Green Man pulls out a pistol*)
GARGA (*takes it*)   We'll have a drink afterwards. Nobody likes
having a boot put in his face.
GREEN MAN   What's he really after?
GARGA (*shrugs his shoulders*)   One fine morning he spat a little
cherry stone in my eye.
GREEN MAN   Unknown?
GARGA   Never saw him before.

GREEN MAN   Careful. Cold blood.
  (*Sound of trains rumbling by above*)
  That's the Pacific-New York. Will he want to dig his heels in?
GARGA   Surely.
GREEN MAN   . . . Have reckoned with you?
GARGA   I turned up out of the blue.
GREEN MAN   Having a drink is undoubtedly better. Sleeping with
  women. Smoking.
GARGA   Baring your teeth isn't bad.
GREEN MAN   If you've got good ones.

The play's literary ancestry
A NOTE BY GERHARD NELLHAUS

At the start of the opening scene Brecht acknowledges, in the
order of their importance, the two writers who particularly in-
fluenced his play. They were the Danish novelist Johannes Vil-
helm Jensen (1873–1950) and the French poet Arthur Rimbaud
(1854–1891). In the note on p. 421 he specifies the works from
which, directly and indirectly, he had drawn: the novel *Hjulet*
(*The Wheel*) and the prose poem *Une saison en enfer*. He knew both
in the German: the former in a translation by Mens published in
1908 under the title *Das Rad*, and Rimbaud's writings in translations by K. L. Ammer (Karl Klammer) and Adolf Christian.

Of the two, the influence of *The Wheel* was the greater in every
way: background and plot, characterizations, imagery, illustrations of which are given in the notes below (which are based on
the German edition published by S. Fischer in 1921, since *Hjulet*
has not been published in English). It is in the main the story of
"a fight between two human beings, two different types of nervous organism, a relentless fight which could only end with the
extermination of one of them, because one was fighting blind and
with all the strength of his basic appetite while for the other it was
a question of life or death" (German edition, pp. 107–8). This was
the continuation of a fight that had begun in a novel *Madam d'Ora*,
which Jensen had written a year earlier, in 1904. In it the lay
preacher Evanston, a self-styled superman, destroyed the re-
nowned scientist Edmund Hall by accusing him of his own murder of one Elly Johnson in London. But later in New York,
Evanston is defeated by the young journalist Lee in a boxing
match, "an encounter . . . which [Evanston] could not possibly
forget. . . [He] came to love Lee . . . to long for [him], to long
for [him] from the moment when [Lee] with a blow of his fist
shut [Evanston's] eyes" (p. 182). Now Evanston, alias Cancer, has

come to Chicago, for this was the hub of the world's wheel, "a grand international center . . . the center of the most materialistic philosophy in the world" (p. 165). Here Evanston starts out in a hole in the wall as a revivalist and becomes the prophet of a mass movement which he hopes to turn into a new religion. For it, Evanston wants Lee to write the new Bible because he knows Lee's "God is in Chicago" as well, since he has read Lee's tract proclaiming Americans as the lost people of God who in America have the opportunity of creating the vital civilization Europe might have become had the Gothic and not the Gallic influence won out.

Evanston's "spiritual rape" of Lee consists not only of stealing the would-be poet's views of life, but of seeking to possess him physically, of alienating him from his fiancée, of charging him with a murder—just as he had done Hall—in an anonymous letter. Evanston can do this because he has studied this "naïve young man" and knows that he is "both a coward and full of self-importance," a "sentimentalist" who, "not being much for women," is "still pure" and yet is engaged to the daughter of Chicago's richest man. A general strike organized by Cancer against the latter fails when Lee kills Evanston, this "long extinct type who existed outside of society," in order to redeem "his city and all his own kind." After fleeing Chicago, first to Japan and then around the world, Lee returns to his pregnant fiancée and, learning of her father's death, quite "sensibly" takes over the business.

By contrast, the relationship between Verlaine and Rimbaud now occupied Brecht less than it had done in *Baal.* He was more concerned with Rimbaud's literary manner, his "concoction of words." The Rimbaud quotations put into the mouth of Garga are often somewhat free; hence the original French is given below wherever possible for comparison. Though in Brecht's "Statement" of 1924 (p. 417 above) he claimed also to have been quoting Verlaine, no lines comparable in style or content have been found.

Page 113   Jane's relationship to the Baboon here and later: Evanston in *The Wheel* (p. 84) says that "it happens to be a female's pleasure to have her ears boxed by as malicious and dirty a baboon as possible."

Page 115   Garga's quotes come from the section "Mauvais Sang" of Rimbaud's *Une saison en enfer*: "Je suis une bête, un nègre. Mais je puis être sauvé. Vous êtes des faux nègres, vous, maniaques, féroces, avares. Marchand, tu es nègre; général, tu es nègre; empereur, vieille démangeaison, tu es nègre: tu as bu d'une liqueur non taxée, de la fabrique de Satan.—Ce peuple est inspiré par la fièvre et le cancer." "Je ne comprends pas les lois; je n'ai pas le sens moral, je suis une brute: vous vous trompez."

Page 125   "Stormy the night and the sea runs high" is a line from a sentimental and trashy song, "The Sailor's Lot," for which, according to information supplied by Dr. Kurt Opitz, Adolf Martel wrote the text (about 1890) and H. W. Petrie the music (1897). It was very popular at the turn of the century, and Brecht heard it often as a child, so that it became for him the quintessence of *Kitsch*. He referred to it in *Drums in the Night* (p. 80 above), in scene 13 of *Mahagonny*, in chapter 14 of *The Threepenny Novel* and in an unfinished essay of the 1950's on popular poetry ("Wo ich gelernt habe") where he noted that it contained "one quatrain of great beauty."

Page 130   Shlink's observation about man's skin: In *The Wheel* (p. 162) Lee says of Evanston, "What was one to do about a man whose nerves hardly reached his skin?"

Page 131   Cf. *The Wheel*, p. 221: "In all the streets people began to move about, all the faithful early risers in the city, people like himself, whom he had always fully comprehended, whether they were driving in their wagons or were striding off with their tools, or were half-running along the sidewalk, a mountain of fresh newspapers on their shoulders." There is a similar echo in Shen Teh's speech in scene 4 of *The Good Woman of Szechwan*.

Page 132   "L'époux infernal" is the subheading of the first 'Délire' in *Une saison en enfer*. The rest of the quotation, if indeed it is one, was not found.

Page 132   "I loved deserts ..." Cf. "Délires II": "J'aimai le désert, les vergers brûlés, les boutiques fanées, les boissons tiédies."

Page 132   "his widow" may derive from "Délires I": "Je suis veuve ... J'étais veuve ..." though the rest of it was not found in Rimbaud.

Page 136 and 137   The source of Garga's quotations on these pages could not be traced.

Page 136   "Drinkers lie": In *The Wheel*, too, Evanston reproaches Lee for drinking.

Page 154   "La montagne est passée: nous irons mieux," i.e., "The mountain has been crossed, things will go easier," said to have been the dying words of Frederick the Great.

Page 157   "You show traces of feeling. You're old": In *The Wheel* Lee refuses Evanston's love because he finds him so unappealing, because he "knew instinctively that Evanston was an old man" (p. 168), "a worm of the past" (p. 245), who fought "with the powers of an ape and mostly with the corruption of age" (p. 297).

Page 157   "I've observed the animals . . ." This key speech echoes both Rimbaud's "J'enviais la félicité des bêtes" and many passages from *The Wheel*. Note Evanston's remark (p. 216) that "the only thing real in this world is sensual (or sexual) lust . . . the only proof I have of being alive is that I die of pleasure." And several times Jensen describes how Evanston confronts Lee "like a beast of prey, baring his teeth" (p. 163), and how "they faced each other like two wild animals" (p. 280).

Page 158   "your drivel," "high-sounding words": Towards the end of their fight, Lee in *The Wheel* complains of his adversary's "endless babbling" (p. 293).

Page 158   "I will go . . .": Rimbaud, *Une saison en enfer*: "Je reviendrai, avec des membres de fer, la peau sombre, l'oeil furieux; sur mon masque, on me jugera d'une race forte. J'aurai de l'or: je serai oisif et brutal. Les femmes soignent ces féroces infirmes retour des pays chauds. Je serai mêlé aux affaires politiques. Sauvé."

Pages 162–163   The final scene recalls what happens at the end of *The Wheel* when Lee decides to devote himself to his dead father-in-law's business: "The everyday had returned with its chances and ways, the everyday and the old taste for work."

THE LIFE OF
EDWARD THE SECOND
OF ENGLAND

Text by Brecht

On Looking Through My First Plays [iv]

Adapting Marlowe's *Edward the Second* was a job which I undertook in collaboration with Lion Feuchtwanger because I had to do
a production at the Munich Kammerspiele. Today it is hard for
me to come to terms with it. We wanted to make possible a
production which would break with the Shakespearean tradition
common to German theaters: that lumpy monumental style
beloved of middle-class Philistines. I am reprinting it without any
changes. The reader may find something to interest him in the
narrative methods of the Elizabethans and in the emergence of a
new stage language.

[From "Bei Durchsicht meiner ersten Stücke." Foreword
to *Stücke I*, all editions except the first. Dated March 1954.]

Editorial Note

No manuscript, typescript or prompt copy of the play has yet
come to the notice of the Brecht Archive. Nor did Brecht write
any formal notes to it. The version which he decided to print
unchanged in the collected *Stücke* was that published by Kiepenheuer in 1924, the year of the play's original production. (There
were in fact some very slight editorial changes, probably not by
Brecht himself.)

The version of Marlowe's play which Brecht and Feuchtwanger used was a German translation by Alfred Walter Heymel,
originally published by Insel-Verlag (Leipzig) before the First
World War. It has been reprinted by Dr. Reinhold Grimm in the
edition suhrkamp volume *Leben Eduards des Zweiten von England.*
Vorlage, Texte und Materialien (Frankfurt, 1968). Miss Louise La-
boulle has calculated that they took over about one sixth of Marlowe's lines, but even where they did so they often changed
Heymel's wording.

In the same volume there is a reprint of the extract originally
published in the Munich literary magazine *Der neue Merkur* in
February 1924, on the eve of the première. This only goes up to
the end of Anne's scene with Mortimer after the (imaginary)
Battle of Killingworth (p. 205), but already contains one or two
major differences from the final version. In particular it follows
Marlowe in having Edward sign the decree banishing Gaveston
when the Archbishop threatens to "discharge these lords/Of duty
and allegiance due to thee." Edward then persuades Anne to
seduce Mortimer as best she can (part of the dialogue was later
brought forward to the catapult-showing scene) to have the decree
rescinded. Gaveston, as in Marlowe, returns from Ireland and is
assaulted by the Peers. In the final version, of course, Edward
refuses to sign, and the battle immediately follows (after a hypo-
thetical gap of nine years).

Other differences include the swapping around of the catapult scene with that where Mortimer is discovered alone with his books, and the omission of Gaveston's monologue when writing his will. In the opening scene a few lines are left of Gaveston's best-known speech from the original ("I must have wanton poets . . ."), which is entirely missing from the final version. Lancaster's comment on Edward's love for Gaveston is also perhaps worth recording: "Goddam!" he says. "That's what I call passion."

The magazine called the play a "History by Bertolt Brecht," without mentioning either Feuchtwanger or Marlowe. Feuchtwanger's name was also apparently missing from the program of the first Berlin production at the end of the same year, and the exact nature and extent of his contribution cannot as yet be judged. Brecht's own note: "I wrote this play with Lion Feuchtwanger. Bertolt Brecht" should be set against the corresponding note three years later to the published version of Feuchtwanger's *Kalkutta. 4 Mai*: "I wrote this play with Bertolt Brecht. Lion Feuchtwanger." (Strictly speaking this was a joint revision, made in 1925, of a play written by Feuchtwanger in 1915.)

No trace has been found of the revised text of 1926 referred to in an undated note (p. 141 of the volume *Im Dickicht der Städte. Erstfassung und Materialien* in the edition suhrkamp series: not included in GW). The relevant passage goes:

> Thus in *Edward* (second version, summer 1926), I have tried to sketch that great somber beast which felt the first shock waves of a mighty global disaster threatening the individual like premonitions of an earthquake. I have shown his primitive and desperate measures, his terrible and anachronistically isolated finish. In those years the last of the saurians loomed up before the eyes of posterity, heralding the Flood.

It is the same idea as in scene 1 of the 1926 revision of *Baal*.

FIVE ONE-ACT PLAYS

Editorial Note

The only one of these five small plays to be performed in Brecht's lifetime was *The Wedding*, which was staged at the Frankfurt-am-Main Schauspielhaus on December 11, 1926, in a double bill with Alexander Lernet-Holenia's farce *Ollapotrida*, a work which had helped earn its author that year's Kleist Prize. Both were directed by the young dramatist Melchior Vischer, one of the runners-up for the same prize in 1923, when Alfred Döblin made the awards. They were not a great critical success.

Brecht's Augsburg friend H. O. Münsterer says that he read the five plays, with the exception of *The Catch*, at the end of November 1919. They were not, however, published until 1966, ten years after Brecht's death. They are unmentioned in the 1,300 pages of his collected theatrical writings and notes. A note to GW says that the first four of them were submitted to a Munich publisher, presumably about the time Münsterer saw them, but were not accepted. To judge from the typescripts in the Brecht Archive (one of *The Beggar* and two of each of the others) *The Catch*, *The Wedding* and *He Drives Out a Devil* were at one stage grouped together, in that order, with a view to possible publication.